P9-EAY-520

Monographs of the
Hebrew Union College
Number 14

Jewish Lore in Manichaean Cosmogony: Studies in the *Book of Giants* Traditions

Monographs of the Hebrew Union College

1. Lewis M. Barth, *An Analysis of Vatican 30*
2. Samson H. Levey, *The Messiah: An Aramaic Interpretation*
3. Ben Zion Wacholder, *Eupolemus: A Study of Judaeo-Greek Literature*
4. Richard Victor Bergren, *The Prophets and the Law*
5. Benny Kraut, *From Reform Judaism to Ethical Culture: The Religious Evolution of Felix Adler*
6. David B. Ruderman, *The World of a Renaissance Jew: The Life and Thought of Abraham ben Mordecai Farissol*
7. Alan Mendelson, *Secular Education in Philo of Alexandria*
8. Ben Zion Wacholder, *The Dawn of Qumran: The Sectarian Torah and the Teacher of Righteousness*
9. Stephen M. Passamaneck, *The Traditional Jewish Law of Sale: Shulḥan Arukh, Ḥoshen Mishpat, Chapters 189–240*
10. Yael S. Feldman, *Modernism and Cultural Transfer: Gabriel Preil and the Tradition of Jewish Literary Bilingualism*
11. Raphael Jospe, *Torah and Sophia: The Life and Thought of Shem Tov ibn Falaquera*
12. Richard Kalmin, *The Redaction of the Babylonian Talmud: Amoraic or Saboraic?*
13. Shuly Rubin Schwartz, *The Emergence of Jewish Scholarship in America: The Publication of the Jewish Encyclopedia*
14. John C. Reeves, *Jewish Lore in Manichaean Cosmogony: Studies in the Book of Giants Traditions*

With warm regards –

John C. Reeves

JEWISH LORE IN MANICHAEAN COSMOGONY

Studies in the *Book of Giants* Traditions

JOHN C. REEVES

Hebrew Union College Press
Cincinnati

© Copyright 1992 by the Hebrew Union College Press
Hebrew Union College–Jewish Institute of Religion

Library of Congress Cataloging-in-Publication Data

Reeves, John C.
Jewish lore in Manichaean cosmogony : studies in the Book of Giants traditions / John C. Reeves.
p. cm. — (Monographs of the Hebrew Union College ; no. 14)
Includes bibliographical references and index.
ISBN 0-87820-413-X
1. Manichaeism—History—Sources. 2. Book of giants—Criticism, interpretation, etc. 3. Judaism—Relations—Manichaeism. 4. Manichaeism—Relations—Judaism. 5. Cosmogony. I. Title. II. Series.
BT1410.R44 1991
299'.932—dc20 90–25661
CIP

Printed on acid-free paper
Manufactured in the United States of America
Distributed by Behrman House, Inc.
235 Watchung Avenue, West Orange, NJ 07052

Contents

Preface and Acknowledgments

The present study is a thorough revision of the author's dissertation submitted to Hebrew Union College–Jewish Institute of Religion in the spring of 1989. It represents the first stage of a comprehensive research project investigating the heterodox Jewish background of early Manichaeism. Much work remains to be done, particularly with regard to Mani's youthful affiliation with the Elchasaite sect and that sect's possible role in the preservation, transmission, and adaptation of Second Temple Jewish literature. I sincerely hope that the present study contributes some potentially fruitful suggestions for lines of further inquiry.

Thanks are initially due to my teachers at Hebrew Union College, to those at whose feet I sat and whose words I thirstily imbibed. My gratitude extends especially to my dissertation referees. Professor Ben Zion Wacholder first recognized the possibilities contained in this topic, and he provided me with constant guidance through a labyrinthine maze of textual sources. Professor Herbert H. Paper, my mentor in Iranian studies, supplied needful encouragement and advice every step of the way.

While engaged in the demanding task of revision, I profited greatly from the suggestions and criticisms offered in the course of my correspondence with several scholars active in Manichaean studies. I am especially indebted to Professor Werner Sundermann of the Zentralinstitut für Alte Geschichte und Archäologie of the Akademie der Wissenschaften in Berlin for his insightful remarks on a variety of problematic issues.

Special thanks are due to Professor Michael A. Meyer, chair of the Publications Committee of Hebrew Union College, and to Ms. Barbara Selya, copyeditor of the Hebrew Union College Press, for their diligent labors in transforming my rough manuscript into the present monograph.

Most of all, I thank my wife Lu Waggoner for her interest in and support of my work. It was her vision that kept me working at a task which, without her confidence and gentle prodding, I might have abandoned long ago. It is to her that I dedicate this book.

John C. Reeves

NOTE: All translations of ancient sources, unless otherwise indicated, are those of the author.

Frequently Cited Abbreviations

APAW	*Abhandlungen der Preussischen Akademie der Wissenschaften in Berlin*
BSOAS	*Bulletin of the School of Oriental and African Studies*
BSOS	*Bulletin of the School of Oriental Studies*
CMC	*Cologne Mani Codex*
CSCO	*Corpus Scriptorum Christianorum Orientalium*
DJD	*Discoveries in the Judaean Desert* (Oxford, 1955–)
EI[2]	*The Encyclopaedia of Islam*, new edition (Leiden, 1960–)
FGrH	*Die Fragmente der griechischen Historiker* (Leiden, 1923–)
GCS	*Griechische Christliche Schriftsteller*
Homilies	*Manichäische Handschriften der Sammlung A. Chester Beatty, Band I: Manichäische Homilien* (Stuttgart, 1934)
HSCP	*Harvard Studies in Classical Philology*
HTR	*Harvard Theological Review*
HUCA	*Hebrew Union College Annual*
IEJ	*Israel Exploration Journal*
JA	*Journal asiatique*
JAOS	*Journal of the American Oriental Society*
JBL	*Journal of Biblical Literature*

JJS	*Journal of Jewish Studies*
JNES	*Journal of Near Eastern Studies*
JQR	*Jewish Quarterly Review*
JRAS	*Journal of the Royal Asiatic Society*
JSJ	*Journal for the Study of Judaism*
JSS	*Journal of Semitic Studies*
JTS	*Journal of Theological Studies*
Kephalaia	*Manichäische Handschriften der Staatlichen Museen Berlin, Band 1: Kephalaia, 1. Hälfte* (Stuttgart, 1934–1940); *2. Hälfte (Lfg.11/12)* (Stuttgart, 1966)
Mir. Man. I,II,III	"Mitteliranische Manichaica aus Chinesisch-Turkestan. I,II,III." *SPAW* (1932–1934)
NGWG	*Nachrichten von der Gesellschaft der Wissenschaften zu Göttingen*
NHC	Nag Hammadi Codex
NTS	*New Testament Studies*
OLZ	*Orientalistische Literaturzeitung*
PAAJR	*Proceedings of the American Academy for Jewish Research*
P.G.	Migne, *Patrologia Graeca*
P.L.	Migne, *Patrologia Latina*
PO	*Patrologia Orientalis*
Psalm-Book	*Manichaean Manuscripts in the Chester Beatty Collection, vol. II: A Manichaean Psalm-Book, pt. II.* (Stuttgart, 1938)
QG	Qumran (Book of) Giants
RAC	*Reallexikon für Antike und Christentum*
RB	*Revue biblique*

REJ	*Revue des études juives*
RHR	*Revue d'histoire des religions*
RQ	*Revue de Qumran*
RSO	*Rivista degli Studi Orientali*
SPAW	*Sitzungsberichte der Preussischen Akademie der Wissenschaften in Berlin*
WZKM	*Wiener Zeitschrift für die Kunde des Morgenlandes*
ZA	*Zeitschrift für Assyriologie*
ZDMG	*Zeitschrift der deutschen morgenländischen Gesellschaft*
ZNW	*Zeitschrift für die neutestamentliche Wissenschaft*
ZPE	*Zeitschrift für Papyrologie und Epigraphik*
ZRGG	*Zeitschrift für Religions- und Geistesgeschichte*

Introduction

Mani belongs to a select group of personalities who share the distinction of having founded a new religion. The "conscious syncretism"[1] of the resultant religion termed Manichaeism is sometimes remarked. Manichaean literature often invokes the names of select biblical patriarchs, Zoroaster, Jesus, and the Buddha as exemplars of and historical testimony to a chain of authoritative witness[2] that culminates in the appearance of Mani as the "apostle of Light"[3] and the "seal of the prophets."[4] Scholars have labored throughout the past two centuries to uncover the historical and cultural presuppositions that allowed Mani to weave such diverse traditional lore into one fabric. This interpretive task has been hampered by the lack of trustworthy sources for Mani's early life and career; little is certain apart from his known *floruit* during the early decades of the Sasanian dynasty and his general activity within the confines of that empire. The pronounced dualistic flavor of Mani's system suggests a strong dependence upon Iranian religious conceptions which, given the time and place of his activity, is hardly a surprising conclusion. Hence a number of influential studies of Manichaeism in this century have stressed the primacy of this presumed Iranian component in Mani's teachings,[5] together with some accretions from Gnostic thought.

This near consensus of assessment was rudely shattered in 1969, however, when a new document purporting to be a "life of Mani" was deciphered at the University of Cologne.[6] This text, henceforth designated the *Cologne Mani Codex*, is in its present form a Greek work of Egyptian provenance which has been dated palaeographically to the fourth or fifth century C.E. In the opinion of its initial editors, the Greek text exhibits hints suggesting that it derived from an Aramaic *Vorlage* which might ultimately stem from Mani himself.[7] The text is autobiographical in form and occasionally quotes from literary sources[8] when seeking to elaborate a specific point. Although badly damaged in parts, the *Codex* yields one hundred and ninety-two pages of fragmentary text which clarify the ideological background of Mani's thought.

Among the more important contributions of the *Codex* to the study of Manichaean origins is its description of the religious community in which Mani was reared during his formative years. Reports concerning this community are tantalizingly brief in two earlier known sources,[9] but the *Codex* now expands our information and confirms the essential verity of this traditional account. The group is identified in the *Codex* as adherents of the teachings of Elchasai,[10] a Jewish-Christian prophet who apparently lived during the early part of the second century C.E. and whose doctrines are otherwise known to us only from the hostile reports of Christian and Muslim heresiologists.[11] These accounts depict Elchasai as a Jewish visionary[12] who was the recipient of a "heavenly book"[13] ultimately derived from the revelatory activity of two gigantic beings, identified as the Son of God (or "angel" or "Great King") and the Holy Spirit.[14] According to the Christian accounts, this book prescribes a firm adherence to Jewish law, supplemented with a rigorous program of repetitive ablutions which are to atone for the recurrent defilements of daily life. Followers of the teachings of Elchasai and/or his book are termed Helkesaites or Elkeseans in the heresiological tradition,[15] and communities of these Elchasaites are placed by the Church Fathers in Palestine, Syria, and the Transjordan, particularly around the region of the Dead Sea.[16] The geographical distribution of these communities, coupled with certain observable similarities between the ritual customs of the Elchasaites and those of the earlier Second Temple Jewish sect of the Essenes as described by Josephus and Philo, have led some scholars to posit a genetic connection between these sects.[17] If such can indeed be established, and there are some important clues affirming this relationship,[18] then one must entertain the possibility that some of the significant formative influences upon the young Mani were not necessarily rooted in Iranian thought, but instead were derived ultimately from sectarian Judaism of the pre-*Ḥurban* era.

An important literary link between Second Temple Jewish sectarianism and the development of Manichaeism is a text entitled by

Manichaean tradition the "Book of Giants." The authorship of the work is ascribed to Mani himself by both authentic Manichaean tradition and hostile heresiologists. No ancient tradent, however, explicitly quotes from Mani's "Book of Giants," and thus the precise character of the work remained unknown to modern students of Manichaeism until the fourth and fifth decades of this century, when portions of a "Book of Giants" were identified among the medieval manuscripts recovered from Turfan in the Tarim Basin of Central Asia. These fragments were collated and published by W.B. Henning in 1943.[19] Three decades later, further light was cast upon the Manichaean Book of Giants from an unexpected quarter — the manuscript remains of the library at Qumran on the western shore of the Dead Sea in Judaea. J.T. Milik identified multiple copies of an Aramaic composition emanating from the Second Temple period of Jewish history which exhibited surprising connections with the later Manichaean work. Milik suggested that this "Qumran Book of Giants" was in fact the primary source utilized by Mani in the compilation of his book.[20]

The present study is devoted to the explication of the importance of the Book of Giants to Manichaean ideology, and in particular to the implications arising from Milik's posited nexus between the two recensions of the Book of Giants for the origins of Manichaeism. Chapter one examines the information that survives in ancient sources regarding the Manichaean Book of Giants; in addition, it gives attention to the speculations of post-Enlightenment scholars concerning the nature of the work. Chapter two provides a thorough exegetical study of the contents of both the Qumran and Manichaean fragments of the Book of Giants, with an emphasis upon the continuity of motifs within the two recensions. Chapter three addresses a series of quotations from an unnamed Manichaean source found in a paschal homily of the sixth-century Monophysite patriarch Severus of Antioch. These citations are commonly identified as stemming from the Book of Giants. Chapter four demonstrates that the fundamental structure of Manichaean cosmogony is ultimately indebted to Jewish exegetical expansions of Genesis 6:1–4. Finally, chapter five summarizes the results of the investigation regarding the probable Jewish background of nascent Manichaeism.

Notes to Introduction

[1]Paraphrasing the characterization of Mani as "ein bewusster Synkretist" by M. Lidzbarski, "Warum schrieb Mani aramäisch?" *OLZ* 30 (1927), 913; repeated by H. Gressmann, *Die orientalischen Religionen im hellenistisch-römischen Zeitalter* (Berlin & Leipzig, 1930), 169.

[2] For a list of textual references to Mani's "forerunners," see H.-C. Puech, *Le manichéisme: son fondateur — sa doctrine* (Paris, 1949), 144–46 n.241.

[3] The designation of Mani as "apostle of Light" (Coptic *apostolos m̄pŏuainĕ*; Parthian *fryštgrwšn*; Chinese *ming-shih*; Arabic رسول النور) appears throughout Manichaean literature, connoting his status as an earthly incarnation of the heavenly entity of the same name. For the Coptic evidence, see *Psalm-Book* 30:17; 139:47–48; *Homilies* 29:8–9; 54:12–13; 55:17,23; 62:14 (should perhaps be restored in 60:28–29); C. Schmidt-H. Polotsky, "Ein Mani-Fund in Ægypten," *SPAW* (Berlin, 1933), 88 ll.3–4. Middle Iranian references can be found in the glossary of F.C. Andreas - W.B. Henning, "Mitteliranische Manichaica aus Chinesisch-Turkestan. II," *SPAW* (Berlin, 1933), 357 s.v. פריסתג, and idem, "Mitteliranische Manichaica aus Chinesisch-Turkestan. III," *SPAW* (Berlin, 1934), 910 s.v. *fryštgrwšn*; These publications are henceforth cited as *Mir. Man. II* and *Mir. Man. III*. For the use of the designation in a Chinese text, see G. Haloun – W.B. Henning, "The Compendium of the Doctrines and Styles of the Teaching of Mani, the Buddha of Light," *Asia Major* 3 (1953), 189–90. Discussions of the expression in G. Widengren, *The Great Vohu Manah and the Apostle of God: Studies in Iranian and Manichaean Religion* (Uppsala, 1945), 29–30; J.P. Asmussen – A. Böhlig, eds., *Die Gnosis III: Der Manichäismus* (Zürich & München, 1980), 68; S.N.C. Lieu, *Manichaeism in the Later Roman Empire and Medieval China: A Historical Survey* (Manchester, 1985; repr. 1988), 204 and 211.

[4] For this alleged self-designation, see the testimonies supplied by al-Bīrūnī, *Athār al-bāqiya 'ani'l-qurūn al-khāliya* (cf. E. Sachau, ed., *Chronologie orientalischer Völker von Albêrûnî* [Leipzig, 1878], 207 l.19), Ibn al-Murtaḍā (*apud* K. Kessler, *Mani: Forschungen über die manichäische Religion* [Berlin, 1889], 349 l.13), and Abu'l Ma'ālī (*apud ibid.*, 371 ll.14–15). It perhaps represents a later reflex (under the influence of *Qur'an* S.33:40) of the phrase "seal of his apostleship" (σφραγὶς αὐτοῦ τῆς ἀποστολῆς), an epithet used in *CMC* 72:6–7, an expression derived in turn from 1 Corinthians 9:2 (ἡ γαρ σφραγίς μου τῆς ἀποστολῆς). For general discussions of the designation "seal of the prophets," see J. Horovitz, *Koranische Untersuchungen* (Berlin & Leipzig, 1926), 53–54; J. Wansbrough, *Quranic Studies* (Oxford, 1977), 64–65; G.G. Stroumsa, "Aspects de l'eschatologie manichéenne," *RHR* 198 (1981), 169 n.28; C. Colpe, "Das

Siegel der Propheten," *Orientalia Suecana* 33–35 (1984–86), 71–83; cf. also A.J. Wensinck, "Muhammed und die Propheten," *Acta Orientalia (Copenhagen)* 2 (1924), 195 for some similar Christian titles applied to Jesus.

[5] The revolutionary impact of the discovery and publication of the Turfan texts prompted H.S. Nyberg to speak of a "Paniranismus" dominating the (then) modern study of Manichaeism; cf. Nyberg, "Forschungen über den Manichäismus," *ZNW* 34 (1935), 81. One thinks in particular of the post-*Poimandres* work of R. Reitzenstein, but see also W. Bousset, *Hauptprobleme der Gnosis* (Göttingen, 1907; repr. 1973), 116 and *passim*; F. Cumont – M. Kugener, *Recherches sur le manichéisme* (Bruxelles, 1908–12), 7ff.; A.V.W. Jackson, *Researches in Manichaeism* (New York, 1932; repr. 1965), 7; H. Jonas, *Gnosis und spätantiker Geist. Teil 1: Die mythologische Gnosis* (Göttingen, 1934), 284–320; G. Widengren, *Mani and Manichaeism* trans. C. Kessler (New York, 1965), 43–73. This accepted primacy of the Iranian component, at least in the formative stages of Manichaeism, was resisted by F.C. Burkitt, *The Religion of the Manichees* (Cambridge, 1925), 71–104; H.H. Schaeder, "Urform und Fortbildungen des manichäischen Systems," in F. Saxl, ed., *Vorträge der Bibliothek Warburg IV* (Leipzig, 1927), 65–157; reprinted in H.H. Schaeder, *Studien zur orientalischen Religionsgeschichte* (Darmstadt, 1968), 15–107; Puech, *Le manichéisme*, esp. 68–72.

[6] A. Henrichs – L. Koenen, "Ein griechischer Mani-Codex (P. Colon. inv. nr. 4780)," *ZPE* 5 (1970), 97–217. For a transcription of the text with a commentary, see Henrichs-Koenen, "Der Kölner Mani-Kodex (P. Colon. inv. nr. 4780). ΠΕΡΙ ΤΗΣ ΓΕΝΝΗΣ ΤΟΥ ΣΩΜΑΤΟΣ ΑΥΤΟΥ. Edition der Seiten 1–72," *ZPE* 19 (1975), 1–85; idem, "...Edition der Seiten 72,8–99,9," *ZPE* 32 (1978), 87–199; idem, "...Edition der Seiten 99,10–120," *ZPE* 44 (1981), 201–318; idem, "...Edition der Seiten 121–92," *ZPE* 48 (1982), 1–59. Photographic plates were published by L. Koenen - C. Römer, eds., *Der Kölner Mani-Kodex: Abbildungen und diplomatischer Text* (Bonn, 1985). See now idem, eds., *Der Kölner Mani-Kodex: Kritische Edition* (Opladen, 1988).

[7] See Henrichs-Koenen, *ZPE* 5 (1970), 104–5; R. Köbert, "Orientalistische Bemerkungen zum Kölner Mani-Codex," *ZPE* 8 (1971), 243–47; A. Henrichs, "Mani and the Babylonian Baptists: A Historical Confrontation," *HSCP* 77 (1973), 35–39; idem, "The Cologne Mani Codex Reconsidered," *HSCP* 83 (1979), 352–53; A. Böhlig, "Der Synkretismus des Mani," in A. Dietrich, ed., *Synkretismus im syrisch-persischen Kulturgebiet* (Göttingen, 1975), 149–50.

[8] "Apocalypses" of Adam (*CMC* 48:16–50:7), Sethel (50:8–52:7), Enosh (52:8–55:9), Shem (55:10–58:5), and Enoch (58:6–60:7); Galatians 1:1 (60:18–23); 2 Corinthians 12:1–5 (61:2–14); Galatians 1:11–12 (61:16–22); Mani's "Epistle to Edessa" (64:8–65:22); Mani's "Gospel" (66:4–68:5; 68:6–69:8; 69:9–70:10).

[9] These sources are: 1) a short notice regarding Mani's youthful residence among a sect of "baptists" in the eleventh *memra* of Theodore bar Konai's *Book of Scholia* (see H. Pognon, *Inscriptions mandaïtes des coupes de Khouabir* [Paris, 1898], 125 ll.13–17; Theodore bar Konai, *Liber Scholiorum* ed. A. Scher [CSCO

scrip. syri, t.66] [Paris, 1912], 311 ll.14–19), and 2) a longer description of the same residence in the *Kitāb al-Fihrist* of al-Nadīm, a tenth-century compendium of medieval Muslim culture (see G. Flügel, *Mani: seine Lehre und seine Schriften* [Leipzig, 1862; repr. Osnabrück, 1969], 49–50 [text].

[10] *CMC* 94:10–12. The name of Elchasai (*'lxs'*) has lately been identified in a Parthian Manichaean text that deals with the early life of Mani. See W. Sundermann, *Mitteliranische manichäische Texte kirchengeschichtlichen Inhalts* (Berlin, 1981), 19 l.26.

[11] The sources are conveniently available in A.F.J. Klijn – G.J. Reinink, *Patristic Evidence for Jewish-Christian Sects* (Leiden, 1973). For interpretations of this data, see W. Brandt, *Elchasai: ein Religionsstifter und sein Werk* (Leipzig, 1912); J. Thomas, *Le mouvement baptiste en Palestine et Syrie* (Gembloux, 1935), 140–56; G. Strecker, "Elkesai," *RAC* (Stuttgart, 1950–), IV 1171–86; G.P. Luttikhuizen, *The Revelation of Elchasai* (Tübingen, 1985).

[12] Epiphanius, *Panarion* 19.1.5: ἀπὸ Ιουδαιών ὁρμώμενος καὶ τὰ Ιουδαίων φρονών. Cf. Brandt, *Elchasai*, 11–12 and 37; Thomas, *Le mouvement baptiste*, 153–54.

[13] Eusebius, *Historia ecclesiastica* 6.38: καὶ βίβλον τινὰ φέρουσιν ἥν λέγουσιν ἐξ οὐρανοῦ πεπτωκέναι. Compare Hippolytus, *Refutatio* 9.13.1–2: Αλκιβιάδης τις καλούμενος... ἐπῆλθε τῇ Ῥώμῃ φέρων βίβλον τινὰ, φάσκων ταύτην ἀπὸ Σηρῶν τῆς Παρθίας παρειληφέναι τινὰ ἄνδρα δίκαιον Ηλχασαΐ ἥν παρέδωκεν τινι λεγομένῳ Σοβιαί, χρηματισθεῖσαν ὑπὸ ἀγγέλου... and Theodoret, *Haereticarum fabularum compendium* 2:7: καὶ βίβλον δὲ τινα συντεθείκασιν, ἥν ἐκ τῶν οὐρανῶν ἔφασαν. For a discussion of the concept of the "heavenly book," see especially G. Widengren, *Muhammad, the Apostle of God, and his Ascension* (Uppsala, 1955), 115–61.

[14] See Hippolytus, *Refutatio* 9.13.2–3; 9.15.1; Epiphanius, *Panarion* 19.4.1–2 (cf. 19.3.4); 30.17.6; 53.1.8. Note the observations of Luttikhuizen, *Revelation of Elchasai*, 62 n.30, 196–99.

[15] "Helkesaites" in Eusebius, *Historia ecclesiastica* 6.38 and later sources dependent upon it; "Elkeseans" (sometimes "Helkeseans") in Epiphanius, *Panarion* 53.1.1 and later sources dependent upon him.

[16] Eusebius, *Historia ecclesiastica* 6.38; Epiphanius, *Panarion* 19.1.1–2; 19.2.2; 20.3.1–2; 53.1.1. Note too John of Damascus, *De haeresibus* 53: ...ἔτι δεῦρο τὴν Αραβιαν κατοικοῦντες καθύπερθεν τῆς νεκρᾶς θαλάσσης κειμένην (B. Kotter, ed., *Die Schriften des Johannes von Damaskos IV* [Berlin, 1981], 34). See the summary provided by Strecker, *RAC*, IV 1178.

[17] See Brandt, *Elchasai*, 155–66; S. Wagner, *Die Essener in der wissenschaftlichen Diskussion* (Berlin, 1960), 185–92. Luttikhuizen conveniently summarizes the older scholarly approaches to the Elchasaite sect and calls attention to the frequent Essene-Elchasaite connections expressed in those studies (*Revelation of Elchasai*, 1–37).

[18] See N. Golb, "The Qumran Covenanters and the Later Jewish Sects," *Journal of Religion* 41 (1961), 38–50; and especially L. Koenen, "Manichäische Mission und Klöster in Ægypten," in *Das römisch- byzantinische Ægypten* (Mainz

am Rhein, 1983), 102–8. For a thorough examination of certain institutional correspondences, see J.C. Reeves, "The 'Elchasaite' Sanhedrin of the *Cologne Mani Codex* in Light of Second Temple Jewish Sectarian Sources," *Journal of Jewish Studies* 42 (1991), 68-91.

[19] W.B. Henning, "Ein manichäisches Henochbuch," *SPAW* (1934), 27–35; idem, "Neue Materialen zur Geschichte des Manichäismus," *ZDMG* 90 (1936), 1–18; idem, "The Book of the Giants," *BSOAS* 11 (1943), 52– 74. Subsequently additional fragments of the Book of Giants were identified and published by W. Sundermann. See his *Mittelpersische und parthische kosmogonische und Parabeltexte der Manichäer* (Berlin, 1973), 76–78; idem, "Ein weiteres Fragment aus Manis Gigantenbuch," in *Orientalia J. Duchesne-Guillemin emerito oblata* (Leiden, 1984), 491–505. For yet another possible fragment, cf. Sundermann, *Kirchengeschichtlichen Inhalts,* 91 ll.1450–55.

[20] J.T. Milik, "Problèmes de la littérature hénochique à la lumière des fragments araméennes de Qumran," *HTR* 64 (1971), 333–78; idem, "Turfân et Qumran, Livre des Géants juif et manichéen," in G. Jeremias, H.-W. Kuhn, and H. Stegemann, eds., *Tradition und Glaube: Das frühe Christentum in seiner Umwelt* (Göttingen, 1971), 117–27; idem, *The Books of Enoch: Aramaic Fragments of Qumrân Cave 4* (Oxford, 1976), 298–339.

Chapter One

A Manichaean Book of Giants?

There are preserved for us, both within Manichaean literature and in the writings of the Manichaeans' opponents, the titles of works purportedly authored by Mani which were subsequently accorded "canonical" status by his church. Both groups of traditions (that is, internal and antithetical) are remarkably uniform in their accounts of the composition of this canon, despite the diverse chronological and geographical settings of these reports. Such correspondence of detail often extends even to the very order in which the books are listed, giving rise to suspicion that tradition also authorized the sequence in which these works were transmitted. External tradition informs us that the language in which Mani originally prepared these writings was "Syriac";[1] perhaps a better description of the dialect of composition, given Mani's homeland and sphere of operation, would be "Eastern Aramaic."[2] Unfortunately, little if any trace of the Aramaic *Vorlagen* of Mani's works survives,[3] a situation due in part to the fanatical repression of the sect in Mesopotamia during the Sasanian and again during the Abbasid periods, but also, ironically, thanks to the missionary fervor of Mani himself, who ordered that the sacred writings be rendered into the vernacular speech of the localities wherein Manichaean evangelists operated.[4] Some Manichaean terminology probably survives in the writings of certain Syrian church fathers who combated the spread of this "abominable heresy"[5] among the local population.

Among these works is a so-called "Book of the Giants." The apparent popularity of this work is reflected in repeated citations of or allusions to this book in a diverse number of textual witnesses which mirror the historical and geographical spread of the

Manichaean religion. An examination of the various places where a "Book of the Giants" is cited will enable us to form a better idea of the role of this work within the Manichaean system and as a transmitter of Manichaean doctrine.

The earliest extant Manichaean references to the book occur in the non-canonical Coptic texts recovered from Medinet Madi in Egypt and which began to be published during the third decade of the present century.[6] The published texts are conventionally designated by modern researchers as the *Homilies*,[7] *Psalm-Book*,[8] and *Kephalaia*.[9] The list of canonical Manichaean writings is recited several times within these works, the most common form of which is as follows:

1	Gospel	*[eu]aggelion*	εὐαγγέλιον
2	Treasure of Life	*thēsauros mpōnh*	θησαυρός
3	Pragmateia	*pr[agma]teia*	πραγματεία
4	Book of Mysteries	*čōme nmmusterion*	μυστήριον
5	Book of Giants	*čō[me n]ngigas*	γίγας
6	Epistles	*epistolaue*	ἐπιστολή
7	Psalms	*psalmos*	ψαλμός

This is the form which the list takes in *Homilies* 25:2–5; restorations of lacunae in the titles have been effected from the other occurrences of the canon in the Coptic Manichaean corpus. Further listings largely identical to this one appear in *Psalm-Book* 46:21–47:4, *Kephalaia* 5:22–26, and *Kephalaia* 148. A fragmentary list at *Homilies* 94:18–95:6(?) appears to transfer the "Epistles" from the sixth position to the third and reverses the positions of the "Pragmateia" and the "Book of Mysteries," a sequence which also appears in the Chinese "Compendium," to be discussed below.

In two places on these lists we encounter differing renderings where we would expect to find the "Book of Giants." These have been interpreted to be alternative designations for the book. At *Psalm-Book* 46:30, the fifth position is filled by the title *čōme nncalašire*, a name which probably represents a translation of the Greek γίγας.[10] The fifth position of the list found at *Kephalaia* 5:22–26 is occupied by an enigmatic work written "on account of the Parthians."[11] Based upon the position of this title in the canon and on testimony regarding the presence of Persian mythologumena in the Book of Giants, C. Schmidt and H. Polotsky declared the work on the Parthians to be identical with the more familiar Book of Giants.[12] A further fragmentary list at *Psalm-Book* 139:54–140:9 has a gap where we would expect mention of either the "Book of Mysteries" or the "Book of Giants." There is, however, an isolated phrase at this point which mentions "the shame of the sons of Error (πλάνη)," a descriptive designation which may very well allude to the Giants.[13] *Kephalaia* 148 groups the "Book of Giants" with the "Pragmateia" and the "Book of Mysteries" (occurring immediately above the "Book of Giants" in the lists) and terms them "the three holy writings which together form a single (work), gifts of the Twin of Light."[14] Hence it may not always be necessary to cite these three works individually at every textual occurrence, although in practice it seems that they were.

The only other place within Manichaean literature that preserves a list of the canonical writings is the so-called Chinese "Compendium," edited and translated by G. Haloun and W.B. Henning.[15] This document is a fragmentary manuscript originally found at Tunhuang by Sir Aurel Stein and later recognized to be the beginning of the "Fragment Pelliot" published by E. Chavannes and P. Pelliot in 1913.[16] The form of the canon as it appears in the "Compendium" is as follows:[17]

1	Gospel	*ying-lun*	εὐαγγέλιον (*'wnglywn*)
2	Treasure of Life	*hsin-t'i-ho*	*symt ḥy'*
3	Epistles	*ni-wan*	*dēwān*
4	Mysteries	*a-lo-tsan*	*rāzān*
5	Pragmateia	*po-chia-ma-ti-yah*	πραγματεία (*prgmṭy'*)
6	Giants	*chü-huan*	*kawān*
7	Psalms	*a-fu-yin*	*āfrīn*

A comparison of the Chinese listing with those contained in the Coptic corpus shows a remarkable agreement, given the widely divergent locales and eras from which these lists derive. The "Gospel" and the "Treasure" occupy, as in the earlier testimonies, the first two positions in the list. The "Epistles" have been shifted from the sixth to the third rank, and the "Mysteries" and the

"Pragmateia" have exchanged places, producing thus a sequence identical with the one reconstructed by Polotsky at *Homilies* 94:18ff.[18] Due to the shifting of the "Epistles," the "Giants" has moved one notch down to the sixth position. The seventh place is unanimously accorded to the "Psalms."

The citation from the "Compendium" demonstrates the fixed character of the Manichaean canon through several centuries of the existence of the Manichaean church. The correspondence between the Coptic and Chinese lists suggests that the canon was promulgated in this form by either Mani himself or by his immediate ecclesiastical successors and transmitted by Manichaean missionaries from Babylonia to emerging communities in both the West and the East.[19] However, the most important information supplied by the Chinese canon concerns the titles of Mani's works preserved in this source. Three of the titles given in Chinese characters transliterate what were probably the original names given by Mani to these tractates. The title *ying-lun*, glossed as "the Great Gospel," is a transparent rendering of the Greek εὐαγγέλιον,[20] early taken over into Syriac.[21] The *po-chia-ma-ti-yah*, glossed by the translator as "the book of instruction which testifies the past," is a transcription of πραγματεία,[22] also a loan word in Syriac.[23] The title *hsin-t'i-ho* is a rendition of the Sogdian transliteration *smṯyh'* of Syriac *symt ḥy'*, or "Treasury of Life."[24] This direct rendition from Syriac allows us to recover what was possibly the original designation for this work.[25]

The four remaining titles represent transcriptions of Middle Persian designations for these works. This is hardly surprising since the Central Asian and Chinese Manichaean communities owed their existence to the evangelistic work of missionaries from eastern Iran and Afghanistan. These titles provide important evidence for the existence of Middle Persian or Parthian versions of the canonical works, evidence which has, happily, been confirmed by the continuing publication of the large manuscript hoard of Middle Persian, Parthian, Sogdian, and Uighur texts from Turfan. *Ni-wan* for "Epistles" represents Middle Persian *dēwān*, "archive, collection." Henning suggests that since this word was borrowed by both Syriac and Mandaic, it may reflect the title given by Mani himself to this work.[26] *A-lo-tsan* is Middle Persian or Parthian *rāzān* "secrets," a word well attested in Hebrew, Jewish Aramaic, and Syriac from an early date.[27] *A-fu-yin* for "Psalms" is Middle Persian *āfrīn*[28] "prayer, praise." Finally *chü-huan*, glossed by the translator as the "book of the strong heroes," represents Middle Persian or Parthian *kawān*,[29] singular *kaw* or *kay*. This word has various senses in the Iranian sphere. *Kaw* and *kay* refer to kings and princes in Zoroastrian tradition (note "heroes" in the Chinese gloss), but in Manichaean literature the word is used for both divine beings and humans, connoting, with regard to the latter, "giants."[30] This term would then correspond to Syriac *gabbara* (= Hebrew גבור) and Greek γίγας.[31]

That the title of *Kawān* is actually used for this work within the Middle Persian Manichaean tradition is proven by a reference to the work within an epistle[32] recovered from the manuscript hoard unearthed at Turfan in Central Asia. Written in Parthian, the letter was apparently sent from some Manichaean church official in Marv (Mar Sisin?) to an unnamed recipient — possibly Mar Ammō, otherwise renowned for his evangelistic work in the East. Herein the writer relates that he has sent a copy of the "Book of the Giants" (*Kawān*) to Mar Ammō in Khurāsān via a trusted messenger. The writer also notes that he has prepared another copy of the work while in Marv.[33] There are further references to Manichaean works by title in the Middle Persian fragments,[34] but as yet no lists of the Manichaean canon have been found among the manuscript remains of Turfan.

The Manichaean Canon as Reported by Hostile Witnesses

For additional testimony concerning the Manichaean canon, we must turn to the heresiological literature authored by the Christian and Muslim opponents of Manichaeism. Traditions regarding the canon within this diverse body of texts might be grouped into three rough categories. There is one group of witnesses whose information is ultimately derived from an early narrative account known as the *Acta Archelai*.[35] This text, presumably composed in the early fourth century,[36] purports to give the proceedings of a public disputation between Mani and a Christian bishop Archelaus in the city of Carchar,[37] along with a jumble of slanderous assertions meant to discredit Mani and his teachings. Herein is set forth a polemical charge that Mani did not himself write the works that circulated under his name, but rather plagiarized certain books that came into his hands from two pagan predecessors named Scythianus and Terebinthus. These books, four in number, were entitled *Mysteriorum, Capitulorum, Euangelium,* and *Thesaurum.*[38] We recognize in these titles three of the works which appear in the Coptic and Chinese versions of the Manichaean canon. The new work, *Capitulorum,* is probably a reference to the Coptic compilation called *Kephalaia* that has been recovered from Medinet Madi.[39]

The information from the *Acta Archelai* was repeatedly utilized (and embellished) by later Christian authors within both the Western and Eastern church traditions.[40] The same four treatises, along with the defamatory biographical frame, reappear in a catechesis of Cyril of Jerusalem[41] that can be dated around 350 C.E. The same tradition was exploited by Epiphanius for the exposé of Manichaeism contained in his *Panarion,* but, surprisingly, he also introduces four additional works that differ in two instances from the list preserved in the *Acta Archelai.*[42] The notion of an authoritative tetrad of Manichaean works was transmitted into Syriac tradition. They appear first in Syriac dress in the seventh-century *Chronicon Maroniticum*[43] in the course of a brief biographical sketch of Mani that is derived in part from the slander of the *Acta Archelai.* Theodore bar Konai paraphrases this account in the heresiological portion of his *Book of Scholia* (eighth century),[44] and from here on, the story becomes a stock feature of the Syriac chronicle tradition.[45]

The Byzantine abjuration formulae comprise a second group of hostile witnesses that are cognizant of a Manichaean canon. These formulae were designed to be recited by former adherents of Manichaeism or other heresies who wished (or who were compelled) to profess an "orthodox" faith. Earlier versions of such formulae were employed in the West by the Latin church. A simple example of such an abjuration is found in Augustine's *Contra Felicem,* to be dated perhaps around 398 C.E.[46] The Latin formulae, however, do not mention the titles of books which the converts were forced to renounce. The first Greek abjuration formula,[47] stemming from the sixth century, does specify a series of works which the erstwhile follower of Mani was expected to anathematize. A parallel catalogue of Manichaean works is contained in the roughly contemporaneous refutation of Mani prepared by Timothy of Constantinople.[48] Both lists shed light on one another, and are accordingly reproduced in tandem.

Short Greek abjuration[49]	Timothy of Constantinople[50]
1) ...τὸ Ζῶν εὐαγγέλιον	1) τὸ ζῶν Εὐαγγέλιον
2) ...τὸν θησαυρὸν τῆς ζωῆς	2) ὁ θησαυρὸς τῆς ζωῆς
3) ...βίβλον...τῶν ἐπιστολῶν ῎Ομοδα	3) ἡ τῶν Ἐπιστολῶν ὁμά
4) ...τὴν τῶν μυστηρίων	4) ἡ τῶν μυστηρίων
5) ...τὴν τῶν πάντων πραγματείαν	5) ἡ ἑπτάλογος Ἀλογίου
?6) ...τὴν...Ἑπτάλογον Ἀγαπίου	6) ἡ τῶν Εὐχῶν
?7) πᾶσαν αὐτῶν βίβλον καὶ πᾶσαν εὐχήν	7) ἡ τῶν κεφαλαίων
	8) ἡ τῶν Γιγάντων πραγματεία

What is noticeable at first glance is the remarkable similarity in content and sequence of these Greek lists of the Manichaean canon to the lists preserved within actual Manichaean literature, and particularly to that list enunciated in the Chinese "Compendium." It will be recalled therein that the first four works were the "Gospel," the "Treasure of Life," the "Epistles," and the "Mysteries," precisely as we have it in both lists here. There is a slight discrepancy between the abjuration and Timothy in the way that "Epistles" is qualified. Timothy refers to "all (ὁμά) of the epistles," while the abjuration might be interpreted as signifying the "epistles to [Mar] Ammō (῎Ομοδα)," otherwise familiar to us as an important figure in the early Manichaean church. It is customary, however, to emend the text of the abjuration so as to conform with the description of Timothy.[51]

From the fifth position on, the two lists diverge rather markedly with respect to each other and from internal Manichaean testimony. The fifth place in the abjuration is filled by a "Treatise (πραγματείαν) Regarding Everything"[52] which exhibits no further qualification. The standard Coptic roster lists the "Book of Giants" in the fifth position; the "Pragmateia" fills this position in the list preserved in the Chinese "Compendium." "Pragmateia" is obviously linguistically coordinate with the πραγματείαν mentioned at the same place in the abjuration, a relationship that would seem to solidify the observable correspondence between the Byzantine and Chinese lists. However, this title as transmitted by the abjuration is apparently corrupt. In the eighth position of the list provided by Timothy, there is mentioned a "Treatise (πραγματεία) on the *Giants* (γιγάντων)." The form of this title suggests that the title preserved in the abjuration is defective: γιγάντων has become πάντων in the course of scribal transmission.[53] Thus we should probably restore the fifth book of the abjuration as "Treatise on the Giants," a combination which conforms to both the Coptic and Chinese evidence when it is recalled that *Kephalaia* 148 plainly states that the "Pragmateia" and the "Book of Giants" formed part of a single work.

The remaining works mentioned in the Greek lists are unimportant for our present purposes. Timothy of Constantinople does add the fourth member of the Manichaean tetrad familiar to us from the *Acta Archelai*, but it is unclear whether he knew the *Kephalaia* (= *Capitulorum*) as an actual book or as a mere title in the earlier heresiological literature. The most significant feature of these Byzantine lists is their awareness of a canonical "Book of Giants" purportedly authored by the founder of Manichaeism and revered as sacred writ by the Manichaean faithful. Although, as we shall see, there are many apparent allusions which suggest such a composition in the older descriptive literature, these are the earliest external witnesses to an actual literary work of this type. We have already seen that these lists, at least with regard to their first five components, are amazingly reminiscent of the authentic recitals of the Manichaean canon. It is very likely that these Greek lists are directly dependent upon Manichaean literature that circulated in Byzantium during the fifth and sixth centuries.

Islamic historians and theologians comprise the third category of witnesses to an official Manichaean canon. A list of Mani's writings is found in the universal history of the ninth-century historian al-Ya'qūbī. He transmits the following account:

> ...and among those (books) which he (Mani) composed was his book which he named "Treasure of Life," (in which) he describes what exists

in the soul (deriving) from the redemptive activity of Light and the corruptive activity of Darkness, and attributes evil deeds to Darkness; and a book which he named "Shaburqan," in which he describes the redeemed soul and the mixture with satans and imperfections...; and a book which he named "Book of Guidance and Organization"; and twelve <read twenty-two> "Gospel(s)," naming each Gospel by a letter of the alphabet, (in which) he spoke of prayer, and what one must necessarily do for the redemption of the spirit; and a "Book of Secrets," in which he discredits the signs of the prophets; *and a "Book of Giants"*; and he has numerous other books and epistles.[54]

Unfortunately al-Ya'qūbī provides us with no clue regarding the contents of the Book of Giants.

The most detailed of the accounts preserved is found in the *Kitāb al-Fihrist* of al-Nadīm,[55] an encyclopaedic survey of the literary culture of the Arab world up to its time of compilation in the late tenth century C.E. The ninth chapter of the *Fihrist* is devoted to an exposition of the teachings and the literature of certain dualistic and Gnostic sects which continued to flourish alongside the religion of the Prophet in the medieval Islamic world.[56] Among the groups discussed are the Manichaeans (*al-Manānīyah*). The compiler provides a list and, in the case of some entries, a minute content-analysis of the works purportedly authored by Mani. The canon is introduced with the notice that Mani composed seven books, one of them written in Persian and the remaining six in Syriac.[57] They are:

1) Book of Mysteries	سفر الاسرار
2) Book of Giants	سفر الجبابرة
3) Precepts for Hearers and for the Elect	فراءص السماعين باب فراءص المجنبين
4) Shabu(r)qan	الشابوقان
5) Book of the Living	سفر الاحياء
6) Pragmateia	فرقماطيا
7) Epistles (?)	الرساءل

Al-Nadīm's catalogue displays some notable affinities with the preceding traditions discussed above. The "Book of Mysteries," "Book of Giants," and "Pragmateia" are familiar to us from both internal Manichaean testimony and selected external witnesses. The "Epistles" are also featured in the earlier lists, but it is unclear whether al-Nadīm intended to include this work in his list at this point since he reserves a separate discussion of the "Epistles" for the section of the *Fihrist* immediately following the list. His incipit specified seven works, but only six titles are given, and one must also reckon with the poor state of preservation of the manuscripts at this point.[58] The "Book of the Living" probably refers to the "Treasure of Life (or Living)" encountered in earlier lists.[59] The two remaining titles are new to the list-tradition. The "Precepts for Hearers (with) a Chapter of Precepts for the Elect" is otherwise unattested under this name and has been compared with certain other Manichaean works mentioned outside of the canonical tradition.[60] By contrast, the "Shabu(r)qan" (= Shabuhragan) is featured in every list transmitted by the Arabic sources.[61] It is the Persian work mentioned in the incipit to this section, and, according to al-Bīrūnī, was composed by Mani for Shapur I,[62] presumably with the intention of winning the favor of the Sasanian monarch for the Manichaean religion.[63]

A further feature of al-Nadīm's list (at least in its original form) was the inclusion of a detailed summary of the content of each of the works enumerated in the canon. Unfortunately, the manuscripts exhibit many lacunae at this portion of the exposition, with the result that the summaries are intact only for the "Book of Mysteries," "Shabu(r)qan," and the "Epistles." Hence no further information can be gained from this source about the content of the "Book of Giants."

In the generation following the compilation of al-Nadīm's *Fihrist*, the learned savant al-Bīrūnī appears as another important witness for the canonical traditions of the Manichaeans.[64] Al-Bīrūnī actually preserves notice of Manichaean sacred literature in two separate places. His best-known work, *Al-Athār al-bāqiya 'an-il-qurūn al-khāliya* ("Vestiges of the Past Generations"),[65] contains a valuable discussion of Manichaean history and doctrine[66] and notes in passing that Mani was the author of "many books" (كتبا كثيرة), listing by name "Gospel," "Shabuhrqan," "Treasure of Life," "Book of Giants," and "Book of Mysteries."[67] A more colorful account of al-Bīrūnī's acquaintance with Manichaean literature is conveyed by his treatise prefacing an index of the writings of the renowned Arab physician al-Rāzī.[68] Therein he speaks of his interest in Manichaean literature having been initially aroused by a passage contained within a work of al-Rāzī entitled *On Divine Knowledge*[69] that discussed Mani's "Book of Mysteries." This citation stimulated his desire to peruse more Manichaean material, but he was unsuccessful in his attempt to satisfy his curiosity immediately, due to his inability to locate any of Mani's books. It was only after the passage of some forty years that he gained access to a "volume filled with the writings of Mani" while in Khwārizm.[70] The works contained in the volume are then listed:[71]

1) Pragmateia	فرقماطيا
2) Book of Giants	سفر الجبابرة
3) Treasure of Life	كنز الاحياء
4) Dawn of Truth and Foundation	ضح اليقين والتاسيس
5) Gospel	الانجيل
6) Shabuhragan	الشابورقان
7) Epistles	رساءل لماني
8) Book of Mysteries	سفر الاسرار

It will be noticed that, aside from the enigmatic "Dawn of Truth and Foundation,"[72] the works discovered by al-Bīrūnī coincide with those titles most frequently attested in the earlier traditions. The most interesting fact revealed by al-Bīrūnī, however, is the continued existence of Manichaean literature (albeit in Arabic translation) in the eleventh century C.E. While the hostility of the ruling powers to the dualist heresies had largely extirpated most if not all of the contemporary representatives of those beliefs in the Muslim world (note al-Bīrūnī's forty-year quest for primary sources!), there were apparently regions remaining (such as eastern Iran or Central Asia) where authentic literature could yet be recovered for perusal by antiquarians and heresiologists. Al-Bīrūnī does utilize some Manichaean sources within his own scholarly works, citing them by name when so employed.[73] Unfortunately, the "Book of Giants" is not one of them,[74] and so we are unable to gain any further information from him about the nature of this book.

Isolated Citations of the "Book of Giants" or "Giants" Traditions?

Apart from the examples of formal lists of the Manichaean canon just reviewed, there are numerous tantalizing references and allusions to individual Manichaean works which provide at times more information regarding the content of a specific writing than a mere mention of a title does. Such citations or characterizations recur throughout every stratum of the heresiological literature. Several of these are quite instructive in gaining a better perspective on the "Book of Giants" and thus demand a closer inspection.

Perhaps the earliest witness to the Manichaean use of traditions concerning "giants" was the Egyptian Neoplatonist Alexander of Lycopolis.[75] This philosopher authored a polemical tract against the teachings of Mani during the late third or early fourth century,[76] a dating that situates his work only a generation or so after the death of Mani himself. Twice in the course of his argument he refers to the credulous utilization by the Manichaeans of γιγαντομαχίαι, or "wars of giants [and gods]," as evidence for the irrational character of the Manichaean "philosophy." This condemnation is dependent, at least from the philosophical standpoint, upon the similar decrial of false teachings about the gods (including, it should be noted, γιγαντομαχίαι) in the Greek philosophical tradition.[77] Whether Alexander knew an actual Manichaean book expounding the battles of the Giants is unclear. His first notice of the Manichaean employment of such material occurs in the course of his initial summary of Manichaean doctrine, where he notes that the better-educated missionaries often make analogies between their teachings and "our own tradition" of Greek mythology: "They also refer to the battle of the giants as told in our poetry, which to their mind proves that the poets were not ignorant of the insurrection of matter against God."[78] One might conclude from this report that the traditions regarding the Giants used by the Manichaeans were derived directly from the familiar Greek fables relating the war between the Titans and/or the Giants and the Olympian deities at the dawn of history,[79] a recurrent theme for allegorical exposition in the Hellenistic world.[80] However, Alexander's second reference to the mythological giants clouds this simple interpretation:

On the other hand, what is told in poetry about the giants is mythological. Those who discourse about these in allegorical form put forth such things hiding the solemnity of their tale behind the form of myth. *For example, when the history of the Jews speaks of the angels who consorted with the daughters of men in order to have sexual intercourse,* this way of telling the story hints at the nurturing faculties of the soul which comes down hither from above. The poets speaking of the giants that came out of the earth in full armour and then, having rebelled against the gods, perished immediately, demonstrating in this allusive way the quickly perishing constitution of the body, adorn their poetry in this way in order to persuade by the marvellousness of their tale. The Manichaeans, however, understand nothing of all this; whenever they are able to come to false conclusions, they appropriate these as a god-send, whatever their origin, making every effort, as it were, to vanquish truth by all possible means.[81]

Here he combines notice of the Greek giant tradition with an explicit citation of the Jewish legend of giants engendered as the illicit offspring of heavenly beings and mortal women — an obvious allusion to the mysterious story reported in Genesis 6:1–4. Whether Alexander combined the Jewish and the Greek giant traditions on his own initiative or, instead, was reacting to Manichaean formulations which already united these traditions is an open question. It is clear from other passages of his treatise that Alexander was acquainted with both Jewish and Christian literature[82] and thus was, himself, perfectly capable of introducing an illustration drawn from an alien tradition. The context of this passage, however, would seem to suggest that Alexander is correcting erroneous assertions uttered by either Mani or his Egyptian missionaries,[83] in which case it follows that the combination of motifs from the Greek and Jewish spheres was already a feature of the Manichaean teachings about the Giants. It is, nevertheless, important to note that our earliest testimony concerning the Manichaean usage of traditions about giants characterizes it as martial in tone: it involves combat between two or more groups of opposed forces, and if the presence of the Jewish tradition is admitted at this stage, the motif of unsanctioned mixture must be considered as well.

Other sources supplement this martial characterization of the Manichaean doctrine regarding the Giants and explicitly link it with a written work. The sixth-century (?) Gelasian Decree condemns as heretical a certain *Liber de Ogia nomine gigante,* whose protagonist was described as "qui post diluvium cum dracone ab hereticis pugnasse perhibetur apocryphus."[84] This "Book of Ogias the Giant" was plausibly identified with the Manichaean Book of Giants even before the discovery of confirming evidence among the Parthian fragments of the latter work.[85] Here it should be noticed that Ogias engages in combat with a dragon, a variation of the aforementioned martial theme. Another writer stemming from a later era and culture, al-Ghadanfar of Tabriz,[86] characterizes Mani's Book of Giants as follows: "The Book of Giants of Mani the Babylonian is full of stories about these giants, among whom are numbered Sām and Narīmān, names which he took from the Avesta of Zoroaster...."[87] Sām and Narīmān are familiar warrior heroes featured in the epic lore of Iran.[88] Al-Ghadanfar goes on to compare Mani's Book of Giants with Indian literature that narrates among other actions "battles" (حروب) with giants.[89] This comparison would hardly be apt had Mani's book not included similar stories about the bellicose behavior of the Giants.

There is, in addition to the persistent testimony that Mani's Book of Giants apparently contained stories involving gigantomachy, a parallel stream of tradition that suggests that the Giants were the products of, or were themselves engaged in, sexual irregularities. The root of this particular facet of the tradition is undoubtedly the Jewish legends clustered around the terse notice preserved in Genesis 6:1–4 about the *beney ha'elohim* and the *benot ha'adam,* particularly as found in 1 Enoch and the Book of Jubilees.[90] We have already seen that Alexander of Lycopolis objects to the Manichaean interpretation of this biblical episode within the general context of the gigantomachy.

Jerome, in his Homily upon Psalm 132, refers to an "apocryphal book" that relates a story about the descent of the sons of God upon Mount Hermon for the purpose of acquiring human wives.[91] Although it is not explicitly stated, this is clearly an allusion to a narrative source much like 1 Enoch 6–11. Jerome then goes on to say: "I have read about this apocryphal book in the work of a particular author who used it to confirm his own heresy."[92] This "particular author," as the context indicates, is Mani, for Jerome continues by declaring that this story of the sexual union of the sons of God and the daughters of men was the "source of the teachings of

Manichaeus the ignorant."[93]

The ninth-century Muslim writer al-Jāḥiẓ[94] is also cognizant of the sexual aspects of Manichaean mythology. He mentions, in his description of the principal features of the Manichaean teaching, their stories about "marriages of the satans (and) copulations of the demons."[95] This is apparently a reference to episodes much like the ones recounted in 1 Enoch 6–11, which describe the sexual aberrations of the Watchers and their progeny the Giants. We would probably not go far wrong in viewing this line from al-Jāḥiẓ as testimony to part of the content of the Manichaean Book of Giants. Another ninth-century source, this one stemming from Byzantium, condemns what Mani "wrote regarding the giants and the abortions."[96] Here the term "abortions" (ἐκτρώματα) betrays a definite dependence by Mani upon a Jewish exegesis of Genesis 6:1–4. This is attested by *Bereshit Rabba* 26:7, wherein the *nephilim* of verse 4 are explained to be *nephalim* ("abortions").[97] The peculiar relationship between the Giants and the "abortions" will be explored in greater detail later. Here, it suffices to note that this Byzantine formula knows a written work authored by Mani which discusses "giants and abortions," surely a reference to his Book of Giants, as known from other sources. This terminology, coupled with the incidental remark of al-Jāḥiẓ about similar sexual adventures, prompts one to conclude that the content of the Book of Giants was based upon events very much like, if not identical with, those narrated by our extant legendary expansions of Genesis 6:1–4.

This survey of actual and possible testimonies to a Manichaean Book of Giants produces the following observations: Manichaean literature ranks a "Book of Giants" among its own canonical scriptures. The epistle to Mar Ammō shows that the dissemination of the Book of Giants formed part of the missionary enterprise of the Manichaean church, hence suggesting an important instructional role for this work. This becomes especially significant when viewed in conjunction with Jerome's assertion that Mani's teaching about the giants was the foundation of his heresy. The Manichaean utilization of stories about "giants," if not an actual book itself, appears in every stratum of the heresiological literature. It can be learned from a variety of sources that the content of the work featured both martial and sexual exploits. Finally, there have been several indications that the narrative of the Book of Giants was related to the Jewish legends which surround the exegesis of Genesis 6:1–4.

Modern Opinions Concerning the Nature of the Book of Giants

Prior to the great manuscript discoveries of this century, scholars had only the aforementioned heresiological notices to guide them in making speculations as to the possible origin and character of Mani's Book of Giants. The first modern student of Manichaeism, the eighteenth-century Huguenot scholar Isaac de Beausobre,[98] devoted some attention to the resolution of this difficulty. While recognizing the possible relevance of the Greek gigantomachy tradition,[99] Beausobre also noticed a passage in the *Chronographica* of the Byzantine historian, Georgius Syncellus, which mentions a γραφὴ τῶν γιγάντων discovered by Kenan,[100] the great-grandson of Noah.[101] Beausobre also called attention to the ancient testimonies concerning a "Book of Enoch"[102] and in particular to a passage in Syncellus that quotes from a work attributed to Enoch bearing the title "On the Watchers."[103] Beausobre suggested that "Manichée pouvoit avoir puisé dans ces mauvaises sources."[104] These remarkably prescient observations would eventually find vindication in the twentieth century. However, they were largely ignored by Beausobre's contemporaries and by succeeding scholars who devoted themselves to the explication of the enigma of the Manichaean Book of Giants.

A careful study of Manichaean doctrine based upon the traditions preserved in the Church Fathers was published by F.C. Baur in 1831.[105] Therein, Baur directed attention to certain descriptions provided by Augustine of some of the actors featured in Manichaean mythology. It appeared that the bodily forms of Primal Man and of his adversaries, the servants of Darkness, were imagined by Mani as being in the form of giants.[106] Baur remarked as cultural parallels the common conception of "Homer and ancient Oriental peoples" who imagined the constellations as "giant forms" stretched out across the nocturnal heavens.[107] Baur noted a passage in Augustine that speaks of the construction of the world from different bodily parts of certain "defeated and bound giants," and cited in this connection the Greek references to Mani's Book of Giants.[108] Baur, however, did not draw any conclusions concerning the identity of these "giants." It would seem, then, that for him the genus "giants" embraced all of the mythological actors in Mani's cosmological drama, whether good or evil, and was not limited to a specific category of malevolent entities such as we find in the Enochic lore invoked by Beausobre.

A new source for the study of Manichaeism was made available to researchers in 1862 when G. Flügel published the section of al-Nadīm's *Fihrist* that treated of Manichaeism.[109] We have already had occasion to notice the canonical list of Mani's works that is preserved in this source. It will be recalled that a "Book of Giants" (سفر الجبابرة) appears in this list, but with a lacuna marring the table of contents customarily supplied by al-Nadīm. In his commentary to this passage, Flügel noted the ancient references to the Book of Giants, repeating an earlier observation of Mosheim to the effect that the book may have possibly described a war between "giants" and God; that is to say, between the principles of good and evil.[110] Flügel, however, doubted the validity of this characterization. He opined instead that the work was concerned mainly with an exposition of Mani's "demonology." According to Flügel, Mani's use of the term "giants" for "demons" reflected a general Oriental conception of infernal spirits as "powerful" and "monstrous." Mani "fantasized" many of his mythological actors to be giant-like.[111] One manuscript of the *Fihrist* suggested that the Book of Giants contained an exhortation, perhaps, Flügel thought, consisting of warnings or admonitions concerning the threat posed to humanity by such demons. Flügel concluded by calling attention to a Manichaean work mentioned by al-Shahrastānī (الجبلة) that is otherwise unattested in the tradition[112] and suggested that the title supplied by al-Shahrastānī was a scribal garbling of the title of the Book of Giants (الجبابرة).[113]

The continuing publication of Oriental texts during the second half of the nineteenth century soon made available to researchers a number of new sources that aided in the reconstruction of Manichaean history and theology. The important, if somewhat erratic, monograph of K. Kessler was one of the first studies that employed the new data gained from the study of medieval Arabic, Syriac, and Persian manuscripts.[114] Kessler's discussion of Mani's Book of Giants marked a notable advance beyond the opinions of Baur and Flügel in that he was willing to consider possible literary influences or models which might lie behind the production of such a work, as opposed to Baur's and Flügel's appeals to the nebulous (and even pejorative) characterizations of "general Oriental conception" or "fantasy." Kessler's suggested reconstruction of the theme of Mani's Book of Giants was primarily dependent upon the notice about this book preserved by al-Ghadanfar that we have mentioned above.[115] It will be recalled that al-Ghadanfar described Mani's Book of Giants as a composition that "is filled with stories about these Giants," two of whom are identified as Sām and Narīmān, characters occurring in ancient Iranian epic. Al-Ghadanfar compared Mani's book to the Indian *Mahābhārata* and characterized the stories about the Giants as being martial in tone. Kessler pointed out that al-Ghadanfar's note occurs in the context of a discussion of the building of the Tower of Babel and of the battles of certain antediluvian giants.[116] Hence he suggested that the "Giants" of Mani are renowned legendary figures of prehistory which the traditions of a later age have endowed with superhuman dimensions.[117] Mani perhaps drew the characters for his narrative from the ancient literatures of Babylonia, Iran, India, and Israel, welding these figures into an eclectic "orientalischen Heldenbuch" which narrated the activities and eventual destruction of this race of powerful, gigantic warriors.[118] Specific sources conceivably utilized by Mani include Berossus, Genesis 6 and 11 (together with subsequent midrashic embellishment), and 1 Enoch 6–11.[119] The actual employment of Iranian and Indian traditions is expressly indicated by al-Ghadanfar. Kessler's creative reconstruction of the possible sources and plot for the work was highly conjectural when he advanced it. The true worth of his efforts will be appreciated when we turn to the study of the actual remains of both the Jewish and the Manichaean Book of Giants in chapter two.

The testimony of al-Ghadanfar also determined the position taken regarding Mani's Book of Giants in the joint study of Manichaean mythology prepared by F. Cumont and M.-A. Kugener.[120]

On the basis of that quote, they declared the book to be largely Iranian in inspiration, with absolutely no relationship to the narratives about Giants contained in the Enochic literature.[121] They also recognized the possible influence upon Mani of the Greek gigantomachy tradition insofar as the latter had already become amalgamated to analogous Iranian motifs in the Mithraic mysteries.[122] The authors also suggested that extracts from the Book of Giants may be present in a polemical homily of the Monophysite bishop Severus of Antioch.[123] This interesting proposal will be examined in more detail in chapter three below.

The important study of Manichaean literature authored by P. Alfaric[124] is distinguished for its comprehensive examination and evaluation of both Western and Eastern sources as it attempts to trace the historical evolution of Manichaean literature. Alfaric interpreted Manichaeism in light of classical Gnosticism, which was, in turn, explained as a combination of Iranian mythology, Jewish biblical interpretations, and Middle Platonist speculation.[125] After a meticulous comparison of the various testimonies regarding the Book of Giants, Alfaric suggested that the *Capitulorum* (or *Kephalaia*) mentioned in the *Acta Archelai* and its dependent literature was identical with the Book of Giants known to Islamic tradition, on the grounds that authors who mention the former work seem ignorant of the latter, and vice versa.[126] The single exception to this geographic pattern of citation in the sources that were available to Alfaric is Timothy of Constantinople, who cites both. Alfaric resolved this difficulty by suggesting that they were, in fact, the same work cited under two separate titles. It is, of course, now known from the Coptic manuscript finds that the *Kephalaia* is distinct from the Book of Giants. Alfaric also identified Mani's Book of Giants with a work known from Chinese Manichaean sources as the "Holy Book of Two Principles,"[127] reasoning that the story of a gigantomachy would have aroused less interest in Central Asia and China amid their Buddhist environment than would a description of the fundamental antithesis of the principles of Good and Evil.[128] Alfaric disputed the value of al-Ghadanfar's testimony pronouncing the background of the Book of Giants to be Iranian by pointing out that Sām and Narīmān are also mentioned in Mandaean sacred literature. He called attention to certain similarities observed between the teachings of the Mandaeans and testimonies regarding the beliefs and practices of the ancient Ṣabians of Ḥarran, and opined that Mani came under considerable influence from these or related sectarian communities.[129] Alfaric noted that traditions concerning Giants circulated among Gnostic sects in tandem with various legends featuring the biblical figures Adam, Seth, Enoch, and Noah, and observed that these patriarchs are also invoked by the Manichaeans in certain contexts.[130] Finally, Alfaric equated the γραφὴ τῶν γιγάντων discovered by Kenan with the "Book of Og" condemned in the Gelasian Decree, and suggested that Mani was possibly inspired to compose his Book of Giants on the pattern of works of this genre.[131]

The Recovery of the Book of Giants

The great manuscript discoveries of the twentieth century revolutionized the study of Manichaean literature. Now, for the first time, scholars could peruse actual Manichaean works and form judgments regarding the reliability of the various reports from opponents of Manichaeism on the basis of these texts. Both the Coptic documents recovered from Medinet Madi and the manuscripts in various Middle Iranian dialects and Central Asian languages found at Turfan and Tun-huang contained many interesting indications of Manichaean dependence upon earlier religious traditions. One of the more surprising constituent elements, although not completely unknown prior to the discoveries, was the important role assigned certain biblical figures in the Manichaean conception of the historical progress of religious revelation. Manichaeism envisioned a type of "prophetic succession" composed initially of biblical patriarchs from the antediluvian and immediately postdiluvian periods (Adam, Seth, Enosh, Enoch, Noah, Shem). This series of authentic prophets, augmented with a series of later religious figures, culminated with the advent of Mani.[132] That the Manichaeans knew not only the names of these patriarchs, but also writings allegedly authored by them, was known from earlier heresiological reports, but the importance of these figures and their "books" had remained obscure. The Turfan and Medinet Madi discoveries clarified the role played by these precursors in Manichaean theology.

A series of important articles by the noted Iranist W.B. Henning[133] established that Mani had read Enochic literature and had utilized characters and narrative events stemming from that tradition. One of the more significant bits of evidence, aside from the explicit citation of the name "Enoch," was the occurrence of the terms *'yr* and *q'w* in some of the fragments from Turfan. Henning understood the latter word to be Middle Persian *kaw* "prince, mighty one," but the former term was puzzling: no Iranian etymology suggested itself. After further study of the fragments, Henning recognized in *'yr* the Aramaic loan-word עיר "Watcher," the well known designation for the heavenly beings that descend to earth in 1 Enoch 6–11 and the word which lies behind Greek ἐγρήγορος in the Enochic work cited by Syncellus as περὶ τῶν ἐγρηγόρων.[134] He therefore reasoned that *kaw* signified the gigantic progeny of the Enochic Watchers. The Turfan association of "Watcher" and "Giant" demonstrates awareness of the story of the birth of the Giants in 1 Enoch 6–11, because these Giants were the products of the sexual union of the Watchers and mortal women.[135] Henning called attention to some of the notices that testify to the existence of a Book of Giants in the Manichaean canon, and suggested that this Book of Giants was a Manichaean version of the stories related in the first section of 1 Enoch.[136] The presence of Aramaic *'yr* in the Iranian text indicated that Mani had used an Aramaic translation of 1 Enoch as the source of his book.

Henning was able to derive further proof for his hypothesis after the publication of the Coptic *Kephalaia*. Therein he pointed to several explicit references to the descent of the Watchers and the appearance of the Giants that confirm Mani's reliance upon 1 Enoch for his own Book of Giants.[137] Henning thought that Mani probably prepared a special edition of 1 Enoch for his disciples from which his Book of Giants was produced as an independent literary creation.[138] His continued study of the Turfan material convinced Henning that he could recover actual fragments from the Book of Giants. The presence of Aramaic elements in these Iranian texts led Henning to hypothesize that Mani had composed the Book of Giants in Syriac and that the Turfan fragments represented a Persian translation of this original work. The simultaneous inclusion of Iranian motifs and terminology, including the title of the book (*Kawān*), suggested that Mani combined the Jewish legend of the Giants with native Iranian mytholegumena, since *Kawān* designates both the Giants and the mythological heroes of Iran's past.[139]

A signal accomplishment was achieved by Henning in 1943, when he published his reconstruction of part of Mani's Book of the Giants from a variety of fragments recovered from Turfan.[140] The biblical origin of the *dramatis personae* and the structure of events contained in the Book of Giants was dramatically confirmed. Mani transformed the *beney ha'elohim* of Genesis 6:1–4 and the ἐγρήγοροι of 1 Enoch into "demons" (Middle Persian and Parthian *dyw'n*) who rebelled against the realm of Light. Two hundred of these demons succeeded in escaping from imprisonment in heaven to the earth. There they engaged in lawless activities, producing as a consequence of their sinful behavior "giants" (*kawān*, corresponding to *gibborim*) and "abortions" (*'bg'ng*, corresponding to *nephilim*).[141] The rebellious Watchers and their progeny are fought and vanquished by four "angels" — Raphael, Gabriel, Michael, and Sariel.[142] The fragments did not permit Henning to reconstruct the remainder of the narrative of the Book of Giants, but he thought that he could detect evidence that the stories in the book underwent influence from local traditions.[143] Henning, however, departed from his earlier opinion that regarded Mani as responsible for blending Iranian mytholegumena with the Jewish substrate. Instead, he now believed that Mani did not employ any Iranian traditions in the original composition. The presence of the intrusive names (such as Sām and Narīmān) was credited to his later disciples. They introduced them into the Book of Giants in order to increase its appeal among the local population.[144] An Aramaic original for the Book of Giants, probably based upon an Aramaic version of 1 Enoch, seemed assured.

Hence a consensus was reached among students of Manichaeism that the Book of Giants was a free literary creation of Mani based upon certain extrabiblical legends that had gathered around the events summarized in Genesis 6:1–4. Mani's immediate source for the composition of his narrative was apparently an Aramaic version of 1 Enoch, a Jewish pseudepigraphical work of the Second Temple period that enjoyed an extensive circulation within both Jewish and Christian religious circles in late antiquity. Barring discovery of Mani's Aramaic *Vorlage*, it seemed that research had reached its limit with regard to the source criticism of Mani's Book of Giants. A further chapter, however, was still to be written.

J.T. Milik astonished the scholarly world in 1971 when he reported that he had discovered, among the Aramaic fragments of 1 Enoch that had been recovered from Qumran, portions of a work that bore a close resemblance to Mani's Book of Giants.[145] His subsequent publication and analysis of part of these fragments confirmed their relationship with the later Manichaean book.[146] Although the remains are exceedingly fragmentary, the surviving references to the protagonists and to narrative events leave no doubt that this Jewish apocryphon is the literary ancestor of the Manichaean Book of Giants. Intriguing questions are raised by this discovery, not the least of which concern the means by which Mani gained knowledge, perhaps even a copy, of a work that now can be traced to the scribal activity of a sectarian Jewish community hundreds of miles from Mesopotamia.

Milik proposed that the "Enochic Book of Giants" (as he christened the newly found work) was originally an integral part of 1 Enoch itself.[147] The book of 1 Enoch has long been recognized to consist of five discrete sections which were at one time independent works of varying provenance which eventually were fused together to form a single composition.[148] Aramaic fragments of four of the five sections of 1 Enoch have been found at Qumran; only the portion designated the "Similitudes" (chapters 37–71), sometimes suspected to be Christian in provenance, was totally lacking at Qumran. Milik suggested that this "Book of Giants" initially stood in the position of the "Similitudes" in the original version of 1 Enoch, being later replaced with the "Similitudes" by Christian scribes who disliked the mythological flavor of the "Book of Giants."[149] Mani became acquainted with this Jewish Book of Giants either through reading an unexpurgated version of the "original" 1 Enoch or by coming across the "Book of Giants" as an independently circulating narrative.

Milik's proposal to view the Qumran Book of Giants as part of a hypothetical "Enochic Pentateuch" encountered sharp criticism from several scholars.[150] While researchers were willing to grant the possibility that the Book of Giants may have circulated at one time as part of a collection of Enochic compositions, including those compositions now represented in the present 1 Enoch, they were opposed to Milik's unwavering advocacy of a "pentateuchal" structure for 1 Enoch and the late dating for the "Similitudes" made necessary by his replacement theory. The resulting furor over the date and provenance of the "Similitudes"[151] largely eclipsed immediate discussion of the significance and character of the Qumran Book of Giants, an issue which is now worthy of attention in its own right.

However, scholars were not slow to posit one possible channel through which Mani might have received knowledge about or even a copy of the Enochic Book of Giants. The decipherment and initial publication of portions of the *Cologne Mani Codex* coincided with Milik's first reports about the Qumran discovery.[152] As stated above, this Greek text purports to be an autobiographical account of the youth and early manhood of Mani, a period of time which, according to the new evidence available in this text, was spent among a sectarian community of Elchasaites in southern Mesopotamia. It has been plausibly suggested that Mani became acquainted with Enochic traditions such as those preserved in the Qumran Book of Giants as a result of his sojourn among this Jewish-Christian sect.[153]

Whatever the channel through whom Mani gained access to this Jewish composition, it is of paramount importance for Manichaean studies that actual fragments of the Book of Giants have now been identified. An examination of the relationship between the Qumran Aramaic and the Turfan Middle Iranian versions of this work should shed new light upon the role of Jewish traditions in the formation of Manichaeism.

Notes to Chapter One

[1] The clearest statement is found in the *Fihrist* of al-Nadīm (cf. G. Flügel, *Mani, seine Lehre und seine Schriften* [Leipzig, 1862; repr. Osnabrück, 1969], 72 ll.10–11: لماني سبعة كتب احدهما فارس وستة سوري بلغة سوريا; "Mani authored seven books, one of them in Persian, and six in Syriac, the language of Syria.") See also Epiphanius, *Panarion* 66.13.3, wherein it is stated that Mani arranged one of his books (to be identified as his Gospel following al-Ya'qūbī and al-Bīrūnī and not Μυστήρια as Epiphanius holds) according to the number of the letters of the Syriac alphabet: βίβλους γὰρ οὕτος διαφόρους ἐξέθετο, μίαν μεν ἰσάριθμον <τῶν> εἴκοσι δύο στοιχείων τῶν κατὰ τὴν τῶν Σύρων στοιχείωσιν δι' ἀλφαβήτων συγκειμεύην. (K. Holl, ed., *Epiphanius; dritter Band* GCS 37 [Leipzig, 1935], 34–35). The form سوري is unusual (although note W. Wright, *A Grammar of the Arabic Language*, 3rd edition [Cambridge, 1896–98; repr. Cambridge, 1979], I §249); the more common terms for the Syriac language are سرياني, سريانية. These are used not only for the language of Syria proper, but for Mesopotamia as well; cf. T. Nöldeke, "Die Namen der aramäischen Nation und Sprache," *ZDMG* 25 (1871), 121; 129–31. Also Titus of Bostra, *Adversus Manichaeos* I 14: τῇ Σύρων φωνῇ χρώμενος (Migne, *Patrologia Graeca* [= *P.G.*] 18, 1085D); *Acta Archelai* 40.5: "Persa barbare, non Graecorum linguae, non Aegyptiorum, non Romanorum, non ullius alterius linguae scientiam habere potuisti, sed Chaldaeorum solam...audire potes" (Hegemonius, *Acta Archelai*, ed. C.H. Beeson GCS 16 [Leipzig, 1906], 59).

[2] See the remarks of F. Rosenthal, *Die aramaistische Forschung seit Th. Nöldeke's Veröffentlichungen* (Leipzig, 1939; repr. Leipzig, 1964), 207–11; G. Widengren, *Mani und der Manichäismus* (Stuttgart, 1961), 77, from which the designation "eastern Aramaic" has been drawn.

[3] A group of Aramaic papyrus fragments discovered in Egypt and which employ the Manichaean script have been published by F.C. Burkitt in his *The Religion of the Manichees* (Cambridge, 1925), 111–19. They are, unfortunately, too fragmentary for conclusions to be reached regarding the *ipsissima verba* of Mani. They probably represent, as Rosenthal suggested (*Forschung*, 208), copies made of Manichaean writings by early Egyptian converts to this system of belief. H.H. Schaeder believed that he had discovered a fragment of Manichaean poetry embedded within the hostile description of Manichaeism penned by Theodore bar Konai, an eighth century Syrian savant: see his "Ein Lied von Mani," *OLZ* 29 (1926), 104–7. Note also the alleged citations from Mani contained in the Syriac version of the refutation of Manichaeism by Titus of Bostra, as interpreted by A. Baumstark, "Der Text der Mani-Zitate in der

syrischen Uebersetzung des Titus von Bostra," *Oriens Christianus*, series 3, no.6 (1931), 23–42.

[4] M. Boyce, "The Manichaean Middle Persian Writings," in E. Yarshater, ed., *The Cambridge History of Iran: Volume 3(2): The Seleucid, Parthian and Sasanian Periods* (Cambridge, 1983), 1197. Cf. M 5794 (= T II D 126 I): *dyn 'yg mn wcyd 'c 'b'ryg'n dyn 'y pyšyng'n pd dḥ xyr fr'y 'wd wyhdr 'st. yk, kw dyn 'y 'hyng'n pd yk šhr 'wd yk 'zw'n bwd; 'yg dyn 'y mn ''d kw pd hrw šhr 'wd pd wysp 'zw'n pyd'g bw'd, 'wd pd šhr'n dwr''n qyšyh'd.* ("The religion that I [i.e., Mani] have chosen is in ten things above and better than the other, previous religions. Firstly: the primeval religions were in one country and one language. But my religion is of that kind that it will be manifest in every country and in all languages, and it will be taught in far away countries.") Text transcription taken from M. Boyce, *A Reader in Manichaean Middle Persian and Parthian* (Leiden & Teheran, 1975), 29; see also Andreas–Henning, *Mir. Man. II*, 295. The translation is that of J.P. Asmussen, *Manichaean Literature* (Delmar, New York, 1975), 12. References to the exhortation to proclaim the Manichaean message to "every place (city, people, etc.)," which would necessarily involve translation, can be found at *CMC* 104:10b–105:8; 124:6–15, and *Kephalaia* 7:9–10; 9:1–10. See also W. Sundermann, *Mitteliranische manichäische Texte kirchengeschichtlichen Inhalts* (Berlin, 1981), 35 ll.328–330.

[5] *ywlpnh msyb'*— the phrase is that of Theodore bar Konai, probably derived from Ephrem, *Ad Hypatium, Manetum, Marcionem et Bardesanem tractatus secundus* (cf. J.J. Overbeck, ed., *S. Ephraemi Syri... Opera Selecta* [Oxford, 1865], 67 l.23): *ywlpn' hn' msyb'.* The primary candidates for such inclusions are Severus of Antioch and Theodore bar Konai. For more details on these writers and the material which they preserve, see below. F. Cumont – M.-A. Kugener, *Recherches sur le manichéisme* (Bruxelles, 1908–12), 161, suggest that Severus extracted from the Book of Giants.

[6] Cf. C. Schmidt – H.J. Polotsky, "Ein Mani-Fund in Ægypten," *SPAW*, Phil.-hist. Klasse (1933), 4–90.

[7] H.J. Polotsky, ed., *Manichäische Handschriften der Sammlung A. Chester Beatty, Band 1: Manichäische Homilien* (Stuttgart, 1934).

[8] C.R.C. Allberry, ed., *Manichaean Manuscripts in the Chester Beatty Collection, Volume II: A Manichaean Psalm-Book, part II* (Stuttgart, 1938).

[9] H.J. Polotsky – A. Böhlig, eds., *Manichäische Handschriften der Staatlichen Museen Berlin, Band 1: Kephalaia, 1. Hälfte* (Stuttgart, 1934–40); A. Böhlig, ed., *2. Hälfte (Lfg. 11/12)* (Stuttgart, 1966).

[10] See Allberry's note to this line in the *Psalm-Book*; Polotsky, *Homilien*, xix, translating *calašire* as "Krieger, Held" (= καλασῖρις? See Polotsky's *index verborum*, 20*, and Herodotus 2.164, which identifies the καλασίρεις as an Egyptian warrior caste). Similarly the Septuagint invariably translates *gibbor* "mighty one" as γίγας.

[11] *tlaice nnparthos*, literally "because of the Parthians." See W. E. Crum, *A Coptic Dictionary* (Oxford, 1939), 151–52. Tardieu asserts that Coptic *laice* is equivalent to Greek αἴτημα, and translates "le livre que j'ai écrit *à la requête des*

Parthes." See M. Tardieu, *Le manichéisme* (Paris, 1981), 59. While his rendition seems an acceptable paraphrase, his conclusions based upon his rendering go beyond the evidence. See the next note.

[12] Schmidt–Polotsky, "Ein Mani-Fund," 39. Also Tardieu, *Le manichéisme*, 59. By identifying the "Parthians" with the eastern mission of Mar Ammō, Tardieu suggests that Mani composed the Book of Giants at the request of this emissary in order to expand upon legends barely mentioned in the Pragmateia.

[13] *Psalm-Book* 4:22–25 is the only other place in the published Coptic Manichaean literature that employs this designation: "[They arose], they that belong to Matter (ὕλη), the children of Error (πλάνη), desiring to uproot thy unshakeable tree and plant it in their land; they strove (?) at the matter, they did not succeed, [those] creatures of shame." Note the collocation of "children of Error" and "shame" in this reference as well. The allusion is either to the original attack of the forces of Darkness (=ὕλη) upon the realm of Light prior to the mixture of the two kingdoms, or to a subsequent rebellion of these same forces of Darkness modeled upon the legendary expansions of Genesis 6:1–4. The Nag Hammadi tractate *On the Origin of the World* (formerly referred to as the *Untitled Treatise*, NHC II.5 and XIII.2) characterizes the era of the Watchers and their offspring (= Genesis 6:1–4) as the era of πλάνη; cf. 123:2–24 and the analysis of M. Tardieu, *Trois mythes gnostiques: Adam, Eros et les animaux d'Egypte dans un écrit de Nag Hammadi (II,5)* (Paris, 1974), 71. Note too the Coptic *Apocryphon of John* 77:16–78:11; especially 77:30–78:2: "They (i.e., the rebellious angels) brought gold and silver and gifts and copper and iron and metal and every kind of these beautiful things, and they tempted mankind with great temptations, those who bound them up with themselves and led them astray into many errors (πλάνη)." (S. Giversen, *Apocryphon Johannis* [Copenhagen, 1963], 102–5). A clue to the source of this designation may be supplied by the wording of Greek 1 Enoch 6:2 in the version of Syncellus: καὶ ἐγένετο, ὅτι ἐπληθύνθησαν οἱ υἱοὶ τῶν ἀνθρώπων, ἐγεννήθησαν αὐτοῖς θυγατέρες ὡραῖαι, καὶ ἐπεθύμησαν αὐτὰς οἱ ἐγρήγοροι <u>καὶ ἀπεπλανήθησαν ὀπίσω αὐτῶν</u>.... A Syriac version of this same text appears in the universal chronicle of Michael the Syrian. Here the key term ἀπεπλανήθησαν is translated by *ṭ'w*; cf. J.B. Chabot, *Chronique de Michel le Syrien, patriarche jacobite d'Antioche, 1166–1199* (3 vols., Paris, 1899–1924; repr. in 4 vols., Brussells, 1963), IV 3.

[14] Schmidt–Polotsky, "Ein Mani-Fund," 34; 72 note n.

[15] G. Haloun – W.B. Henning, "The Compendium of the Doctrines and Styles of the Teaching of Mani, the Buddha of Light," *Asia Major* n.s. 3 (1953), 184–212.

[16] E. Chavannes – P. Pelliot, *Un traité manichéen retrouvé en Chine* (Paris, 1913); reprint of *JA* 18 (1911), 499–617; 20 (1913), 99–199; 261–339; P. Pelliot, "Two New Manichaean Manuscripts from Tun-Huang," *JRAS* (1925), 113.

[17] Haloun–Henning, 194–95.

[18] Henning speculates upon this basis that *Homilies* 94:18ff. preserves the original sequence of the canon; ibid., 205.

[19] Ibid., 204.

[20] Ibid., 194 n.61; 205. Referred to in Middle Persian as *ewangelyōn zīndag* "Living Gospel"; cf. Boyce, *Reader*, 33. The form *ewangelyōn* betrays its Syriac origin.

[21] A. Schall, *Studien über griechische Fremdwörter im Syrischen* (Darmstadt, 1960), 133–34.

[22] Haloun–Henning, 194 n.61; 207; S.N.C. Lieu, *Manichaeism in the Later Roman Empire and Medieval China: A Historical Survey* (Manchester, 1985; repr., 1988), 204.

[23] R. Payne Smith, *Thesaurus Syriacus* (Oxford, 1879–1901), 3235–36; C. Brockelmann, *Lexicon Syriacum* 2nd ed. (Halle, 1928), 592. Unfortunately none of the sources cited therein are earlier than the sixth century.

[24] Haloun–Henning, 194 n.61; 206–7. This work is referred to in Middle Persian as *niyān ī zīndagān* "Treasure of Life"; cf. Boyce, *Reader*, 41 l.2.

[25] The use of this designation is confirmed by certain Syriac testimonia to the life and teachings of Mani. Therein Mani is portrayed as promulgating several written works, one of which bears the title *symt'* "Treasury(s)." See *Chronicon Maroniticum* 59 l.12 (I. Guidi, ed., *Chronica Minora* CSCO scrip. syri series III vol.4 [Paris, 1903]); Theodore bar Konai, *Liber Scholiorum* ed. A. Scher CSCO scrip. syri, t.66 (Paris, 1912), 312 l.8. This term corresponds to the Latin *Thesaurum* (= Greek θησαυρός) of *Acta Archelai* 62.6 (ed. Beeson, 91). See now Sundermann, *Kirchengeschichtlichen Inhalts*, 35 l.345 and n.8.

[26] Haloun–Henning, 207.

[27] Ibid., 207. The title *rāzān* remains unattested in the Turfan fragments. *Raz* "secret, mystery" frequently appears in the Hebrew sectarian literature from Qumran; cf. K.G. Kuhn, *Konkordanz zu den Qumrantexten* (Göttingen, 1960), 203–4, and F. Nötscher, *Zur theologischen Terminologie der Qumran-Texte* (Bonn, 1956), 71–75. Aramaic *raz, raz'a* appears already in the Aramaic portion of Daniel, 1QapGen 1:2–3, and 4Q Mess ar 1:8. Abundant Syriac references in Payne Smith, *Thesaurus*, 3871–73, and Brockelmann, *Lexicon*, 722.

[28] Haloun-Henning, 208.

[29] Ibid., 194 n.61; 207–8.

[30] The fundamental study is that of A. Christensen, *Les Kayanides* (Copenhagen, 1931). See also idem, *L'Iran sous les Sassanides* (Copenhagen, 1936), 193 n.4, and M. Boyce, *A History of Zoroastrianism* (Leiden, 1975–), I 11.

[31] W.B. Henning, "Ein manichäisches Henochbuch," *SPAW* (1934), 30; *idem*, "The Book of the Giants," *BSOAS* 11 (1943), 53; Widengren, *Mani und der Manichäismus*, 81.

[32] M 5815 II (= T II D 134 II); cf. Boyce, *Reader*, 49; Andreas–Henning, *Mir. Man. III*, 857–60; Asmussen, *Manichaean Literature*, 23–24.

[33] *'wm 'w's 'w zmb wsyyd kyrd, 'wd fryh mry'mw 'wd hwr's'n nyrd fršwd; 'wd k'w'n 'wd 'rdhng nyrd bwrd. 'wd mn 'ny kw'n 'wd ''rdhng 'ndr mrg kyrd.* (Boyce, *Reader*, 49) ("And I have now let him go to Zamb and sent him to dear Mar Ammō and Khorasan, and (the Book of) the Giants and the Ardahang he has taken with him. And I have made another (copy of the Book of) the Giants and the

Ardahang in Marw.") Translation is that of Asmussen, *Manichaean Literature*, 23. For discussion of the mission of Mar Ammō, see Lieu, *Manichaeism*, 78–80.

[34] See above notes 20 and 24.

[35] Hegemonius, *Acta Archelai* [ed. Beeson] (see n.1 above). According to Jerome (*De viris illustribus* 72; see Migne, *Patrologia Latina* [= *P.L.*] 23, 719B) the work was originally composed in Syriac by the bishop Archelaus who is featured in the narrative, but this provenance is almost universally rejected. The work survives in its entirety only in a Latin version of what was almost certainly a Greek original, fragments of which are preserved in Epiphanius, *Panarion* 66. For a concise discussion of the work see A. Harnack, *Geschichte der altchristlichen Literatur bis Eusebius* (Leipzig, 1904) II.2, 163–64.

[36] The use of data contained in the *Acta* by Cyril of Jerusalem provides a *terminus ad quem*; see below, note 41.

[37] Qualified as "civitate Mesopotamiae" (*Acta Archelai* 1.1 [ed. Beeson, 1]). Cf. Socrates, *Hist. eccl.* 1.22: Κασχάρων, μιᾶς τῶν ἐν Μεσοποταμίᾳ πόλεων. The precise identification of this city is much disputed. For a thorough discussion of the various options, see Flügel, *Mani*, 19–26.

[38] *Acta Archelai* 62–65 (ed. Beeson, 90–95). For the titles of the books, see Beeson, 91 ll.4–7.

[39] Epiphanius, *Panarion* 66.2.9 transmits the titles as Μυστήρια, Κεφάλαια, Εὐαγγέλιον, and Θησαυρός. See Schmidt–Polotsky, "Ein Mani-Fund", 5.

[40] For a comprehensive list of sources which utilize and perpetuate the *Acta* see H.-C. Puech, *Le manichéisme: son fondateur — sa doctrine* (Paris, 1949), 99 n.10.

[41] Cyril of Jerusalem, *Catecheses* 6.22–30 (Migne, *P.G.* 33, 576A–93A).

[42] Epiphanius, *Panarion* 66.13.6 transmits Μυστήρια, Θησαυρός, τὸν μικρὸν δὴ θησαυρὸν οὕτω καλούμενον, τὴν περὶ ἀστρολογίας. It is unclear whether there is any relationship between these four titles and the works mentioned at *Panarion* 66.2.9 (cf. note 39 above).

[43] *Chronicon Maroniticum*, 59 ll.10–13 (cf. note 25 above).

[44] Theodore bar Konai, *Liber Scholiorum*, 311 l.12–313 l.9 (see note 25 above).

[45] See Puech, *Le manichéisme*, 100.

[46] Text in A. Adam, ed., *Texte zum Manichäismus* 2. Auflage (Berlin, 1969), 90.

[47] Ibid., 93–97. The list of works can be found at 94 ll.24–34. For a thorough study of the abjuration-formulae, see especially S.N.C. Lieu, "An Early Byzantine Formula for the Renunciation of Manichaeism — The Capita VII Contra Manichaeos of <Zacharias of Mitylene>," *Jahrbuch für Antike und Christentum* 26 (1983), 152–218.

[48] Timothy of Constantinople, *De receptione haereticorum* (Migne, *P.G.* 86:1, 20–24). The list of works can be found at 21C.

[49] The abjuration expressly states that "five books" (πέντε βίβλοις) were to be anathematized, and then goes on to provide the further material listed in positions 6 and 7 of the catalogue above.

[50] Timothy provides five additional titles which were held in esteem by the

Manichaeans: the Gospel of Thomas, the Gospel of Philip, the Acts of Andrew, the 15th Epistle to the Laodiceans, and the Infancy Narrative.

[51] I. de Beausobre, *Histoire critique de Manichée et du Manichéisme* (Amsterdam, 1734–39; repr. Leipzig, 1970), I 430; Schmidt–Polotsky, "Ein Mani-Fund," 25; Adam, *Texte*², 94. There are no "epistles to Mar Ammō" mentioned in the catalogue of Mani's letters preserved in al-Nadīm's *Fihrist* (*apud* Flügel, *Mani*, 73–76).

[52] For πραγματεία signifying "treatise," see K. Kessler, *Mani: Forschungen über die manichäische Religion* (Berlin, 1889), 205; H.H. Schaeder, [Review of Schmidt–Polotsky, "Ein Mani-Fund"], *Gnomon* 9 (1933), 347; Puech, *Le manichéisme*, 67.

[53] P. Alfaric, *Les écritures manichéennes* (Paris, 1918–19), II 58–59; Schmidt–Polotsky, "Ein Mani-Fund," 38.

[54] وممّا وضع كتابه الذى يسمّيه كنز الاحياء يصف ما فى النفس من الاخلاص النورى والفساد الظلمى وينسب الافعال الرديّة الى الظلمة وكتاب يسمّه الشابر قان يصف فيه النفس الخالصة والضحتلطة بالشياطين والعلل . . . وكتاب يسميه كتاب الهدى والتدبير واثنا عشر انجيلا يسمى كل انجيل منها بحرف من الحروف ويذكر الصلوة وما ينبغي ان يستعمل لخلاص الروح وكتاب سفر الاسرار الذى يطعن فيه على آيات الانبياء وكتاب سفر الجبابرة وله كتب كثيرة ورساءيل .

Text cited from Aḥmad ibn Abī Ya'qūb ibn Wāḍiḥ al-Ya'qūbī, *[Ta'rīkh] Ibn Wadih qui dicitur al-Ja'qubi historiae...* ed. M.T. Houtsma (Leiden, 1883), 181 ll.3–12.

[55] Abū al-Faraj Muḥammad ibn Isḥāq Abū Ya'qūb al-Warrāq al-Nadīm, *Kitāb al-Fihrist* ed. G. Flügel (Leipzig, 1871–72). An English translation was produced by B. Dodge, *The Fihrist of al-Nadim* 2 volumes (New York, 1970). Al-Nadīm's treatment of Manichaeism was the subject of a separate study by Flügel (see n.1 above).

[56] In addition to the Manichaeans, al-Nadīm also includes discussion of the Ḥarranian Ṣabians, the followers of Bardaiṣan, the Marcionites, and various other smaller, more obscure sects.

[57] See n.1 above. The list of Mani's works appears in Flügel, *Mani*, 72–73.

[58] For the most recent discussion of the manuscript tradition of the *Fihrist* together with references to the earlier treatments, see Dodge, *Fihrist*, I xxiii–xxxiv. See also F. Sezgin, *Geschichte des arabischen Schrifttums* (=*GAS*) (Leiden, 1967–), I 385–88.

[59] See Flügel, *Mani*, 367–69; Kessler, *Mani*, 203–4.

[60] For a list of possible equations with other Manichaean works, see Flügel, *Mani*, 363–65; Kessler, *Mani*, 201–3; Alfaric, *Les écritures*, II 54–58. The "Precepts" are most commonly identified with the so-called *Epistula fundamenti* refuted by Augustine; cf. his *Contra epistulam quam vocant fundamenti* ed. J. Zycha (Corpus Scriptorum Ecclesiasticorum Latinorum 25) (Vienna, 1891–92), 191–248.

[61] Citations of Manichaean works which include the Shabuhragan are found

in al-Ya'qūbī, al-Mas'ūdī, al-Nadīm, 'Abd al-Jabbār, al-Bīrūnī, al-Shahrastānī, and Ibn al-Murtaḍā. See al-Ya'qūbī, *Ta'rīkh* (ed. Houtsma), 181 ll.6–8; al-Mas'ūdī, [*Kitāb al-tanbīh wa-l-išrāf*] *Le livre de l'avertissement et de la revision* trans. B. Carra de Vaux (Paris, 1896), 188; Aḥmad ibn Yaḥya ibn al-Murtaḍā *apud* Kessler, *Mani*, 346 ll.4–5. For 'Abd al-Jabbār, see G. Vajda, "Le témoignage d'al-Māturidī sur la doctrine des Manichéens, des Dayṣanites et des Marcionites," *Arabica* 13 (1966), 121. For the list-traditions of al-Bīrūnī see below. Passages from the Shabuhragan are quoted by 'Abd al-Jabbār, al-Bīrūnī (cf. note 73 below), and al-Shahrastānī. For the latter see Muḥammad ibn 'Abd al-Karim al-Shahrastānī, *Kitāb al-milal wa-al-niḥal: Book of Religious and Philosophical Sects* ed. W. Cureton (London, 1842–46), 192 l.2. Some portions of the book have been recovered from Turfan. See M. Boyce, *A Catalogue of the Iranian Manuscripts in Manichaean Script in the German Turfan Collection* (Berlin, 1960), 31–32; D.N. MacKenzie, "Mani's Šābuhragān," *BSOAS* 42 (1979), 500–534; 43 (1980), 288–310; Sundermann, *Kirchengeschichtlichen Inhalts*, 92ff.

[62] E. Sachau, ed., *Chronologie orientalischer Völker von Albêrûnî* (Leipzig, 1878), 207 l.9. English translation in E. Sachau, ed., *The Chronology of Ancient Nations* (London, 1879), 190.

[63] Al-Ya'qūbī relates that Shapur was led astray by the teachings of Mani for ten years. See al-Ya'qūbī, *Ta'rīkh* (ed. Houtsma), 180–81.

[64] On al-Bīrūnī see D.J. Boilot, "al-Bīrūnī," *The Encyclopaedia of Islam*, new edition (=*EI*^{2}) (Leiden, 1960–), I 1236–38.

[65] Cf. n.62 above.

[66] Sachau, *Chronologie*, 207 l.8 – 209 l.10.

[67] Ibid., 208 ll.13–14.

[68] The text of this treatise (*risālah*) appears in Sachau, *Chronologie*, XXXVIII–XXXXVIII; cf. also X–XV. A new edition was prepared by P. Kraus, *Epître de Beruni, contenant le répertoire des ouvrages de Muhammad b. Zakariya ar-Razi* (Paris, 1936). For discussion and partial translations of the treatise, see J. Ruska, "Al-Bīrūnī als Quelle für das Leben und die Schriften al-Rāzī's," *Isis* 5 (1923), 26–50; R. Köbert, "Die Einführung Bīrūnīs zu seinem Verzeichnis der Schriften Rāzīs," *Orientalia* 27 (1958), 198–202; and D.M. Dunlop, *Arab Civilization to A.D.1500* (New York, 1971), 238–39. On al-Rāzī see Dodge, *Fihrist*, II 701–9; P. Kraus – S. Pines, "al-Rāzī," in *Enzyklopaedie des Islam* (Leiden, 1913–38), III 1225–27; and Sezgin, *GAS* (cf. n.57 above), III 274–94.

[69] كتاب العلم الالهي. This work is mentioned by Maimonides; see his *The Guide for the Perplexed* trans. M. Friedländer, 2nd revised ed. (London, 1904; repr. New York, 1956), 267. See also the reference to this work in R. Dozy – M.J. De Goeje, "Nouveaux documents pour l'étude de la religion des Harraniens," in *Actes de la sixième session du congrès international des orientalistes à Leide* (Leiden, 1884–85), pt.II sect.I, 312. The book has not survived, but for a reconstruction of its content based on various references to it, see M. Mohaghegh, "Razi's Kitab al-Ilm al-Ilāhi and the Five Eternals," *Abr-Nahrain* 13 (1972–73), 16–23.

[70] Al-Bīrūnī, *Risālah* (*apud* Sachau, *Chronologie*, XXXIX) ll.10–19:

> ...and this I read (in) his book on 'Divine Knowledge,' and he begins with arguments against the books of Mani, especially his book called 'Book of Mysteries.' The title enticed me in the same way that another is enticed by (the colors) white and yellow in (the practice of) alchemy. The novelty, or rather, the inaccessability of the truth stimulated me to search for these 'Mysteries' among my acquaintances in (various) countries and regions, but I remained in a state of longing (for this work) some forty years until there came to me in Khwārizm a soldier from Hamadān bearing books which Faḍl ibn Sahlān had come across, and he informed me that they (these books) were very dear to him. Among them was a volume filled with the writings of the Manichaeans, containing the Pragmateia, the Book of Giants, the Treasure of Life, the Dawn of Truth and Foundation, the Gospel, the Shabuhragan, and a number of epistles of Mani, and the goal of my search, the Book of Mysteries. Happiness over this discovery overwhelmed me, as those who are thirsty are overwhelmed at the sight of a drink, but also sadness in the end, as when one is stricken with gas from contaminated (water?), and I experienced the truth of the word of God Most High: 'He to whom God does not grant light has no light' (Sura 40:24).

[71] Ibid., ll.15–17.

[72] It is unclear whether this should be interpreted as one title or two. Ruska (see n.68 above) understands two separate works: 1) the "Dawn of Truth" 2) the "Book of Foundation(s)." On the other hand, it might correspond to the similar dually constructed title "Precepts for Hearers and for the Elect"; see n.60 above and Alfaric, *Les écritures*, II 14–17 and 55.

[73] For quotations and/or allusions to the "Gospel," see Sachau, *Chronologie*, 23 ll.10–14; 207 ll.18–19. For quotations from the Shabuhragan, see ibid., 118 ll.12–21; 207 ll.14–18; 208 ll.8–12. Quotation from the "Book of Mysteries" in E. Sachau, *Alberuni's India* (London, 1888; repr. London, 1910), I 54–55; from the "Treasure of Life" in ibid., I 39; and from unnamed Manichaean sources in ibid., I 48,55,381; II 169.

[74] Unless a further reference to Mani's teachings regarding the existence of "jinns and demons" can be taken as an allusion to this work; see Sachau, *Chronologie*, 237 ll.7–12.

[75] Regarding Alexander of Lycopolis, see now the excellent detailed study by A. Villey, *Alexandre de Lycopolis: Contre la doctrine de Mani* (Paris, 1985).

[76] A. Brinkmann, ed., *Alexandri Lycopolitani contra Manichaei opiniones disputatio* (Leipzig, 1895) is the critical edition of the Greek text. An English translation based on this edition was provided by P.W. van der Horst – J. Mansfeld, *An Alexandrian Platonist Against Dualism* (Leiden, 1974). For the dating circa 300 C.E. see Brinkmann, XIIIff. and H.H. Schaeder, "Urform und Fortbildungen des manichäischen Systems," in F. Saxl, ed., *Vorträge der Bibliothek*

Warburg IV (Leipzig, 1927), 106–7, reprinted in H.H. Schaeder, *Studien zur orientalischen Religionsgeschichte* (Darmstadt, 1968), 56–57. Van der Horst–Mansfeld suggest that the treatise was composed prior to the edict against Manichaeism issued by the emperor Diocletian in 297 C.E. (p.5, n.8).

[77] Xenophanes B 1.19–24 (cf. H. Diels, ed., *Die Fragmente der Vorsokratiker* [Berlin, 1912], I 55–56); Plato, *Euthyphro* 6b–c; *Republic* 378a–c.

[78] Alex. Lycop., *Contra Man.* 5: ἐκ δὲ τῶν ποιήσεων τῆς γιγαντομαχίας, ὅτι μηδὲ αὐτοὶ ἠγνόησαν τὴν τῆς ὕλης κατὰ τοῦ θεοῦ ἀνταρσιν (Brinkmann, 8). The English translation is that of van der Horst–Mansfeld, 57.

[79] For information on the development of these stories, see M. Mayer, *Die Giganten und Titanen in der antike Sagen und Kunst* (Berlin, 1887); F. Vian, *La guerre des géants* (Paris, 1952); H.J. Rose, *A Handbook of Greek Mythology* (London, 1928; repr. New York, 1959), 56–62.

[80] Already Plato, *Sophist* 246a–b. See especially Philo, *De Gigantibus* 58–67; J. Pépin, *Mythe et allégorie: Les origines grecques et les contestations judéo-chrétiennes* 2nd ed. (Paris, 1976), 128; 402–3. Note the comment of J. Bidez regarding the cosmogonical tradition reported in Book 1 of the *Babyloniaka* of Berossus: "la gigantomachie où Bel triompha d'Omorka, représentait la victorie de la lumière et de l'ordre sur les ténèbres et le chaos...." This observation is taken from his important study "Les écoles chaldéennes sous Alexandre et les Séleucides," *Annuaire de l'institut de philologie et d'histoire orientales* (Bruxelles) 3 (1935), 49. A "modern" allegory for the γιγαντομαχία is provided by G. Murray, *Five Stages of Greek Religion* 3rd ed. (Boston, 1951; repr. Garden City, 1955), 58–59.

[81] Alex. Lycop., *Contra Man.* 25 (Greek text of Brinkmann, 37 l.13–38 l.6): Ἃ δὲ λέγεται ὑπο τῶν ποιήσεων περὶ τῶν Γιγάντων, ἄντικρυς μῦθός ἐστιν. οἱ μὲν γὰρ περὶ τούτων διατάττοντες ἐν ἀλληγορίαις τὰ τοιαῦτα προφέρονται τὸ σεμνὸν τοῦ λόγου ἀποκρύπτοντες τῇ τοῦ μύθου ἰδέᾳ οἷον ὅταν ἡ τῶν Ἰουδαίων ἱστορία φῇ τοὺς ἀγγέλους ταῖς θυγατράσι τῶν ἀνθρώπων εἰς ἀφροδισίων συνεληλυθέναι μῖξιν, τὰς γὰρ θρεπτικὰς δυνάμεις τῆς ψυχῆς ἀπὸ τῶν ἄνω ἐπὶ τὰ τῇδε <... > ἡ τοιαύτη προφορὰ τοῦ λόγου σημαίνει. οἱ ποιηταὶ δὲ ἐκ γῆς ἐνόπλους ἀνασχεῖν λέγοντες τούτους εἶτ' εὐθὺς πρὸς θεοὺς ἀντάραντας ἀπολωλέναι, τὸ ταχὺ καὶ ἐπίκηρον τῶν σωμάτων ὑποδηλοῦντες, οὕτω τὴν ποίησιν εἰς ψυχαγωγίαν τῷ θαύματι κατακοσμοῦσιν. οἳ δὲ οὐδὲν εἰδότες τούτων, ἔνθα δᾶν παραλογισμοῦ τινος εὐπορῆσαι δύνωνται, ὁπόθεν δήποτε ἐκεῖνο ἕρμαιον ἑαυτῶν ποιοῦνται, ὥσπερ διαπραγματευόμενοι τὸ ἀληθὲς πάσῃ τέχνῃ καταγωνίσασθαι. English translation from van der Horst–Mansfeld, 95. A similar criticism occurs in a polemical hymn of Ephrem: "Mani hated truth and believed fiction...he gave credence to (the narrative) about the Giants, and believed (the doctrines of) the Chaldaeans." See E. Beck, ed., *Des heiligen Ephraem des Syrers: Hymnen contra Haereses* CSCO 169 (Louvain, 1957), 29 ll.16–18 (text).

[82] For a Jewish source in addition to the passage just cited, note the reference to the *'Aqedah* at the end of chapter 24 (Brinkmann, 36). There are

numerous references to "Christ" and "Christians"; see especially chapter 1 (Brinkmann, 3) and chapter 16 (Brinkmann, 24). Alexander is cognizant of the existence of Christian "sects" (αἱρέσεις) (Brinkmann, 4), and apparently classified Mani as a Christian sectarian leader. See R. Reitzenstein, "Eine wertlose und eine wertvolle Ueberlieferung über den Manichäismus," *NGWG*, Phil.-hist. Kl. (1931), 40 and 56 n.2.

[83] Chapter 25 of Alexander's exposition is devoted to the refutation of Manichaean asceticism, and features a constant interplay between Manichaean assertion and Alexander's philosophical ridicule. The allusion to the gigantomachy forms the concluding part of this section. A further reference to a "war with giants" or gigantomachy appears approximately half a century later in the anti-Manichaean treatise of Serapion of Thmuis, although this witness supplies little information regarding this motif beyond what is contained in Alexander and perhaps derives his information on this point from the Neoplatonist writer: καὶ τοιούτου μὲν τοιοῦτος ὁ ἔλεγχος, ἵνα πολλὴν συστείλωμεν ὁμιλίαν, τὰς προβολὰς αὐτῶν, τὰς μάχας, τὰς μυθοποιίας ἐκείνας καὶ γιγαντομαχίας σιωπῶντες.... See R.P. Casey, *Serapion of Thmuis Against the Manichees* (Cambridge, Mass., 1931), 52.

[84] Migne, *P.L.* 59, 162–63. See E. von Dobschütz, ed., *Das Decretum Gelasianum: De libris recipiendis et non recipiendis* [Texte und Untersuchungen zur Geschichte der altchristlichen Literatur 38] (Leipzig, 1912), 54 and cf. his discussion, 305–6. J.T. Milik thinks that this work was a Latin translation of the Manichaean Book of Giants. See his "Problèmes de la littérature hénochique à la lumière des fragments araméennes de Qumrân," *HTR* 64 (1971), 367; *idem*, "Turfan et Qumran: Livre des Géants juif et manichéen," in G. Jeremias, H.-W. Kuhn, and H. Stegemann, eds., *Tradition und Glaube: Das frühe Christentum in seiner Umwelt* (Göttingen, 1971), 118. Lieu speculates that it may have been a Latin translation of either the Manichaean or Jewish Book of Giants (*Manichaeism*, 88).

[85] Migne, *P.L.* 59, 162 n.19.; Alfaric, *Les écritures*, II 32; cf. Henning, *BSOAS* 11 (1943), 71–72 (Parthian N). Henning identifies Ogias with Ohya (*'why'*), one of the two Giant sons of Shahmīzād (i.e., Shemiḥazah, the leader of the rebellious Watchers in 1 Enoch) mentioned in the Middle Iranian versions of the Book of Giants. Noting v. Dobschütz's identification of Ogias with Og of Bashan, the biblical Amorite king of gigantic stature (see Deuteronomy 3:11), Henning suggests that "stories that primarily appertained to Ogias were transferred to the better known Og, owing to the resemblance of their names" (p.54). The name "Ohya" is now attested in the Qumran fragments of the Jewish Book of Giants (*'whyh*); see chapter two below. For the relationship of Og of Bashan to the antediluvian (and postdiluvian!) generation(s) of Giants, see bT Niddah 61a; Targum Pseudo-Jonathan to Deuteronomy 3:11.

[86] Abū Isḥāq 'Ibrāhīm ben Muḥammad al-Tibrizī, called al-Ghadanfar, is an otherwise obscure author whose *floruit* was apparently the mid-thirteenth century C.E. See Sachau, *Chronologie*, XV.

[87] وكتاب سفر الجبابرة لماني البابليّ مملؤ من قصص هؤلاء الجبابرة الذين
منهم سام ونريمان وكانّه قد أخذ هذين الاسمين من كتاب افدستاك
لزردشت الاذربجاني...

See Sachau, *Chronologie*, XIV and Kessler, *Mani*, 199–200.

[88] Sām and Narīmān are generally considered to be Saka (i.e., Scythian) heroes that have been grafted into indigenous Iranian epic lore. The Iranian historical traditions are particularly difficult to unravel, for we possess no contemporary historical sources that aid us in discriminating between legendary and historical events. Karshāsp (Avestan Kərəsāspa) is the most celebrated warrior of the Avestan legends. His epithet *naire.manah* "of manly mind" became personified in later tradition in the forms "Nīram," "Narīmān" and thus evolves into a separate figure. The Avestan Kərəsāspa bears the clan name Sāma which in turn is transformed into a separate hero "Sām" in the *Shāh-nāma*. In the later tradition (cf. *Bundahishn*) Sām = Karshāsp and appropriates some of the martial exploits associated with the latter hero. Narīmān also partially replaces Karshāsp in Persian epic and becomes a link in the genealogy Sām – Narīmān – Zāl – Rustam, the last named of course being the most prominent hero of the *Shāh-nāma*. For an excellent discussion of the Iranian epic tradition see E. Yarshater, "Iranian National History," in E. Yarshater, ed., *The Cambridge History of Iran: Volume 3(1): The Seleucid, Parthian and Sasanian Periods* (Cambridge, 1983), 359–477. See also T. Nöldeke, *Das iranische Nationalepos*[2] (Berlin, 1920), 9–12; Christensen, *Kayanides* (cf. n.30 above), 129–32; and Boyce, *History* (cf. n.30 above), I 100–104.

[89] Cf. Kessler, *Mani*, 200. The text speaks of a book composed by Vyasa consisting of 120,000 verses which narrates stories about the Giants. To Vyasa is traditionally ascribed the authorship of the *Mahābhārata* as well as the four Vedas and the Puranas; see M. Winternitz, *A History of Indian Literature* trans. V.S. Sarma (Delhi, 1981), 301–3. The destruction of the Giants is credited to Vasudeva (i.e., Kṛṣna) during the time when the Bharata clan flourished. For an earlier allegation that Mani had borrowed ideas from India, see Ephrem, *Hymnen contra Haereses* (ed. Beck; cf. n.81 above), 12 ll.12–13. Note Beausobre, *Histoire*, II 304.

[90] 1 Enoch 6–11; 69:4–5; 86–88; Jubilees 5:1–9; 7:20–27; 10:1–14. Another stream of tradition present in both 1 Enoch and Jubilees identifies the sin of the rebellious angels as their unauthorized impartation of "hidden" knowledge to humanity.

[91] Jerome, *Tractatus de Psalmo CXXXII* (cf. G. Morin, ed., *S. Hieronymi Presbyteri Opera: Pars II: Opera Homiletica* Corpus Christianorum Series Latina 78 [Turnholt, 1958], 280): "*Sicut ros Ermon, qui descendit in montem Sion.* Ros Ermon. Legimus quendam librum apocryphum, eo tempore quo descendebant filii Dei ad filias hominum, descendisse illos in montem Ermon, et ibi inisse pactum, quomodo uenirent ad filias hominum, et sibi eas sociarent. Manifestissimus liber est, et inter apocryphos conputatur ...."

[92] Ibid., 281: "Legi in cuiusdam libro de isto libro apocrypho suam haeresim

confirmantis." Translation is taken from *The Homilies of Saint Jerome: Volume I (1–59 On the Psalms)* trans. M.L. Ewald (Washington, 1964), 338.

[93] Jerome, *De Psalmo CXXXII* (ed. Morin, 281): "Videtis quomodo nescitis Manichaei dogma consurgit?"

[94] On al-Jāḥiẓ see C. Pellat, "al-Djāḥiẓ," *EI²*, II 385–87; *idem*, "Le témoignage d'al-Jāḥiẓ sur les manichéens," in C.E. Bosworth, et al., eds., *Essays in Honor of Bernard Lewis: The Islamic World, from Classical to Modern Times* (Princeton, NJ, 1989), 269–79.

[95] تناكح الشياطين وتسافد العفاريت Al-Jāḥiẓ *apud* Kessler, *Mani*, 368 ll.4-5.

[96] καὶ ὅσα αὐτῷ ἐπραγματεύθη περὶ γιγάντων καὶ ἐκτρωμάτων. This phrase comes from the so-called "long" Greek abjuration formula. The complete text can be found in Adam, *Texte²*, 97–103; the phrase quoted here from 98 ll.19–20.

[97] *Bereshit Rabba* 26:7: אמר ר׳ לעזר בר׳ שמעון...נפילים שהיפילו את העולם ונפלו מן העולם ושמלאו את העולם נפלים מן הזנות שלהם (Theodor–Albeck, 254). See also *Leqaḥ Ṭob* to Genesis 6:4; Rashi to Genesis 6:4; and compare Tanḥuma Buber, *Bereshit* §40. Cf. T. Nöldeke, [Review of Kessler, *Mani*] *ZDMG* 43 (1889), 536; G.A.G. Stroumsa, *Another Seed: Studies in Gnostic Mythology* (Leiden, 1984), 65–70; 160–61; B.A. Pearson, "The Problem of 'Jewish Gnostic' Literature," in C.W. Hedrick – R. Hodgson, Jr., eds., *Nag Hammadi, Gnosticism, & Early Christianity* (Peabody, MA, 1986), 23.

[98] Beausobre, *Histoire* (see n.51 above). For the importance of Beausobre's contribution to the scientific study of Manichaeism, see H.S. Nyberg, "Forschungen über den Manichäismus," *ZNW* 34 (1935), 72; G. Widengren, "Der Manichäismus: Kurzgefasste Geschichte der Problemforschung," in B. Aland, ed., *Gnosis: Festschrift für Hans Jonas* (Göttingen, 1978), 278–79.

[99] Beausobre, *Histoire*, II 303–4.

[100] Beausobre, *Histoire*, I 429 n.6, referring to the so-called Kenan *deuteros*. Kenan (קינן) as son of Arpachshad and father of Shelah appears in LXX Genesis 10:24, LXX Genesis 11:12–13, LXX Alexandrinus 1 Chronicles 1:18, and in the Lucan genealogy of Jesus (Luke 3:36); he is listed as *brother* of Arpachshad (and hence son of Shem) in LXX Genesis 10:22. Kenan ben Arpachshad also appears in the Ethiopic Version of Genesis 11:13. These sources report nothing about Kenan's alleged discovery. The earliest reference to this story is found in Jubilees 8:1–4:

> And in the twenty-ninth jubilee, in the first week (of years), at its outset, Arpachshad took in marriage a woman whose name was Rasuya, daughter of Susan, daughter of Elam, and she bore him a son in the third year of that week, and he named him Qaynam. The boy grew, and his father taught him the art of writing, and he departed seeking a place where he might acquire a city for himself. And he discovered an inscription which previous (generations) had inscribed on a stone, and read what was on it, and he copied it, and thus erred due to what was on it, because there was on it the

> teaching of the Watchers by which they instituted divination (using) sun, moon, and stars among all the signs of heaven. He copied it, but did not speak about it; for he was afraid to tell Noah about it lest the latter should be angry with him about it.

According to B. Beer, Jubilees is dependent upon the testimony of the Septuagint for the insertion of this patriarch. See his *Das Buch der Jubiläen und sein Verhältniss zu den Midraschim* (Leipzig, 1856), 17. However, it should be noted that Jubilees includes this extra patriarch for the purpose of making a theological point: "Twenty-two heads of humanity from Adam up to Jacob, and twenty-two kinds of thing(s) were created up to the seventh day. This (i.e., the Sabbath) is blessed and holy; and that one (i.e., Jacob) is blessed and holy, and both together are for consecration and praise" (Jubilees 2:23). Without the insertion of Kenan into the genealogy, there would be only twenty-one patriarchs and thus the symmetry established with the created order and the Sabbath (according to Jubilees' enumeration) would be marred. There would seem to be no such justification for the presence of Kenan in the Septuagintal chronology, and hence the question of dependence is hardly resolved. The so-called *Midrash Tadshe* (cf. A. Jellinek, *Bet ha-Midrasch* [Leipzig, 1853–1877; repr. Jerusalem, 1938], III 169) also seems cognizant of the patriarchal sequence presupposed by Jubilees: כ"ב מינים נבראו בעולם בז' ימים ...כנגד כ"ב אותיות שבא"ב וכנגד הכ"ב דורות מאדם עד שבא יעקב.

It is assumed that the report of Kenan's discovery contained in Syncellus (and subsequent Byzantine histories) is derived from a later version of Jubilees 8:1–4; see A.-M. Denis, *Introduction aux pseudépigraphes grecs d'ancien testament* (Leiden, 1970), 153. Knowledge of the tradition in this particular form is exhibited by the *Syriac Chronicon ad 1234* where the "writing of the Watchers" (Jubilees) or the "Book of Giants" (Syncellus) is termed "a book which the ancient ones (*qdmy'*) wrote." See J.-B. Chabot, ed., *Chronicon ad annum Christi 1234 pertinens* CSCO scrip. syri 3.14 (Paris, 1920), 46 ll.3–22 and compare I.E. Rahmani, ed., *Chronicon civile et ecclesiasticum anonymi auctoris...* (Charfé, 1904) as cited in E. Tisserant, "Fragments syriaques du livre des Jubilés," *RB* 30 (1921), 206–7.

[101] Καϊνᾶν ... εὗρε τὴν γραφὴν τῶν γιγάντων καὶ ἔκρυψε παρ' ἑαυτῷ ("Kenan found the Book of Giants and hid (it) for himself" [Cf. Jubilees 8:4]). Syncellus citation taken from A.A. Mosshammer, ed., *Georgii Syncelli Ecloga Chronographica* (Leipzig, 1984), 90. Compare also Georgius Cedrenus, *Compendium Historiarum* ed. I. Bekker (Bonn, 1838), 27: Καϊνᾶν ἐν τῷ πεδίῳ εὗρε τὴν γραφὴν τῶν γιγάντων.... These sources are conveniently juxtaposed in A.-M. Denis, ed., *Fragmenta Pseudepigraphorum quae supersunt Graeca* (Leiden, 1970), 85–86.

[102] Beausobre, *Histoire*, I 429. A valuable collection of ancient witnesses to the "Book of Enoch" is provided by H.J. Lawlor, "Early Citations From the Book of Enoch," *Journal of Philology* 25 (1897), 164–225.

[103] περὶ τῶν ἐγρηγόρων. Beausobre, *Histoire*, I 428–29 n.3.

[104] Ibid., I 429.

[105] F.C. Baur, *Das manichäische Religionssystem nach den Quellen neu untersucht und entwickelt* (Tübingen, 1831). Baur also utilized the pagan testimonies of Alexander of Lycopolis and Simplicius. For the importance of Baur's research, see Widengren, "Der Manichäismus" (cf. n.98 above), 279–81.

[106] Baur, *Religionssystem*, 77, citing Augustine, *De natura boni* 46 and *Contra Faustum* 20.14. Baur's n.17 also calls attention to the immense form attributed to Ahriman, the principle of Evil, in Zoroastrian writings.

[107] Baur, *Religionssystem*, 77. See also ibid., 66 n.14.

[108] Ibid., 78.

[109] Flügel, *Mani* (see n.1 above).

[110] J.L. Mosheim, *De rebus christianorum ante Constantinum Magnum commentarii* (Helmstedt, 1753), 767: "Agebat sine dubio in illo de principe daemonum ejusque satellitibus ac ministris, atque ea, quae de gigantum cum Diis bello veteres referunt, ad pugnam boni malique principii trahebat," as cited in Flügel, *Mani*, 362. Also noticed by Baur, *Religionssystem*, 78 n.18.

[111] Flügel, *Mani*, 362.

[112] Al-Shahrastānī, *Milal* (cf. n.61 above), 192 ll.1–2: وذكر الحكيم ماني في باب الالف من الجبلة... "And Mani the sage mentions in the first chapter of the *Jblh* ...." This title was simply transliterated by Haarbrücker in his German translation of al-Shahrastānī as "al-Dschibilla"; see T. Haarbrücker, *Abu-'l-Fath' Muhammad asch-Schahrastâni's Religionspartheien und Philosophen-Schulen* (Halle, 1850–51), I 290; II 422.

[113] Flügel, *Mani*, 362–63; also Kessler, *Mani*, 198–99. The citation of "chapter one" (*bāb ālaf*) suggests that the correct reading of this title is انجيل "Gospel," which according to al-Ya'qūbī and al-Bīrūnī consisted of twenty-two chapters corresponding to the letters of the Syriac alphabet. See D. Gimaret – G. Monnot, eds., *Shahrastani: Livre des religions et des sectes I* (n.p., 1986), 660 n.35.

[114] Kessler, *Mani* (cf. n.52 above). See also Nöldeke, *ZDMG* 43 (1889), 535–49.

[115] See nn.87–90 above.

[116] Kessler, *Mani*, 199, referring to the summary in Sachau, *Chronologie*, XIV.

[117] Kessler, *Mani*, 200.

[118] Ibid., 200–201.

[119] Ibid., 200.

[120] Cumont–Kugener, *Recherches* (see n.5 above).

[121] Ibid., 3–4 and n.1; 41–42 n.4.

[122] Ibid., 4 n.1. The authors refer to Cumont's magisterial *Textes et monuments relatifs aux mystères de Mithra* (Bruxelles, 1896–99), I 45 n.1 and 158.

[123] Cumont–Kugener, *Recherches*, 161. The 123rd homily of Severus, a sixth-century patriarch of Antioch, is extant in two Syriac versions which were translated from a Greek original. Cumont–Kugener partially reproduce the version of Jacob of Edessa (7th–8th century) in their *Recherches*, 89–150; the complete homily (in this version) is available in M. Brière, "Les Homiliae

Cathedrales de Sévère d'Antioche, traduction syriaque de Jacques d'Edesse CXX à CXXV," *PO* 29 (1960), 124–89. Another Syriac version prepared by Paul of Callinicus (6th century) was published by I.E. Rahmani, *Studia Syriaca IV. Documenta de antiquis haeresibus* (Beirut, 1909), 48–89.

[124] Alfaric, *Les écritures* (see n.53 above).

[125] Note particularly Alfaric's "Préface" and his initial chapter "Origine des écritures manichéennes" (I 1–31), which launches into an examination of the Gnostic literary milieu based on the testimony of the patristic sources.

[126] Alfaric, *Les écritures*, II 31.

[127] Entitled *Erh-tsung san-chi ching*, or the "Sutra of the Two Principles and the Three Moments." According to a Buddhist source, this Manichaean work was later adopted into the Taoist Canon. The work is now thought to be a Chinese version of the Shabuhragan. See Chavannes–Pelliot, *Un traité* (see n.16 above), 157–69, 174–76; and Lieu, *Manichaeism* (cf. n.22 above), 225–28.

[128] Alfaric, *Les écritures*, II 32.

[129] Ibid., 31. On the presumed presence of Manichaeans in Harran, see now M. Tardieu, "Ṣābiens coraniques et «Ṣābiens» de Ḥarrān," *JA* 274 (1986), 23–25 n.105.

[130] Alfaric, *Les écritures*, II 31, calling attention to Augustine, *Contra Faustum* 19.3.

[131] Ibid., 32. v. Dobschütz, *Decretum Gelasianum*, 305 n.4 notes the parallel but does not identify the two works.

[132] Note *CMC* 47:1–48:15:

> Furthermore, let him who is willing hearken and pay attention to how each one of the primeval patriarchs communicated his own revelation to a select (group) whom he chose and gathered together from that generation during which he appeared, and after writing (it down), he left it for future generations. Each (patriarch) revealed (information) about his heavenly journey, and they (i.e., the chosen group) promulgated beyond...to record and display afterwards, and to laud and extol their teachers and the truth and the hope that was revealed to them. Thus each one spoke and wrote down a memoir recounting what he saw, including (an account) about his heavenly journey, during the period and cycle of his apostleship.

This introduction is then followed by citations from written revelations received by Adam, Sethel (= Seth), Enosh, Shem, Enoch, and the Christian apostle Paul (!). Cf. Shahrastānī, *Milal*, 192 ll.8–12 and *Kephalaia* 12:9ff. for additional listings of apostles who preceded Mani. For a comprehensive discussion, see especially Puech, *Le manichéisme*, 144–46 n.241. Compare the Qur'anic rosters of prophets who preceded the advent of Muhammad in Suras 19:42–59; 6:83–86; 3:30; and 4:163ff. For discussions of the relationship between the Manichaean and Islamic concepts of "earlier" revelations, see T. Andrae,

Mohammed: The Man and his Faith (New York, 1936; repr. New York, 1960), 94–113 and G. Widengren, *Muhammad, the Apostle of God, and his Ascension* (Uppsala, 1955), 7–24 and especially 115–61.

133 Henning, *SPAW* (1934), 27–35; idem, "Neue Materialen zur Geschichte des Manichäismus," *ZDMG* 90 (1936), 1–18; *idem, BSOAS* 11 (1943), 52–74.

134 Henning, *SPAW* (1934), 29–30.

135 Note particularly the verso of M625c as reproduced in ibid., 29: *'wd drxt'n [ky] 'wzyd hynd h'n 'yr 'wd q'w hy[nd] ky 'c znyn 'wzyd hynd 'wd...* («...und die Bäume, [die] herausgegangen sind, das sind die *'yr* und die *q'w*, die aus den Weibern hervorgegangen sind und...»).

136 Ibid., 30–32.

137 Henning notes particularly *Kephalaia* 92:27ff. and 93:24ff.; cf. *ZDMG* 90 (1936), 3.

138 Henning, *ZDMG* 90 (1936), 3.

139 Henning, *SPAW* (1934), 29; *idem, ZDMG* 90 (1936), 3.

140 Henning, *BSOAS* 11 (1943), 52–74.

141 Ibid., 53.

142 Ibid., 54. The names of Jewish archangels appear in other Manichaean works as well. See, for example, W.B. Henning, "Two Manichaean Magical Texts with an Excursus on the Parthian ending *-endeh*," *BSOAS* 12 (1947), 39–66, and Boyce, *Reader*, 187–92. Note the intriguing occurrence of "Samael" in *Mir. Man. III*, 882, l. 2.

143 Henning, *BSOAS* 11 (1943), 55.

144 Ibid., 52–53. G. Widengren has argued that an amalgamation of Iranian and Semitic narrative traditions can already be traced to the Parthian period. According to Widengren, one of the more important indications of such activity is the semantic (and eventually "historical") identification of Semitic *gibbor*, *gabbara* "Giant" and Iranian *kaw* "prince, ruler," evidenced in the oriental evolution and transformation of the biblical Nimrod-legend. Widengren asserts, *contra* Henning, that Mani inherited this "Giant-*kaw*" assimilation from earlier Iranian narrative sources, and was consequently dependent upon Iranian material for the formulation of his Book of Giants. See his *Iranisch-semitische Kulturbegegnung* (Köln & Opladen, 1960), 42–49; *idem, Mani und der Manichäismus* (see n.2 above), 81–82.

145 Milik, *HTR* 64 (1971), 333–78; *idem*, "Turfan et Qumran" (cf. n.84 above), 117–27.

146 J.T. Milik, *The Books of Enoch: Aramaic Fragments of Qumrân Cave 4* (Oxford, 1976), 298–339. Milik identified six separate copies of the Book of Giants at Qumran.

147 Ibid., 58.

148 The five-fold division of the contents of the Ethiopic Book of Enoch (1 Enoch) was first propounded by R.H. Charles and is universally accepted today. Cf. R.H. Charles, *The Book of Enoch* (Oxford, 1893), 25–32; idem, "Book of Enoch," in *idem*, ed., *The Apocrypha and Pseudepigrapha of the Old Testament* (Oxford, 1913), II 168–70.

[149] Milik, *HTR* 64 (1971), 334.

[150] See especially J.C. Greenfield – M.E. Stone, "The Enochic Pentateuch and the Date of the Similitudes," *HTR* 70 (1977), 51–65; idem, "The Books of Enoch and the Traditions of Enoch," *Numen* 26 (1979), 89–103; J.C. VanderKam, "Some Major Issues in the Contemporary Study of 1 Enoch," *MAARAV* 3 (1982), 85–97.

[151] J.H. Charlesworth, "The SNTS Pseudepigrapha Seminars at Tübingen and Paris on the Books of Enoch," *NTS* 25 (1979), 315–23; M.A. Knibb, "The Date of the Parables of Enoch: A Critical Review," *NTS* 25 (1979), 345–59; C.L. Mearns, "Dating the Similitudes of Enoch," *NTS* 25 (1979), 360–69; D.W. Suter, *Tradition and Composition in the Parables of Enoch* (Missoula, 1979), 11–33.

[152] A. Henrichs – L. Koenen, "Ein griechischer Mani-Codex (P. Colon. inv. nr. 4780)," *ZPE* 5 (1970), 97–217.

[153] J.C. Greenfield, "Prolegomenon" to the Ktav reprint of H. Odeberg, *3 Enoch or The Hebrew Book of Enoch* (Cambridge, 1928; repr. New York, 1973), XLVII n.54. The citation of passages from "Apocalypses" of Adam, Seth, Enosh, Shem, and Enoch in the *Cologne Mani Codex* (48:16–60:12), particular compositions which are not extant in any other source, has suggested to some that the Elchasaites possessed a library of Jewish pseudepigraphical works. See M. Tardieu, *Le manichéisme*, 41; I. Gruenwald, "Manichaeism and Judaism in Light of the Cologne Mani Codex," *ZPE* 50 (1983), 35. For a suggestive demonstration of Manichaean acquaintance (via the Elchasaites?) with the so-called "Astronomical Enoch" (1 Enoch 72–82), see J. Tubach, "Spuren des astronomischen Henochbuches bei den Manichäern Mittelasiens," in P.O. Scholz and R. Stempel, eds., *Nubia et Oriens Christianus: Festschrift für C. Detlef G. Müller zum 60. Geburtstag* (Köln, 1988), 73–95.

Chapter Two

The Qumran Fragments of the Book of Giants

At least six separate copies of the Aramaic Book of Giants have been identified by J.T. Milik among the Qumran literary remains. These six are 1Q23, 6Q8, 4QEnGi[a], 4QEnGi[b], 4QEnGi[c], and an unpublished manuscript, 4QEnGi[e], in the possession of J. Starcky.[1] The fragments of 1Q23 had been previously published by Milik in the first volume of the *Discoveries in the Judaean Desert* (= *DJD*) series as one of "deux apocryphes en araméen."[2] Similarly, 6Q8 had been edited by M. Baillet in *DJD* III and assigned to the Genesis Apocryphon (1QapGen).[3] After incorporating some new readings of doubtful letters, Milik reproduced portions of these texts alongside his publication of the thirteen fragments of 4QEnGi[a] in *The Books of Enoch.*[4] In addition to these fragments, Milik also transcribed and presented portions of two manuscripts (4QEnGi[b], 4QEnGi[c]) which had been entrusted to J. Starcky for publication.[5] These transcriptions were reproduced, however, without corroborative photographic plates. Milik also alludes to a third manuscript in the Starcky collection (4QEnGi[e]) as well as two groups of small fragments (4QEnGi[d], 4QEnGi[f]) also contained in the latter lot.[6] Unfortunately, neither photographs nor transcriptions are available for these documents. Finally, Milik suggests that three further manuscripts may in fact stem from the Book of Giants, but that there is not sufficient evidence to guarantee a positive identification. These are 1Q24, 2Q26, and 4QEn[c] 2–3.[7]

The palaeographic dating of these manuscripts produces mixed and inconclusive results. The majority of the identified remnants of the Book of Giants have yet to appear in a format that allows the application of the principles of palaeographic analysis. 6Q8 was identified by F.M. Cross as emanating from the last half of the first century B.C.E.[8] Cross also had access to the unpublished fragments of 4QEnGi[b], and he characterized this text as belonging to the first half of the first century B.C.E.[9] Neither Cross nor Milik hazard an opinion regarding the relative dating of 1Q23.

Milik dates 4QEnGi[a] to the last third of the first century B.C.E.[10] However, Milik's analysis of the ductus and provenance of 4QEnGi[a] must be viewed in conjunction with his study of the third copy of the Aramaic *Vorlage* of 1 Enoch found at Qumran, 4QEn[c].[11] This latter manuscript contains portions of the Book of Watchers (1 Enoch 1–36), the Book of Dreams (1 Enoch 83–90), and the Epistle of Enoch (1 Enoch 91–108), three of the five traditional subsections of 1 Enoch known to us from the Ethiopic recension of the book. Milik noted some physical and orthographic similarities between 4QEn[c] and 4QEnGi[a], and determined that the same scribe was responsible for the production of both texts. On the basis of these correspondences, he pronounced that 4QEnGi[a] was originally part of the same scroll as 4QEn[c].[12] However, he placed the Giants text not at the beginning or end of the scroll, but directly after the Book of Watchers in place of the traditional Book of Similitudes.[13] This decision, of course, is connected with his conviction mentioned above that the Book of Similitudes (1 Enoch 37–71) is a late Christian replacement within 1 Enoch for the original Book of Giants.

Milik goes on to state that this copy of 4QEn[c] (including 4QEnGi[a]) was made from an older exemplar "doubtless belonging to the last quarter of the second century B.C."[14] Why "doubtless"? Because Milik has already determined on exegetical grounds that the Book of Giants must have been composed during that period. Milik called attention to the record of Enochic literary production contained in Jubilees 4:17–24,[15] a passage wherein most commentators perceive allusions to separate Enochic works later combined to form the book of 1 Enoch.[16] Milik detected no mention of the Book of Giants in this passage, and concluded that the book was not yet written when the text in Jubilees was composed. Milik dates the Book of Jubilees to the period 128–125 B.C.E. Milik also referred to a short passage in the Damascus Covenant (CD) which mentions the Giants, and in fact opined that CD quotes from the Book of Giants (in Hebrew!) at this point.[17] Milik dates the Damascus Covenant to the period 110–100 B.C.E. For Milik, therefore, the Book of Giants must have been composed sometime between Jubilees and CD, or in other words, circa 125–100 B.C.E.[18] Hence 4QEn[c], which contained 4QEnGi[a], "doubtless" must stem from this same period.

Several problems mar Milik's proposal for the dating of the Aramaic Book of Giants. Since his exegetical argument serves as the basis of his overall scheme, analysis should focus upon that point. As mentioned above, Milik situates the Book of Giants between the composition of the Book of Jubilees and the compilation of the Damascus Covenant. Milik dates Jubilees to the period 128–125 B.C.E. because he believes that Jubilees 34:2–9 and Jubilees 38:1–14 mask, under the figures of Jacob and his sons, the military campaigns of John Hyrcanus following the death of Antiochus VII Sidetes in 129 B.C.E.[19] This dating of Jubilees to the reign of Hyrcanus follows influential arguments advanced by R.H. Charles, who also asserted that the extrabiblical battle narratives in Jubilees veil allusions to the Hasmonean wars of conquest.[20] However, other scholars have argued more convincingly that the battle narratives of Jubilees 34 and 38 need not be interpreted in so strict a manner. Some have suggested that a greater number of parallels can be discerned between the Jubilean battles and the campaigns of Judas Maccabeus.[21] However, it seems more plausible to view the conflicts of Jubilees 34 and 38 as typical Jubilean narrative expansion and embellishment of cryptic biblical allusions and by no means as necessarily tied to the military endeavours of any contemporary Jewish ruler.[22]

Shorn of this problematic exegetical anchor, the dating of Jubilees cannot be fixed with the certitude exhibited by Milik. More evidence, however, can be brought to bear which suggests that Jubilees should be dated much earlier than Milik allows. Significant palaeographical data is supplied by some as yet unpublished Qumran fragments of Jubilees that have been studied by F.M. Cross. He has determined that the semi-cursive script in which these fragments are written dates from *circa* 125–75 B.C.E., thus making them the oldest representative of the text of Jubilees.[23] Cross also established that this script should be situated in the evolutionary line of development between 4QXII[a] (*circa* 150–100 B.C.E.) and 4QDan[c] (*circa* 100–50

B.C.E.). J.C. VanderKam concluded on the basis of this evidence that Jubilees "was almost certainly written before 100 B.C.," provided that these fragments are not part of the book's autograph.[24] One might go beyond VanderKam's rather conservative estimate by utilizing the plus-or-minus fifty-year margin of error to its fullest potential. That is to say, if we accept 100 B.C.E., along with Cross and VanderKam, as the mean date for the emergence of this copy of Jubilees, there is little to prevent us from adding to this figure the fifty-year margin of error presumed by Cross to arrive at 150 B.C.E. as the earliest date for the production of this manuscript. If we employ Cross's upper limit of 125 B.C.E. as our starting point, the resulting date of production is 175 B.C.E. Furthermore, it must be recalled that these fragments are in all probability part of a *copy* of a yet earlier text of Jubilees. One suggested rule-of-thumb regarding the copying of manuscripts is to allow at least a fifty-year interval between the initial composition of a work and subsequent copying activity,[25] since a significant amount of time had to have elapsed before a relatively new work amassed the respect implied by its reproduction and promulgation. If we accordingly adjust our dates above, we arrive at the period 225–200 B.C.E. for a possible date of composition for Jubilees. Even if we begin with 75 B.C.E. (Cross's lower limit) as our point of entry, we arrive at 175 B.C.E. as the latest possible date for the composition of Jubilees.

Adopting the period 225–175 B.C.E. as the era during which Jubilees was composed conforms with the internal concerns of the book. Many scholars have viewed the book's strident polemic against intercourse with Gentiles and its exhortation to adhere to the revealed Law as evidence of a reaction to the crisis created by Antiochus Epiphanes in 167–164 B.C.E.[26] However, it is of paramount importance to note that there is no reference in Jubilees to the desecration of the Temple by the Seleucid monarch, nor is there any mention of persecution resulting from faithful observance of the Law.[27] The concerns expressed by Jubilees need not be confined to the so-called "Hellenistic crisis": the Gentile presence in Palestine certainly antedated the invasion of Antiochus or for that matter Alexander, and the pre-Hellenistic period Books of Ezra-Nehemiah and Chronicles abound in exhortatory admonitions toward the observance of the Law. Scholars are increasingly accepting this and other coordinate evidence as indications that Jubilees probably should be assigned to the period 225–175 B.C.E.[28]

It will be recalled that Milik also bases his decision to date the Book of Giants after the composition of Jubilees upon the apparent absence of any reference to the former work in the description of the literary activity of Enoch contained in Jubilees 4:17–24. An initial difficulty with this argument is Milik's unquestioned assumption that Enoch would have been considered to be the author or compiler of the Book of Giants. Milik, of course, assumes Enochic authorship because his theory of the literary history of 1 Enoch dictates such a position. Yet no fragment of the Book of Giants in either its Jewish or Manichaean recensions can be cited to support this assumption. In fact, as we have learned earlier, Manichaean tradition ascribed the authorship of the Book of Giants to Mani himself, an eventuality which would have been difficult to justify had any trace of an alleged Enochic authorship survived in the transmitted text. Nevertheless, Milik's contention that Jubilees 4:17–24 and, by extension, the remainder of the Book of Jubilees does not know the Book of Giants can be challenged. There are several notable differences distinguishing the treatment of the story of the Watchers and Giants in the Book of Jubilees from the treatment accorded the same topic in the various components of 1 Enoch.[29] These divergences are so marked that the possibility of an independent source underlying the narrative of Jubilees must be considered. It seems possible that the Book of Giants (or an earlier version thereof) may have been such a source.

Similar objections can be raised against Milik's use of the Damascus Covenant as a chronological peg for the fixing of the date of composition of the Book of Giants. His selection of 110 B.C.E. as the earliest date for the appearance of the Damascus Covenant depends upon palaeographical evidence recovered from Qumran as well as upon his exegetical interpretation of the chronological timetable contained within that work.[30] Neither argument is particularly compelling. Palaeographical data is notoriously flexible, as has been illustrated above.[31] Furthermore, the internal chronological indications of the Damascus Covenant are a *crux interpretum* of Qumran research. In contrast to Milik, some scholars now consider the Damascus Covenant to be a pre-Qumranic composition reflecting the ideological currents of the first half of the second century B.C.E.[32] Perhaps the least disputed issue in the continuing controversy surrounding the dating of the Damascus Covenant is the almost unanimous recognition that the treatise postdates the Book of Jubilees, since a passage of the Damascus Covenant appears to refer to Jubilees by name.[33] A more precise determination above and beyond this relative positioning cannot be established at present.

Further discussion of the relationship of the Book of Giants to presumably contemporary Jewish literature must await a detailed examination of the fragments themselves. Reproduced below are the texts that Milik has identified as belonging to the Giants corpus, followed by a fresh translation and extended commentary. The transcriptions printed here follow in the main the published works of Milik and K. Beyer.[34] Photographs of the fragments have been consulted and compared with these transcriptions where available. Due to the sometimes poor quality of these reproductions, the author has usually followed Milik or Beyer under the assumption that their readings can be physically justified in some way. All readings and restorations have been subjected to a thorough critical analysis.

The arrangement of the fragments of the Book of Giants calls for some comment. Milik's publication of this material provides only minimal suggestions for the narrative ordering of the fragments.[35] Beyer's study of the fragments goes further in attempting to establish a coherent sequence of events.[36] The author is indebted to the observations of Beyer regarding the structuring of the textual material, but has nevertheless felt compelled to alter Beyer's sequence on the basis of both internal and external criteria. These will be justified in the course of our textual presentation.

Transliteration of the Aramaic Fragments of the Book of Giants

QG1 (4QEnGi[c] 2nd frag + 1Q23 1.9.14.15)

1) ...]' *ṭmyw* [...
2) ...] *gbryn wnpylyn* [...
3) ...] *'wldw w'lw kw*[*l* ...
4) ...]*dmh w'l yd mh*[...
5) ...]*n dy l' śpq lhwn wl*[...
6) ...] *wb'yn lm'kl śgy' ml*[...
7) ... vacat ...
8) ...]*mḥwh npyly'* ... [...
9) ...] *wyd'w r*[...]*h rbh b'r''* [...]*bh wqṭlw lśgy*[*'yn* ...] *gbryn m*[...]*h* ... *l dy* ... [...

QG2 (4QEn[e] 2; 4QEn[e] 3 + 4QEnGi[e]; 4QEnGi[b])

2) ...]*yn wkl* [... *'tḥ*]*zyt lḥnwk s*[*pr prš'* ...]*dm m* ... *rb*[...
3) ... *lš*] *qrh* [*b*] *'r''* *kl* ... *mt'št* ... *bh dm hwh špyk* (*mštpk*) *wkdbyn hww m*[ ]*yn b* ... *mbwl 'l 'r''* ... [...
4)–9) unpublished
10) ... *npšt qṭy*]*lyn qbln 'l qṭlyhwn wmz'qn* [...

QG3 (4QEnGi[a] 9:1–8; 4QEnGi[a] 10)

I.

1) ...] *kwl* [...
2) ...] *'lyn mn qwdm hdr yq*[...
3) ...]*rk dy kwl rzy' yd*[' ...
4) ...] *wkwl ṣbw l' tqptkh* [...
5) ... *q*]*wdmykh* vacat *wk'n* [...
6) ...] *mlkwt rbwtkh lš*[...
7) ...
8) ...

II.

1) ... *w*]*k'n mry* [...
2) ...] *śgyt wh*[...
3) ...] *tṣb' wk*[...

QG4A (4QEnGi[b] 2)

3) ...] *b'dyn ḥlmw tryhwn ḥlmyn*
4) *wndt šnt 'ynyhwn mnhwn w*[...
5) *w'tw 'l* [...] *ḥlmyhwn*
6) ... *b*] *ḥlmy hwyt ḥz' blyly' dn*
7) [*w'lw/w'rw/wh'* ...] *gnnyn hww' mšqyn*
8) ... *šr*] *šyn rbrbyn npqw mn 'qrhn*
9) ... *wḥz'*] *hwyt 'd dy* [...] *mn*
10) ...] *kl my' wnwr' dlq bkl*
11) [*prds'*(?)/*gn'*(?)/*'r''*(?)] ...
12) ...] *'d k' swp ḥlm'*
13) ... *l'*] *hškḥw gbry' lḥwy' lh*[*wn*(?)]
14) ... *lḥnwk*] *lspr prš' wypšwr ln'*
15) *ḥlm'* vacat *b'dyn* [*hw*] *h hwdh 'ḥwhy 'whyh w'mr qdm gbry' 'p*
16) *'nh ḥzyt bḥlmy blyly' dn gbry' h' šlṭn šmy' l'r'' nḥt*
17)–19) unpublished
20) ...] *'d k' swp ḥlm'* [...] *dḥlw kl gbry'*
21) ... *w*] *q*[*r*] *w lmhwy w'th l*[...] *gbry' wšlḥwhy 'l ḥnwk*
22) ...]*' w'mrw lh 'zl* [...] *wmwt' lkh dy*
23) ...] *šm'th qlh w'mr lh* [...]*r ḥlmy'*

QG4B (6Q8 2)

1) *tltt šršwhy* [... *wḥz'*]
2) *hwyt 'd dy 'tw* [...
3) *prds' dn klh wl*[...

QG5 (4QEnGi[b] 3)

3) *b'ḥt 'rkt gbry'* [...
4) *k'l'wlyn wprḥ bydwhy* [...] *knš*[*r'* ...
5) *ḥld wḥlp lšhwyn mdbr' rb'* [...
6) *w*[*ḥ*]*zh ḥnwk wz'qh w'mr lh mhwy* [...

7) *ltn' wlkh tnynwt lmḥwy b'[yt ...*
8) *l[m]lyk wkl npyly 'r'' hn hwbl [...*
9) *mn ywm[y ...] thwn wytws[...*
10) *...n] nd' mnk pšrh[w] n [...*
11) *...gn]nyn dy mn šmyn n[ḥtw ...*

QG6 (6Q8 1 + 1Q23 1.29)

2) *...] 'why' w'mr lmhwy [...*
3) *...] wl' mrtt mn 'ḥzyk kl' '[...*
4) *... l'] why' brq'l 'by 'my hwh [...*
5) *...] l' šyṣy mhwy [l'] št'yh mh dy [...*
6) *...] h 'rw tmhyn šm't hn yldt sry[...*

QG7 (4QEnGi[a] 7 ii)

5) *lkh m[...*
6) *ltry lwḥy' [...*
7) *wtnyn' 'd k'n l' qry[...*

QG8 (4QEnGi[a] 8)

1) *sp[...*
2) vacat
3) *pršgn lwḥ' t[nyn]' dy 'y[...*
4) *[... ']l yd ḥnwk spr prš' [...*
5) *wqdyš' lšmyḥzh wkwl ḥ[brwhy ...*
6) *ydy' lhw' lkwn d[y ...*
7) *w'wbdkwn wdy nšykwn [...*
8) *'nwn [w] bny[hwn] wnšy' d[y ...*
9) *bznwt[k] wn b['] r'' whwt ['] lyk[wn ...*
10) *wqblh 'lykwn 'l 'wbd bnykwn [...*
11) *ḥbl' dy ḥbltwn bh [...*
12) *'d rp'l mṭh 'rw 'bd[n' ...*
13) *wdy bmdbry' wd[y] bymy' [...*
14) *' lykwn lb'yš wk'n šrw' 'syrkwn m[...*
15) *wṣlw* vacat

QG9 (4QEnGi[c])

3) ...] *gbr wbtqwp ḥyl dr'y wbḥsn gbwrty*
4) [*k*] *wl bśr w'bdt 'mhwn qrb brm l'*
5) [*m*] *škḥ 'nh 'mn l'štrrh db'ly dyny*
6) ... *bšmy*] *' ytbyn wbqdšy' 'nwn šryn wl'*
7) ... *'nw*] *n tqypyn mny* vacat
8) ...] *rh dy ḥywt br' 'th w'wš br' qryn*
9) ...] *wkdn 'mr lh 'whyh ḥlmy 'nsn*[*y*]
10) [*wndt mny š*] *nt 'yny lmḥz'* [*ḥz*] *wh 'rw yd' 'nh dy 'l*
11) ...
12) ... *g*] *lgmyš* [...

QG10 (1Q23 1.6)

2) ...] *ḥmryn m'tyn 'rdyn m'*[*tyn* ...
3) *'n m'tyn tyšyn m'*[*tyn* ...
4) *br' mn kl ḥwh w'q*[...
5) *'l mzg* [...

QG11 (4QEnGi[a] 1–4; 7 i; 13; 4QEnGi[b]; 4QEnGi[c])

I.

1) *kdy 'q*[...
2) *brq'l* [...
3) *'npy 'wd* [...
4) *'nh q'm* [...

II.

1) *'lyhwn* [...
2) vacat
3) ...] *h mhw*[*y* ...

III.

1) ...
2) *ḥbrwh*[*y* ...
3) *ḥwbbš w'dk*[...

4) *wmh ttnwnny lq*[...

IV.

1) ...] *bhwn* [...
2) vacat
3) ...] *w'mr 'whyh lh*[*hyh* ...
4) ...] *wmn 'lwy 'r'' wš*[...
5) ... *'r*] '' vacat *k*[...
6) ...] *šwyw wbkw qwd*[*m* ...
7) ...

V.

1) ...
2) ...
3) *wtwqp*[*k*] *h* [...
4) vacat
5) *b'd*[*yn 'mr*] *'whyh lhhy*[*h* ...
6) *ln'* ... *l'z'* [*z*] *l w'bd* [...
7) *gbry' w*[...] *'ytnšwn kwl hb*[...

VI.

1) ...] *'dyn 'nw ṭly'*
2) ...] *'yryn*
3) ...] *lh 'gnn' wtqp* [*'*] *ly*[*n'*]

VII.

1) ...] *yw mn* [*q*] *wd*[*m* ...
2) ...] *yn 'mr lh*[...
3) ...] *'yty lkh š*[...
4) ...] *l' hwh* [...

Translation

QG1 (4QEnGi[c] 2nd frag + 1Q23 1.9.14.15)

1) ... they became defiled ...
2) ... Giants and Nephilim ...
3) ... they begat, and behold, all ...
4) ... its blood (?) and by means of tu[rmoil(?) ...
5) ... for it was not enough for them and ...
6) ... and they sought to consume much ...
7) ... *vacat* ...
8) ... the Nephilim smote it ...
9) ... and they knew ... much ... upon earth ... and they killed many ... Giants ... which

QG2 (4QEn[e] 2; 4QEn[e] 3 + 4QEnGi[e]; 4QEnGi[b])

2) ... and all ... [was revealed] to Enoch [the scribe set apart] ...
3) ... [to practice deceit upon] the earth, all ... resolving ... blood was shed upon it, and deceptions were being ... a flood upon the earth ...

10)... [the souls of the slain] cried out against their killers and called out ...

QG3 (4QEnGi[a] 9:1–8; 4QEnGi[a] 10)

I.

1) ... all ...
2) ... before the majesty ...
3) ... for all mysteries are kno[wn ...
4) ... and no thing is too difficult for you ...
5) ... b]efore you. *vacat* And now ...
6) ... your great kingdom ...
7) ...
8) ...

II.

1) ... now my Lord ...
2) ... you have increased ...
3) ... you desire ...

QG4A (4QEnGi[b] 2)

3) ... Then both of them dreamed dreams
4) and the sleep of their eyes fled from them and ...
5) and they came to ... their dreams
6) ... in] my dream (which) I saw tonight
7) [and behold ...] gardeners were watering
8) ... great [shoo]ts came forth from their root(s)
9) ... and I continued [looking] until ...(?)... from
10) ... all the water, and fire burned in all
11) [the garden(?)/the world(?)] ...
12) ... so far the end of the dream.
13) ... the Giants were [un]able to explain to [them (?)]
14) ... to Enoch] the scribe set apart, and he will interpret for us
15) the dream. *vacat* Then his brother 'Ohyah acknowledged and said before the Giants, Also
16) I have beheld in my dream tonight. O Giants, behold, the ruler of heaven descended to earth
17)–19) [unpublished]
20) ... so far the end of the dream. ... All the Giants were afraid
21) ... and] they [sum]moned Mahaway, and he came to ... Giants, and they sent him to Enoch
22) ... and they said to him, Go ... to you that
23) ... you have heard his voice, and say to him ... the dreams

QG4B (6Q8 2)

1) three of its shoots ...
2) I continued [looking] until there came ...
3) this garden, all of it ...

QG5 (4QEnGi^{b} 3)

3) in one (hand) the authorization (?) of the Giants ...
4) as the storms, and he flew with his hands ... like an eag[le ...
5) land (?), and he passed by the wastelands, the great desert ...
6) and Enoch [s]aw and called out to him, and Mahaway said to him ...
7) here, and for you the second (tablet?) to declare (an interpretation?) [I se]ek ...
8) for your [wo]rds, and all the Nephilim of the earth, whether he (?) brought ...
9) from the day[s ...] of their ...
10) ... we] might learn from you their interpretation ...
11) ... gard]eners (?) who de[scended] from heaven ...

QG6 (6Q8 1 + 1Q23 1.29)

2) ... 'Ohyah and said to Mahaway ...
3) ... and do not tremble. Who showed you all (this)? ...
4) ... to 'O]hyah, Baraq'el my father was with me ...
5) ... Mahaway had not finished relating that which ...
6) ... behold, I have heard frightening portents. If(?) I(?) begat ...

QG7 (4QEnGi^{a} 7 ii)

5) to you ...
6) two tablets ...
7) and the second has not been read until now ...

QG8 (4QEnGi^{a} 8)

1) ...
2) *vacat*
3) copy of the second tablet which ...
4) b]y Enoch the scribe set apart ...
5) and Holy One, to Shemiḥazah and all [his associates] ...
6) let it be known to you that ...
7) and your action, and that your wives ...

8) they [and their] sons and wives who ...
9) in your fornication upon the earth, and upon you there has ...
10) and complained against you regarding the action of your sons ...
11) the destruction which you have perpetrated upon it ...
12) has reached Raphael. Behold, ruin (?)...
13) and those in the deserts and those in the seas
14) upon you for (your?) wickedness. And now, free your prisoners ...
15) and pray! *vacat*

QG9 (4QEnGi[c])

3) ... Giant(?), and with the strength of my powerful arm and with the power of my might
4) ... a]ll flesh, and I did battle with them, but I [am] not
5) able to prevail for us(?), for my adversaries
6) sit [in heaven], and they dwell with the holy ones, and no
7) ... the]y are stronger than I. *vacat*
8) ... of the wild animal has come, ...(?)... crying out
9) ... and then 'Ohyah said to him, My dream baffled [me]
10) [and the sleep] of my eyes [fled] to behold a vision. Now I know that regarding
11) ...
12) ... G]ilgamesh ...

QG10 (1Q23 1.6)

2) ... asses, two hundred onagers, tw[o hundred ...
3) of the flock, two hundred he-goats, tw[o hundred ...
4) apart from every animal ...
5) on account of ...

QG11 (4QEnGi[a] 1–4; 7 i; 13; 4QEnGi[b]; 4QEnGi[c])

I.

1) When ...
2) Baraq'el ...

3) face of ...
4) I rise ...

II.

1) over them ...
2) *vacat*
3) ... Mahawa[y] ...

III.

1) ...
2) [h]is associates ...
3) Hobabish and ...
4) and what you will give me ...

IV.

1) ... in them ...
2) *vacat*
3) ... 'Ohyah said to H[ahyah ...
4) ... and above the earth ...
5) ... ear]th. *vacat* ...
6) ... they sat and wept befo[re ...
7) ...

V.

1) ...
2) ...
3) and [your] might ...
4) *vacat*
5) The[n] 'Ohyah [said] to Hahy[ah ...
6) us ... for Aza[z]el and he did ...
7) Giants ... they have forgotten all ...

VI.

1) ... then the children answered
2) ... Watchers
3) ... he imprisoned us and has power [ov]er [us]

VII.

1) ... from [be]fo[re ...
2) ... said ...
3) ... there is for you ...
4) ... there is not ...

Commentary to QG1

QG1 is placed at the beginning of the fragments of the Book of Giants because it appears to narrate the events that immediately transpire after the descent of the heavenly Watchers to earth. The references to defilement (l.1), birth (l.3), Giants and Nephilim (ll.2,8,9), bloodshed (ll.4 (?),9), and insatiable hunger (ll.5,6) cohere well with the parallel descriptions of this antediluvian era contained in 1 Enoch 7–9 and Jubilees 5. In both of these latter sources the appearance of the Giants upon earth is accompanied by widespread slaughter, destruction, and moral corruption. These motifs are explored in greater depth in the detailed textual commentary that follows.

1) *ṭmyw* —> *ṭm'* "be unclean." The form can be parsed as either a *Pe'al* passive third masculine plural "become unclean, be rendered unclean" or a *Pa'el* third masculine plural "make unclean, defile." Milik reads the letters on this line together as one word (*'ṭmyw*) and thus understands the word as an *Ithpe'el* form ("they defiled themselves").[37] The stem *ṭm'* was largely replaced in later Jewish Aramaic by *s'b*: "[*ṭm'*] in Targ. raro usurpatur, vox sueta est *s'b.*"[38] However, note 4QEn^a 1 ii 13 (= 1 Enoch 5:4) *ṭmtkn* "your defilement, uncleanness"[39] (cf. Greek ἀκαθαρσίας ὑμῶν)[40] and 1QapGen 20:15: *w'l yšlṭ blyly' dn* <u>*lṭmy' 'ntty mny*</u> "may he (i.e., Pharaoh) not have the power *to defile my wife* tonight ..."[41] This last example alludes to the defilement that would result from cohabitation with the Gentile ruler.[42] One should also note that the infrequent usage of *ṭm'* in the Targumim is for the most part limited to matters involving corpse-uncleanness (*ṭmy npš'*),[43] association with menstruous women (*'yt'*

ṭwm'h, ṭwm't'),[44] or idolatry,[45] issues commonly brought up in discussions of or allusions to the unclean status of the Gentile.[46]

The setting presupposed by the Book of Giants is Genesis 6:1–4, in which the *beney ha'elohim* descend from heaven and conjugally unite with the *benot ha'adam.* The suggested mixture of the two separate realms of the divine and the human, tolerated and even prized in Greek mythology, was abhorred by Jewish tradition as an illicit disruption of the created demarcation between the spheres of the sacred and the profane.[47] Transgression against these boundaries by the Watchers is expressed most clearly in the condemnation uttered by God to Enoch when the latter was transported to heaven to make intercession on behalf of the repentant Watchers:

> Why have you left the high and holy heaven, which is eternal, and lain with women? (Why have) you defiled yourselves with mortal women? (Why have) you acquired wives and acted like earthly mortals, engendering giant sons? Although you were holy, spiritual, (and) endowed with eternal life, you instead defiled yourselves with <the blood of>[48] women and engendered (offspring) with the blood of flesh, and lusted for the flesh of humanity, and behaved like those who are made of flesh and blood, those who die and perish. Therefore I have given them wives so that they might sow seed within them and engender offspring with them in order that nothing decreases upon earth. However, you were previously spiritual, endowed with eternal life, destined to live through all the generations of the world. For this reason I did not institute marriage for you, since the spiritual beings of heaven have their (proper) abode in heaven. [1 Enoch 15:3–7]

The resultant defilement of the angelic "nature" makes it impossible for the Watchers to return to their former status,[49] or even, as is suggested in the above quote, to return to their heavenly place of origin.[50] This motif is picturesquely developed in a Syriac tradition that recounts the story of the illicit mixture of the *beney ha'elohim* (= sons of Seth) and *benot ha'adam* (= daughters of Cain):

> And when the daughters of Cain beheld the beauty of the sons of Seth, they set upon them like rapacious beasts and defiled their bodies, and (so) the sons of Seth caused their souls to perish through fornication with the daughters of Cain. And when they sought to reascend the holy mountain after they had descended and fallen, the rock of the holy mountain was (as) fire [in their sight], for [God] did not permit them

to return to that place as they had defiled <their souls> with the filth of fornication.[51]

The theme of angelic defilement is an important motif in the narrative expansions of Genesis 6:1–4. A question remains as to the precise nature of the defilement perpetrated or incurred by the Watchers. Some traditions do stress that the angels produce uncleanness as a result of their sexual activity.[52] This interpretation is perhaps linked to the disruptive behavior and illegitimate status[53] of the gigantic offspring of this unholy union. However, the bulk of the evidence seems to suggest that the angels themselves became defiled on account of their experience. References to their defilement occur at 1 Enoch 7:1a; 9:8; 10:11; 12:4; 15:3–4 and Jubilees 4:22; 7:20–21; and 20:3–5. The Greek versions of 1 Enoch employ the middle-passive stem of μιαίνεω "pollute, defile," the verb most often used to translate Hebrew *ṭm'* in the Septuagint. Thus 1 Enoch 7:1a: καὶ ἔλαβον ἑαυτοῖς γυναῖκας ... καὶ ἤρξαντο εἰσπορεύεσθαι πρὸς αὐτὰς καὶ μιαίνεσθαι ἐν αὐταῖς "and they took for themselves wives ... and began to go into them *and defile themselves by them.*" The Ethiopic versions of 1 Enoch and Jubilees generally render this expression with the verb *rak*^{w}*sa* "be polluted, unclean."[54]

The defilement of the angels can be viewed as deriving from three factors. First, the Watchers' descent from heaven and sojourn upon earth defiles their essential angelic, heavenly nature: they lower their original holy status by their imitation of human behavior. This represents a breach in the divinely constituted ordering of heaven and earth.[55] Another aspect of the angelic defilement reflects the possibility that the angels contracted uncleanness through their cohabitation with menstruous women. This is suggested by the wording of 1 Enoch 10:11[56] and the Greek version of 1 Enoch 15:4.[57] Finally, one might note that according to later interpretation, transgression against the expressed will of God is sufficient to produce an unclean state among those who are disobedient.[58]

2) *gbryn wnpylyn* — "Giants and Nephilim." The term *gbryn* is the Aramaic form of Hebrew *gibborim* (singular *gibbor*), a word whose customary connotation in the latter language is "mighty hero, warrior,"[59] but which in some contexts later came to be interpreted

in the sense of "giants."[60] *Gbryn, gbry'* are the most common designations for the Giants in the Qumran Giants fragments.[61] Similarly, *npylyn* is the Aramaic form of Hebrew *np(y)lym* (i.e., *nephilim*), an obscure designation used only three times in the Hebrew Bible. Genesis 6:4 refers to the *nephilim* who were on the earth as a result of the conjugal union of the *beney ha'elohim* and *benot ha'adam* and further qualifies their character by terming them *gibborim*.[62] Both terms are translated in LXX Genesis 6:4 by γίγας and in Targum Onkelos by *gbry'*. Numbers 13:33 reports that gigantic *nephilim* were encountered by the Israelite spies in the land of Canaan;[63] here the *nephilim* are associated with a (different?) tradition concerning a race of giants surviving among the indigenous ethnic groups that inhabited Canaan.[64] A further possible reference to both the *nephilim* and *gibborim* of Genesis 6:4 occurs in Ezekiel 32:27. The surrounding pericope presents a description of slain heroes who lie in Sheol, among whom are a group termed the *gibborim nophelim me'arelim.* The final word, *me'arelim,* "from the uncircumcized," should probably be corrected on the basis of the Septuagint (ἀπ' αἰῶνας) to *me'olam,* and the whole phrase translated "those mighty ones who lie there from of old." *Gibborim nophelim me'olam* bears a striking resemblance to the phraseology of Genesis 6:4, and indeed C.H. Cornill suggested long ago that *nophelim* should be repointed to *nephilim*.[65] There is, however, even without Cornill's emendation, an apparent wordplay upon the mythological tradition of Genesis 6:4.

The conjunction of *gbryn wnpylyn* in QG1 1.2 may be viewed as an appositional construction similar to the expression *'yr wqdyš* "Watcher and Holy One" (e.g., Daniel 4:10,14, etc.). However, the phrase might also be related to certain passages that suggest there were three distinct classes (or even generations) of Giants, names for two of which are represented in this line. Note the Greek version of 1 Enoch 7:1c–2 preserved in the Byzantine chronographer Syncellus: καὶ ἔτεκον αὐτοῖς γένη τρία. πρῶτον γίγαντας μεγάλους. οἱ δὲ γίγαντας ἐτέκνωσαν Ναφηλειμ, καὶ τοῖς Ναφηλειμ ἐγεννήθησαν Ελιούδ ... and compare Jubilees 7:22: "And they bore children, the Nāphidim (*sic*) ... and the Giants killed the Nāphil, and the Nāphil killed the 'Elyo, and the 'Elyo (killed) human beings, and humanity (killed) one another." This conception is probably also reflected in 1 Enoch 86:4, where the three classes of Giants are symbolized by elephants, camels, and asses.

The word *npylyn* is used twice more within the Giants fragments as a designation for the Giants.[66] It was noted above that early Jewish tradition as reflected in the Septuagint, Jubilees, and Targum Onkelos understood the *nephilim* as "Giants." Another strand of Jewish tradition interpreted the *nephilim* of Genesis 6:4 to signify *nephalim* "abortions."[67] This particular exegesis of the *nephilim* as "abortions" was taken over by Mani into his cosmogonical and anthropogonical systems.[68] Although the word *nephilim* does not appear in Manichaean literature, beings designated "abortions" figure in contexts that parallel the Jewish expansions of Genesis 6:1–4. The invaluable description of Manichaean cosmogony supplied by Theodore bar Konai, important because its Syriac composition may preserve authentic terminology used by Mani, reports of pregnant female archons (= Watchers? *benot ha'adam*?) whose fetuses "abort" (*yḥṭ*) and "fall" (*npl*!) to the earth and which then consume the sprouting buds of the trees planted there.[69] Theodore's account of the "descent" of the abortions is verified by authentic Manichaean sources in Coptic and Middle Persian. *Kephalaia* 92:12–93:32 contains an account of the revolt of the Watchers (ἐγρήγοροι as in the Greek fragments of 1 Enoch) that also refers to the abortions (Coptic *nhŏuhĕ*).[70] These abortions are portrayed as being the first stage of "fleshly existence,"[71] and are usually identified in Manichaean tradition with animal life.[72] The abortions are also closely associated with the "archons" who wield authority over the realm of Darkness and the corrupted material world, especially those archons who are responsible for the creation of humanity. According to Theodore bar Konai, a being named Ashaqlūn, further qualified as a "son of the ruler of Darkness," creates with the aid of a female archon and the fallen abortions the first human couple, Adam and Eve.[73] This same being also appears in the *Kephalaia* bearing the name Saklas (Σακλᾶς) and is there explicitly identified as an "abortion."[74] In classical Gnostic tradition, as represented in the Nag Hammadi texts, Sakla(s) is one of the designations applied to the demiurge responsible for the creation of the earth and its inhabitants.[75] There, too, this deity or archon is viewed as the product of an aborted birth or as an "abortion."[76] This denigrating appellation was intended to disparage those entities produced in turn by the "abortion"; namely, the material, fleshly life upon this earth.

While it seems clear that the source of both the Gnostic and the Manichaean exegeses of *nephilim* is a tradition similar to what is found in *Bereshit Rabba* 26:7, it remains possible that Mani did not receive this tradition directly from Jewish tradents, but instead encountered it in Gnostic literature. Upon examination of the relevant Gnostic texts, it seems likely that Mani used a more primitive form of the motif of the "abortions" than appears in classical Gnostic mythology. Stroumsa has suggested that the absence of a figure corresponding to the Sophia/Barbelo hypostasis (the mother of the "abortion" Yaldabaoth) in Manichaean cosmogony indicates that Mani utilized a simpler (and possibly earlier) form of the "abortion" tradition.[77] To this suggestion, we might add a further observation. Manichaean cosmogony operates with a conception of a plural number of abortions. This corresponds to the plural number of *nephilim* mentioned in Genesis 6:4 and to the numerous Giants that are produced in the Jewish narrative expansions of Genesis 6:1–4, including most notably the Qumran Book of Giants. By way of contrast, classical Gnostic tradition features only one abortion: the creator deity/archon Yaldabaoth. Jewish tradition nowhere conceives of God the Creator being one of the *nephilim*, but in Manichaean mythology the being responsible for the formation of Adam and Eve is often identified as one of the "abortions." Given this evidence, it seems likely, as Stroumsa has indicated, that the Manichaean formulation of the story of the abortions represents an intermediate stage in the evolution of this particular tradition from its Jewish roots to its Gnostic inversion. If this is the case, it augments the evidence for Mani's dependence upon Jewish traditions.

3) *'lw* — Cf. Daniel 2:31; 4:7,10; 7:8 (*bis*). This interjection is probably related to Imperial Aramaic *hlw*; cf. *KAI* 233 ll.9,11,13; 270A l.1; 270B l.4[78] and possibly Hermopolis 1:7.[79] The by-form *'rw* also is employed in Daniel (7:2,5,6,7,13) as well as in the Giants fragments[80] and in other contemporary Jewish Aramaic literature.[81] This is probably why Milik chooses to translate *'lw* as if it were *'illu* "if" and why Beyer attempts to read the word as a third masculine plural form of *'l'* "lament, wail." Given the presence of both forms in the

text of Daniel and possibly in Imperial Aramaic texts,[82] there is little reason to follow their suggestions.[83]

4) *'l yd* — The expression *'l yd* occurs in Imperial Aramaic with the meaning of "into the hand (of), to"[84] and in later Aramaic dialects in the sense of "by, through, by means of."[85] The broken context of this line does not permit a definitive conclusion regarding the import of the phrase here. Beyer translates "unter der Leitung von," Milik "according to the power," and Uhlig "nach der Hand (= Macht?)."

mh- — A possible restoration for this word might be *mh[m']* or *mh[wmt']* "noise, turmoil, commotion." Note 11QtgJob 32:6: *yḥ'k 'l* <u>*mhm'*</u> *tqp qry'* "he laughs at the loud *commotion* of the city." Cf. also Targum Isaiah 17:12 and Targum Esther 1:10. The stem *hwm* "be troubled" already appears in *KAI* 226 l.6. References to "noise" upon the earth, with regard to the activity of the Giants, can be found at 1 Enoch 8:4; 9:1–2,10; 65:4,9; 87:4.

5) *l' śpq lhwn* — "insufficient for them"; i.e., for the gargantuan appetites of the Giants. The stem *śpq* is spelled with *samekh* in later Hebrew and Aramaic dialects, but with *śin* in Imperial Aramaic as in Driver 7:3,7.[86] The notion that the resources upon earth were too meager to support the appetites of the Giants is reflected in 1 Enoch 7:3–4: "who consumed all the products of human labor *to the extent that humans were unable to support them,* with the result that the Giants turned upon them (and) devoured humankind." See also *Clementine Homilies* viii.15: "Therefore, God recognizing ... *that the world had not sufficient means for their satiety* (for it was created in proportion to humans and to human need), *in order that they might not, driven by hunger,* turn to the eating of animals ... God all-powerful showered them with manna."

6) *wb'yn lm'kl śgy' ml[...* — For the syntagm *b'y* plus infinitive see Daniel 6:5; 1QapGen 19:15,19; 20:9. The spelling of *śgy'* with *śin* is characteristic of the older dialects of Aramaic. Hunger now drives the Giants to more desperate measures in their unceasing quest for nourishment. Various sources describe how the Giants progress from the consumption of vegetable life to the slaying and eating of

animals, human beings, and even each other.[87] The voracious appetites of the Giants are reflected in the Manichaean stories about the "abortions." It will be recalled from above that Theodore bar Konai recounts how the abortions consumed the buds of the trees that grew upon earth, and that when the abortions were preparing to create the first human couple, Ashaqlūn and Namrael devoured the offspring of the ravenous abortions.[88] Theodore's testimony is confirmed from a Middle Persian Manichaean fragment that describes the same episode: "And they (i.e., the abortions) came down to the earth and began to rise on the earth. And they devoured the fruits and the fruit from the trees and grew bigger ...."[89] It will be noticed that, with one exception, the diet of the abortions agrees in every detail with that of the Enochic Giants. The exception is the consumption of human beings. Since, according to the Manichaean myth, humanity has yet to appear upon earth, the abortions cannot indulge in anthropophagy.

8) *mḥwh npyly'*- "the Nephilim smote it." *Mḥwh* appears to be the third masculine plural Perfect of the stem *mḥy* plus the third feminine singular suffix.[90] The feminine suffix (read *ha*?) presumably refers to *'r'* "the earth."[91] The era of the Giants upon earth was almost universally depicted in Jewish literature as a period of destruction, oppression, corruption, and bloodshed. *Mḥy* is employed in 1QapGen to describe the ravages of the four allied kings who invade Canaan; cf. 21:28 (*bis*); 21:30; 22:4. The bellicose behavior of the Giants achieves an afterlife in their transformation after the Deluge into evil spirits. Note 1 Enoch 15:11: "Also the spirits of the Giants ... who oppress, corrupt, fell, fight, and crush the earth ...."

9) Beyer inserts this line (which stems from a different manuscript) here, while Milik treats it as a separate fragment.[92] In light of its apparent subject matter, the suggestion of Beyer is followed here.

]*wyd'w r*[— Milik restores *r*[*zy* "mysteries," but the broken context does not permit us to follow him.

wqṭlw lśgy[*'yn* — "and they slew many"; i.e., the Giants killed many creatures upon earth, presumably denoting humans. Compare 4QEn[a] 1 iii 19 (= 1 Enoch 7:4): *wšryw lqṭlh l'nš'* "and they (the Giants) began to slay humanity."

gbryn — "Giants" as opposed to Beyer's "Männer." It is true that the forms are identical, but the Enoch literature appears to make a terminological distinction between "men" and "Giants," employing forms of *'nš'* for the former and *gbryn*, *npylyn*, etc. for the latter. Note 4QEn[a] 1 iii 18–19 (= 1 Enoch 7:3–4); 4QEn[c] 4 10 (= 1 Enoch 89:36); 4QEn[e] 1 xxii 1,4 (= 1 Enoch 22:5); 4QEn[g] 1 ii 23 (= 1 Enoch 92:1); 4QEn[g] 1 v 17,22 (= 1 Enoch 93:12–14); 4QEnastr[b] 23 8 (= 1 Enoch 77:3); 4QEnastr[b] 26 5 (= 1 Enoch 78:17).

One might now profitably compare with QG1 some relevant passages from the published fragments of the Manichaean Book of Giants in Middle Persian and Parthian.

Sundermann 20 (= M 8280)[93]

Verso/I/

1. They [descended?] to earth because
2. of the beauty of the female beings[94]
3. [li]ke assailants among
4. ... they came down (?) from

Verso/II [Superscription]

1. flesh ...
2. blood ...
3. ...
4. ...
5. hairstyle[95] (?) ...
6. great distress (?) ...
7. ...

Henning Fragment i 100–111[96]

(100) ... and ravished them. They chose beautiful [women], and demanded ... them in marriage. Sordid ... (103) ... all ... carried off ... severally they were subjected to tasks and services. And they ... from each city ... and were ordered to serve the ... The Mesenians

[were directed] to prepare the Khuzians to sweep [and] (110) water, the Persians to ...

Henning Fragment j 23–32[97]

... Virōgdād[98] ... Hōbābiš[99] robbed Ahr[100] ... of -naxtag, his wife. Thereupon the giants began to kill each other and [to abduct their wives]. The creatures, too, began to kill each other. Sām[101] ... before the sun, one hand in the air, the other ... (30) ... whatever he obtained, to his brother ... imprisoned ...

Commentary to QG2

QG2 appears to continue the description of the depradations committed upon earth occasioned by the descent of the Watchers and the birth of the Giants. The references to bloodshed (ll.3,10) and deception (l.3) match other parallel accounts of this violent era. The mention of Enoch in this context is somewhat surprising. Enoch does not figure in the narrative describing the initial wickedness of the Watchers and Giants in 1 Enoch 6–11. According to 1 Enoch 12:1, Enoch had been removed from human society "before these things" (πρὸ τούτων τῶν λόγων); i.e., prior to the woeful events of chapters 6–11. The suggested restoration of [*'tḥ*]*zyt* "was revealed" in line 2,[102] if correct, presupposes that Enoch did not have experiential knowledge of what was transpiring upon earth. Hence it is possible that QG2 preserves an account of an angelic (or divine) revelation to Enoch of the earthly deeds of the Watchers and Giants similar to that recounted in 1 Enoch 12:3–6.

2) *lḥnwk s*[*pr prš'*] - Restoration of this particular epithet is based on QG4A 14 and QG8 4. The meaning of the phrase *spr prš'* remains problematic. Milik translates as "scribe of distinction," explaining that the adjective probably connotes Enoch's ability to provide clear interpretations of obscure oracles or texts (compare Ezra 4:18 *mprš qry qdmy* "*clearly* read in my presence").[103] Note the use of *mprš'* in connection with writing in Targum Onkelos to Exodus 28:11, 21, 36;

39:6, 14, 30 with the meaning "(an inscription) clearly written like the engraving of a seal." See also Targum Onkelos to Exodus 32:16, where *mprš'* translates Hebrew *ḥrwt* "engraved." The verb *pryš* renders Hebrew *b'r* in Targum Onkelos to Deuteronomy 1:5 and 27:8 ("set forth clearly, explain"). Beyer translates *spr prš'* as "der Schreiber, der deuten kann"; Uhlig "[der] bestimmte Schreiber."[104] The epithets applied to Enoch's scribal office in Greek are not helpful here: ὁ γραμματεὺς τῆς δικαιοσύνης "scribe of righteousness" (1 Enoch 12:4; Testament of Abraham (Recension B) 11:3) or ὁ γραμματεὺς τῆς ἀληθείας "scribe of truth" (1 Enoch 15:1). Both of these Greek designations probably reflect an Aramaic substrate of *spr qwšṭ'*.[105]

More promising for the explication of *spr prš'* may be a designation applied to the patriarch Joseph in Targum Onkelos to Genesis 49:26 and Deuteronomy 33:16. This Targum renders the Hebrew *nezir 'eḥaw* ("a Nazirite [or prince?] among his brothers")[106] as *gbr' pryš' d'ḥwhy* "the man *set apart from* his brethren."[107] The reference in both the Hebrew and Aramaic versions of these texts is apparently to the distinguished position Joseph achieves in the government of Egypt after having been separated from his family in Canaan.[108] This "separation" or indeed "removal" of Joseph recalls the analogous "removal" of Enoch from human society: "Before all (these) events (transpired) Enoch disappeared, and there was no human being who knew where he was concealed, or where he lived, or what had happened to him" (1 Enoch 12:1). Does *prš'* refer to Enoch's status as one "separated" from intercourse with mortal men? According to traditions in 1 Enoch, Jubilees, and other Jewish literature, Enoch dwelt apart from other humans in localities variously identified as heaven itself, the Garden of Eden, or the fabulous land of Parwayyim.[109] The interpretation of *prš'* to connote Enoch's physical "separation" from human society seems a distinct possibility for the solution of this opaque epithet.[110]

3) *lš*] *qrh* [*b*] *'r'*— "[to practice deceit upon] the earth." Milik restores *l<u>b</u>*] *qrh* "to examine" here,[111] but the reference to *kdbyn* "lies" later in this fragment as well as the characterization of the era of the Giants as one of "deception" in other texts makes Beyer's restoration of *lš*] *qrh* attractive.[112] The Aramaic fragments of the so-called

Apocalypse of Weeks (1 Enoch 93:1–10 + 91:12–17) describes the period of the Giants as [*šbwʿ*] *tnyn dy bh šqr' wḥms' yṣmḥ* [... "the second [week] in which *deceit* and violence will spring up" (4QEn^g 1 iii 25 = 1 Enoch 93:4).[113] In a vision granted to Baruch, history is periodized into eras of "truth" and "deceit," and the era of the Watchers and Giants apparently falls under the aegis of "deceit" (2 Baruch 56:2,9–16).[114] According to Sibylline Oracles 1.177–178, the generation of the Deluge contains "liars" and "slanderers"; compare also Targum Job 4:8 (*dr' dṭwbʿn' ʿbdy šqr' wplḥy lyʿwt'*). Note, too, the similar Gnostic tradition appearing in the *Apocryphon of John*: "And they (i.e., the Watchers) steered the people who had followed them into great troubles, *by leading them astray with many deceptions*" (29:33–30:2).[115] One might recall in this connection the polarity evidenced in Iranian religious thought between the concepts of *aša* "righteousness, justice" and *drug* "deceit," the former associated with Ahura Mazda and the latter with Angra Mainyu (Ahriman).[116] A linkage of *drug* with the notions of "rebelliousness" or "disobedience" already appears in the Bisitun Inscription of Darius I, where it is stated that the "Lie" (Old Persian *drauga*) was responsible for fomenting dissension and rebellion among unruly subject peoples.[117] Whether this Iranian polarization of the concepts of righteousness and deceit exerted any influence upon analogous Jewish descriptions of conflicts between the "righteous" and the "wicked" (note the Syriac Apocalypse of Baruch cited above, as well as Noah's characterization as *'iš ṣaddiq tamim hayah bedorotaw* [Genesis 6:9]) remains an unresolved question.[118]

Another Aramaic fragment recovered from Cave 4 at Qumran[119] also mentions *šqr'* in what appears to be a context of either primeval or eschatological destruction. The fragment reads as follows:

1. *zrʿk wyšt'rwn kl ṣdyqy' wyšy*[...
2. *ʿwl wkl šqr l' ʿwd yštkḥ* [...
3. *wkʿn sb lwḥy' wqry' kwl'*[120] [...
4. [*k*] *l ʿqty wkl dy yt' ʿl*[*y*[121] ...
5. [ ] *lwḥ' mn* [...

1. your seed, and all the righteous ones will remain and ...

2. wickedness, and deceit will not be found any more ...
3. and now, take the tablets and read everything ...
4. ... all my distress and all that has come upon [me ...
5. ... the tablet from ...

One should note that this fragment characterizes the period of the "righteous ones" as an era in which there is no deceit. The period under discussion could be either the era after the Flood, in which case the *zr'* of line 1 signifies the progeny of Noah, or it could refer to the eschatological End of Days. However, the mention of "tablets" in lines 3 and 5 suggests a connection with other texts that allude to "tablets" in the context of the Deluge, especially the Qumran Book of Giants.[122] Other Jewish texts also report the discovery or recovery of tablets inscribed with antediluvian wisdom after the Flood waters have receded.[123] The conjunction of "deceit" and "tablets" coupled with the demonstrated presence of the motif of "deceit" during the final antediluvian generations suggests that this Aramaic fragment belongs to a work concerned with the description of events leading up to the judgment of the Deluge; in short, a work very much like the Book of Giants. Perhaps it is not too daring to suggest that this fragment actually stems from the Book of Giants.

mt'št — Milik reads the phrase as *mn b'št* "on account of the wickedness of,"[124] but the letters read by Milik as final *nun* and *beth* appear in the photograph to be one letter (*taw*? *he*? *ḥeth*?); a final *nun* is certainly not present.[125] Similarly, the letter read as *aleph* seems too small to be that letter, but some distortion must be taken into account due to the bunching of the manuscript at this point. Beyer reads the whole collection of letters as *mt'št* "planend"[126] from the stem *'št* "to intend, resolve," a verb used in Cowley 30:23 and Daniel 6:4.[127] In light of the photographic evidence, this is a better reading and is hence adopted here.

bh dm hwh špyk — "blood was shed upon it," the "it" presumably referring to the earth. Compare 4QEn[a] 1 iv 7 + 4QEn[b] 1 iii 8 (= 1 Enoch 9:1): *dm sgy šp*[*y*]*k* [ʿ]*l 'r'* "much blood shed upon the earth"[128] alongside the Greek (αἷμα πολὺ ἐκχυννόμεν[ον] ἐπὶ τῆς γῆς) and Ethiopic (*bezuxa dama za-yetka'awu ba-diba medr*) versions of the same verse. See also Jubilees 7:23–24. Milik has identified a scrap of 4QEnGi[e] that substantially reproduces this fragment of 4QEn[e] save for the grammatical variant *mštpk* in place of *špyk.*[129]

wkdbyn hww m[ ]*yn b*[... — For the significance of *kdbyn*, see the discussion above regarding *šqr'*. Further support for the notion that "deceit" and "lying" were endemic to the generation of the Flood can be gathered from the second column of 1QapGen. Therein, Lamech suspects that his new-born son Noah may actually be the product of an illicit liason between his wife Batenosh and a fallen Watcher or Giant. Lamech repeatedly badgers Batenosh to reveal the truth of the matter to him: *'d kwl' bqwšṭ' tḥwynny* "everything will you truthfully tell me" (2:5); *tḥwynny wl' bkdbyn* "you will tell me *without lies*" (2:6); *'d bqwšṭ 'my tmllyn wl' bkdbyn* "you will speak truthfully to me *and not with lies*" (2:7). Even after Batenosh has assured Lamech that the child is his own, Lamech remains unconvinced of the verity of her disclaimers until he has the opportunity to consult his grandfather Enoch "to learn from him the truth of the whole matter" (*lmnd' mnh kwl' bqwšṭ'* [2:22]). The intensity of Lamech's suspicion, coupled with its final alleviation only through the mediation of Enoch (who it will be recalled does not dwell among his corrupt human brethren), suggests that *kdbyn* "lies" were the order of the day during the final antediluvian generation. One might note as a more distant parallel the repeated communal condemnations of Noah as a "liar" (كاذب) in the Qur'an; see Suras 11:29 (compare 7:58) and 54:9 (compare 7:62; 10:74).

Milik restores within the lacuna *m*[*t'*]*bdyn*,[130] probably upon the basis of 1 Enoch 9:1b,[131] but the photograph provides little support for his suggestion.

mbwl 'l 'r' — "Deluge upon the earth." The Hebrew term *mbwl* is used thirteen times in the Hebrew Bible[132] and refers almost exclusively to the universal Deluge said to have taken place in the generation of Noah.[133] It appears as the loan-word *mbwl'* in some Aramaic texts,[134] but is more often rendered by Aramaic *ṭwpn'*[135] or *ṭwb'n'*[136] in the Targumic traditions. Aramaic *ṭwpn'* in turn was borrowed by both Arabic[137] and Mandaic[138] literature to designate the same cataclysmic event. A reference to the Flood at this point in the Book of Giants tends to support the suggestion voiced earlier to view QG2 as presenting the content of an angelic or divine revelation to Enoch along the lines of 1 Enoch 12:3–6. Although the Flood is not mentioned in the latter passage, its evocation here could be viewed as the natural culmination of the destruction pictured in verse 6.[139] Thus the reference to the Flood may serve as a proleptic warning of the impending judgment that Enoch would be expected to communicate to the Watchers and Giants in due course.

10) According to Milik, this line is found in 4QEnGi[b] and almost literally corresponds to 1 Enoch 9:10: "... the souls of those who have died are crying and making their suit to the gates of heaven ...."[140]

Corresponding to the same era of destruction and malice portrayed in QG2 are two descriptions of antediluvian terror contained in the Manichaean witnesses to the Book of Giants.

Coptic M[141]

Now attend and behold how the Great King of Honour[142] who is ἔννοια, is in the third heaven. He is ... with the wrath ... and a rebellion ..., when malice and wrath arose in his camp, namely the Egrēgoroi of Heaven who in his watch-district (rebelled and) descended to the earth. They did all deeds of malice. They revealed the arts in the world,[143] and the mysteries of heaven to the men. Rebellion and ruin came about on the earth ...

Sogdian H[144]

... and what they had seen in the heavens among the gods, and also what they had seen in hell, their native land, and furthermore what they had seen on earth,—all that they began to teach (*hendiadys*) to the men. To Šahmīzād[145] two (?) sons were borne by .... One of them he named "Ohya"; in Sogdian he is called "Sāhm, the giant." And again a second son [was born] to him. He named him "Ahya"; its Sogdian (equivalent) is "Pāt-Sāhm." As for the remaining giants, they were born to the other demons and Yaksas. (*Colophon*) Completed: (the chapter on) "The Coming of the two hundred Demons."[146]

Commentary to QG3

In 1 Enoch 6–16, the description of the destruction and carnage resulting from the birth of the Giants (chapters 7–8) is immediately followed by a petition addressed to God by the four principal archangels imploring his intervention upon earth (chapter 9). A similar structuring of narrative events appears to be operative in the Qumran Book of Giants. QG3 consists of a series of fragmentary lines which possess certain correspondences with the other prayers found in early Aramaic literature. Two particularly close parallels are present in 1 Enoch 9:4–5 and 84:2–6. 1 Enoch 9:4–5 reproduces the introductory paean of praise offered to God by Michael, Uriel, Raphael, and Gabriel which precedes their report of the sins of the Watchers and Giants. 1 Enoch 84:2–6 is an intercessory prayer uttered by Enoch after he had experienced an especially frightening vision of cosmic destruction (1 Enoch 83). His grandfather Mahalalel advises Enoch to petition God for mercy, and Enoch accordingly addresses God with the prayer of 84:2–6.[147] God responds to Enoch's plea by vouchsafing him yet another vision, the so-called "Animal Apocalypse" (chapters 85–90). The speaker(s) of QG3 is not identified in the text, but if we are correct in our hypothesis that QG2 reflects either a vision or an oral report of earthly woe presented to Enoch, then it seems likely that Enoch is the one who makes this prayer. The setting of QG2–QG3 would thus be analogous to what is found in 1 Enoch 83–84.

I. 2)] *ʿlyn mn qwdm hdr yq*[— "... before the majesty ...." Milik does not venture to restore the first word; Beyer suggests [*r*] *ʿlyn* "zittern."[148] The motif of "trembling" in the presence of a theophanic vision is common in Jewish apocalyptic literature and is based upon biblical antecedents.[149] However, the stem *rʿl* is sparsely attested in Jewish Aramaic literature and so one cannot confidently follow Beyer in his restoration. The phrase *hdr yq*[... can probably be read with both Milik and Beyer as *hdr yq*[*rkh* "majesty of your glory." For the collocation of these terms, note Daniel 4:27: *wlyqr hdry* "and my majestic honor"; 4:33: *wlyqr mlkwty hdry* "and the glory of my majestic kingdom"; 5:18: *wyqr' whdr' yhb lnbkdnṣr 'bwk* "glory and majesty he granted to Nebuchadnezzar your father." See also 11QtgJob 34:6 (=

Job 40:10): *wzwy* [*sic*!] *whdr wyqr tlbš* "put on grandeur and majesty and glory."

3) ...]*rk dy kwl rzy' yd*[' — "... for all mysteries are kno[wn (by you?)]." The knower is presumably God.[150] Compare 1 Enoch 84:3e–f: "and you know, see, and hear everything; there is nothing hidden from you, because you see everything"; also, 1 Enoch 9:11a: "and you know everything before it happens ...."

4) ...] *wkwl ṣbw l' tqptkh* [... — "and no thing is too difficult for you." This line has an exact parallel in 1 Enoch 84:3b: *wa-'i-yeṣana'aka gebr wa-'i-'aḥadu wa-'i-'aḥatti* "and nothing is too hard for you." For *ṣbw* in the sense of "thing," see Daniel 6:18 and Bodleian fragment column d 18 of the Aramaic Testament of Levi.[151]

6) *mlkwt rbwtkh lš*[... — "your great kingdom ...." Compare possibly 1 Enoch 84:2c: *wa-malakotka wa-mangeštka wa-'ebayka yenbar la-'ālam wa-la-'ālama 'ālam* "and *your* lordship and *kingdom* and *greatness* endure forever."

II. 1) ...*w*]*k'n mry* [... — "[and] now, my Lord ...." M.A. Knibb draws attention to the possible relationship of this fragment with 1 Enoch 84:6, also beginning "and now, my Lord ...."[152] Unfortunately the remainder of QG3 is too fragmentary to pronounce upon the likelihood of this suggestion.

The Manichaean Book of Giants preserves a passage which may supply a setting for the prayer uttered in QG3:

Fragment g 86–94[153]

(86) ... And (in) another place I[154] saw those that were weeping for the ruin that had befallen them and whose cries and laments rose up to heaven. (90) And also I saw another place [where there were] tyrants and rulers ... in great number, who had lived in sin and evil deeds, when ...[155]

If we are correct in interpreting QG2 as the remnant of either a divine or angelic revelation of the current earthly woes to a sequestered Enoch, then this Middle Persian fragment could very well form part of that same revelatory discourse. A reconstruction of the sequence of events presupposed in QG2–3 might take the following form. Either God speaks, or a heavenly messenger travels to Enoch and communicates the news about the corruption of the earth and an intended punishment (QG2). Enoch views the situation upon earth from his separate abode (Fragment g 86–94), and, moved by compassion for the suffering, addresses an intercessory prayer to God on the earth's behalf (QG3).

Commentary to QG4A

The response of God to the carnage upon earth (QG1–2) and the intercessory prayer of Enoch (QG3) now follows. In 1 Enoch 10:1–16, God reacts to this deplorable situation by dispatching his four principal archangels to earth. Sariel[156] arrives with a message for Noah to prepare himself for the onset of the Deluge, while Raphael, Gabriel, and Michael are sent to execute divine punishment upon Azazel, the Giants, and Shemiḥazah and his Watcher colleagues. In the Qumran Book of Giants, the wheel of retribution revolves more slowly. Herein two dreams presaging universal destruction are sent by God to Hahyah and 'Ohyah, the two Giant sons of Shemiḥazah. Neither Giant is able to fathom the actual significance of his dream for himself. The frightening character of the dreams lead them to recount what they have seen before an assembly of the remaining Giants. Thoroughly alarmed but still puzzled, the Giants resolve to consult Enoch in order to receive an authoritative interpretation of the visions. They accordingly commission the Giant Mahaway to bear their oracular request before Enoch.

3) *ḥlmw tryhwn ḥlmyn* — "both of them dreamed dreams." Compare the wording of Targum Onkelos Genesis 40:5: *wḥlmw ḥlm' trwyhwn* .... The two sons of Shemiḥazah also experience symbolic dreams in the medieval Jewish *Midrash of Shemhazai and Azael.* For further discussion of this work, see below.

4) *wndt šnt ʿynyhwn mnhwn* — "and the sleep of their eyes fled from them." Note QG9 10 below. Compare Daniel 6:19: *wšnth ndt ʿlwhy* and the Aramaic Testament of Levi Bodleian a 6–7: *tnwd šnt ʿyn'*. Note the analogous Hebrew expressions in Genesis 31:40 (*wtdd šnty mʿyny* [Targum Onkelos reads *wndt šnty myʿyny*]), Esther 6:1 (*nddh šnt hmlk*), and Daniel 2:1 (*wšntw nhyth ʿlyw*).

5) *'tw ʿl*— "they came to ...." For this syntagm see Ezra 4:12; 5:3; 1QapGen 20:21; 22:1–2.[157] Note that these examples use *'t' ʿl* to denote a journey whose objective is a person or group of persons. By contrast, the construction *'t' l-* is usually employed when a place or locality is the object.[158] The former usage would support the restoration of the personal name of a Giant or Watcher as the object of *'tw ʿl*. Milik restores the name Shemiḥazah;[159] Beyer does not hazard a guess here.

6) *b*] *ḥlmy hwyt ḥz' blyly' dn* — "[in] my dream (which) I saw tonight." Compare the similar idioms in Daniel 2:31: *'nth mlk' hzh hwyt* ...; 7:2: *hzh hwyt bḥzwy ʿm lyly'* ...; and 7:6: *b'tr dnh hzh hwyt* .... These clauses are all followed by the copula and interjection *w'lw/w'rw* "and behold!" which introduces the narrative description of the dream itself, and hence this term seems a plausible restoration for the beginning of line 7.[160] An alternative candidate for restoration would be the interjection *h'*. Note line 16 below, as well as 1QapGen 19:14: *wḥzyt bḥlmy wh'* ... ("and in my dream I saw, behold ...") and 4QEn[e] 4 i 16 (= 1 Enoch 89:2): [*whywt*] *ḥzh wh'* ... ("[and I] saw, behold ..."). We learn from line 15 below that the recipient of this first dream is the Giant Hahyah.

The recountal of the first dream now follows in lines 7–12. We reproduce here the entire dream narrative in order that the constituent elements of Hahyah's vision can be viewed in relation to each other and to the similar dream narrative contained within the medieval *Midrash of Shemhazai and Azael.*

7) [*w'lw/w'rw/wh'* ...] *gnnyn*[161] *hww' mšqyn*
8) ...*šr*] *šyn rbrbyn npqw mn ʿqrhn*
9) ... *wḥz'*[162]] *hywt ʿd dy* [...] *mn*

10) ...] *kl my' wnwr' dlq bkl*
11) [*prds'*(?)/*gn'*(?)/*'r''*(?)] ...
12) ...] *'d k' swp ḥlm'*[163]

7) [and behold ...] gardeners were watering
8) ... great [shoo]ts[164] came forth from their root(s)
9) ... and I continued [looking] until ... (?) ... from
10) ... all the water, and fire burned in all
11) [the garden(?)/the world(?)] ...
12) ... so far the end of the dream.

Despite the fragmentary condition of the dream narrative, the sequence of events, along with their significance, are not difficult to reconstruct. Hahyah dreams of a garden or grove that is tended by an unspecified number of "gardeners." The vegetation flourishes under their care, producing large "shoots" and presumably much fruit. However, something disturbs the balance of this ecosystem which leads to the garden's destruction by both water and fire. With this arresting climax the dream comes to an end.

The information within this dream narrative should be compared with a similar dream recounted within the *Midrash of Shemhazai and Azael.*[165] This medieval text, alleged to have been part of the no longer extant *Midrash Abkir,*[166] relates a tale that possesses some astonishing parallels with this particular portion of the Qumran Book of Giants. Therein also the angel Shemhazai[167] (= QG Shemiḥazah) is credited with fathering two Giant sons from mortal women named Hiwwa (*hyww'*) and Hiyya (*hyy'*).[168] The former name corresponds to that of 'Ohyah (*'hy'/h*) in the Qumran Book of Giants, while the latter appellation is equivalent to that of his brother Hahyah (*hhyh*).[169] The evil perpetrated upon earth due to the corrupt actions of the Watchers and Giants provokes God into dispatching a messenger[170] to Shemhazai to apprise him of the impending judgment of the Deluge. Chastened by this ominous message, Shemhazai repents of his wicked deeds.[171] Warnings, however, are also sent to the two sons of Shemhazai in the form of symbolic dreams. Neither Giant is capable of deciphering the precise significance of his dream, but they are sufficiently impressed and disturbed by the symbolism to repeat their dreams before their father. Recognizing their import, Shemhazai reveals to his sons that their dreams presage a universal destruction that will consume everything upon earth except for Noah and his three sons. He consoles their despair with the promise that the names Hiwwa and Hiyya would never be forgotten.[172]

According to the midrash, the dream experienced by Hiyya was as follows:

> And the other (i.e., Hiyya) saw in his dream a large and flourishing garden, and the garden was planted with every type of tree and all sorts of delightful (plants), and then angels came bearing hatchets and cut down all the trees, leaving only one tree which had three branches.[173]

One notes that this dream also speaks of a garden of incredible fertility that undergoes sudden divine destruction. The mode of destruction is disparate, however. In Hahyah's dream contained in the Qumran Book of Giants, the garden is apparently wiped out by the complementary action of water and fire, but in the midrash the destruction occurs at the hands of axe-wielding angels. Similarly, the midrash speaks of the survival of a three-pronged tree which serves as a symbol for the preservation of Noah and his three sons during the Deluge. QG4A 7–12 does not preserve a reference to this event, but a fragment from another copy of the Qumran Book of Giants (QG4B)[174] does feature this specific motif:

1) *tltt šršwhy* [... *wḥz'*]
2) *hwyt 'd dy 'tw* [...
3) *prds' dn klh wl*[...

1) three of its shoots ...
2) I continued [looking] until there came ...
3) this garden, all of it ...

This text, which in all probability must be viewed as another textual fragment from this very dream, will be examined in greater detail below.

A question naturally arises regarding the possible relationship of these two dream narratives — one Qumranic and eventually Manichaean in provenance, the other belonging to the realm of medieval Jewish midrash. Does the medieval midrash reflect knowledge of either the Qumranic or the Manichaean form of this dream? Milik has suggested that the *Midrash of Shemhazai and Azael* represents a Hebrew retroversion (from Syriac) of part of the Manichaean Book of Giants,[175] but this hypothesis seems unlikely.[176] We know of only a few examples where Jewish scholars demonstrate their familiarity with Manichaean mythology, despite that literature's biblical roots and imagery.[177] For example, the magical bowl corpus from southern Mesopotamia attests how distinctive religious personae or concepts were freely shared among the Jewish, Christian, and Mandaean communities of that region, with little or no regard for their original religious identity. However, the appearance of a Mandaean deity on a Jewish bowl does not indicate that Mandaean literature was translated or even perused by the Jewish community. With regard to the relationship between the Book of Giants and the midrash, it seems much more plausible to assume that these stories are both textual expressions of an early exegetical tradition circulating in learned groups during the Second Temple era. One version appeared in Aramaic at Qumran and was presumably the version later studied and adapted by Mani. Another version of the same tradition recurs in Hebrew in the early Middle Ages. Still other versions (if not one of the two aforementioned ones) apparently influenced Islamic exegetes of the Qur'anic passage regarding the sins of Hārūt and Mārūt (Sura 2:96).[178]

The discrepancy over the mode of destruction may perhaps be explained in light of the relative age of the two texts. The Qumran passage reflects an eschatological conception well attested in the Hellenistic era of a dual cosmic destruction, one of which employs water (*mabbul shel mayim*) and the other fire (*mabbul shel 'esh*).[179] This particular doctrine exhibits several distinct forms. The oldest, although not necessarily the source for later Jewish and Christian speculations, appears in Plato's *Timaeus*, where it is imparted to the Greek sage Solon by an Egyptian priest.[180] Therein it is stated that the sublunary world periodically undergoes destruction by both conflagrations and floods. Destruction by fire is caused by the position of certain heavenly bodies vis-à-vis the earth, an astronomical phenomenon symbolized in Greek lore by the myth of Phaethon.[181] Floods, on the other hand, are attributed simply to the purgative whims of the gods.

The idea of a recurrent destruction of the earth by water and fire is also expressed in a purported fragment of the astrological teachings of the Babylonian priest Berossus excerpted in the *Quaestiones Naturales* of Seneca.[182] This passage asserts that the earth is periodically destroyed (and presumably renewed) at calculable intervals by an alternating action of fire and water. The imminence of each destruction is foreshadowed by planetary conjunctions in the signs of Cancer and Capricorn, respectively.[183]

Another distinctive form of this teaching largely discards the cyclical character of the previously discussed pattern, instead positing that there are only two universal destructions within each cosmic revolution or "Great Year." One already occurred during the present era, when the world was flooded in the age of Noah-Deukalion-Xisuthros. Another universal destruction, however, is fated to transpire at the appointed end of time. At this juncture the world as we know it will come to a fiery end.[184] Depending upon one's philosophical or religious view, the final conflagration could be perceived as the final termination of a corrupt world order (Jews, Christians, Manichaeans) or as a necessary purgative step leading to an identical reconstruction of the world order (Stoics).

Yet another form of this doctrine might be characterized as exegetical. In this schema, the destructions by fire and water are "historicized" by connecting them with significant events reported in the sacred literature of a religious community.[185] For those communities who employed the Jewish Bible as sacred scripture, the destructions by water and fire were illustrated in the story of Noah (Genesis 6:5–9:17) and in the tale regarding the destruction of Sodom and Gomorrah (Genesis 19:24–28). The concept of eschatological destruction by water or fire could thus be signaled by a literary reference to the appropriate legend. An important development within this tradition is marked by a textual linkage that evolves between these two originally unrelated stories. The Deluge and the fiery destruction of Sodom amalgamate, so to speak, to form a rhetorical *topos* that is much invoked in both Jewish and Christian literature.[186] The welding of these two narrative traditions can probably be traced to an early interpretation of Genesis 14:5, a verse which remarks in passing that *repha'im* (LXX τοὺς γίγαντας; Targumim *gybry'* "giants") are among the populace of the Cities of the Plain.[187] The common motif of "Giants" thus unites these two disparate pericopae.

By contrast, the medieval text may have patterned its destruction-motif upon the biblical models of Ezekiel 31:1–14 and Daniel 4:1–25. In both of these pericopae, important ruling kingdoms are likened to great trees whose temporal destruction is accomplished by a divine command ordering that these trees be cut down. A similar motif is also present in 1QapGen 19:14–17, a passage in which Abram dreams of a cedar and a date-palm, which symbolize himself and Sarai, his wife. Men come forward intent upon hewing down the cedar (Abram), but the date-palm (Sarai) protests and persuades the woodcutters to spare the cedar. This dream functions as a warning of the danger Abram and Sarai face from the covetous Pharaoh, a threat that is fully borne out by subsequent events. The dream of Hahyah performs a similar task in the Qumran Book of Giants.

13) [*l'*] *hškḥw gbry' lḥwy' lh*[*wn*(?)] — "the Giants were [un]able to explain to [them (?)]." The plot communicated in the following lines demands that the negative [*l'*] be inserted before the verb, else there would be no reason for consulting Enoch regarding the interpretation of the dreams. For *hškḥ/'škḥ* in the sense of "to be able,"[188] see also QG9 5 below as well as 4QEn^{a} 1 ii 8–9 (= 1 Enoch 4): *wlm*] *drk 'l 'prh w*['] *l* [*kp*] *yh l' tškḥwn mn* [*ḥmth*][189] "you will be unable to step upon its dirt or its rock due to its heat," and 1QapGen 21:13: *w'śgh zr'k k'pr 'r'' dy l' yškḥ kwl br 'nwš lmmnyh*[190] "I will multiply your seed (to be) like the dust of the ground which no man is able to count." The verb *ḥwh* "explain, recount, interpret" is used often in Daniel to refer to the "setting forth" of an "interpretation" (*pšr'*) of a dream or visual enigma. See Daniel 2:9–11; 2:24; and 5:7 for examples of this usage. Milik restores *lh*[*wn*] and translates "for themselves" at the end of this line, but this reflexive translation is impossible here. Beyer prefers the singular *lh* "to him," understanding the whole line to describe a futile attempt by the assembled Giants to interpret the dream for Hahyah. In the absence of photographic evidence, either pronominal reading is possible. Presumably the word *ḥlm'* or phrase *pšr ḥlm'* should be restored at the beginning of line 14.

14)–15a) *lḥnwk] lspr prš' wypšwr ln' ḥlm'*— "to Enoch] the scribe (who is) set apart, and he will interpret the dream for us." The speakers are apparently the Giants, represented in the preceding line as unable to decipher the meaning of Hahyah's dream. Recourse shall thus be made to Enoch for an authoritative interpretation of the puzzling vision. For Enoch's epithet *spr prš'*, see the discussion of QG2 2 above. The stem *pšr* "to interpret" is used as a verb and as a noun in biblical Aramaic; for the former, see Daniel 5:12,16, and the latter, Daniel *passim.* The normal Hebrew reflex of this stem is *ptr*, as is evident from the Joseph narrative in Genesis, but *pšr* also appears as a loan-word from Aramaic in Hebrew compositions of the Second Temple period (see Ecclesiastes 8:1 and the Qumran *pesharim*).[191]

15) *b'dyn [hw]h hwdh 'ḥwhy 'whyh w'mr qdm gbry'*— "then his brother 'Ohyah acknowledged and said before the Giants." The use of *hwdh* in the sense of "make declaration, confession" is rather curious here. *Hwdh/'wdh* is normally employed in Jewish Aramaic to express gratitude or thanksgiving for divine deliverance and care.[192] However, the *Ithpa'el* form of the stem *w/ydy* does apparently connote the practice of making a public verbal profession of evidence suitable for a legal document. In an Aramaic promissory note emanating from the cache of documents found at Murabba'at, the initial lines state: *bṣwyh 'ytwdy 'bšlwm br ḥnyn mn ṣwyh bnpy mnyh 'my ... ksp zwzyn 's[ry]n*[193] "at Siwaya, Absalom bar Hannin of Siwaya *has declared* in my presence (that) there is on account with me ... the sum of 2[0] zuzin." Perhaps such a legal formulation has influenced the language of QG4A 15. Beyer has regarded this expression with suspicion, proposing to read instead ['n]*h twbh.* The use of *twb/twbh* "furthermore, again" is sporadically attested in Egyptian Aramaic,[194] but appears in no Jewish texts contemporary with the Giants fragments.

16a) *'p 'nh ḥzyt bḥlmy blyly' dn gbry'*— "I also have beheld in my dream tonight, O Giants." Given the frequent orthographic ambiguity of *waw* and *yod* in Qumran texts, the reading *gbry'* "Giants" as a vocative may be preferable to the more difficult *gbrw'* of both Milik and Beyer. Milik translates *gbrw'* as "an extraordinary thing"; similarly Beyer.[195]

The dream of 'Ohyah now follows:

16b) *h' šlṭn šmy' l'r'' nḥt*
17)–19) unpublished
20a) ...] *'d k' swp ḥlm'*

16b) behold, the ruler of heaven descended to earth
17)–19) [unpublished]
20a) ... so far the end of the dream.

Unfortunately, fewer details regarding 'Ohyah's dream have survived or have been made available to readers by its modern editor. According to Milik, lines 17–19 recount a scene of judgment similar to that found in Daniel 7:9–10.[196] The absence of these lines inhibits further discussion of 'Ohyah's vision. However, let us return to the *Midrash of Shemhazai and Azael* and examine the dream ascribed there to the Giant Hiwwa, a figure corresponding to the 'Ohyah of the Qumran Giants fragments. According to the midrash, Hiwwa's dream was as follows:

> One of them (i.e., Hiwwa) beheld in his dream a large stone spread out over the earth like a table, and the whole of it was chiseled and inscribed with many rows (of characters). *Then an angel descended from heaven* with a type of knife in his hand, and scraped and effaced all of the rows (of characters), leaving only one row containing four words.[197]

While there is no scene of judgment corresponding to that of Daniel 7:9–10 in Hiwwa's dream, there does emerge from this narrative one important parallel with the dream of 'Ohyah in the Qumran Book of Giants. In both visions a divine being descends from heaven to earth. This figure is designated *šlṭn šmy'*[198] "ruler of heaven" in the Giants fragment as opposed to *mal'ak* "angel" in the midrash. The Giants fragment does not impart the mission of this heavenly being (presumably for judgment, if we accept Milik's report), but a clearer clue can perhaps be gained from the description in the midrash. There, the angel approaches a large stone tablet engraved with rows of written characters and proceeds to erase all of the inscribed lines save for one row that contains four words.[199] These four words are presumably the names of Noah and his three sons, just as in the preceding dream of Hahyah/Hiyya a tree with three shoots connoted the same individuals. Thus we see that in the midrash the two separate dreams of the Giant progeny of Shemhazai relate an identical message via differing symbolic structures — namely, the imminent arrival of a universal cataclysm which only Noah and his seed would survive. Given the demonstrable correspondences of motifs among the dreams in both sources, it does not seem too hazardous to suppose that the dream of 'Ohyah was equally consonant with the preceding dream of Hahyah in that it imparted an identical message of universal destruction.

20b) *dḥlw kl gbry'* — "all the Giants were afraid." This report confirms the suspicion outlined above that the symbolism of the second dream was in thematic accord with the disturbing scenario of destruction contained in Hahyah's initial vision. One might compare a similar notice in the *Midrash of Shemhazai and Azael*: *kywn šnn'rw mšntm 'mdw bbhlh* ...[200] "when they (i.e., Hiyya and Hiwwa) awoke from their sleep, they arose *terrified* ...." In the Qumran Book of Giants, the entire assembly of Giants shares the dreamers' fright.

21) ... *w*] *q*[*r*] *w lmhwy w'th l*[...] *gbry' wšlḥwhy*[201] *'l ḥnwk* — "... and] they [sum]moned Mahaway, and he came to [...] Giants, and they sent him to Enoch." Desperate for an authoritative interpretation of the dream symbolism, the Giants commission one of their number, a Giant named Mahaway (*mhwy*), to bear their request for decipherment to Enoch. Mahaway identifies himself in a later fragment (QG6 4) as the son of Baraq'el, one of the twenty fallen Watchers listed by name in 1 Enoch.[202] Mahaway is expressly cited at least five times in the extant fragments of the Qumran Book of Giants,[203] and his prominence as an actor in the Giants drama is indicated by his retention as a character in the Middle Persian, Sogdian, and Uighur remnants of the Manichaean recension of the book.[204] For the locution *šlḥ 'l*, see Ezra 4:11, 17, 18; 5:6, 7, 17.

22) *w'mrw lh 'zl* ... — "and they said to him, Go ...." The formal

commissioning of Mahaway now takes place. For this form of the imperative, see Ezra 5:15 and 4QEn^c 5 ii 29 (= 1 Enoch 107:2): *wk'n 'zl n' 'd lmk* [*br*]*k*[205] "and now, go to Lamech your son." With the obvious goal of Mahaway's journey being the habitation of Enoch, the lacuna following *'zl* can perhaps be restored [*'d ḥnwk* ... or something similar. The remainder of this line is too uncertain for further comment.

23) ...] *šm'th qlh w'mr lh* [...]*r ḥlmy'*— "... you have heard his voice, and say to him ... the dreams." Beyer understands this final passage to signify (and reconstructs accordingly) that Mahaway was the only Giant capable of executing this mission due to his personal acquaintance with Enoch.[206] However, there is no evidence either from the Book of Giants or other related literature that any one Giant enjoyed a special relationship with Enoch. It seems better to interpret this line as connoting particular travel instructions imparted by the Giants to Mahaway. They appear to be telling Mahaway that he will have reached his destination *when* he hears the voice of Enoch calling out to him. Such an understanding emerges from the subsequent narrative of QG5, which describes the actual journey of Mahaway to Enoch. While relating some of the sights and localities that Mahaway passes over, there suddenly intrudes *w[ḥ]zh ḥnwk wz'qh*[207] "and Enoch saw him and called out to him." A Manichaean fragment preserved in Uighur paralleling QG5 also contains this motif of the "calling out" of Enoch to Mahaway.[208] Hence, we should probably understand QG4A 23 as follows: "[and *when*] you hear his voice, *then* you shall recount to him ... the dreams." The Giants may thus be alerting Mahaway as to how he would know when he had arrived at the dwelling of Enoch.

A parallel to the dream of Hahyah as reported in QG4A (and QG4B?) is present in a fragment from the Manichaean Book of Giants.

Fragment j 39–41[209]

Narīmān[210] saw (in his sleep)[211] a gar[den full of] trees in rows. Two hundred[212]... came out, the trees ...

Commentary to QG4B

The papyrus fragment labeled here QG4B was introduced above during the discussion of Hahyah's dream which featured the sudden destruction of a grove of trees. While QG4A stems entirely from Cave 4, QG4B was discovered in Cave 6[213] and apparently was part of another copy of the Book of Giants. Both Milik and Beyer recognize that this fragment belongs with the longer dream narratives of QG4A.[214] In view of the material contained within it, it seems very likely that QG4B preserves a few further details of Hahyah's dream related in QG4A 7–12.

1) *tltt šršwhy [... wḥzh*[215]]
2) *hwyt ʿd dy*[216] *ʾtw*[217] [...
3) *prds' dn klh wl*[...

1) three of its shoots ...
2) I continued [looking] until there came ...
3) this garden, all of it ...

If we combine the evidence accumulated from QG4A 7–12, QG4B, Henning Fragment j 39–41, and the *Midrash of Shemhazai and Azael,* a reasonably coherent structure for the dream of Hahyah can be reconstructed. Hahyah beholds in his vision a grove of trees carefully attended by gardeners. This tranquil scene is interrupted by the sudden appearance (or transformation?) of two hundred figures within this garden. The result of the invasion was the production of "great" (*rbrbyn*)[218] shoots sprouting up from the roots of the trees. While Hahyah viewed this scene, emissaries from Heaven arrived[219] and ravaged the garden with water and fire, leaving only one tree bearing three branches as the sole survivor of the destruction. With this image, the dream apparently ended.

The symbolism of this dream is relatively transparent. The grove represents the earth, and the trees planted therein symbolize the earth's antediluvian population. The "gardeners" (*gnnyn*) who nurture the trees have been identified as angelic protectors,[220] but it seems possible that this symbol connotes the Watchers themselves prior to their apostasy. A tradition preserved in the Book of Jubilees relates that God originally dispatched the Watchers to earth for the purpose of instructing humanity in proper ritual and ethical conduct.[221] Only after their arrival and sojourn among human beings were the Watchers corrupted and led astray by the irresistible beauty of mortal women. The statement that "the gardeners were watering" (QG4A 7) may be an allusion to the initial educational mission of the Watchers, given the common exegetical nexus in Jewish literature between "water" and "Torah."[222] The "great" shoots springing up from the roots of the trees indicate the birth of the Giants. Perhaps we should understand that these shoots were so large that they threatened to choke out the original inhabitants of the garden. The eventual destruction by water and fire symbolizes the coming Deluge, and the surviving tree with its three branches represents Noah and his three sons.

This final image of the lone tree with its three shoots or branches is not without significance for the later transmissional history of the Qumran Book of Giants. Archaeological exploration of the Tarim Basin in Central Asia during the first decade of this century uncovered a veritable treasure trove of beautifully illuminated manuscripts and wall-paintings produced by the Manichaean communities in that region.[223] Among the Buddhist cave-temple complex at Bäzäklik, A. Grünwedel exhumed two sanctuaries which, upon later analysis, proved to display traces of an earlier Manichaean occupation. In the sanctuary designated Cave 25, Grünwedel's attention was arrested by a curious composition adorning the farther end of the sanctuary wall.[224] The painting depicted a tree with three trunks growing out of a circular, basin-like object. The tree possessed large stylized leaves, some flowers, and several enormous grape-clusters dangling from its branches. On either side of the tree were a series of kneeling human figures in attitudes of prayer or adoration. A thick horizontal line marked the lower border of the composition. This painting was first reproduced in the excavation report of S. von Oldenburg.[225]

The painting was initially interpreted to be a representation of the enlightenment of the Buddha, the tree signifying the *bodhi*-tree beneath which the Buddha achieved his insight, and the basin-like object from or behind which the tree springs a stylized rendering of the vacant throne (*vajrāsana*) symbolizing the presence of the Buddha.[226] However, the *bodhi*-tree never displays the peculiar attributes of this form in either earlier or contemporary Buddhist art. Further study of the costumes of the adoring figures in this painting, coupled with the presence of similar representations of a three-stemmed tree among the Manichaean textual fragments recovered from Qočo, convinced scholars that the painting was actually Manichaean in provenance.[227] Two manuscript illuminations are particularly important in this regard.[228]

The first, discovered in Ruin α at Qočo,[229] contains a stylized tree featuring three primary branches sprouting off from the main trunk. The source from which the trunk springs is unfortunately lost, and Le Coq suggested that a lotus-throne or garlanded basin may have been depicted there. The three shoots branch off in three directions: one to the right, one to the left, and the third straight upward, ultimately lost to view due to damage. Each branch bears buds and huge flowers similar to the foliage adorning the tree at Bäzäklik, and the two side branches each terminate in a large blossom upon which a Manichaean priest is seated. The termination point of the middle branch is missing, but the remains of a "stool-like" structure which survive suggested to Le Coq that Mani himself (or alternatively his vacant *bēma*-seat[230]) may have been pictured on this topmost branch. The two Manichaean priests wear the customary garb of the *electi*. The priest to the right is seated in the fashion of a Buddha with arms and hands arranged in the classic *dharma-cakra mudrā*.[231] The priest on the left holds open before him a handsomely bound volume of writings. Le Coq has plausibly suggested that this priest is engaged in the reading of a sacred text which his opposite number then expounds to an attendant crowd of *auditores* below.[232]

A second illumination from Ruin K at Qočo[233] displays two rows of Manichaean priests divided by a column of text. Each of the priests is pictured at a desk with pen in hand. Behind the seated priests on both sides rise the trunks of two trees, their canopies featuring the large blossoms and grape-clusters familiar from the Bäzäklik painting. The manuscript is heavily damaged, but it has seemed plausible to at least one interpreter to reconstruct a three-stemmed tree in this situation as well.[234]

The significance of the peculiar tree for Manichaean theology remained obscure to early researchers. None of the Manichaean texts recovered from Turfan make reference to such a symbol. Yet the tree clearly occupied an important place in the religious conceptions of the Manichaean community of that region, given its iconographic prominence in the fragmentary remains and the reverent postures assumed by the Bäzäklik attendants. Hackin termed it a "sacred" tree and sought to align it more closely with contemporary Buddhist representations of the *bodhi*-tree.[235] As Hackin was publishing the results of his investigation, further light was shed upon the tree from an unexpected quarter. Several passages from the newly discovered Coptic Manichaean corpus recovered from Medinet Madi in Egypt made mention of a "good tree" and a "worthless tree," also designated "Tree of Life" and "Tree of Evil (or) Death," as symbols, respectively, for the two great opposed realms undergirding Manichaean cosmology, the Kingdom of Light and the Kingdom of Darkness.[236] It seemed possible that the tree beneath which the Manichaean faithful gathered in adoration was in fact this "Tree of Life,"[237] designed as an iconographic rendering of the Kingdom of Light to which every pious Manichaean aspired to return.

Further refinement of the Tree of Life interpretation was afforded by some curious extracts purportedly cited from a Manichaean treatise by the sixth-century Monophysite bishop Severus of Antioch in a Syriac homily directed against the Manichaeans.[238] Although Severus does not name the Manichaean text that he is quoting, it has been widely assumed since the fundamental investigation of F. Cumont and M.-A. Kugener[239] that the extracts stem from Mani's Book of Giants.[240]

In the extracts of Severus, the Kingdoms of Light and Darkness are described respectively as a Tree of Life and a Tree of Death. A wealth of descriptive detail is provided that is lacking in the Coptic allusions. Most significant for the present discussion are the fragments' textual depiction of these "Trees." The Tree of Life extends over *three* regions of the cosmos — east, west, and north. By contrast, the Tree of Death exercises dominion over the south, a quarter depicted as the region *below* the Kingdom of Light.[241] If one recalls the composition of the tree imagery preserved at both Bäzäklik and Qočo, it is astonishing how similar the textual description contained in Severus is to the iconographic representations in Central Asia. One must entertain the possibility that the mysterious three-stemmed tree of Manichaean art is a representation of the Manichaean Tree of Life.

The curious appearance of a tree with "three shoots" in the Qumran Book of Giants has increased interest in the Tree of Life symbolism. H.-J. Klimkeit has vigorously championed a direct link between the "three shoots" of QG4B and the three-stemmed tree of Central Asian provenance.[242] Klimkeit argues that the three-stemmed tree depicted in the Bäzäklik painting was based upon a description of the Tree of Life once contained in Mani's Book of Giants. The plausibility of such an inclusion within the Book of Giants is based upon the alleged testimony of Severus of Antioch. However, Klimkeit goes on to suggest that the Manichaean image of the tri-stemmed Tree of Life (reconstructed from Severus and Central Asian iconography) is ultimately dependent upon the textual description of Noah and his three sons in the Qumran Book of Giants, the presumed *Vorlage* for Mani's work of the same name. Despite the absence of Noah (or any other biblical personage) in the fragments cited by Severus, and the silence of the Turfan remains of the Book of Giants regarding a Tree of Life, the possibility advanced by Klimkeit of a transmissional link between the heirs of the Qumran Giant tradition and Mani's early community is real. Furthermore, the conception of Noah and his three sons as a "Tree of Life" is an appealing one, given his family's role in the repopulation of the decimated earth.

Additional evidence can be brought to bear on the possible designation of Noah and his progeny as a "Tree of Life" from Jewish literature. *Bereshit Rabba* 26:1 exegetes Genesis 5:32, the verse which refers to the birth of Noah's three sons, with the aid of Psalm 1, a composition that likens the pious believer to a well-watered, fruitful tree. Here are the relevant lines of this interpretation:

> "And when Noah was five hundred years old, he fathered Shem, Ham, and Japhet" (Gen 5:32). [This verse is to be exegeted by] "Blessed is the man who does not follow the counsel of the wicked" (Ps 1:1). "Blessed is the man": this [man] is Noah .... "*And he is like a tree* planted by streams of water" (Ps 1:3), for God "planted" him in the ark, "which produces its fruit in due season" (ibid.): this [fruit] is Shem; "whose foliage does not wither" (ibid.): this [foliage] is Ham; "and all that it produces thrives" (ibid.): this [production] is Japhet. "Thus Noah fathered (*three sons*): Shem, Ham, and Japhet" (Gen 5:32b).[243]

A further expression of this arboreal symbolism is found in the immediately succeeding pericope:

> "They (i.e., the righteous[244]) are planted in the Temple of the Lord; they produce sprouts in the courts of our God" (Ps 92:14). "Planted in the Temple of the Lord": this is Noah, for God "planted" him in the ark. "They produce *sprouts* in the courts of our God": [this refers to the verse] "*Noah fathered Shem, Ham, and Japhet*" (Gen 5:32b). "Still producing fruit in old age" (Ps 92:15a): this is Noah. "They are luxuriant and green" (Ps 92:15b): [this refers to the verse] "Noah fathered Shem, Ham, and Japhet" (Gen 5:32b).[245]

These two passages demonstrate that the comparison of Noah and his progeny with a tree and its fruits or sprouts was not foreign to Jewish exegetical genius during the early centuries of the Common Era. This typology is ultimately rooted in biblical metaphors that speak of the righteous individual or community as a "plant" or as having been "planted" by God, a use of language already visible in Psalm 1 above.[246] During the Second Temple era, a refinement of this imagery took place, in that specific individuals or groups featured in Jewish history were singled out as especially deserving of the epithets "plant," "eternal plant," or "plant of righteousness." Significantly, one of the recipients of these designations was Noah and his progeny.

An important passage employing this typology is the "original" version[247] of 1 Enoch 10:3, preserved in its entirety only by Syncellus. 1 Enoch 10:1–3 relates the divine commission of Sariel to inform Noah of the impending Deluge. Verse 3 as transmitted by the Greek Codex Panopolitanus and the Ethiopic recension states: "And [now] instruct him (i.e., Noah) so that he will escape and his seed will remain throughout all generations."[248] However, the same passage in Syncellus reads: "Instruct the righteous one what to do, the son of Lamech, that he might preserve his life and escape forever, *and from him a plant shall be planted and established* for all the generations of the world."[249] Similarly 1 Enoch 10:16, when describing the postdiluvial era, refers to Noah as the "*plant of righteousness and truth.*"[250] This typology is employed again in the petition for mercy uttered by Enoch in 1 Enoch 84:2–6 when he pleads: "But establish the flesh of righteousness and uprightness[251] *(as) a plant of the eternal seed*" (1 Enoch 84:6b).[252] Finally, this image is also familiar to the author of the Book of Jubilees. Among the instructions which Noah issues his sons is the following exhortation: "And now, my children, give heed: act (with) justice and righteousness *so that you may be truly planted* upon the surface of all the earth ..." (Jubilees 7:34).[253]

The last citation from Jubilees 7:34 illustrates a further facet of this botanical symbolism. The designation of "plant," etc. is also applied to those descendents of Noah who are distinguished for their pious or righteous behavior. "Act justly and righteously,"[254] Noah exhorts, "so that you may be planted in righteousness," or in other words, so that you also might be designated "righteous plants." This theme surfaces in a passage from the Apocalypse of Adam, a Gnostic text recovered from Nag Hammadi, when it states that the third manifestation of the "Luminary" (*phōstēr*) will leave behind on earth "fruit-bearing trees" from the seed of Noah, Ham, and Japhet.[255] The descendents of Noah, however, were less capable of maintaining the ideal status of the exemplary *ṣaddiq*, save for Abraham, who inherited the botanical title of Noah for himself and his posterity.[256] Further lapses into apostasy and lawlessness (from the sectarian perspective) by the progeny of Abraham only serve to highlight the exemplary conduct of those few persons who concerned themselves with the proper observance of the Torah imparted to the "righteous plants" and to Moses. The Qumran community eventually adopts the metaphor of "plant" to describe their own group in relationship to the surrounding culture,[257] thus explicitly declaring themselves the "true" heirs of Noah and Abraham. Significantly both Noah and Abraham were considered by later tradition to be the paradigmatic exponents of orthodox piety and cult in their respective generations.[258] By their appropriation of the "plant" metaphor, the Qumran sect expressed their own religious isolation from their allegedly "deviant" contemporaries.

It is hardly a great semantic leap to shift from designating the pious believer a "plant" or "fruitful tree" to terming him a "tree of life." This terminological development is already visible in Jewish literature of the Second Temple era, and was destined to achieve further prominence in Christian writings of Syrian and Mesopotamian provenance. An important example illustrative of this synonymity is Psalms of Solomon 14:1–5, wherein those persons who order their lives in accordance with the Torah are designated "the garden of the Lord" (ὁ παράδεισος τοῦ κυρίου) and "trees of life" (τὰ ξύλα τῆς ζωῆς) (verse 3b). A Qumran composition also exploits this metaphor by contrasting "trees of life" (*'eṣey ḥayyim*) to other trees which, although planted by water (*'eṣey mayim*), neither bear fruit nor flourish.[259] The "trees of life" in this hymn are undoubtedly the members of the sect who are nurtured by the proper interpretation of the Torah (= water) expounded by the leaders of the sect.

The preceding extended excursus allows us to make the following observations: 1) the designation of Noah and his progeny as "plant" was a popular image in Jewish literature of the Second Commonwealth; 2) the appellation of "plant" could in turn be assumed by subsequent individuals or groups perceived to be heirs of the righteousness of Noah; and 3) "plant" in this restricted sense came to be synonymous with the designation "tree of life."

In Manichaean discourse, the term "tree of life" was applied to exemplary bearers of revelation in salvation history (for example, Jesus or Mani) as well as to the locale proclaimed as the *summum bonum* of Manichaean cosmology, the Kingdom of Light. The former usage appears to be dependent conceptually upon the latter, in that the Kingdom of Light or "Tree of Life" is the source from whence specially chosen individuals receive their commissions as "apostles of Light." One detects a subtle shift here from the Jewish conception of the "plant" or "tree" being nourished by revelation (Torah) to the "plant" as an actual bearer of revelation, a "shoot" or "fruit," so to speak, of the original heavenly Tree of Life transplanted among humanity to propagate more of its own kind.[260] Interestingly, Noah is often included in the roster of human messengers who temporally preceded Mani in the proclamation of authentic revelation.[261]

Commentary to QG5

Having received his commission from the assembly of Giants, Mahaway now sets forth in quest of Enoch, hoping to receive an interpretation of the ominous dreams. QG5 describes some of the geographical details of his journey and reproduces his initial meeting with the sequestered sage.

3) *b'ḥt 'rkt gbry'* — "in one (hand) the authorization (?) of the Giants." The translation is that of Fitzmyer-Harrington,[262] ultimately dependent upon a paraphrase by Milik.[263] Milik's interpretation of *'rkt* (> *'rk'*) as "a letter granting full powers on behalf of the giants" is apparently based upon the Palmyrene term *bt 'rk'* (cf. Syriac *byt 'rk'*) "library" or "archives," *'rk'* being the Greek loan-word ἀρχή.[264] This explanation of line 3, however, is extremely doubtful. There is no other example of Greek vocabulary in the published Hebrew or Aramaic texts stemming from Qumran.[265] Furthermore, it could hardly be expected that Enoch would demand written credentials from a messenger eager to consult his expertise. Perhaps aware of these difficulties, Beyer transcribes the text *b'ḥry 'rkt gbry'* and translates "schliesslich die Lebensdauer der Riesen."[266] In other words, Beyer understands this enigmatic line as forming the conclusion of the commissioning of Mahaway in QG4A, being a request by the Giants to discover from Enoch their expected lifespans. Contextually, Beyer's suggestion seems more plausible than that of Milik, but in the absence of photographs no final decision can be reached. His interpretation of *'rkt gbry'* as "lifespan of the Giants" remains somewhat forced. Perhaps a better explanation of *'rkt gbry'* is signaled by Targum Onkelos Genesis 6:3b, where we read *'rk' yhybt lhwn m'h w'śryn šnyn 'm ytwbwn* "a span of 120 years I will grant them (to see) if they repent," a reference to a period of probation for the generation of the Flood.[267] It is possible that a similar allusion to a probationary period for the repentance of the Giants is designated here by the phrase *'rkt gbry'*. Perhaps the Giants, entertaining suspicions that the dreams presaged their annihilation, requested a period of respite during which they might repent.

4) *k'l'wlyn* — "as the storms." Plural form of *'l'wl'*, a word which literally signifies a "whirlwind" or "storm,"[268] but also used to connote "trouble" or "mishap" in general.[269] Interestingly, the use of the simile "like storms" appears also in the Gnostic treatise entitled *Hypostasis of the Archons*. There the wicked archons create Adam and attempt to give him the power of movement by "breathing into his

face" (compare Genesis 2:7), but their efforts remain unsuccessful even though "*like storm winds* they persisted (in blowing) ...."[270] Here in QG5 the image of the "storms" apparently refers to the speed of Mahaway's flight. Alternatively, one might read the initial *kaph* as *beth* and translate "in" or "through" storms. Then the word might signify a meteorological hazard braved by Mahaway on his journey.

wprḥ bydwhy — "and he flew with his hands." Mahaway possesses the power of flight, a credential which perhaps explains his selection as the messenger of the Giants. Wings are ascribed to Mahaway in the Uighur fragments of the Manichaean Book of Giants; see below.

5) *ḥld* — "land" (?) This word occurs several times in biblical Hebrew as a synonym for *'ereṣ*, but appears nowhere else in published Aramaic texts. The reading should perhaps be questioned here.[271]

wḥlp lšhwyn mdbr' rb' — "and he passed by the wastelands, the great desert." The stem *ḥlp* denotes the passage of time in Daniel (cf. Daniel 4:13, 20, 22, 29), but is used to signify travel from one place to another in 1QapGen. Compare 1QapGen 19:12: [*wḥ*] *lpt šb't r'šy nhr' dn* "I [cro]ssed the seven branches of this river" as well as 19:13: *k'n ḥlpn' 'r'n' w'ln' l'r' bny ḥm l'r' mṣryn* "now we passed out of our land and entered the land of the children of Ham, the land of Egypt." *Šhwyn* is apparently the plural form of *šhw'* or *šhwyh*[272] "wasteland, desert," synonymous with the *mdbr' rb'* that follows. It is unclear whether the *mdbr' rb'* "great desert"[273] is to be considered a feature of mythical or mundane geography. "Deserts" (*mdbryn*) are placed near the region of the "paradise of righteousness" (*prds qwšṭ'* = Hebrew *gan 'eden*) in the Astronomical Book of Enoch.[274] 1 Enoch 28:1 and 29:1 also locate a desert adjacent to the Garden. Yet the phrase *mdbr' rb'* is used in 1QapGen to designate a familiar geographical locale: the Syrian desert. There we read: *wkwl mdbr' rb' dy mdnḥ ḥwrn wšnyr 'd pwrt* "and the whole of *the great desert* which is east of Hauran and Senir as far as the Euphrates" (1QapGen 21:11–12). The legendary association of the Watchers and Giants with the environs of Mt. Hermon (= Senir) and Abel Mayyin in northern Palestine[275] coupled with one tradition placing Enoch's abode in Paradise to the east or northeast of Eretz Israel[276] suggests that the *mdbr' rb'* of our passage may be identical with the Syrian desert.

6) *w[ḥ]zh ḥnwk wz'qh w'mr lh mhwy*—"and Enoch [s]aw and called out to him, and Mahaway said to him ...." Mahaway finally reaches the goal of his journey. Enoch espies Mahaway, cries out to him, and Mahaway begins to narrate the message he bears from the Giants. Milik interprets the sequence of action differently, viewing Mahaway as the subject of the verbs *ḥzh* and *z'q*, and translating: "and he caught sight of Enoch and he called out to him and said to him."[277] From the limited context of this line, Milik's interpretation is certainly possible. However, as noted above, when the Giants issue their instructions to Mahaway, they make reference to "hearing the voice" of Enoch. It was suggested there that the Giants were informing Mahaway as to how he would know when he had reached his journey's end. Similarly the Uighur fragments of the Manichaean Book of Giants also make mention of the "voice of Enoch" addressing Mahaway while the latter was yet airborne. These circumstantial factors render it probable that it is Enoch and not Mahaway who "sees" and "cries out,"[278] at which point Mahaway descends and begins to relate his message.

7) *ltn' wlkh tnynwt lmḥwy b'[yt*— "here, and for you the second (tablet?) to declare (an interpretation?) [I se]ek." Both Milik and Beyer interpret the word *tnynwt* to refer to "a second (time),"[279] thus implying that this was not the first time that Mahaway had approached Enoch for information. However, if Mahaway had visited Enoch prior to this occasion, there would have been no need for the Giants to provide him with travel instructions. It seems better to link this mention of "the second" with the existence of a "second tablet" discussed in QG7 and QG8 3 below.

10) *n]nd' mnk pšrh[w]n* — "[we] might learn from you their interpretation." Mahaway, speaking on behalf of all the Giants, either prepares to relate the contents of the dreams or concludes his narration.

11) *gn]nyn dy mn šmyn n[ḥtw*— "gard]eners(?) who de[scended] from heaven ...." Is the speaker Mahaway or Enoch? The preceding line is ambiguous. Given the fragmentary nature of the text, the possibility that Enoch is now providing his interpretation of the

dreams should not be excluded.[280] Milik restores the initial word of this line as *'yl*] *nyn* "trees," noting that the Watchers in one fragment of the Manichaean Book of Giants are symbolized by "trees" in a dream-narrative reported there.[281] Beyer prefers to reconstruct *lš*] *nyn*, interpreting the word as a reference to "tongues of fire" which will accompany the imminent Deluge.[282] Given the central role of the "gardeners" (*gnnyn*) in the dream of Hahyah (QG4), it seems equally possible to reconstruct that word at this point, especially if one equates these "gardeners" (as we have done above) with the original office of the heavenly commissioned Watchers. Thus *gn*] *nyn dy mn šmyn n*[*ḥtw* would refer to the initial episodes of Hahyah's dream.

The relevant parallel narratives from the Manichaean Book of Giants now follow.

Uighur B[283]

(First page) ... fire was going to come out. And [I saw] that the sun was at the point of rising, and that [his?] centre without increasing (?) above was going to start rolling. Then came a voice from the air above. Calling me, it spoke thus: "Oh son of Virōgdād,[284] your affairs are lamentable (?). More than this you shall [not] see. Do not die now prematurely, but turn quickly back from here." And again, besides this (voice), I heard the voice of Enoch, the apostle,[285] from the south, without, however, seeing him at all. Speaking my name very lovingly, he called. And downwards from ... then

(Second page) ... "...for the closed door of the sun will open, the sun's light and heat will descend and set your wings alight. You will burn and die," said he. Having heard these words, I beat my wings and quickly flew down from the air. I looked back: Dawn had ..., with the light of the sun it had come to rise over the Kögmän mountains.[286] And again a voice came from above. Bringing the command of Enoch, the apostle, it said: "I call you, son of Virōgdād, ... I know ... his direction ... you ... you .... Now quickly ... people ... also ....

Middle Persian D[287]

... outside ... and ... left ... read the dream we have seen. Thereupon Enoch thus ... and the trees that came out,[288] those are the Egrēgoroi (*'yr*),[289] and the giants that came out of the women.[290] And ... over ... pulled out ... over ....

Commentary to QG6

Upon concluding his consultation with Enoch, Mahaway returns to the Giants bearing two tablets[291] inscribed with the interpretations of the ominous dreams. Prior to his appearance before the assembly of Giants, Mahaway apparently encounters the Giant 'Ohyah[292] and imparts to him the gist of Enoch's message. QG6 relates a portion of their conversation in exceedingly fragmentary form. The parallel narratives of this dialogue in the Middle Persian and Sogdian remains of the Book of Giants suggest that 'Ohyah reacted to the message of Mahaway with some hostility.[293]

2) ...] *'whyh w'mr lmhwy* — "... 'Ohyah and said to Mahaway ...." Assuming 'Ohyah to be the speaker, we should probably reconstruct *'nh] 'whyh w'mr lmhwy.*

3) ...] *wl' mrtt* — "and do not tremble." Fitzmyer-Harrington parse the form *mrtt* as a *Pa'el* participle (active?) of the stem *rtt* "tremble, quake."[294] However, the passive participle would have the identical form. Perhaps the phrase should be translated "and do not be afraid."[295] Presumably 'Ohyah is still the speaker in this line.

mn 'ḥzyk kl' '[... — "who showed you all (this)? ...." Compare 4QEn[c] 5 ii 26 (= 1 Enoch 106:19): *yd' 'nh brzy* [...] *qdyšyn 'ḥwywny* <u>*w'ḥzywny*</u>[296] "I know the mysteries ... the holy ones have informed me *and shown me.*" Given 'Ohyah's presence at the original assembly that commissioned Mahaway, it is unclear why he here questions Mahaway's authority.

4) *brq'l 'by 'my hwh* — "Baraq'el my father was with me." This

statement indicates that Mahaway is now the speaker. Baraq'el was one of the twenty principal Watchers who descended to earth (1 Enoch 6:7), and was responsible for instructing humankind in the forbidden science of astrology (1 Enoch 8:3). The name Baraq'el, "lightning of God," is simply translated in the later Middle Persian editions of the Book of Giants as Virōgdād (*Wrwgd'd*).[297] The identification of Mahaway as the son of Baraq'el is confirmed by Henning Fragment c 14, a passage where Māhawai (= Aramaic Mahaway) also refers to "my father, Virōgdād."[298]

5) ...] *l' šyṣy mhwy [l']št'yh mh dy* [... — "Mahaway had not finished relating that which ...." For *l'št'yh* as "narrate, relate, tell" compare 1QapGen 19:18: *w'mrt ly 'št'y ly ḥlmk w'nd' wšryt l'št'yh lh ḥlm' dn*[299] "and she said to me, tell me your dream that I might know (it), and so I began to relate this dream to her."

6) *'rw tmhyn šm't*— "behold, I have heard frightening portents." The word *tmh'* "marvel, portent" appears three times in Daniel, each time in parallel with *'t'* (= Hebrew *'wt*) "sign, wonder." There the designation *'tyn wtmhyn* connotes the mighty acts performed by the God of Israel on behalf of his worshipers.[300] One might compare with this meaning the use of *tmh'* in 11Q Targum Job IV.5 (= Job 21:6b): *wtmh' 'ḥd ly* " and consternation seized me," where *tmh'* renders Hebrew *plṣwt* "shuddering, shaking." The *tmhyn* of QG6 6 probably reflect both the concepts of fear and awesome power illustrated in these contemporary Aramaic examples. The *tmhyn* are perhaps the momentous actions God is planning to set in motion for the eradication of the Giants. The speaker is apparently 'Ohyah in light of the interruption signaled in the preceding line.

hn yldt sry[... — "if(?) I(?) begat ...." The interpretation of this line is obscure. Milik restores the final word as *sry[qh]* "empty" and translates "if an unpregnant (woman) could give birth ...," understanding this phrase to be the first of a series of improbable occurrences used to cast doubt upon the message brought back by Mahaway.[301] Given the broken context, it remains impossible to determine just what is being said here.

The corresponding parallels from the Manichaean Book of Giants underscore the hostile reaction of 'Ohyah to the message of

Mahaway.

Sundermann Fragment L I Recto 1–9[302]

The demons.[303] ... do not exist. Again he[304] said: Bring there (?) what is written[305] (upon?) these two stone tablets.[306] First bring the message to Narīmān.[307] Why do you run thus in fright?[308] Now I have come and brought these two tablets that I might read aloud before the Giants the one about the demons.

Henning Fragment c 1–22[309]

... hard ... arrow ... bow, he that ... Sām said: Blessed be ... had [he?] seen this, he would not have died. Then Shahmīzād said to Sām, his [son]: All that Māhawai ..., is spoilt (?). Thereupon he said to ... We are ... until ... and ... that are in (?) the fiery hell (?) ... As my father, Virōgdād, was[310] ... Shahmīzād said: It is true what he says. He says one of thousands. For one of thousands[311] ... Sām thereupon began ... Māhawai, too, in many places ... until to that place ... he might escape (?) and ...

Sogdian C[312]

(First page) ... I shall see. Thereupon now S[āhm, the giant] was [very] angry, and laid hands on M[āhawai, the giant], with the intention: I shall ... and kill [you]. Then ... the other g[iants ... (Second page) ... do not be afraid,[313] for ... [Sā]hm, the giant, will want to [kill] you, but I[314] shall not let him ... I myself shall damage ... Thereupon Māhawai, the g[iant], ... was satisfied ...

Commentary to QG7 and QG8

As we have seen, Mahaway returns to the Giants bearing two tablets which contain the message of Enoch upon them. Prior to his rendezvous with the assembled Watchers and Giants, Mahaway meets 'Ohyah and imparts (apparently) a specific response to that Giant's query. 'Ohyah reacts violently to Enoch's oracle of doom and apparently threatens Mahaway with physical harm. Mahaway, however, escapes this predicament, perhaps with the aid of his father Baraq'el,[315] and proceeds to the waiting assembly of Watchers and Giants.

Although only fragmentarily preserved, QG7 serves to introduce the scene presented in QG8 when the second tablet is actually read before the Watchers and Giants. The speaker in QG7 is presumably Mahaway.

5) *lkh m*[... — "to you ...." For this form,[316] see also QG4A 22; QG5 7; and QG11 VII 3 below. Compare also 4QTLevi ar[a] I 18: *wqrbny lmhw' lkh* "and bring me near to be *for you* ...,"[317] and 1QapGen 5:9: *wk'n lk' 'nh 'mr* ... "and now I say *to you* ...," where the *aleph* is an orthographic variant of *he*.

6) *ltry lwḥy'* ... — "two tablets ...." These are the two tablets upon which the message of Enoch to the Giants is contained. This is proven by the Sundermann fragment of the Manichaean Book of Giants that was quoted above: "Now I have come and brought *these two tablets* that I might read aloud before the Giants the one about the demons." One might recall in this connection the reference to "tablets" (*lwḥy'*) in the so-called 4Q Testuz discussed above in the commentary to QG2. That text mentions the survival of the pious and the eradication of evil and deceit, a collocation of motifs which have a demonstrable relationship with the universal Deluge.[318] An unnamed auditor is bidden to "take *the tablets* and read everything," the "everything" presumably referring to the events that are destined to transpire upon the earth. It seems possible that the "tablets" of 4Q Testuz are identical with the "two tablets" of QG7, and that the unnamed auditor in 4Q Testuz is in fact Mahaway. If so, the unidentified speaker in 4Q Testuz 1–3 is probably Enoch. 4Q Testuz might thus preserve a fragment of Mahaway's consultation with Enoch, other portions of which survive in QG5 above.[319]

7) *wtnyn' 'dk'n l' qry*[... — "and the second has not been read until now ...." See especially QG8 3 below, as well as the Sundermann fragment cited above.[320]

Given the close connection of QG7 with the actual delivery of the oracle in QG8, the commentary to the latter passage is placed here without further introduction.

3) *pršgn lwḥ' t*[*nyn*] *'dy 'y*[... — "copy of the se[cond] tablet which ...." The import of the two tablets has been discussed above. The use of the word *pršgn* "copy" suggests that Enoch's message was not simply an *ad hoc* response to the queries of the Giants, but indeed an official transcription of an archival document.[321] Perhaps Enoch employed the "heavenly tablets" in the formulation of his interpretation, regarding which we are informed: "And the judicial sentence for all of them is set forth and recorded on the heavenly tablets ... all their sentences are set forth, recorded, and engraven" (Jubilees 5:13–14).

4) [... ⌉*l yd ḥnwk spr prš'* ... — "[b]y Enoch, the scribe set apart." Milik reads the initial word in this line as *bktb,* while Beyer proposes the reading *kk*[*t*] *b*.[322] An examination of the photograph discloses no trace of the first three letters supplied by these exegetes. Moreover, the letter identified as *beth* by both Milik and Beyer is very similar in shape to the lower portion of a *lamed,* an example of which appears in the immediately preceding line in the word *lwḥ'.* If this final letter is indeed *lamed,* a restoration which easily suggests itself is [⌉*l yd ḥnwk* "[b]y Enoch," the idea being that the message read by Mahaway was inscribed by Enoch himself. Compare the language of Sundermann Fragment L I Recto 10–11: "Shahmīzād said: Read *the handwriting which Enoch the wise [scribe?]* ...."[323] For a discussion of the sobriquet *spr prš',* see the commentary to QG2 2 above.

5) *wqdyš'* — "and Holy One ...." This epithet is almost surely a reference to God himself,[324] the source of the judgment pronounced in the message communicated to the Watchers and Giants. Note especially 1 Enoch 10:1: *'amēhā le'ul* <*yebē*>[325] *'abiy wa-qeddus tanāgara* "then the Most High, Great *and Holy One,* spoke ..." and 1 Enoch 97:6: *wa-yetnabbab k^wellu nagara 'ammaḍākemu qedma 'abiy wa-qeddus* "and the full account of your wrongdoing will be read before the Great *and Holy One.*" Upon the basis of this testimony,

one could presumably reconstruct the epithets "[Great] and Holy One" ([*rb'*] *wqdyš'*) here as well. For the reversal of these epithets (i.e., "Holy and Great One"), see 1 Enoch 1:3; 14:1; 25:3; 84:1; 92:2; 98:6 and 104:9. Compare also the expression *qdyš' rb'* "Great Holy One" in 1QapGen 2:14, and the address *lmrh šmy' l'l 'lywn lqdyš' rb'* "to the Lord of the heavens, to God Most High, to the Great Holy One" in 1QapGen 12:17.

lšmyḥzh wkwl ḥ[*brwhy* ... — "to Shemiḥazah and all [his associates ...." For similar phraseology, compare 4QEn^b 1 iv 9 (= 1 Enoch 10:11a) *lšm*[*yḥz*] *' wlk*[*wl ḥbrw*]*hy* with Greek Panopolitanus 1 Enoch 10:11a (Σεμιαζᾷ καὶ τοῖς λοιποῖς τοῖς σὺν αὐτῷ) and Ethiopic (*lasemyāzā wa-la-kāle'ān 'ella meslēhu*). With the publication of the Aramaic fragments of 1 Enoch and of the Book of Giants, the orthography of the name of the Watcher who instigated the descent of two hundred of his fellows to earth is now clear.[326] The form of this name has undergone considerable distortion in the course of textual transmission. Most scholars now interpret the designation Shemiḥazah to mean "the Name seeth," with "Name" (*šm*) serving as a circumlocution for "God."[327] No one, however, explains how such an interpretation of the chief Watcher's name accords with the narrative events depicted in 1 Enoch 6–16. A. Caquot has recently reintroduced the interesting option of interpreting the initial component of this name as "heavens" (*šmy*[']), translating *šmyḥzh* as "les cieux du Voyant."[328] However, rather than understanding the "Voyant" to be a reference to God (so Caquot), it seems possible that one might view *ḥzh* as a reference to Shemiḥazah's initial status as a "seer" or "Watcher," and translate the name as "heavenly seer" or "heavenly Watcher." Such a proposal provokes an intriguing possibility for interpreting 1 Enoch 13:5, a text which states why the fallen Watchers (including Shemiḥazah) were unable to approach God for repentance: "For they (the Watchers) henceforth were unable to speak *or to raise their eyes toward heaven* due to the disgrace of their transgression, for which they had been condemned." It is possible that this verse alludes ironically to the original meaning of the name *šmyḥzh*. The chief of the fallen Watchers whose very name emphasizes his "watching" function can now, in his state of sin, no longer exercise this privilege. The "heavens" are forever veiled from his view.

This loss of status may help explain one puzzling aspect regarding the name of this prominent Watcher. Several scholars have observed that certain versions or reflexes of the story of the rebellion of the Watchers transmit a variant name in place of that of Shemiḥazah. For example, the exegetical school of Rabbi Ishmael explained that the scapegoat designated for Azazel on the Day of Atonement makes expiation for the action(s) of "Uzza (*ʿwzʾ*) and Azael."[329] The reference to Azael indicates that the story of Shemhazai and Asael forms the background for this explanation.[330] A variant designation "Azza" (*ʿzʾ*, *ʿzh*) also figures in certain narrative fragments that recall the rebellion of the Watchers.[331] Due to this synonymity, it has been suggested that Uzza/Azza and Shemiḥazah are in fact identical.[332] The phonetic similarity between the last component in the name Shemiḥazah (*ḥzh*) and the designations Uzza (*ʿwzʾ/h*) or Azza (*ʿzʾ/h*) is indeed striking. Might one speculate that the form Uzza/Azza represents a later abbreviation of the form Shemi<u>ḥazah</u>? The initial component may have been removed either to establish assonance with his fellow Watcher Asael/Azael (*<u>ʿs</u>/zʾl*), or to purge the name of this impious rebel of any reference to the "heavens" or to the "Name."[333]

Be that as it may, the full form Shemhazai (with many variant spellings) is also well attested in Jewish literature. In addition to the important *Midrash of Shemhazai and Asael* examined above, the name Shemhazai also figures in single passages from the Bavli[334] and the Targum.[335] Interestingly, his name survives within medieval Syriac historiography in its treatment of the antediluvian era, but his presence in these works results from their use of the fifth-century Alexandrian chronologist Annianus, who was in turn dependent upon the Greek text of 1 Enoch.[336] The name apparently appears once in a magic bowl text recovered from Nippur.[337] However, the most significant evidence for the preservation of the name Shemiḥazah comes from the Manichaean fragments of the Book of Giants found at Turfan. Therein his name is simply transliterated as *šhmyzʾd*[338] in Middle Persian and *šγmyzʾty*[339] in Sogdian.

6) *ydyʿ lhwʾ lkwn d[y* — "let it be known to you that ...." This phrase imitates the language of an official proclamation or epistle as

known to us from Achaemenid records. Compare Ezra 4:12: *ydy' lhw' lmlk' dy* ... "let the king be informed that ..."; see also 4:13 and 5:8. Note Driver 4:3 *kn yd[y] 'yhwh lk* "thus let it be kn[ow]n to you," and Driver 7:8 *kn ydy' yhwy lk.*[340] Compare also the sarcastic employment of this formula in the response of the three Jewish youths to Nebuchadnezzar in Daniel 3:18.

7) *w'wbdkwn wdy nšykwn* — "and your action, and that your wives ...." Milik's plural rendering "your works" should probably be corrected to the singular "your deed" or "your action";[341] note in particular the expression *'l 'wbd bnykwn* in line 10 below. The "deed" (*'wbd'*) perhaps in mind here is the Watchers' descent to earth for the purpose of satisfying their carnal lust. Compare the wording of 1 Enoch 6:3–4: "And Semyāzā, who was their chief, said to them: I fear that you possibly will not want to do *this deed* (Ethiopic *zentu gebr*; Greek τὸ πρᾶγμα = Aramaic *'wbd' dn*?) ... they all answered him: We will all swear an oath ... that we will not turn back from this plan, but that we will do *this planned deed*" (Ethiopic *la-zāti mekr gebra*; Greek τὸ πρᾶγμα). "Your wives" (*nšykwn*) refers to the mortal women taken in marriage by the heavenly Watchers (see 1 Enoch 7:1–2).

9) *bznwt[k]wn b[']r'' whwt [']lyk[wn* ... — "in your fornication upon the earth, and [against] you there has ...." The charge of *znwt'* "fornication, improper intercourse" refers to the Watchers' fundamental transgression against the divinely established boundaries of creation, as is made clear by Jubilees 7:21: "For on account of these three (things) the Deluge took place upon earth: *on account of fornication* (*zemmut*), *for the Watchers contrary to their commanded regulations* had illicit intercourse with mortal women ...." Ethiopic *zemmut* is the philological correspondent of Aramaic *znwt'*.[342] See also the commentary to QG1 and QG2 above.

10) *wqblh 'lykwn 'l 'wbd bnykwn* [... — "and has complained against you regarding the action of your sons ...." The subject of *qblh* may be *'r''* "earth" of the preceding line. Note 1 Enoch 7:6: "Then *the earth laid accusation* against the wrongdoers (i.e., the Giants)." *Qbl* in the sense of "accuse, complain" has already appeared in QG2 10 above.

11) *ḥbl' dy ḥbltwn bh* [... — "the destruction which you have perpetrated upon it ...." For a similar paronomastic construction, see the Greek version of 1 Enoch 12:4b: 'Αφανισμὸν μέγαν ἠφανίσατε τὴν γῆν "*You have wrought* great *destruction* on the earth." The "it" (*bh*), as in 1 Enoch 12:4b, is presumably the earth.

12) *'d rp'l mṭh* — "... has reached Raphael." Analogous syntax is displayed in Daniel 7:13: *w'rw 'm 'nny šmy' kbr 'nš 'th w'd 'tyq ywmy' mṭh* "and behold, one like a human being came with heavenly clouds, and *reached the Ancient of Days.*" The subject of *mṭh* is missing.[343] Beyer is probably correct in postulating that it was the report of the calamities taking place upon earth (*'wbd', znwt', ḥbl'*) that "reached" Raphael in heaven.[344] Compare the initial verses of 1 Enoch 9 which describe how the cries and lamentations of suffering humanity attract the attention of Michael, Sariel, Raphael, and Gabriel. These archangels then convey the report of the earthly tragedy to God. A similar intercessory function is attested for Raphael in the Book of Tobit. When Raphael finally reveals his true identity to Tobit and Tobias, he declares: "When you and your daughter-in-law Sarah prayed, *I brought mention of your prayer before the Holy One* ... I am Raphael, one of the seven holy angels *who convey the prayers of the pious* and who enter into the presence of the glory of the Holy One" (Tobit 12:12, 15). Raphael's appearance in the Book of Giants is confirmed by the later Manichaean fragments. He is identified there as the slayer of the Giant 'Ohyah.[345]

'rw 'bd[*n'*(?)... — "behold, ruin (?) ...." This phrase may signal a transition in Enoch's account from his rehearsal of the charges laid against the Watchers and Giants to his pronouncement of their judgment. If *'bd*[*n'*] "ruin, destruction" is the correct reading here, it probably refers to the impending Deluge. The same word is employed in 1QapGen to designate the Flood: ... *lmrh šmy' l'l 'lywn lqdyš' rb' dy pltn' mn 'bdn'* ... "... (I [i.e., Noah] prayed) to the Lord of the heavens, to God Most High, to the Great Holy One *who delivered us from destruction* ..." (1QapGen 12:17; compare Jubilees 10:3c).

13) *wdy bmdbry' wd*[*y*] *bymy'* [... — "and those in the deserts and those in the seas ...." These words perhaps indicate the totality of the destruction that is to come. Not even the most remote locales will provide refuge from the Deluge.

14) *'lykwn lb'yš* — "upon you for (your?) wickedness." The following *wk'n* suggests that these two words belong with the preceding sentence. Apparently we should understand that the destruction (*'bdn'*) of the earth and all who dwell upon it is the punishment decreed for the wickedness (*b'yš'*) of the Watchers and Giants.

wk'n šrw' 'syrkwn m[... — "and now, free your prisoner(s) (?) ...." This is one of the more puzzling clauses in the Aramaic Book of Giants. Were the Watchers and Giants holding one or more captives? Milik chose to read *'swrkwn* "bonds" and translated "now loosen your bonds ...," explaining that the Watchers must have already been fettered prior to the delivery of Enoch's message.[346] However, Milik's proposal does not cohere with the order of narrative events contained in 1 Enoch 6–16. There the binding of the Watchers does not take place until after Enoch has pronounced his oracles of doom and has even engaged in a futile attempt at intercession on their behalf.[347] Moreover, the development of events in the Book of Giants also speaks against Milik's interpretation. We have had no indication in the preceding narrative that the heavenly archangels had already executed their mission of punishment. Instead, we must consider the possibility that the problematic word in fact signifies "prisoners" held by the rebels. Unfortunately, none of the Jewish sources that deal with this episode make mention of any enslaving activity effected by the Watchers or Giants. However, the Manichaean fragments of the Book of Giants retain some isolated references to "prisoners" or "slaves." For example, Henning Fragment i lines 103–111 mentions the subjection of certain national groups (Mesenians, Khuzians, Persians) to forced labor, presumably at the command of the fallen Watchers.[348] There are several further references, unfortunately lacking context, to slaves and imprisonment.[349] Whether these later passages are connected with the reference to *'syr*[*yn*] here cannot be proven at this time.

15) *wṣlw* — "and pray!" Presumably this is an imperative completing the sentence beginning *wk'n šrw'* in the preceding line. Enoch thus advises the Watchers and Giants to supplicate God and perhaps mitigate his intended punishment. 1 Enoch 12:6b may preserve knowledge of this tradition: "and should (the Watchers) petition forever, they will receive neither mercy nor peace."

The Manichaean fragments of the Book of Giants that parallel or supplement this Aramaic pericope now follow.

Sundermann Fragment L I Recto 10–13[350]

Shahmīzād said: Read the handwriting which Enoch the wise [scribe?] ... which on account of the speech [regarding the demons].

Henning Fragment l 43–49[351]

... Enoch, the apostle, ... [gave] a message to [the demons and their] children: To you ... not peace.[352] [The judgment on you is] that you shall be bound for the sins you have committed. You shall see the destruction of your children. ... ruling for a hundred and twenty [years][353] ...

Ḥenning Sogdian E[354]

(First page) ... [when] they saw the apostle,[355] ... before the apostle ... those demons that were [timid], were very, very glad at seeing the apostle. All of them assembled before him. Also, of those that were tyrants and criminals, they were [worried] and much afraid. Then ...

(Second page) ... not to .... Thereupon those powerful demons spoke thus to the pious apostle: If ... by us any (further) sin [will] not [be committed?], my lord, why? ... you have ... and weighty injunction ...

Commentary to QG9

The dire message of Enoch now provokes a reaction among the Watchers and Giants. Some manifest fright, others are thrown into a fit of depression, but a significant group seems to have expressed an unrepentant defiance of the command of God. Apparently one or more Giants waged battle with the archangels whom God had commissioned to reclaim the earth (line 4 below). QG9 seems to preserve some lines that reflect the initial confrontations between the archangels and the Giants.

3) ...] *gbr wbtqwp ḥyl dr'y wbḥsn gbwrty* — "...(?), and with the strength of my powerful arm, and with the power of my might." It is unclear whether the initial word *gbr* is to be understood as a verbal ("he strengthened, prevailed") or nominative ("man," "Giant") form. The confident, even boasting character of the remainder of the clause accords well with several testimonia contained in Jewish sources that stigmatize the "pride" or "arrogance" of the Giants. 3 Maccabees 2:4 states: "Those who formerly practiced lawlessness, among whom were *Giants confident of (their) might and boldness,* you (i.e., God) utterly destroyed (by) bringing upon them immeasurable water(s)." Note also Wisdom of Solomon 14:6: "For also in the beginning, *while arrogant Giants were dying,* the hope of the world found refuge upon a ship ...." Josephus is also familiar with this motif: "For many angels of God had sexual intercourse with (mortal) women (and) engendered sons who were arrogant and contemptuous of all that was good, *placing confidence in their strength* ..." (*Antiquities* 1.73). Compare finally CD 2:17–19: *blktm bšryrwt lbm ... wbnyhm 'šr krwm 'rzym gbhm wkhrym gwywtyhm ky nplw* "*by persisting in their own stubborness* ... their sons whose heights were as tall as cedars and whose bodies were like mountains also fell (into destruction)." The unidentified speaker, probably a Giant, illustrates this traditional motif of pride.

4) [... *k*]*wl bśr w'bdt 'mhwn qrb* — "... [al]l flesh, and I did battle with them." The unnamed Giant[356] continues to speak. He has apparently already engaged in combat at least one time with the punitive forces of heaven. For the syntagm *'bd qrb 'm X,* see line 32

of the Aramaic version of Darius the Great's Bisitun Inscription: *'ḥr d[drš ']zl 'bd qrb 'm mrg[w]y'* "Then Da[darshu w]ent (and) *joined battle with* the Marg[i]ans."[357] Note also Daniel 7:21: *wqrn' dkn 'bd' qrb 'm qdyšyn* "and that horn *did battle with* the holy ones."

4)–5) *brm l'[m] škḥ 'nh 'mn l'štrrh*— "but I [was] not able to prevail for us (?)." For *škḥ* in the sense of "to be able," see the discussion of *hškḥ* in QG4A 13 above. The form *'štrrh* is the *Ethpa'al* infinitive of the stem *šrr* "to be strong." The connotation of "prevail" commends itself from later Syriac usage of this verb.[358]

5)–6) *db'ly dyny [... šmy] 'ytbyn wbqdyšy' 'nwn šryn wl'*— "for my adversaries sit [in (?) heave]n and dwell with the holy ones, and no ...." This phrase identifies the opponents of the Giant(s) as the heavenly archangels.

7) ... *'nw] n tqypyn mny*— "[the]y are stronger than I." The "they" presumably designates the heavenly army. It remains possible that the negative *wl'* of the preceding clause belongs with this phrase, in which case we would have to translate along the lines of "although my opponents derive their power from heaven, they are still not stronger than I." Such a sentiment would accord well with the traditional arrogance of the Giants. However, this possibility of interpretation conflicts with the defeatist statement of lines 4–5.

8) ...] *rh dy ḥywt br' 'th w'wš br' qryn*— "... of the wild animals has come and ... (?) ... crying out." It is unclear how this sentence is to be interpreted in this context. The subject of *'th* is apparently missing. Moreover, the reading of the latter portion of the line is problematic. Milik rendered *w'wš br' qryn* as "and the multitude of the wild animals began to cry out," but offered no justification or defense for this translation.[359]

9) ...] *wkdn 'mr lh 'whyh ḥlmy 'nsn[y]* — "... and then 'Ohyah said to him: My dream baffled[360] [me] ...." Is this a reference to the earlier dream of 'Ohyah? Or did 'Ohyah have another dream after the decree of punishment had been promulgated? Interestingly, the verso text of the Sundermann fragment (see below) also contains an

account of a dream experienced by Sām (= 'Ohyah) after the reception of Enoch's message. Unfortunately the content of 'Ohyah's dream is missing from QG9, and so it is impossible to determine whether these two dreams are the same. One might alternatively reason that the whole of QG9 provides further details of the initial dreams experienced by Hahyah and 'Ohyah in QG4A–B above. The battle-scene of lines 3–7 may actually form part of a dream-narrative that is being recited before one or more Giants. If so, one would then want to position QG9 among the aforementioned dream-narratives in QG4A–B. However, the intriguing testimony of the Sundermann fragment to a later dream at precisely this position in the narrative flow speaks in favor of the sequence retained here.

12) ...*g*] *lgmyš* — "[G]ilgamesh." Note also 4QEnGi[b] *glgmys*[361] "Gilgames." This is apparently the epic hero familiar from Mesopotamian literature. The identification of Gilgamesh as a Giant would be entirely appropriate in light of the ancient tradition that Gilgamesh was the offspring of a divine being and a human.[362] Gilgamesh is characterized in the standard Babylonian version of the *Gilgamesh Epic* as *šit-tin-šú ilu*(*DINGIR*)*-ma* [*šul-lul-ta-šú a-me-lu-tu*] "two-thirds of him is god, one-third of him is human" (Tablet I ii 1; cf. IX ii 16).[363] Moreover, a fragmentary Hittite recension of the introduction to the *Epic* emphasizes the stupendous physical size of the hero: "his stature ... in he[ight] was eleven cubits; his chest was nine ... wide; his ... (part of body) was three (?) ... long." [364]

Copies of the *Gilgamesh Epic* and cuneiform references to his person were produced down into the Arsacid period — that is, to the second or first centuries B.C.E.[365] The appearance of Gilgamesh as a character in the Book of Giants (as well as Humbaba and possibly Utnapishtim, see below) suggests that one or more Aramaic versions of the *Gilgamesh Epic* may have circulated among literate circles in the ancient Near East.[366] There currently exist at least three further (and later) references to Gilgamesh outside of the cuneiform tradition. The Greek naturalist Aelian (*circa* 200 C.E.) transmits a legend that recounts the marvelous rescue from death of an infant son of a Babylonian princess. The child was raised by a gardener (!), and eventually acceded to the throne of Babylon. The name of this child was "Gilgamesh" (Γίλγαμος).[367] Six centuries later, the Nestorian bishop Theodore bar Konai includes among his *scholia* to the book of Genesis a list of postdiluvian monarchs that is synchronized with the generations from Peleg to Abraham. The tenth name on this roster is that of "Gilgamesh."[368] Finally, the fifteenth-century Arab polymath al-Suyūṭī transmits an incantation of Solomon that includes in its list of invoked spiritual entities the name "Gilgamesh" (جلجميش).[369] This latter employment of the name of Gilgamesh in a ritual context must ultimately derive from the similar usage of his name in first-millenium Babylonian incantations.[370]

Parallels from the Manichaean Book of Giants now follow.

Sundermann Fragment L I Verso 1–12[371]

Sām, one of the Giants (superscription). Then Sām said to the Giants: Come here that we might eat and be happy! On account of sorrow,[372] no bread was consumed. They slept. Māhawai went to Atambīš[373] (and) related everything. Again Māhawai came. Sām saw a dream.[374] He came up to heaven. Upon earth fever broke out. All of the water was swallowed up. From the water wrath went out.[375] (The tutelary spirits?) were invisible. He (Sām) beheld before him the rulers of heaven[376] ...

Henning Fragment k 57–66[377]

... father ... nuptials (?) ... until the completion of his ... in fighting ... and in the nest (?) Ohya and Ahya ... he said to his brother: "get up and ... we will take what our father has ordered us to. The pledge we have given ... battle." And the giants ... together ...

Henning Sogdian I[378]

... manliness, in powerful tyranny, he (or: you?) shall not die. The giant Sāhm and his brother will live eternally. For in the whole world in power and strength,[379] and in ... [they have no equal].

Commentary to QG10

The opening of hostilities signaled in QG9 leads one to anticipate now a description of the decisive battle between the heavenly archangels and the Giants, perhaps recounted in tandem with the story of the Deluge. The Manichaean remnants of the Book of Giants preserve extensive testimony regarding this conflict. By contrast, no parallels to the final combat survive in the Qumran fragments. The absence of such material can probably be attributed to the sparsity of the preserved remains. There is, however, some evidence which suggests that the story of the Flood formed part of the content of the Book of Giants. QG10 contains a list of animals which might represent a portion of the cargo that Noah loads upon the ark. The Aramaic fragment reads "... [two hundred] asses, two hundred onagers, tw[o hundred ...] of the flock, two hundred he-goats, tw[o hundred ...] apart from every animal ...." It might legitimately be objected that the number "two hundred" is too large a figure to reconcile with the biblical evidence, which mentions "two" or at the most "seven" animals from each species.[380] However, a parallel to this very passage survives among the Manichaean fragments of the Book of Giants. There we read a similar list: " ... wild ass, ibex ... ram, goat (?), gazelle, ... oryx, *of each two hundred, a pair* ... the other wild beasts, birds, and animals ...."[381] The mention of "a pair" in this fragment reminds one of the loading of the ark in the Genesis narrative. Moreover, it should be noted that a further small piece of the Aramaic fragment contains the line *rbw myn ʿl ʾrʿ* "the waters increased upon the earth,"[382] a statement that clearly situates the roster of animals within the Flood story.

The descriptions of the final battle between the archangels and the Giants that survive in the Manichaean remnants now follow.

Henning Sogdian G[383]

...they took and imprisoned all the helpers that were in the heavens.[384] And the angels themselves descended from the heaven to the earth. And (when) the two hundred demons saw those angels, they were much afraid and worried. They assumed the shape of men and hid themselves. Thereupon the angels forcibly removed the men from the demons, laid them aside, and put watchers over them ... the giants ... were sons ... with each other in bodily union ... with each other self- ... and the ... that had been born to them, they forcibly removed them from the demons. And they led one half of them eastwards, and the other half westwards, on the skirts of four huge mountains, towards the foot of the Sumeru mountain,[385] into thirty-two towns[386] which the Living Spirit had prepared for them in the beginning. And one calls (that place) Aryān-waižan.[387] And those men are (or: were) ... in the first arts and crafts. ... they made ... the angels ... and to the demons ... they went to fight. And those two hundred demons fought a hard battle with the [four angels], until [the angels used] fire, naphtha, and brimstone ...

Henning Fragment i 95–99[388]

... many ... were killed, four hundred thousand Righteous ... with fire, naphtha, and brimstone[389] ... And the angels veiled (or: covered, or: protected, or: moved out of sight) Enoch.[390] *Electae et auditrices*[391] ...

Sundermann 22 (= M 5900)[392]

(recto) Then Atambīš two hundred ... he seized ... he cut off (?) before (?) ... he smashed and he tossed [to] the four end[s] of the ea[rth]. And he ... (?) ... he took. And those three Giants who were with Atambīš were slain. And he came (?) before those Wa[tch]ers and Giants who were with him. And when thos[e ... Atambīš ... (verso) ... and (?) ... which by height ... helmet ... he arrived ... mountains ... and those who (?) ... (?) he made. Slain, slain was that angel who was great, their watcher (?). Dead were those who were joined with flesh, and defeated were those who were ... (?) with ... (?) were slain, those who ... with one step (?) ...

Henning Parthian T (first page)[393]

... mirror ... image ... distributed. The men ... and Enoch was veiled (= moved out of sight). They took ... Afterwards, with donkey-goads ... slaves, and waterless trees (?). Then ... and imprisoned the demons. And of them ... seven and twelve.

Kephalaia 93:23–28[394]

On account of the malice and rebellion that had arisen in the watch-post of the Great King of Honour, namely the Egrēgoroi who from the heavens had descended to the earth, — on their account the four angels received their orders: they bound the Egrēgoroi with eternal fetters in the prison of the Dark (?), their sons were destroyed upon the earth.[395]

Commentary to QG11

QG11 consists of very fragmentary pieces whose precise position in the narrative sequence of the Book of Giants is impossible to determine. We shall therefore focus only upon two personal names that appear among these fragments — Azazel and Hobabiš.

III. 3) *ḥwbbš w'dk*[... — "Hobabiš and ...." The initial name, as Milik has plausibly suggested,[396] is that of the monster Humbaba (Sumerian and Old Babylonian Ḫuwawa), fearsome guardian of the Cedar Mountain and adversary of Gilgamesh and Enkidu in the early portion of the *Gilgamesh Epic.* The literary descriptions of Huwawa/ Humbaba focus upon his awesome ferocity and power,[397] qualities appropriate for an arrogant Giant. Humbaba also frequently figures in incantation literature as a demonic entity who exercises authority over other demons.[398] The inclusion of Humbaba among the antediluvian Giants may result from that monster's geographical association with the "Cedar Mountain." According to 1 Enoch 13:9, the penitent Watchers (and presumably their frightened progeny) assembled at Ubelseyael (corrupt for Abilene?),[399] a locality placed "between Lebanon and Senir" — that is, Lebanon and Hermon. The "Cedar Mountain" which Humbaba protects is identified in an Old Babylonian fragment of the *Gilgamesh Epic* as "Hermon and Lebanon" (*sa-ri-a ù la-ab-na-am*),[400] an interesting coincidence of identity. Such a similarity in setting, if known to the author of the

Book of Giants, may have stimulated the inclusion of Humbaba among his cast of characters.

Like Gilgamesh, Humbaba also seems to have survived outside of cuneiform tradition. The mention of the name "Hōbābiš" in one of the Manichaean fragments of the Book of Giants is probably directly dependent upon its occurrence in the Qumran Book of Giants.[401] There is an apparent survival of his name in Greek literature as well. In the second-century Herodotean parody *De Dea Syria* ("The Syrian Goddess") attributed to Lucian of Samosata, there appears an aetiological legend which describes the foundation of the temple and cultus of Hierapolis (Mabbug). A prominent actor in this legend is named Kombabos (Κομβάβος).[402] This Kombabos is portrayed as a handsome young courtier who sacrifices his manhood in order to avoid any possibility of sexual compromise with a beautiful queen who had been placed in his charge. Given the similarities in geographical setting and the "guarding" function assigned to both Humbaba and Kombabos, many scholars assume that Humbaba and Kombabos are in fact the same personage.[403]

However, the most intriguing possibility for the survival of the name Huwawa/Humbaba/Hobabiš has gone almost unrecognized. Muslim polemic against Manichaean doctrine usually includes a description of the beings or substances associated with the Two Realms of Light and Darkness. An entity frequently identified as the "Spirit of Darkness" bears the curious appellation "Hummāmah" (الهمامة).[404] Who is this "Hummāmah?" The name does not appear in either Manichaean literature or non-Muslim polemical sources. Muslim commentators themselves were puzzled by the expression, and one sage explicitly rejected an Arabic derivation for the word, suggesting instead that it was a technical designation of Manichaean mythology.[405] Is it possible that "Hummāmah" represents a somewhat distorted rendering of an original "Humbaba" or "Hobabiš?"[406] A relatively uninformed reader of Manichaean literature may have confused the Giant Humbaba/Hobabiš with either Shemiḥazah or Azael. In fact, evidence for such confusion appears in a report about Manichaean eschatology provided by al-Nadīm, wherein the final imprisonment of Hummāmah displays several points of contact with the narrative about the judgment of Aza(z)el contained in 1 Enoch 10:4–6.[407] The tradent from which most Muslim heresiographers received their information about Manichaeism was Abū 'Isā al-Warrāq.[408] This latter figure, usually castigated as a proponent of "dualist heresy," may have been a convert to Manichaeism.[409] The name "Hummāmah," and perhaps the confusion of role, probably stem from the work of this authority,[410] especially if we assume he had access to a copy of Mani's Book of Giants.

The appearance of pagan actors like Humbaba, Gilgamesh, and perhaps Utnapishtim in the Qumran Book of Giants attests the vitality of Mesopotamian literary traditions among learned scribal circles in the final centuries before the Common Era. Knowledge of their lives and deeds among Jewish tradents should probably be attributed, as suggested above, to the existence of an Aramaic version of the *Gilgamesh Epic.* Fully cognizant of the semi-divine status of these pagan heroes and villains, the Jewish scribe(s) responsible for the composition of the Book of Giants excerpted their names and integrated them among the wicked Giants who flourished upon earth during the final years of the biblical antediluvian era. From an exegetical standpoint, this represents a bold polemical thrust against the revered traditions of a rival culture, analogous to the denigration of pagan deities or idol-worship found in Jewish writings like the Book of Jubilees or Bel and the Dragon. The demigods of pagan tradition perished in the universal Deluge, and they merit no respect or honor from later generations.

V. 6) *ln'* ... *l'z'*[*z*]*l w'bd* ... — "us (Giants?) ... for Aza[z]el, and he did ...." According to 1 Enoch 6–16, Shemiḥazah and Aza(z)el were the two principal leaders of the angelic rebellion against God. The latter's name is written *'s'l* in 4QEn^{a} 1 iii 9 (= 1 Enoch 6:7) and *'ś'*[*l*] in 4QEn^{c} 1 ii 26 (= 1 Enoch 6:7).[411] The identification of this "Asael" (also "Azael" in rabbinic sources) with biblical "Azazel" is guaranteed by 1 Enoch 10:4–5, wherein Asael's place of punishment is called the "wilderness of Dudael," an almost certain reflex of "Bet Ḥidudo," the locale in the wilderness where the Sages say that the goat for Azazel was taken.[412] One might also recall that the medieval *Midrash of Shemhazai and Azael* examined above explicitly identifies the Watcher "Azael" with the "Azazel" of Leviticus 16.[413] Finally, Azazel (spelled *'zz'l*) appears in a Hebrew text recovered from

Qumran. Therein, too, Azazel is brought into association with the "angels" who fathered Giants.[414] As far as we can tell, no reference to the various forms of the name "Azazel" survives in the Manichaean fragments of the Book of Giants.

This concludes our examination of the Qumran remnants of the Book of Giants in conjunction with the most important parallels gathered from the later Manichaean fragments. Sufficient evidence has been accumulated to demonstrate that the Manichaean Book of Giants was based, at least in part, upon a text very similar to that recovered from Qumran. The appearance of such distinctive *dramatis personae* as Shemiḥazah, Baraq'el, 'Ohyah, Hahyah, Mahaway, Hobabiš, and Enoch in both works — works, it will be recalled, that are far removed from each other temporally, geographically, and theologically — cannot be ascribed to chance. We have also observed the continuity of narrative motifs that link the earlier Jewish composition and the later Manichaean recension. Both works focus upon the evil consequences that result from the descent of the Watchers to earth and their unsanctioned mixture with the inhabitants below. Both works dwell at length upon the unparalleled ferocity and wickedness of the progeny that emerge from this mixture, the Giants. Both works utilize dreams and the quest for the proper interpretation of these dreams as the means for advancing the flow of the narrative. Both works also preserve indications that the biblically based story of the Deluge was included in the narrative as well. The relationship between the two versions of the Book of Giants is so close at times that reconstructions of missing narrative can plausibly be offered. It is clear that Mani had access to a copy or later recension of the Qumran text.

Unfortunately, given the fragmentary nature of both the Qumran narrative and the Manichaean witnesses, it remains more difficult to discern how Mani adapted this originally Jewish story to his distinctive ideological requirements. Mani's Book of Giants is not merely a copy of the Qumran prototype. The Henning fragments suggest that Mani exegeted the story of the Watchers and Giants by interspersing allegorical observations within the "historical" recountal of the battle between Heaven and the rebels upon earth. Indeed, the thematic structure of the story of the Watchers and Giants that is recounted in texts like 1 Enoch 6–11 and the Qumran Book of Giants encourages this interpretive procedure. The dichotomy between heaven and earth presupposed in the Enochic account of the manifestation of evil, the rebellion of the Watchers against God, the unsanctioned mixture between the two separate realms of heaven and earth, the magnification and promulgation of wickedness by the bastard Giants, and the steps taken by God to remove evil from the created order all find ready analogues in mature Manichaean ideology. The question raised by these correspondences is the possible role of this Jewish legend in the genesis of the Manichaean worldview. Had Mani already formulated his particular ideas about the pernicious effect of unlawful mixture for the history of the cosmos prior to his acquaintance with Enochic motifs, or was the story of the Watchers and Giants fundamentally instrumental in the formulation of nascent Manichaeism? The formulation of a response to this query will occupy the remainder of our study.

Notes to Chapter Two

[1] J.T. Milik, *The Books of Enoch: Aramaic Fragments of Qumrân Cave 4* (Oxford, 1976), 309.

[2] D. Barthélemy – J.T. Milik, *Discoveries in the Judaean Desert of Jordan I: Qumran Cave I* (Oxford, 1955), 97 and plate XIX.

[3] M. Baillet, J.T. Milik, and R. de Vaux, *Discoveries in the Judaean Desert of Jordan III: Les "petites grottes" de Qumrân* (Oxford, 1962), 116–19. Cf. plate XXIV of the separate volume of plates for a photographic reproduction of these fragments.

[4] Milik, *Books of Enoch*, 300–17. Photographs of 4QEnGi^{a} appear as plates XXX–XXXII at the end of the volume.

[5] Ibid., 303–8.

[6] Three lines of 4QEnGi^{e} that apparently overlap with 4QEn^{e} 2 are transcribed by Milik, ibid., 237. The sigla 4QEnGiants^{d} and 4QEnGiants^{f} are used in the "Addendum" to J.A. Fitzmyer, *The Dead Sea Scrolls: Major Publications and Tools for Study* (Missoula, Mont., 1977) for the "two groups of small fragments entrusted to the Starcky edition" (Milik, *Books of Enoch*, 309).

[7] Milik, *Books of Enoch*, 309. 1Q24 appears in *DJD I*, 99 and plate IX; 2Q26 in *DJD III*, 90–91 and plate XVII; and 4QEn^{e} 2–3 in Milik, *Books of Enoch*, 236–38 and plate XIX.

[8] F.M. Cross, Jr., "The Development of the Jewish Scripts," in G.E. Wright, ed., *The Bible and the Ancient Near East: Essays in Honor of William Foxwell Albright* (New York, 1961; repr. Garden City, 1965), 190, Figure 4, line 6.

[9] Ibid., Figure 4, line 3.

[10] Milik, *Books of Enoch*, 178.

[11] Ibid., 178–217.

[12] Ibid., 178–81, 310.

[13] Ibid., 182–83.

[14] Ibid., 183.

[15] Ibid., 57.

[16] Cf. R.H. Charles, *The Book of Jubilees* (London, 1902), xliv, lxviii–lxix; P. Grelot, "Hénoch et ses écritures," *RB* 82 (1975), 484–88; J.C. VanderKam, "Enoch Traditions in Jubilees and Other Second- Century Sources," *Society of Biblical Literature Seminar Papers* (1978), I 231–36; idem, *Enoch and the Growth of an Apocalyptic Tradition* (Washington, 1984), 180–88; M. Küchler, *Frühjüdische Weisheitstraditionen* (Göttingen, 1979), 72–73.

[17] CD 2:17–19: בלכתם בשרירות לבם נפלו עירי השמים בה נאחזו אשר לא שמרו מצות אל ובניהם אשר כרום ארזים גבהם וכהרים גויותיהם כי נפלו. See Milik, *Books of Enoch*, 57–58.

[18] Milik, *Books of Enoch*, 58.

[19] Ibid., 58 n.1. Note also the criticism of K. Berger, *Das Buch der Jubiläen* (Gütersloh, 1981), 300–301 n.13.

[20] Charles, *Jubilees*, lviii–lxvi. See also M. Testuz, *Les idées religieuses du Livre des Jubilés* (Geneva, 1960), 34–35.

[21] Also Charles, *Jubilees*, lvi, lxii–lxiii, but expressed earlier by W. Bousset, "Die Testamente der zwölf Patriarchen," *ZNW* 1 (1900), 202–5. See particularly J.C. VanderKam, *Textual and Historical Studies in the Book of Jubilees* (Missoula, 1977), 214–38.

[22] The story of the war with the Amorite kings at Shechem (Jubilees 34:1–9) can be viewed as an aggadic expansion of the curious notice in Genesis 48:22: "And I give to you *škm 'ḥd* more than your brothers *which I captured from the Amorites with my sword and bow.*" The enigmatic *škm 'ḥd* was often interpreted as referring to the city of Shechem; cf. Septuagint and Targum Pseudo-Jonathan to this verse, the commentaries of Rashi and Ibn Ezra, and the tradition ascribed to R. Nehemiah in *Bereshit Rabba* 97:6 (Theodor – Albeck, 1249). The war of the sons of Jacob with the sons of Esau (Jubilees 37–38) is one possible literary expression of the antipathy existing between Judaea and Edom in the exilic and post-exilic periods. See G.W.E. Nickelsburg, *Jewish Literature Between the Bible and the Mishnah: A Historical and Literary Introduction* (Philadelphia, 1981), 76.

[23] VanderKam, *Studies*, 216.

[24] Ibid.

[25] See B.Z. Wacholder, *The Dawn of Qumran: The Sectarian Torah and the Teacher of Righteousness* (Cincinnati, 1983), 206.

[26] The following authors vary regarding the date of the final redaction of Jubilees, but agree that the Hellenistic crisis precipitating the Maccabean revolt exerted a profound influence upon the content of the book: H.H. Rowley, *The Relevance of Apocalyptic* 3rd ed. (New York, 1964), 99–105; VanderKam, *Studies*, 216–85; K. Berger, *Jubiläen*, 298–300; E. Schwarz, *Identität durch Abgrenzung: Abgrenzungsprozesse in Israel im 2. vorchristlichen Jahrhundert und ihre traditionsgeschichtlichen Voraussetzungen* (Frankfurt am Main, 1982), 99–129; Nickelsburg, *Jewish Literature*, 78–79; idem, "The Bible Rewritten and Expanded," in M.E. Stone, ed., *Jewish Writings of the Second Temple Period* (Assen & Philadelphia, 1984), 101; J.C. Endres, *Biblical Interpretation in the Book of Jubilees* (Washington, 1987), 13.

[27] L. Finkelstein, "Pre-Maccabean Documents in the Passover Haggadah," *Harvard Theological Review* 36 (1943), 19–24; Nickelsburg, "The Bible Rewritten", 102–3.

[28] E. Meyer, *Ursprung und Anfänge des Christentums* (Stuttgart, 1921), II 45–47; W.F. Albright, *From the Stone Age to Christianity* 2nd ed. (Garden City, 1957), 20 and 347; Wacholder, *Dawn*, 41–42; J.A. Goldstein, "The Date of the Book of Jubilees," *PAAJR* 50 (1983), 63–86; E.J. Bickerman, *The Jews in the Greek Age* (Cambridge, Mass., 1988), 211. G.L. Davenport identifies three distinct stages of composition within Jubilees and dates the first stage in the late third or early second centuries B.C.E.; cf. his *The Eschatology of the Book of Jubilees* (Leiden,

1971), 10–14. Nickelsburg, [Review of VanderKam, *Studies*], *JAOS* 100 (1980), 84 suggested that a date prior to 168 B.C.E. was defensible, but does not repeat this suggestion in the works cited in n.26 above.

[29] Note the observations of VanderKam, "Enoch Traditions," 242–45.

[30] Milik, *Books of Enoch*, 58 n.2 refers to his earlier analysis in his *Ten Years of Discovery in the Wilderness of Judaea* (London, 1957), 58–60; 88–92. A convenient summary of the scholarly discussion regarding the date of the Damascus Covenant can be found in P.R. Davies, *The Damascus Covenant: An Interpretation of the "Damascus Document"* (Sheffield, 1983), 3–47.

[31] A trenchant critique of the use of palaeographical data for the determination of absolute dates is offered by R. Eisenman, *Maccabees, Zadokites, Christians and Qumran* (Leiden, 1983), 28–31; 78–91.

[32] An early dating was advanced prior to the Qumran discoveries by E. Meyer, "Die Gemeinde des neuen Bundes im Lande Damaskus: Eine jüdische Schrift aus der Seleukidenzeit," *APAW*, Phil.-hist. Kl., IX (1919), 1–65; idem, *Ursprung* (see n.28 above), II 47–49; E. Taübler, "Jerusalem 201 to 199 B.C.E.: On the History of a Messianic Movement," *JQR* 37 (1946–47), 1–30; 125–37; 249–63. See now Wacholder, *Dawn*, 178–84; Davies, *Damascus Covenant* (cf. n.30 above); idem, *Behind the Essenes: History and Ideology in the Dead Sea Scrolls* (Atlanta, 1987).

[33] CD 16:2–4: "And the exact statement of the epochs of Israel's blindness to all these, behold it can be learnt in the Book of the Divisions of Times into their Jubilees and Weeks." Translation is that of C. Rabin, *The Zadokite Documents* second revised edition (Oxford, 1958), 74. For a list of scholars who view this description as a reference to the Book of Jubilees, see B.Z. Wacholder, "The Date of the Eschaton in the Book of Jubilees," *HUCA* 56 (1985), 87 n.1.

[34] Milik, *Books of Enoch*, 300–317 and plates XXX–XXXII; also 236–38 and plate XIX; K. Beyer, *Die aramäischen Texte vom Toten Meer* (Göttingen, 1984), 258–68. Portions of the Aramaic fragments were initially published by Milik in his "Turfan et Qumran: Livre des Géants juif et manichéen," in G. Jeremias, H.-W. Kuhn, and H. Stegemann, eds., *Tradition und Glaube: Das frühe Christentum in seiner Umwelt* (Göttingen, 1971), 117–27 and plate I. This preliminary publication was drawn upon by J.A. Fitzmyer and D.J. Harrington for the collection of Giants fragments in their *A Manual of Palestinian Aramaic Texts* (Rome, 1978), 68–79. A separate translation of the Giants fragments (without an edition of the text) is provided by S. Uhlig, *Das Æthiopische Henochbuch* (Gütersloh, 1984), 755–60.

[35] Milik, *Books of Enoch*, 308–9; 311–17.

[36] Cf. Beyer, *Texte*, 258–68.

[37] Milik, *Books of Enoch*, 308.

[38] A. Merx, *Chrestomathia Targumica* (Berlin, 1888), 206.

[39] Milik, *Books of Enoch*, 341 l.13.

[40] Unless otherwise noted, citations from the Greek fragments of 1 Enoch are taken from M. Black, ed., *Apocalypsis Henochi Graece* (Leiden, 1970).

[41] J.A. Fitzmyer, *The Genesis Apocryphon of Qumran Cave 1* second revised

edition (Rome, 1971), 64.

42 Note the language of Jubilees 30:2: "And there they (i.e., the Shechemites) kidnapped Dinā, daughter of Jacob, (taking her) to the house of Sēkēm, son of 'Emor the Hivvite, ruler of the land, and he lay with her *and defiled her* ...." Ethiopic *rak*^{w}*sa* translates the Hebrew *ṭm'* that underlies this expression (cf. Genesis 34:5); the same verb is featured in the Ethiopic versions of 1 Enoch and Jubilees to describe the defilement of the Watchers.

43 Targum Onkelos to Leviticus 22:4; Onkelos to Numbers 5:2; 9:6, 7, 10; Targum Haggai 2:13. Unless otherwise noted, all references to Targum Onkelos and Targum Jonathan rely upon A. Sperber, ed., *The Bible in Aramaic* (Leiden, 1959–68), Volumes I and II.

44 Targum Onkelos to Leviticus 20:18 and Targum Isaiah 30:22 with reference to the *'šh dwh*, and Targum Ezekiel 22:10 in rendering *ṭm't hnddh.*

45 Targum Psalm 106:39. Unless otherwise noted, all references to the Targumim to the Ketuvim rely upon the edition of P.A. de Lagarde, *Hagiographa Chaldaice* (Leipzig, 1873).

46 The halakhic discussions concerning the unclean status of the Gentile have been collected and studied by A. Büchler, "The Levitical Impurity of the Gentile in Palestine Before the Year 70," *JQR* n.s. 17 (1926–27), 1–81 and G. Alon, "The Levitical Uncleanness of Gentiles," in his *Jews, Judaism and the Classical World* (Jerusalem, 1977), 146–89.

47 Note that the Watchers are termed "sons of heaven" in 1 Enoch 6:2; 13:8; 14:3; 101:1, and cf. "heavenly Watchers" in 1 Enoch 12:4. The expression *beney šamay'* does not signify a biological status, but instead denotes membership in the class of beings that inhabit the heavens with God and share in his holiness. Compare the frequent angelic appellation *qdšyn, qdšy'* "holy ones" (Greek οἱ ἅγιοι). For references and discussion see W. Bousset – H. Gressmann, *Die Religion des Judentums im späthellenistischen Zeitalter* (Tübingen, 1926), 321.

48 Ethiopic reads *ba-diba 'anest rak*^{w}*askemu* "you have defiled yourselves *upon* women," but *ba-diba* "upon, onto" is usually explained here as a corruption of *ba-dama* "with the blood." Compare the corresponding Greek version: ἐν τῷ αἵματι τῶν γυναικῶν ἐμιάνθητε. Cf. J. Flemming, *Das Buch Henoch: Æthiopischer Text* (Leipzig, 1902), 19 and M.A. Knibb, *The Ethiopic Book of Enoch* (Oxford, 1978), II 100.

49 A possible allusion to an alteration of the angelic "nature" may be present in 4QEn^c 5 ii 18 (= 1 Enoch 106:14?): *šnyw lm'*[*l*] ... "they changed (their nature) to go in (?) ..."; cf. J. Barr, "Aramaic – Greek Notes on the Book of Enoch (I)," *JSS* 23 (1978), 187. Note *Testament of Naphtali* 3:5: ὁμοίς δὲ καὶ οἱ ἐγρήγοροι ἐνήλλαξαν τάξιν φύσεως αὐτῶν "likewise, the Watchers also altered the order of their nature." Text cited from the critical edition of M. de Jonge, *The Testaments of the Twelve Patriarchs* (Leiden, 1978), 117. Compare *Pirqei de Rabbi Eliezer* 22: ...המלאכים שנפלו ממקום קדושתן מן שמים ראו את בנות קין "the angels *who fell from their holy station, from heaven,* beheld the daughters of Cain ..." (cited from the edition of M. Higger, *Horeb* 9 [1946], 146); Jude 6: ἀγγέλους τε τοὺς μὴ τηρήσαντας τὴν ἑαυτων ἀρχὴν ἀλλὰ ἀπολιπόντας τὸ ἴδιον οἰκητήριον

"and the angels who did not keep to their own domain, instead abandoning their proper place of dwelling ...." Note too the statement attributed to Bardaiṣan in the "Book of the Laws of Countries": "For we must admit with regard to the angels that if they did not also (together with humans) possess free will, they would not have had intercourse with human women, and so would not have sinned or have fallen (*nplyn*!) from their (proper) stations" (Syriac text attributed to Bardaiṣan translated from the edition of F. Nau, "Bardesanes: Liber Legum Regionum," in R. Graffin et al., eds., *Patrologia Syriaca* [Paris, 1894–1926], II 548), and *Debarim Rabba* 11 (end): מאצל שכינתך ממרום ירדו שני מלאכים עוזה ועזאל וחמדו בנות ארצות והשחיתו דרכם על הארץ "From the Divine Presence on high there descended two angels, Uzza and Azael, and they lusted for human women and so corrupted their (own) nature upon the earth."

[50] 1 Enoch 14:5a: "And henceforth you shall not ascend to heaven ever again ..." and 1 Enoch 13:5: "For they henceforth were unable to speak (with God) or to raise their eyes toward heaven due to the disgrace of their transgression, for which they had been condemned." Compare *Clementine Homilies* viii.13: "they no longer had the power to ascend to the heavens" and note the rabbinic references cited by L. Ginzberg, *The Legends of the Jews* (Philadelphia, 1913–38), V 172. Compare also one version of the story of the angels Hārūt and Mārūt recounted by al-Ṭabarī in his *Tafsīr* to the Qur'an, summarized by B. Heller, "La chute des anges: Schemhazai, Ouzza et Azaël," *REJ* 60 (1910), 207–8.

[51] C. Bezold, *Die Schatzhöhle «Mĕʻārath Gazzē»* (Leipzig, 1883–88; repr. Amsterdam, 1981), 66–68 (text).

[52] For example, Justin, *First Apology* 5.2: "In ancient days evil demons appeared and defiled women ...." See also 2 Enoch 18:4 (long version).

[53] Note that the Greek version of 1 Enoch 10:9 refers to the Giants as μαζήρεοι, long recognized to be a transliteration of Hebrew *mamzerim* "bastards." Similarly *Sefer Noaḥ* (A. Jellinek, *Bet ha-Midrasch* 2. Aufl. [Jerusalem, 1938], III 55) terms the spirits of the deceased Giants *ruḥot hamamzerot*; cf. also 4Q510 1 l.5: *ruḥot mamzerim* (M. Baillet, ed., *Discoveries in the Judaean Desert VII: Qumrân grotte 4, III (4Q482–4Q520)* [Oxford, 1982], 216 l.5). Compare Jubilees 10:1, where they are called *'agānent rekusan* "unclean genii" and *Clementine Homilies* viii.15,18 νόθοι "bastards." R. Akiba applied the epithet *mamzer* to the offspring of any marriage prohibited in the Torah (bT Yebamot 49a). Cf. D.W. Suter, "Fallen Angel, Fallen Priest: The Problem of Family Purity in 1 Enoch 6–16," *HUCA* 50 (1979), 118–19.

[54] Exceptions to this usage occur at 1 Enoch 7:1a; 10:11; and 12:4. In 1 Enoch 7:1a, the verb *tadammara* "be married, mixed" is employed. Knibb postulates that this reflects a confusion in the Aramaic *Vorlage* between *ṭmʻ* "sink, be mixed" and *ṭm'* (Knibb, *Enoch*, II 97). The verb *māsana* "ruin, corrupt" is used in 10:11 and 12:4; forms of this verb normally correspond to Hebrew *šḥt, hšḥyt* and Aramaic *ḥbl.* A comparison of the latter usage can be found in VanderKam, *Studies*, 35–38.

[55] A. Dillmann, *Das Buch Henoch* (Leipzig, 1853), 110–11; P.D. Hanson,

"Rebellion in Heaven, Azazel, and Euhemeristic Heroes in 1 Enoch 6–11," *JBL* 96 (1977), 195–233; D.W. Suter, *Tradition and Composition in the Parables of Enoch* (Missoula, 1979), 79–80; C. Molenberg, "A Study of the Roles of Shemihaza and Asael in 1 Enoch 6–11," *JJS* 35 (1984), 139–40.

56 μιανθῆναι ἐν αὐταῖς ἐν ἀκαθαρσίᾳ αὐτῶν (Ethiopic *kama yemāsnu meslēhon ba-kʷellu rekʷsa zi'ahon*). See Suter, *HUCA* 50 (1979), 118–19.

57 See n.48 above.

58 Maimonides, *The Guide for the Perplexed,* trans. M. Friedländer (London, 1904; repr. New York, 1956), 368–69, with reference to Sifra Leviticus 11:44 (Weiss 57b) and 19:2 (86c). Note S. Schechter, *Aspects of Rabbinic Theology* (New York, 1909 ; repr. New York, 1961), 205–9, who also refers to *Bamidbar Rabba* 17:6. CD 2:16–18 states that the primary sin of the Watchers was their failure to obey the *miṣwot 'el.*

59 F. Dexinger, *Sturz der Göttersöhne oder Engel vor der Sintflut?* (Vienna, 1966), 50; H. Kosmala, "*gābhar,*" in G.J. Botterweck – H. Ringgren, eds., *Theological Dictionary of the Old Testament* (Grand Rapids, Mich., 1977–), II 373–77.

60 Hebrew *gibbor, gibborim* is translated seventeen times in the Septuagint by Greek γίγας; cf. E. Hatch – H.A. Redpath, *A Concordance to the Septuagint* (Oxford, 1897), I 256 for references.

61 Besides here, *gbryn, gbry'* designates the Giants in QG1 9; QG4A 13, 15, 16, 20, 21; QG5 3; QG9 3 (?); QG11 V 7.

62 The relationship between these two terms has often been debated. One popular approach has been to view the clauses that contain these designations (i.e., verse 4a and 4c) as remnants of two distinct narrative traditions that have been combined by a later redactor. Others have argued that the reference to *nephilim* in Genesis 6:4 was necessitated by the sudden appearance of *nephilim* in Numbers 13:33. A comprehensive summary of these arguments is provided by C. Westermann, *Genesis 1–11: A Commentary,* trans. J.J. Scullion (Minneapolis, 1984), 377–79. Westermann himself inclines toward the first view. Perhaps the observation of H. Gunkel comes closest to the mark when he states that the obscure term *nephilim* of verse 4a was glossed in verse 4c by the less mythological designation *gibborim.* Cf. his *Genesis* 5. Aufl. (Göttingen, 1922), 58.

63 Numbers 13:33: "And we saw there also the *nephilim*— the sons of 'Anaq are part of the *nephilim*— and being in our own sight as grasshoppers, so we must have appeared to them." LXX: "And there we saw *giants* (γίγαντας) ..."; Targum Onkelos: "And there we saw *giants* (*gbry'*) —the sons of 'Anaq are part of the *giants* (*gbry'*) ...." See also Rashi to Numbers 13:33: "The 'Anaqim were part of the progeny of Shemhazai and Azael who fell (*shenaphlu*!) from heaven during the era of Enosh"; cf. Ramban *ad loc.* and Ibn Ezra to Genesis 6:4.

64 The *nephilim* in Numbers 13:33 are termed *beney 'Anaq,* a group who are further qualified in LXX Deuteronomy 1:28 as "sons of the Giants." Note that LXX Numbers 13:33 lacks the interpretative gloss that mentions the *beney 'Anaq.* Another name used in Hebrew historiographic literature for the aboriginal race of giants is *repha'im,* which the Septuagint translates as "giants" in Genesis 14:5;

Joshua 12:4; 13:12; 1 Chronicles 20:4; see also Jubilees 29:9. The Targumim render almost every occurrence of these ancient names with forms of *gbry'* "giants."

65 C.H. Cornill, ed., *Das Buch des Propheten Ezechiel* (Leipzig, 1886), 390. See also Suter, *Tradition and Composition*, 78.

66 See below line 8 and QG5 8.

67 *Bereshit Rabba* 26:7 (Theodor–Albeck, 254). See above, chapter one, n.97.

68 The author agrees with G.A.G. Stroumsa that Mani's understanding of the *nephilim* as "abortions" is clearly dependent upon Jewish exegesis. See his excellent analysis of the "abortion" motif in his *Another Seed: Studies in Gnostic Mythology* (Leiden, 1984), 65–70; 156–63.

69 Theodore bar Konai (ed. A. Scher), 317, ll.5–6: "He (i.e., Mani) says that these daughters of Darkness were previously pregnant of their own nature, and when they beheld the beautiful forms of the Messenger, their embryos aborted and fell to the earth. These ate the buds of the trees." The abortions are termed *yḥṭ'* (l.7).

70 "Abortions" also appear in *Kephalaia* 138:1–5, 17–18; 171:19–21; 246:8–16; *Psalm-Book* 108:24–26.

71 Augustine, *Contra Faustum* 6.8; Andreas – Henning, *Mir. Man. I*, 182–83; 191–92.

72 W.B. Henning, "The Book of the Giants," *BSOAS* 11 (1943), 53.

73 Theodore bar Konai (ed. Scher), 317, ll.7–15: "Then the abortions took counsel together and recalled the form(s) of the Messenger that they had seen and said, 'Where is the form(s) that we saw?' And Ashaqlūn, son of the King of Darkness, said to the abortions, 'Give me your sons and daughters, and I will make for you a form like the one you saw.' They brought (them) and gave (them) to him. He ate the males, and the females he gave to Namrael his wife. Namrael and Ashaqlūn then united together, and she became pregnant from him and gave birth to a son, naming him Adam. She (again) became pregnant and bore a daughter, naming her Eve."

74 *Kephalaia* 137:15–22; 138:1–5,17–18 terms Saklas "the archon who is the ruler of the [abortions]." Stroumsa has commented upon the use of the term "abortion" in Manichaeism to refer to animal life, archons, Watchers, and Giants; see his *Another Seed*, 160–63.

75 Sakla(s) is an alternate name for Yaldabaoth, the most common designation for the creating deity/archon in Gnostic cosmology, and who was identified by the Gnostic exegetes with the Jewish God. Note especially *Apocryphon of John* 11:15–22: "Now this dim ruler (i.e., the Demiurge) has three names: the first name is Ialtabaoth; the second, Saklas; the third, Samael. And the ruler is impious, in its madness that is with it. For it said, It is I who am god, and no other god exists apart from me ..." (translation taken from B. Layton, *The Gnostic Scriptures* [Garden City, N.Y., 1987], 36–37). See also *Hypostasis of the Archons* 95:4–8; *Gospel of the Egyptians* 57:16–59:1; *Apocalypse of Adam* 74:3–26; and *Trimorphic Protennoia* 39:26–31. Saklas as the "archon of fornication"

appears in Epiphanius, *Panarion* 26.10.1. The name "Sakla(s)" itself is usually understood to be Aramaic *skl'* "fool"; cf. B. Barc, "Samaël-Saklas-Yaldabaôth: Recherche sur la genèse d'un mythe gnostique," in B. Barc, ed., *Colloque international sur les textes de Nag Hammadi (Quebec, 22–25 août 1978)* (Quebec & Louvain, 1981), 123 n.4.

[76] Apparently Marcion argued that the revealer of the Jewish Law was an ἔκτρωμα; cf. F.C. Baur, *Das manichäische Religionssystem nach den Quellen neu untersucht und entwickelt* (Tübingen, 1831), 356, citing Titus of Bostra. Ἔκτρωμα is also the term used by the Valentinians according to Hippolytus, *Refutatio* 6.31.2 (Hippolytus, *Refutatio omnium haeresium*, ed. M. Marcovich [Berlin and New York, 1986], 241); cf. also 6.36.3 (Marcovich, 251). See the version of *Apocryphon of John* 13:32 (Layton, 38) preserved in *Papyrus Berolinensis 8502* 46:10: "But when the mother realized that the *abortion* (i.e., Yaldabaoth) of darkness was not perfect ..." (W.C. Till – H.-M. Schenke, *Die gnostische Schriften des koptischen Papyrus Berolinensis 8502* 2. Aufl. [Berlin, 1972], 133) and compare *Hypostasis of the Archons* 94:15–16. For a good general discussion see K. Rudolph, *Gnosis: The Nature and History of Gnosticism*, trans. and ed. R. McL. Wilson (San Francisco, 1983), 71–87; also Stroumsa, *Another Seed*, 65–70.

[77] Stroumsa, *Another Seed*, 163.

[78] A. Dupont-Sommer, "L'Ostracon araméen d'Assour," *Syria* 24 (1944–45), 44. *KAI* citations refer to H. Donner – W. Röllig, *Kanaanäische und aramäische Inschriften* (Wiesbaden, 1962–64). See also R.A. Brauner, *A Comparative Lexicon of Old Aramaic* (Ph.D. diss., Dropsie University, 1974; repr. Ann Arbor, 1984), 138. For a list of references to *hlw* in Egyptian Aramaic, see P. Leander, *Laut- und Formenlehre des Ægyptisch-aramäischen* (Göteborg, 1928), 128.

[79] J.T. Milik, "Les papyrus araméens d'Hermoupolis et les cultes syro-phéniciens en Egypte perse," *Biblica* 48 (1967), 549; S.A. Kaufman, *The Akkadian Influences on Aramaic* (Chicago, 1974), 69. The text of Hermopolis 1 is conveniently available in B. Porten – J.C. Greenfield, eds., *Jews of Elephantine and Aramaeans of Syene* (Jerusalem, 1974), 152.

[80] QG6 6; QG8 12; QG9 10; 1Q23 7 (*DJD* I, 97 and plate XIX).

[81] 4QEn^{c} 1 v 19 (= 1 Enoch 12:3); 11QtgJob 3:6; 4:3; 5:7; 13:4; 18:7; 21:1,3; 22:6,7; 24:2; 25:8; 26:8; 27:3; 28:1,4,8; 29:8. Given the orthographic similarity of *yod* and *waw* in 1QapGen, M. Sokoloff would add to this list 1QapGen 3:3; 19:16; 20:20,22; 21:14. See his *The Targum to Job From Qumran Cave XI* (Ramat-Gan, 1974), 109–10.

[82] *'rh* "behold!" occurs in Hermopolis 1:5,8 possibly in tandem with *hlw* in 1:7 (see n.79 above). Note *KAI* 233 l.19:] *'rh ml'kty 'šlḥ lk* "*behold*, I will send my message to you," provided that *'rh* is an independent word. See M. Lidzbarski, "Ein aramäischer Brief aus der Zeit Ašurbanipals," *ZA* 31 (1917–18), 202; R.A. Bowman, "An Interpretation of the Asshur Ostracon," in L. Waterman, *Royal Correspondence of the Assyrian Empire: Part IV* (Ann Arbor, 1936), 282; Donner–Röllig, *KAI* II 286.

[83] M. Sokoloff, "Notes on the Aramaic Fragments of Enoch From Qumran Cave 4," *MAARAV* 1/2 (1978–79), 209 also understands *'lw* here as "behold!"

[84] Cowley 2:3,13; 26:21 (cf. A. Cowley, *Aramaic Papyri of the Fifth Century B.C.* [Oxford, 1923 ; repr. Osnabrück, 1967]). See C.-F. Jean – J. Hoftijzer, *Dictionnaire des inscriptions sémitiques de l'ouest* (Leiden, 1965), 104.

[85] G. Dalman, *Grammatik des jüdisch-palästinischen Aramäisch* (Leipzig, 1905; repr. Darmstadt, 1960), 233. Cf. Targum Pseudo-Jonathan to Genesis 6:20: *tryn mkwl' yy‘lwn lwwtk ‘l yd ml'k' d'ḥd wm‘l ythwn lk* "two of every (species) will come to you *by means of* an angel who will seize and lead them to you"; to Genesis 30:6: *whykdyn ‘tyd lmydn ‘l yd šmšwn br mnwḥ dmn zr‘ytyh* "and thus he (i.e., Dan) is destined to judge *through* Samson bar Manoah who will be of his seed"; to Genesis 37:33: *l' ḥywt br' 'kltyh wl' ‘l yd bny nš' 'ytqtl* "a wild beast has not eaten him nor was he slain *by* a human being"; to Genesis 40:12: *mtprqyn ‘l yd tlt r‘yyn* "they will be delivered *by* three shepherds"; to Numbers 33:1: *kd 'yt‘bydw lhwn nysyn ‘l yd mšh w'hrn* "when miracles were performed for them *by* Moses and Aaron." All citations from Targum Pseudo-Jonathan rely upon D. Rieder, *Targum Jonathan ben Uziel on the Pentateuch* (Jerusalem, 1974). *‘l yd* in Syriac also connotes "by, through." For references see R. Payne Smith, *Thesaurus Syriacus* (Oxford, 1877–1901), 1549 and C. Brockelmann, *Lexicon Syriacum* (Halle, 1928), 295.

[86] G.R. Driver, *Aramaic Documents of the Fifth Century B.C.* (Oxford, 1957), 29.

[87] 1 Enoch 7:3–5; 86:6; Jubilees 5:2; 7:22; *Clementine Homilies* viii.15–16.

[88] See above nn.69 and 73.

[89] Andreas-Henning, *Mir. Man. I*, 183; republished in M. Boyce, *A Reader in Manichaean Middle Persian and Parthian* (Leiden & Teheran, 1975), 65. Translation is that of J.P. Asmussen, *Manichaean Literature* (Delmar, N.Y., 1975), 125. For cannibalism among the abortions, cf. *Mir. Man. I*, 194–95 (= Boyce, *Reader*, 72).

[90] Beyer, *Texte*, 621–22. For a list of similar forms, see Dalman, *Grammatik*, 367.

[91] Milik, *Books of Enoch*, 308.

[92] Ibid., 302.

[93] W. Sundermann, *Mittelpersische und parthische kosmogonische und Parabeltexte der Manichäer* (Berlin, 1973), 76–77. Sundermann suggests that this fragment should probably be placed near the beginning of Mani's Book of Giants. The recto side contains some lines which apparently belong to an account that narrates stories about Adam and Eve.

[94] This motivation for the descent of the Watchers coheres with Genesis 6:2; 1 Enoch 6:1–6; Jubilees 5:1; and *Pirkei de Rabbi Eliezer* 22.

[95] Note Targum Pseudo-Jonathan to Genesis 6:2: *'rwm špyrn hynyn wcḥln wpqsn wmhlkn bgylwy byśr'* "for (the women) were beautiful and wore cosmetics and *coiffured hair* and walked about nude." The stem *pqs* can refer to either facial rouge or curled hair; cf. J. Levy, *Chaldäisches Wörterbuch über die Targumim und einen grossen Teil des rabbinischen Schrifttums* (Leipzig, 1867–68), s.v. *pqs* and *kḥl*; P.S. Alexander, "The Targumim and Early Exegesis of 'Sons of God' in Genesis 6," *JJS* 23 (1972), 70. However, M. Grünbaum rejects the connotation of "hair-style"; see his *Gesammelte Aufsätze zur Sprach- und Sagenkunde* (Berlin, 1901), 192–

93.

[96] Henning, *BSOAS* 11 (1943), 62. Note that lines 100–102 belong to the recto portion of the fragment, while lines 103–11 appear on the verso. Given the small size of the surviving fragments, it is unlikely that lines 103–11 can be placed in the same narrative context as the recto portion. However, lines 95–99 of Fragment i also clearly belong to a separate narrative context from lines 100–102 despite their collocation on this fragment. Lines 95–99 deal with the punishment meted out by the heavenly forces upon the rebellious Watchers, an event which occurs later in the story. Therefore it is possible that lines 100–102 represent a recapitulation of the condemnation levelled against the Watchers by God or an archangel. If this is the case, then Fragment i should be positioned later in the narrative among the other fragments that recount the punishment of the Watchers.

[97] Ibid., 60.

[98] Virōgdād (*Wrwgd'd*) "vom Blitz gegeben" was perceptively identified by Henning as a translation of the proper name Baraq'el (*Brq'l*); see Henning, "Neue Materialen zur Geschichte des Manichäismus," *ZDMG* 90 (1936), 4. Baraq'el was one of the twenty principal Watchers who descended to earth (1 Enoch 6:7) and was responsible for instructing humankind in the forbidden science of astrology (1 Enoch 8:3). Significantly the name Baraq'el also appears in the Aramaic fragments of the Book of Giants. According to QG6 4 and Henning Fragment c 14, Baraq'el is the father of a Giant named Mahaway. Curiously, Baraq'el is also the father of Dinah, wife of Mahalalel, the grandfather of Enoch, according to Jubilees 4:15.

[99] Henning (*ZDMG* 90 [1936], 3; *BSOAS* 11 [1943], 61) equated Hōbābiš (*Hwb'byš*) with a Watcher whose name appears in the fourth position of the list of Watchers supplied by Syncellus as Χωβαβιήλ (cf. Syncellus, *Chronographica* [ed. Mosshammer], 12). The Aramaic name of this fourth Watcher has since been identified to be Kokab'el (*Kwkb'l*); see 4QEn^{a} 1 iii 7 (= 1 Enoch 6:7). The correct analogue to Hōbābiš now appears in QG11 III 3 as *Ḥwbbš*. It will be argued below that this is the name of a Giant and that it is derived from the Mesopotamian deity/demon Humbaba who appears in the Gilgamesh epic.

[100] Regarding Ahr-, compare one isolated Qumran fragment containing the name *'ḥyrm* "Ahiram."

[101] According to Henning Fragment Sogdian H, Sām is the Sogdian equivalent for a Giant named Ohyah (Henning, *BSOAS* 11 [1943], 70). Ohyah appears in the Qumran Giants fragments as 'Ohyah (*'whyh*); cf. QG4A 15; QG6 2,4; QG9 9; QG11 IV 3; V 5.

[102] Beyer, *Texte*, 260. Milik suggests either [*'tḥ*]*zyt* or [*'ḥ*]*zyt* (*Books of Enoch*, 237).

[103] Milik, *Books of Enoch*, 262.

[104] Beyer, *Texte*, 648; Uhlig, *Henochbuch* (cf. n.34 above), 759.

[105] Cf. Milik, *Books of Enoch*, 191; M. Black, *The Book of Enoch or I Enoch* (Leiden, 1985), 139, 143.

[106] See J. Skinner, *A Critical and Exegetical Commentary on Genesis*, rev. ed.

(New York, 1925), 532–33; Gunkel, *Genesis* (cf. n.62 above), 487.

107 Note especially Rashi to Genesis 49:26. Rashi explains the Targumic phrase *gbr' pryš' d'ḥwhy* to mean that Joseph was "separated from his brothers" (*shenibdal me'eḥaw*).

108 This is the explicit interpretation of Targum Pseudo-Jonathan to Genesis 49:26.

109 For heaven, see 1 Enoch 12:2; 70–71, and compare Sura 19:58: ورفعناه مكانا عليّا. Note also the phrase فرفعه الى السماء in Saadia al-Fayyūmī's translation of Genesis 5:22–24, as reproduced by P.A. de Lagarde, *Materialen zur Kritik und Geschichte des Pentateuchs* (Leipzig, 1867), I 6. On Enoch's residence in the Garden of Eden, see Jubilees 4:23 and the excursus in VanderKam, *Enoch* (cf. n.16 above), 184–88. Parwayyim may be equivalent to the Garden of Eden; this designation of Enoch's abode appears in 1QapGen 2:23. The parallel source of 1 Enoch 106:8 (see also 1 Enoch 65:2) defines Enoch's residence as at "the ends of the earth." For a discussion of this last locale, see P. Grelot, "La géographie mythique d'Hénoch et ses sources orientales," *RB* 65 (1958), 44–45.

110 Another possible understanding of *spr prš'* suggested to me by Professor B.Z. Wacholder would be to read *spr* not as "scribe" but "book," and thus translate "book of interpretation." See Wacholder, *HUCA* 56 (1985), 88.

111 Milik, *Books of Enoch*, 237.

112 Beyer, *Texte*, 260.

113 Milik, *Books of Enoch*, 264.

114 In the Syriac version of 2 Baruch, the polarization is expressed as one between *šrr'* "truth" and *nkl'* "deceit." The Arabic translation distinguishes between those who practice "truth" (صدق) and "falsehood" (كذب). Syriac quotations from 2 Baruch are taken from S. Dedering, "Apocalypse of Baruch," in *Vetus Testamentum Syriace iuxta simplicem Syrorum versionem* Pars IV, fasciculus iii (Leiden, 1973), [1]–[44]. The Arabic evidence relies upon F. Leemhuis – A.F.J. Klijn – G.J.H. van Gelder, *The Arabic Text of the Apocalypse of Baruch* (Leiden, 1986).

115 Translation cited from J.M. Robinson, ed., *The Nag Hammadi Library in English* (San Francisco, 1977), 115.

116 See M. Boyce, *A History of Zoroastrianism* (Leiden, 1975–), I 200–201.

117 Note DB IV.33–34,36–39 as cited in R.G. Kent, *Old Persian: Grammar – Texts – Lexicon*, second rev. ed. (New Haven, 1953), 129–31. The Aramaic version of the Bisitun Inscription employs the stem *kdb* to render Akkadian *parāṣu* and Old Persian *duruj-*, *drauga*; cf. J.C. Greenfield – B. Porten, eds., *The Bisitun Inscription of Darius the Great: Aramaic Version* [Corpus Inscriptionum Iranicarum Part I Volume V Text I] (London, 1982), 46.

118 Compare especially the suggestive bifurcation expressed in Qumran ideology between followers of the so-called "Teacher of Righteousness" (*moreh [ha]ṣedeq*) and adherents of the "Man of the Lie" (*'iš hakazab*).

119 First published by M. Testuz, *Semitica* 5 (1955), 38 and fig.1 (note that the plate is upside-down), and henceforth referred to as 4Q Testuz. The fragment was later reproduced in Fitzmyer – Harrington, *Manual*, (cf. n.34

above), 126. Milik has recently suggested that this fragment, combined with several joins of manuscript scraps effected by himself and J. Starcky, represents a hitherto unattested literary composition which he entitles *Visions de Jacob* (4Q AJa); cf. his "Ecrits préesséniens de Qumrân: d'Hénoch à Amram," in M. Delcor, ed., *Qumrân: sa piété, sa théologie et son milieu* (Paris, 1978), 103–4. In the absence of photographic evidence (apart from 4Q Testuz), the hypothesis of Milik remains impossible to verify. Beyer accepts the transcriptions which Milik provides regarding the joins, but suggests instead that the fragment stems from a later portion of 1QapGen that treated of Jacob's dream at Bethel; see Beyer, *Texte,* 186. Both Milik and Beyer appeal to Jubilees 32:21ff. as support for their new identifications, but apart from a common reference to "tablets," there is no connection between the two texts. A different provenance for 4Q Testuz is suggested below.

[120] Reading with Milik and Beyer in place of Testuz's *yqry' ky l'* [....

[121] Reading with Milik and Beyer in place of Testuz's *yt"l* [....

[122] Cf. QG7 6; QG8 3 and a Turfan fragment of the Book of Giants published by W. Sundermann, "Ein weiteres Fragment aus Manis Gigantenbuch," in *Orientalia J. Duchesne-Guillemin emerito oblata* (Leiden, 1984), 495–97.

[123] Josephus, *Antiquities* 1.70–71; Jubilees 8:1–3; Life of Adam and Eve 50. Compare the directions given by Bel to Xisuthros reported in Berossus (*FGrH* 680 F4 14; compare F4 15 and 17). *FGrH* refers to the magisterial collection of F. Jacoby, *Die Fragmente der griechischen Historiker* (Leiden, 1923–; repr. Leiden, 1957–).

[124] Milik, *Books of Enoch,* 237.

[125] Cf. ibid., plate XIX 3 i.

[126] Beyer, *Texte,* 260.

[127] Ibid., 666. Note that the lemma *'tš* (*sic!*) should be corrected to *'št.*

[128] Milik, *Books of Enoch,* 157, 171.

[129] Ibid., 237.

[130] Ibid.

[131] The Ethiopic version of 1 Enoch 9:1b reads *wa-k^wello 'ammaḍā za-yetgabbar ba-diba medr* "and every sort of wickedness which was being done upon earth"; Ethiopic *gabra* often renders Hebrew *'śh* and Aramaic *'bd.* The Aramaic version of this verse does not correspond to the Ethiopic, reading instead that the earth "was filled" (*'tmlyt*) with wickedness.

[132] Genesis 6:17; 7:6, 7, 10, 17; 9:11 (*bis*), 15, 28; 10:1, 32; 11:10; Psalm 29:10.

[133] In Psalm 29:10, the term *mbwl* seems to refer to the primeval waters of the creation as opposed to the more specific referent of Noah's Flood.

[134] 1QapGen 12:10; 4Q Pseudo-Daniel A b2 (cf. J.T. Milik, "«Prière de Nabonide» et autres écrits d'un cycle de Daniel," *RB* 63 [1956], 412); Targum Habakkuk 3:6; Targum Sheni 3:7; Targum Pseudo-Jonathan to Genesis 6:3; and rabbinic sources (e.g., *Bereshit Rabba* 32:10) *passim.*

[135] Targum Onkelos to Genesis verses cited in n.132 and Targum Isaiah 54:9. One should note that there is divergence between the readings of *ṭwpn'*

and *mbwl'* in the manuscripts of Targum Psalm 29:10; compare Lagarde, *Hagiographa Chaldaice* (see n.45 above), 15, with J. Levy, *Chaldäisches Wörterbuch* (see n.95 above), s.v. *mbwl'*.

[136] Targum Job 4:8; 6:17; 22:17 and Targum Pseudo-Jonathan to Genesis verses cited in n.132.

[137] Arabic طوفان was recognized by S. Fraenkel to be Aramaic *ṭwpn'*; see his *Die aramäischen Fremdwörter im Arabischen* (Leiden, 1886), 220. The word already appears in the works of the pre-Islamic poets al-A'shā and Umayya b. Abi-ṣ-Ṣalt; for the former, see *Diwan* 13:59 in R. Geyer, ed., *Gedichte von Abû Baṣîr Maimûn Ibn Qais al- 'A'šâ* (London, 1928), 86 (text), and for the latter, see F. Schulthess, *Umajja ibn Abi ṣ Ṣalt* [*Beiträge zur Assyriologie* 8.3] (Leipzig, 1911), XXVI:1; XXX:10. In Sura 29:13, طوفان refers to the universal Deluge, but the same word is curiously employed to designate the first of the ten Egyptian plagues in Sura 7:130. For further discussion of this word, see J. Horovitz, *Koranische Untersuchungen* (Berlin, 1926), 23 and A. Jeffery, *The Foreign Vocabulary of the Qur'an* (Baroda, 1938), 207.

[138] E.S. Drower – R. Macuch, *A Mandaic Dictionary* (Oxford, 1963), 178 *s.v. ṭupania.*

[139] Compare 1 Enoch 10:2: "<Go to Noah and> say to him in my name, Hide yourself! And disclose to him the end that is coming, because the whole earth will be destroyed, and the waters of *the Deluge* will come *upon the* whole *earth*, and that which is on it will be destroyed."

[140] Milik, *Books of Enoch*, 230.

[141] Henning, *BSOAS* 11 (1943), 71. The passage quoted is *Kephalaia* 92:24–31.

[142] The "Great King of Honor" is one of the five "sons" of the Living Spirit, an evocation of the Ruler of Light who exercises the role of Demiurge in the Manichaean system.

[143] Equivalent to 1 Enoch 7:1; 8:1–3; 65:6–11; 69:4–12.

[144] Henning, *BSOAS* 11 (1943), 69–70.

[145] Šahmīzād is Shemiḥazah, the leader of the rebellious Watchers in 1 Enoch 6. He also appears in the Qumran Book of Giants; see QG8 5 and the commentary below.

[146] Compare 1 Enoch 6:6: "And there were in all *two hundred* (Watchers), and they descended <during the era of Yared> to the summit of Mount 'Armon (i.e., Hermon) ...."

[147] Compare 1 Enoch 12:3 ("And I, Enoch, was offering praise to the Great Lord, the Eternal King, and behold, the Watchers cried out to me ...") with 1 Enoch 84:1 ("And I raised my hands in righteousness and praised the Holy and Great One ..."). It seems possible that the prayer which follows in 84:2–6 was suggested by the activity of Enoch in 12:3; or, in other words, that the *Sitze-im-Leben* of both chapters are identical. Knibb, *Enoch*, II 193–94 also recognizes a possible connection between QG3 and 1 Enoch 84.

[148] Beyer, *Texte*, 266.

[149] Exodus 19:16, 19; Job 4:12–16; Daniel 10:7. Cf. 1 Enoch 14:13–14 and

2 Enoch 21:4.

150 A similar knowledge of "mysteries" (*razin*) is predicated of Noah (?) in the Aramaic fragments designated 4Q Messianique. Cf. 4Q Mess ar 1:8: *wyd' rzy 'nš' wḥwkmth lkwl 'mmy' thk wyd' rzy kwl ḥyy'* "and he will know the mysteries of mankind, and his wisdom will go forth to all nations, and he will know the secrets of all living beings." Text of 4Q Mess ar cited from Beyer, *Texte*, 269.

151 Note that the Greek Mt. Athos manuscript of this source translates *l'… ṣbw* as μηθέν. Cf. R.H. Charles – A. Cowley, "An Early Source of the Testaments of the Patriarchs," *JQR* o.s. 19 (1906–07), 574; R.H. Charles, *The Greek Versions of the Testaments of the Twelve Patriarchs* (Oxford, 1908), 250.

152 Knibb, *Enoch*, II 195.

153 Henning, *BSOAS* 11 (1943), 62.

154 That is, Enoch.

155 Henning suggests that these visions relate to the punishment executed against the fallen Watchers and their Giant progeny. He accordingly positions this fragment after the description of the divine judgment. It seems equally plausible, however, to interpret this fragment as descriptive of the oppressive situation upon the earth *prior* to the divine judgment. Thus the "lamenters" of lines 86–89 are the human inhabitants of the corrupted earth. Cf. 1 Enoch 8:4; 9:2–3; and especially 9:10: "the souls of those who died *are crying out* and laying accusation *before the gates of heaven*, and *their outcry has ascended* and does not pass away before the wicked deeds which are taking place upon the earth." Similarly, the sinful "tyrants" of lines 90–94 are none other than the fallen Watchers and Giants prior to their overthrow by the forces of God.

156 According to 4QEn^{b} 1 iii 7 (= 1 Enoch 9:1), Sariel (*śry'l*) is the original name of this archangel, as opposed to the later Greek and Ethiopic variants "Uriel," "Is(t)rael," or "Suryal." Compare 1QM 9:14–16 for another early roster of the names of the four archangels. For a discussion of these names, see Milik, *Books of Enoch*, 172–74. Manichaean tradition also preserves the name of this archangel as Sariel (*sr'yl*). See F.W.K. Müller, "Handschriften-Reste in Estrangelo-Schrift aus Turfan, Chinesisch-Turkistan," *SPAW* (1904), 351; I. Scheftelowitz, *Die Entstehung der manichäischen Religion und des Erlösungsmysteriums* (Giessen, 1922), 35; W.B. Henning, "Two Manichaean Magical Texts with an Excursus on the Parthian Ending *-endeh*," *BSOAS* 12 (1947), 50. For a further attestation of Sariel, see G. Vermes, "The Archangel Sariel: A Targumic Parallel to the Dead Sea Scrolls," in J. Neusner, ed., *Christianity, Judaism and Other Greco-Roman Cults: Studies for Morton Smith at Sixty* (Leiden, 1975), III 159–66.

157 Ezra 4:12: *yhwdy' dy slqw mn lwtk 'lyn' 'tw lyrwšlm*; Ezra 5:3: *bh zmn' 'th 'lyhwn ttny pḥt 'br nhr'…*; 1QapGen 20:21: *b'dyn 'th 'ly hrqnwš*; 1QapGen 22:1–2: *w'th ḥd mn r'h 'nh … 'l 'brm.*

158 Ezra 4:12 (see preceding note) illustrates both usages (*'lyn' 'tw lyrwšlm*). Note also 1QapGen 22:13: *'th lšlm* "he came to Salem." Numerous examples of this usage can be culled from the Targumim.

159 Milik, *Books of Enoch*, 304.

160 Beyer, *Texte*, 264.

161 "Gardeners" (*gnnyn*) also appear in two other isolated fragments stemming from the Qumran Book of Giants; cf. Milik, *Books of Enoch*, 304.

162 Restored with Beyer. Note also Daniel 2:34 and 7:4.

163 Compare Daniel 7:28: *'d kh swp' dy mlt'*. This phrase formally marks the conclusion of the eschatological vision of Daniel 7.

164 Literally "roots," but when used as here in conjunction with *'iqqar* "root," it probably denotes "shoots" or "sprouts" which are visible to the dreamer. Note especially QG4B 1 below, as well as the phrase *'qr šršwhy* "root of its shoots" in Daniel 4:12,20,23. In the latter passages, it is the *'iqqar* that is left "in the ground." Note also Fitzmyer – Harrington, *Manual*, 75, 79, 340 and Milik, *Books of Enoch*, 304, 309.

165 *The Midrash of Shemhazai and Azael* is presently extant in at least four recensions, the oldest of which can be traced to the compilational activity of R. Moshe ha-Darshan of Narbonne in the eleventh century C.E. The most accessible form of this midrash is the version preserved in *Yalqut Shim'oni* 44, detached and reprinted in A. Jellinek, *Bet ha-Midrasch* (Leipzig, 1853–77; repr. Jerusalem, 1938), IV 127–28, and J.D. Eisenstein, *Otzar midrashim* (New York, 1915), II 549–50. Other slightly variant versions appear in Ch. Albeck, *Midrash Bereshit Rabbati* (Jerusalem, 1940), 29–31; M. Gaster, *The Chronicles of Jerahmeel* (London, 1899; repr. New York, 1971), 52–54 (English translation only); and R. Martini, *Pugio Fidei adversus Mauros et Judaeos* (Leipzig, 1687), 937–39. A synoptic edition of these four versions was prepared by Milik; cf. his *Books of Enoch*, 322–26. For a comprehensive discussion of these texts as well as certain other reflexes of the *Midrash of Shemhazai and Azael* in rabbinic literature, see A. Marmorstein, "Midrash 'Abkir," *Debir* 1 (1923), 141.

166 Regarding *Midrash Abkir* see L. Zunz – Ch. Albeck, *Haderashot be-yisrael* (Jerusalem, 1946), 430 nn.33–34; H.L. Strack, *Introduction to the Talmud and Midrash* (New York, 1931; repr. New York, 1980), 216; Marmorstein, *Debir* 1 (1923), 113–44; and J.S. Spiegel, "Ha'edut ha'aḥaronah le-Midrash 'Abkir," *Kiryat Sefer* 45 (1970), 611–14. Surviving passages from *Midrash Abkir* are collected and published in Abraham ben Elijah of Vilna, *Sefer Rab Pe'alim* (Warsaw, 1894), 133–47.

167 *šmḥz'y* (*Jerahmeel, Bereshit Rabbati, Yalqut*); *šmḥwzy* (Martini); *šmḥzy* (some texts of *Yalqut*). Compare the Qumran orthography *šmyḥzh*. Note also the curious spelling *šmḥz'l* in Bahya ben Asher, *Be'ur 'al hatorah* (repr. Jerusalem, 1966–68), III 159.

168 This is the spelling supplied by the *Yalqut*. The remaining versions furnish a range of variants which substitute *ḥeth* for *he*, *yod* for *waw* (or vice versa), and *aleph* for *he* (or vice versa). All of these forms are apparently the result of the vicissitudes of textual transmission.

169 'Ohyah and Hahyah are of course still known to the Middle Persian and Sogdian redactors of the Manichaean Book of Giants.

170 Identified as Metatron in the midrash. The so-called *3 Enoch* or "Hebrew Book of Enoch" states that Metatron is in fact Enoch himself (4:1–3). Cf. also Targum Pseudo-Jonathan to Genesis 5:24 and Albeck, *Bereshit Rabbati*, 26–28.

[171] The mode of penance adopted by Shemhazai (suspending himself upside-down between heaven and earth) apparently influences the tale of the punishment meted out by God on the two fallen angels of Islamic tradition, Hārūt and Mārūt (cf. Sura 2:96 and n.178 below). According to a tradition reported by al-Qazwīnī (see L. Jung, *Fallen Angels in Jewish, Christian and Mohammedan Literature* [Philadelphia, 1926], 129–30), these angels were chained upside-down within a pit in Babylon awaiting their final punishment at the End of Days.

[172] Cf. S. Spiegel, "Noah, Danel, and Job: Touching on Canaanite Relics in the Legends of the Jews," in the *Louis Ginzberg Jubilee Volume* (New York, 1945), 341–55 for some interesting observations on the names of these Giants alongside an abundance of comparative lore.

[173] א<חד> מהם ראה בחלמו פרדס גדול ומשובח והיה אותו פרדס נטוע מכל מיני אילנות ומכל מיני מגדים והיו מלאכים באים וקרדומים בידם והיו קוצרים את האילנות עד שלא נשאר אלא אילן אחד של שלשה ענפים (Albeck, *Bereshit Rabbati*, 30 ll.19–22).

[174] QG4B derives from Cave 6 while QG4A stems from Cave 4. Photographs for the latter have unfortunately not been published.

[175] Milik in fact actually identifies a Jewish "author" for his hypothetical retroversion — R. Joseph bar Hiyya, a fourth century Babylonian Amora. Cf. his *Books of Enoch*, 335–39.

[176] Also questioned by J.C. Greenfield – M.E. Stone, "The Books of Enoch and the Traditions of Enoch," *Numen* 26 (1979), 102; Stroumsa, *Another Seed*, 167.

[177] Under the influence of Mu'tazilī *kalām*, medieval Jewish theologians sometimes include a discussion of Manichaean ideology under the rubric of "dualism." Note S. Landauer, ed., *Kitāb al-Amānāt wa'l-I'tiqādāt von Sa'adja b. Jūsuf al-Fajjūmī* (Leiden, 1880), 48–55 (English translation: Saadia Gaon, *The Book of Beliefs and Opinions* trans. S. Rosenblatt [New Haven, 1948], 58–66), and the perceptive analysis of J. Guttmann, *Die Religionsphilosophie des Saadia* (Göttingen, 1882), 53–58; Ya'qūb al-Qirqisānī, *Kitāb al-Anwār wa-l-marāqib*, ed. L. Nemoy (New York, 1939–43), II.6.6; III.9.9; III.20.4; Yūsuf al-Baṣīr, *Kitāb al-Muḥtawī* XIII, made available by G. Vajda, "La démonstration de l'unité divine d'après Yūsuf al-Baṣīr," in *Studies in Mysticism and Religion Presented to Gershom G. Scholem on his Seventieth Birthday* (Jerusalem, 1967), 288–306; reprinted in G. Vajda – D.R. Blumenthal, *Al-Kitāb al-Muḥtawī de Yūsuf al-Baṣīr* (Leiden, 1985), 123–41. For a further discussion of these and other medieval sources, see S. Stroumsa – G.G. Stroumsa, "Aspects of Anti-Manichaean Polemics in Late Antiquity and Under Early Islam," *Harvard Theological Review* 81 (1988), 37–58. G. Scholem speculated that the "gnosticism" of the *Bahir* might be indebted to Mesopotamian Manichaean communities; see his *Origins of the Kabbalah* (n.p., 1987), 192–93.

[178] A. Geiger, *Was hat Mohammed aus dem Judenthume aufgenommen?* (Bonn, 1833; repr. Leipzig, 1902), 104–6; Horovitz, *Koranische Untersuchungen*, 147. For convenient collections, in translation, of interpretations of Sura 2:96, see E. Littmann, "Hārūt und Mārūt," in *Festschrift Friedrich Carl Andreas* (Leipzig,

1916), 70–87, and L. Jung, *Fallen Angels*, 126–39. See also G. Vajda, "Hārūt wa-Mārūt," *EI*², III 236–37, and T. Fahd, "Anges, démons et djinns en Islam," in *Génies, anges et démons* «Sources Orientales VIII» (Paris, 1971), 173–74.

[179] Bousset–Gressmann, *Religion des Judentums*, 281–82; 502–4; P. Volz, *Die Eschatologie der jüdischen Gemeinde im neutestamentlichen Zeitalter* (Tübingen, 1934), 336; T.F. Glasson, *Greek Influence in Jewish Eschatology* (London, 1961), 77–80; D.S. Russell, *The Method and Message of Jewish Apocalyptic* (Philadelphia, 1964), 215–16; 280–81; M. Hengel, *Judaism and Hellenism* trans. J. Bowden (Philadelphia, 1974), I 191–93; A.F.J. Klijn, *Seth in Jewish, Christian and Gnostic Literature* (Leiden, 1977), 121–24; Stroumsa, *Another Seed*, 106–13.

[180] Plato, *Timaeus* 21E–22E.

[181] "There is a story which even you [i.e., the Greeks] have preserved, that once upon a time Phaethon, the son of Helios, having yoked the steeds in his father's chariot, because he was not able to drive them in the path of his father, burned up all that was upon the earth, and was himself destroyed by a thunderbolt." Translation is that of B. Jowett *apud* E. Hamilton – H. Cairns, *The Collected Dialogues of Plato* (Princeton, 1961), 1157.

[182] Seneca, *Nat. Quaest.* III.29.1. This passage was labeled "Pseudo-Berossus" by F. Jacoby; cf. his *FGrH* 680 F21. However, the authenticity of the passage has been asserted by E. Schwartz, "Berossos," in *Paulys Real-Encyclopädie der klassischen Altertumswissenschaft* (Stuttgart, 1897), III.1 316; P. Schnabel, *Berossos und die babylonisch-hellenistische Literatur* (Leipzig, 1923; repr. Hildesheim, 1968), 17–19 and especially 94ff.; R. Drews, "The Babylonian Chronicles and Berossus," *Iraq* 37 (1975), 50–55; S.M. Burstein, *The Babyloniaca of Berossus* (Malibu, 1978), 31–32; J.J. Collins, "The Development of the Sibylline Tradition," in W. Haase, ed., *Aufstieg und Niedergang der römischen Welt*, Teil II: Principat, Band 20.1. (Berlin, 1987), 425 n.20.

[183] "Berosus [*sic*], the interpreter of Belus, affirms that the whole issue [i.e., the Great Year] is brought about by the course of the planets. So positive is he on this point that he assigns a definite date both for the conflagration and the deluge. All that the earth inherits will, he assures us, be consigned to flame when the planets, which now move in different orbits, will assemble in Cancer, so arranged in one row that a straight line may pass through their spheres. When the same gathering takes place in Capricorn, then we are in danger of the deluge." Translation taken from Burstein, *Babyloniaca*, 15. According to Censorinus (fourth century C.E.), Aristotle also theorized about an alternating pattern of conflagrations and floods. See the discussion of W. Adler, *George Syncellus and His Predecessors: Ante-Diluvian History in the Chronicle of Syncellus and His Acknowledged Authorities* (Ph.D. diss., University of Pennsylvania, 1982; repr. Ann Arbor, 1984), 138–40.

[184] Cf. 1 Enoch *passim*; Sibylline Oracles 2.196–205; 3.84–92; 4.171–78; Life of Adam and Eve 49:3–50:2; Josephus, *Antiquities* 1.69–71; 1QH 3:29–36; 2 Peter 3:5–13; Hystaspes *apud* Justin Martyr, *First Apology* 1.20 (cf. J. Bidez – F. Cumont, *Les mages hellénisés* [Paris, 1938], II 361 and 376, and F. Cumont, "La fin du monde selon les mages occidentaux," *RHR* 103 [1931], 92–93); Hippolytus,

Refutatio 9.27.3 (where this doctrine is attributed to the Essenes). For the biblical background of the final destruction of the cosmos by fire, see Amos 7:4; Zephaniah 1:18; 3:8; Isaiah 66:15–16; Malachi 3:19, and in general, R. Mayer, *Die biblische Vorstellung vom Weltenbrand* (Bonn, 1956). On the Stoic doctrine of ἐκπύρωσις see Zeno, frgs. 107–9; Chrysippus, frgs. 620, 623–25 in H. von Arnim, *Stoicorum Veterum Fragmenta* (Leipzig, 1903–24), and K. Seeliger, "Weltalter," in W.H. Roscher, ed., *Ausführliches Lexikon der griechischen und römischen Mythologie* (Leipzig, 1924–37), VI 426–30.

[185] For example, Celsus identifies the destruction by flood with the myth of Deukalion and Pyrrha, and the destruction by fire with the myth of Phaethon. See Origen, *contra Celsum* 4.11–12; 20–21 (compare also 1.19–20).

[186] Jubilees 20:5; Testament of Naphtali 3:4–5; 3 Maccabees 2:4–5; Mekhilta de R. Ishmael, *Beshallaḥ* 4 (Horowitz-Rabin, 103 ll.5–8); Luke 17:26–30; Jude 6–7; 2 Peter 2:4–6; Apocalypse of Adam 69–70; 75:9–15.

[187] See also Jubilees 29:9–10: "However, in former days they called the land of Gala'ad (Gilead) the land of the Rephai<m>, for it was the land of the Rephaim, and (there) the Rephaim were born, Giants whose stature was ten, nine, eight, and not less than seven cubits. And their place of habitation (extended) from the land of the Ammonites to Mount Hermon, and their palaces were at Qarnaim, Ashtaroth, 'Aderā'a, Misur, and Bewon."

[188] Cf. Fitzmyer, *Genesis Apocryphon*^{2}, 150–51; idem, "The Study of the Aramaic Background of the New Testament," in his *A Wandering Aramaean: Collected Aramaic Essays* (Chico, Calif., 1979), 24 n.66; M. Black, *An Aramaic Approach to the Gospels and Acts* (Oxford, 1967^{3}), 133–34, corrected by J.C. Greenfield, *JNES* 31 (1972), 60–61; Knibb, *Enoch*, II 64.

[189] Milik, *Books of Enoch*, 146.

[190] Fitzmyer, *Genesis Apocryphon*^{2}, 68.

[191] On the complicated relationship involving Akkadian *pašāru*, Aramaic *pšr*, and Hebrew *ptr* (as well as other cognates), see A.L. Oppenheim, *The Interpretation of Dreams in the Ancient Near East* (Philadelphia, 1956), 217–20; Kaufman, *Akkadian Influences on Aramaic*, 81; M.P. Horgan, *Pesharim: Qumran Interpretations of Biblical Books* (Washington, 1979), 230–37.

[192] For example, Daniel 2:23; 6:11; 1QapGen 21:3; Targum Onkelos Exodus 15:1,21.

[193] Mur 18 ar 2–4. Cf. P. Benoit, J.T. Milik, and R. de Vaux, *Discoveries in the Judaean Desert II: Les grottes de Murabba'at* (Oxford, 1961), 101; Fitzmyer – Harrington, 138; Beyer, *Texte*, 306. On the use of the verb *wdy*, see R. Yaron, "The Murabba'at Documents," *JJS* 11 (1960), 158 and E. Koffmahn, *Die Doppelurkunden aus der Wüste Juda* (Leiden, 1968), 83–84.

[194] Cowley 1:7; 9:12; Driver 12:11; Ahiqar 44.

[195] Milik, *Books of Enoch*, 305; Beyer, *Texte*, 264. See also E. Qimron, *The Hebrew of the Dead Sea Scrolls* (Atlanta, 1986), 21 n.13.

[196] Actually, Milik states that the description of judgment "is drawn from Dan. 7:9–10" (ibid., 305). Given the uncertain chronological relationship between Daniel and the Giants fragments, one should perhaps not be so hasty

in excluding the converse possibility.

[197] א<חד> מהם ראה בחלום שלו אבן גדולה פרוסה על הארץ כשלחן והיתה כלה חרותה וכתובה שטות שטות והיה מלאך יורד מן הרקיע ובידו כמין סכין והיה גורר ומוחק כל אותן שטות ולא היה משייר בה אלא שטה אחת של ארבע תיבות (Albeck, *Bereshit Rabbati*, 30 ll.16–19).

[198] Cf. Daniel 4:23: *mn dy tnd' dy šlṭn šmy'* "as soon as you recognize that the *heavens rule.*" Here the "heavens" serve as a circumlocution for God who is portrayed as the ultimate ruling authority. However, the *šlṭn šmy'* of QG4A 16 appears to be a subordinate figure dispatched at the behest of the deity. Beyer (*Texte*, 710) and A. Hultgård ("Théophanie et présence divine dans le judaïsme antique," in A. Caquot, ed., *La littérature intertestamentaire: Colloque de Strasbourg (17–19 octobre 1983)* [Paris, 1985], 51) identify the *šlṭn šmy'* with God himself.

[199] Milik thinks that another fragment possibly stemming from the Qumran Book of Giants (2Q26) may allude to this "erasing" activity of the angel; see his *Books of Enoch*, 334–35. Unfortunately the passage is quite fragmentary.

[200] Albeck, *Bereshit Rabbati*, 30 l.22.

[201] Read *wšlḥwhy* with Sokoloff, *MAARAV* 1/2 (1978–79), 201 and Beyer, *Texte*, 265 in place of Milik's *wšlḥwhw.*

[202] Cf. 1 Enoch 6:7; 8:3; 69:2. Regarding Baraq'el and his appearance in the Manichaean fragments of the Book of Giants under the guise of Virōgdād, see above n.98.

[203] QG4A 21; QG5 6; QG6 2,5; QG11 II 3.

[204] His name is not translated but simply transcribed from Aramaic. He appears as *m'hw'y* in Middle Persian (Henning fragment c 7 and 19) and as *m'h'wy* in Sogdian (Henning Sogdian C first page line 4; second page line 15). In Henning Uighur B he is designated "son of Virōgdād." Henning's early suspicion that the name Mahaway was non-Iranian and simply borrowed from an Aramaic exemplar (see *BSOAS* 11 [1943], 55 n.3) is now confirmed by the Qumran fragments.

[205] Milik, *Books of Enoch*, 210.

[206] He translates lines 22–23 as follows: "Geh [zu Henoch! Denn dazu] besitzt (nur) du die Fähigkeit, weil du [ihn schon gesehen und] seine Stimme schon gehört hast" (*Texte*, 265).

[207] QG5 6.

[208] Henning, *BSOAS* 11 (1943), 65. This fragment is studied in more detail below.

[209] Ibid., 60.

[210] Narīmān, the second son of Shahmīzād (= Shemiḥazah), corresponds to Hahyah of the Qumran Book of Giants.

[211] The preceding context of Fragment j makes it clear that this was a dream.

[212] According to 1 Enoch and presumably the Book of Giants as well, the fallen Watchers were two hundred in number. See n.146 above.

[213] It was initially published under the siglum 6Q8 2 in *DJD* III. See above n.3.

[214] Milik, *Books of Enoch*, 309; Beyer, *Texte*, 265.

[215] Should probably be restored on the basis of the other dream recitations.

[216] Note *wḥz'*] *hwyt 'd dy* ... of QG4A 9.

[217] A reference either to the advent of the two hundred Watchers or a punishing host of divine emissaries.

[218] An almost certain allusion to the large stature of the Giants.

[219] As we have seen, the *Midrash of Shemhazai and Azael* reports that "axe-wielding angels" descend and proceed to demolish the grove. Cf. n.217 above.

[220] So Milik, *Books of Enoch*, 304, who refers to the angelic "shepherds" of the Animal Apocalypse (1 Enoch 85–90). Yet if these "gardeners" were indeed guardian angels, why could they not defend the grove from the invasion of the Watchers?

[221] Note Jubilees 4:15: "... the angels of God descended to earth, those who are named Watchers, *in order to instruct human beings and to act (with) justice and righteousness upon earth.*" See also Jubilees 5:6: "And against *his angels whom he had sent to earth* ...."

[222] For example, see Ben Sira 24:23, 30; CD 3:16–17; 6:3–9; M. Aboth 1:11; Sifre Deuteronomy §48; bT Ta'anit 7a; Baba Qamma 82b; and in general I. Heinemann, *Altjüdische Allegoristik* (Breslau, 1936), 31–32.

[223] For a description of the finds, see A. von Le Coq, *Buried Treasures of Chinese Turkestan* (London, 1928); L. Hambis – M. Bussagli, "Manichaean Art," in *Encyclopedia of World Art* (New York, 1968), IX 433–43; and H.-J. Klimkeit, *Manichaean Art and Calligraphy* (Leiden, 1982).

[224] Cf. A. Grünwedel, *Altbuddhistische Kultstätten in Chinesisch-Turkistan* (Berlin, 1912), 279.

[225] S. von Oldenburg, *Russkaja Turkestanskaja Ekspedicija* (St. Petersburg, 1914). I have been unable to consult this work. The painting was subsequently reproduced as plate XII in J. Hackin, *Recherches archéologiques en Asie centrale* (1931) (Paris, 1936); also Klimkeit, *Manichaean Art*, plate XI.

[226] On the development of this iconography, see A.K. Coomaraswamy, *History of Indian and Indonesian Art* (New York, 1927; repr. New York, 1965), 31.

[227] Note especially Hackin, *Recherches*, 20–21.

[228] A. von Le Coq, *Die buddhistische Spätantike in Mittelasien II: Die manichäischen Miniaturen* (Berlin, 1923).

[229] Ibid., 46–48 and Tafel 7b. It is also reproduced as color plate I in Rudolph, *Gnosis* (see n.76 above).

[230] The bēma — Greek βῆμα — was an empty throne used to symbolize the presence of Mani at the most important festival of the Manichaean liturgical year, the so-called "Bema Feast," which commemorated the death of Mani. See C.R.C. Allberry, "Das manichäische Bema-Fest," *ZNW* 37 (1938), 2–10; H.-C. Puech, "Fêtes et solemnités manichéennes: le Bêma," *Annuaire du Collège de France* 72 (1972), 322–26; J. Ries, "La fête de Bêma dans l'église de Mani," *Revue des études augustiniennes* 22 (1976), 218–33.

[231] That is, the "preaching" *mudrā* associated with the Buddha's exposition of his First Sermon after his enlightenment. Compare the posture of the priest in this illustration with figures 161 and 278 in Coomaraswamy, *Indian Art*.

Sanskrit *mudrā*, literally "seal," designates a series of stylized gestures employed in iconographic representations of Indian religious figures which either identify specific deities or, as in this case, evoke particular episodes within sacred hagiography. The best study of this symbolism is E.D. Saunders, *Mudrā: A Study of Symbolic Gestures in Japanese Buddhist Sculpture* (New York, 1960).

232 The iconography of this fragment is analyzed differently by Klimkeit, *Manichaean Art*, 38–39.

233 Le Coq, *Miniaturen*, 56–57 and Tafel 8[b]b. Reproduced as color plate II in Rudolph, *Gnosis* (see n.76 above).

234 Klimkeit, "Der Buddha Henoch: Qumran und Turfan," *ZRGG* 32 (1980), 373; idem, *Manichaean Art*, 38.

235 Hackin, *Recherches*, 20. See also G. Widengren, *Mani und der Manichäismus* (Stuttgart, 1961), 115.

236 Cf. *Kephalaia* 16:33–23:13, a tractate entitled "The second chapter, on the parable of the trees." This discussion opens with a query directed to Mani concerning the interpretation of the "good tree" and the "worthless tree" of Luke 6:43–44 (compare Matthew 7:15–20 and Gospel of Thomas logion 45), a passage wherein Mani discerns allusions to the opposed Kingdoms of Light and Darkness or alternatively of Life and Death. See also *Psalm-Book* 4:22–24; 66:26–28; and 219:24–30. Regarding these allusions, see V. Arnold-Döben, *Die Bildersprache des Manichäismus* (Köln, 1978), 8–10. Both Jesus and Mani himself are also designated "Tree(s) of Life" in Manichaean literature; see especially G. Widengren, *Mesopotamian Elements in Manichaeism* (Uppsala, 1946), 123–57.

237 Arnold-Döben, *Bildersprache*, 37–40.

238 His 123rd Homily, available in M. Brière, "Les Homiliae Cathedrales de Sévère d'Antioche, traduction syriaque de Jacques d'Edesse CXX à CXXV," *PO* 29 (1960), 124–89.

239 F. Cumont – M.-A. Kugener, *Recherches sur le manichéisme* (Bruxelles, 1908–12), 83–172.

240 This issue will be explored more fully in the following chapter.

241 See the following chapter for a translation and discussion of these passages.

242 Klimkeit, *ZRGG* 32 (1980), 372–75; idem, "Der dreistämmige Baum: Bemerkungen zur manichäischen Kunst und Symbolik," in *Kulturwissenschaften: Festgabe für Wilhelm Perpeet zum 65. Geburtstag* (Bonn, 1980), 252–60; *idem*, *Manichaean Art*, 31.

243 *Bereshit Rabba* 26:1 (Theodor–Albeck, 243–44). I have omitted the short discussion regarding the identification of the "wicked" in Psalm 1:1–2. The same interpretation is repeated in *Midrash Tehillim* 1:12.

244 Referring back to the *ṣaddiq* of the preceding verse of the psalm, who on the basis of Genesis 6:9 (*noaḥ 'ish ṣaddiq: tamim hayah bedorotaw*), is identified with Noah.

245 *Bereshit Rabba* 26:2 (Theodor–Albeck, 244). One might note here the interesting description of Ephrem; cf. E. Beck, ed., *Des heiligen Ephraem des Syrers: Hymnen contra Haereses* CSCO 169 (Louvain, 1957), 30 l.10.

[246] For example, Isaiah 60:21; 61:3. On this theme see especially S. Fujita, "The Metaphor of Plant in Jewish Literature of the Intertestamental Period," *JSJ* 7 (1976), 30–45; F. Dexinger, *Henochs Zehnwochenapokalypse und offene Probleme der Apokalyptikforschung* (Leiden, 1977), 164–69.

[247] 4QEn[a] 1 v 4 (= 1 Enoch 10:3), although extremely fragmentary, apparently confirms the reliability of Syncellus at this point (*contra* Dillmann, *Henoch,* 99). Cf. Milik, *Books of Enoch,* 161–62.

[248] 1 Enoch 10:3 (Ethiopic): *wa-[ye'ezēni] mahharo kama yenfaṣ wa- yenbar zar'u la-k[w]ellomu tewledd* (Flemming); Codex Panopolitanus: καὶ δίδαξον αὐτοῦ ὅπως ἐκφύγῃ, καὶ μενεῖ τὸ σπέρμα αὐτοῦ εἰς πάσας τὰς γενεὰς τοῦ αἰῶνας.

[249] δίδαξον τὸν δίκαιον τί ποιήσει, τὸν υἱὸν Λαμεχ, καὶ τὴν ψυχὴν αὐτοῦ εἰς ζωὴν συντηρήσει, καὶ ἐκφεύξεται δι' αἰῶνος, καὶ ἐξ αὐτοῦ φυτευθήσεται φύτευμα καὶ σταθήσεται πάσας τὰς γενεὰς τοῦ αἰῶνος.

[250] "Destroy all oppression from the face of the earth, and let all evil deeds disappear, and let the plant of righteousness and truth be revealed. It shall be a blessing, a righteous and upright work planted in joy forever" (1 Enoch 10:16). This "plant of righteousness and truth" (Aramaic [*n*]*ṣb' qwšṭ',* Greek τὸ φύτον τῆς δικαιοσύνης καὶ τῆς ἀληθείας, Ethiopic *takla ṣedq wa-ret'*) is usually interpreted by scholars to refer to the righteous community of Israel at the End of Days. See Dillmann, *Henoch,* 102; R.H. Charles, *The Book of Enoch* (Oxford, 1893), 76; G. Beer, "Das Buch Henoch," in E. Kautzsch, ed., *Die Apokryphen und Pseudepigraphen des Alten Testaments* (Tübingen, 1900), II 243; F. Martin, *Le livre d'Hénoch* (Paris, 1908), 26; Uhlig, *Henochbuch,* 530; G.W.E. Nickelsburg, "Apocalyptic and Myth in 1 Enoch 6–11," *JBL* 96 (1977), 390. However, the context of 1 Enoch 10, coupled with the testimony of Syncellus on verse 3, makes it clear that the "plant" is Noah and his progeny. Similarly, Black, *The Book of Enoch,* 139. Note that one Ethiopic manuscript glosses this plant as "Noah" (cf. Martin, *Hénoch,* 26).

[251] A certain allusion to Noah. So too Fujita, *JSJ* 7 (1976), 37.

[252] *wa-šegā ṣedq wa-ret' 'aqem la-takla zar' la-'ālam* (Flemming).

[253] *wa-ye'ezēni weludya sem'u gebaru fetḥa wa-ṣedqa kama tetakkalu ba-ṣedq westa gaṣṣa k[w]ellu medr* (Charles). One might note here also 4 Ezra 9:20–21, a passage which describes Noah as "one *plant* saved from the *forest,*" an image curiously reminiscent of the scenario presented in the Qumran Book of Giants and *Midrash of Shemhazai and Azael.* See too the obscure expression *tḥlyp* applied to Noah in the Hebrew text of Ben Sira 44:17. If Box and Oesterley are correct in their interpretation of this word as "one who puts forth fresh branches or sprouts" (cf. R.H. Charles, ed., *The Apocrypha and Pseudepigrapha of the Old Testament* [Oxford, 1913], I 483), one discerns here yet another instance of the botanical symbolism associated with Noah.

[254] *gebaru fetḥa wa-ṣedqa* = Hebrew *'aśu mishpaṭ uṣedeqah.* Cf. Jeremiah 22:3; Ezekiel 45:9; and compare Isaiah 56:1.

[255] Apocalypse of Adam 76:11–15. Scholars have rightly observed the correspondence here with the Jewish characterization of the righteous elect as

a "plant" or "tree." See G.W.E. Nickelsburg, "Some Related Traditions in the Apocalypse of Adam, the Books of Adam and Eve, and 1 Enoch," in B. Layton, ed., *The Rediscovery of Gnosticism: Proceedings of the International Conference on Gnosticism at Yale ... Volume II: Sethian Gnosticism* (Leiden, 1981), 536; C.W. Hedrick, *The Apocalypse of Adam: A Literary and Source Analysis* (Chico, 1980), 125; F. Morard, *L'Apocalypse d'Adam (NH V,5)* (Quebec, 1985), 96–97.

256 1 Enoch 93:5: "And afterwards, in the third week, at its end, a man will be chosen as *the plant of righteous judgment*, and his posterity (will be) *a plant of righteousness* forever." The context makes it clear that this man is Abraham. Similarly Jubilees 16:26b: "... for he (God) knew and recognized that from him (Abraham) would come *the plant of righteousness* for the eternal generations, and from him (would come) a holy seed that would become like him who created all things."

257 1QS 8:4–7; CD 1:7–8. For further references and discussion, see E. Cothenet, "Le document de Damas," in J. Carmignac *et al.*, *Les textes de Qumran* (Paris, 1961–63), II 150–51; D. Flusser, "The Apocryphal Book of *Ascensio Isaiae* and the Dead Sea Sect," *IEJ* 3 (1953), 38 n.23.

258 For Noah, see Genesis 6:9; 7:1; Ben Sira 44:17; 4 Ezra 3:11; Targum Isaiah 65:8. Regarding Abraham, see Jubilees 11:16–17 and Josephus, *Antiquities* 1.155–57. The succession of "righteousness" from Noah to Abraham figures in the traditional commentaries of Rashi and Ibn Ezra to Genesis 6:9; compare M. Aboth 5:2; Aboth de R. Natan A 33; and Tanḥuma Buber, *Bereshit* §30; §32; *Noaḥ* §1; §6. See the discussion of J. Mann, *The Bible as Read and Preached in the Old Synagogue Volume 1: The Palestinian Triennial Cycle: Genesis and Exodus* (Cincinnati, 1940; repr. New York, 1971), 63–68. Note also the narrative embellishment of the medieval *Sefer Hayashar* which portrays Abraham as receiving his instruction in true piety from Noah and Shem (*Sefer Hayashar* [repr. Brooklyn, 1960], 33). The exemplary status of Noah and Abraham among their contemporaries is also emphasized in Islamic tradition; cf. Sura 57:26 and the remark of T. Fahd, *Le panthéon de l'Arabie centrale à la veille de l'Hégire* (Paris, 1968), 28 n.3.

259 1QH 8:4–14.

260 Arnold-Döben, *Bildersprache*, 25–30. Note in this connection the *berakhah* addressed to Mani that is quoted in the *Fihrist* of al-Nadīm: "Praise be to you, o shining one, Mani our guide, *root of light and branch of life*, great tree which is entirely (for) healing." Text found in G. Flügel, *Mani, seine Lehre und seine Schriften* (Leipzig, 1862; repr. Osnabrück, 1969), 65 ll.1–2; also reproduced by Widengren, *Mesopotamian Elements* (cf. n.236 above), 155. Compare *Kephalaia* 20:3–5: "The *fruits* of the Good Tree are Jesus, the lordly Splendor, the Father of all Apostles."

261 *Psalm-Book* 142:6; Augustine, *Contra Faustum* 19.3; Shahrastānī (ed. Cureton), 191 ll.9–10; Ibn al-Murtaḍā (*apud* K. Kessler, *Mani: Forschungen über die manichäische Religion* [Berlin, 1889], 349 ll.11–12; Abou'l Ma'alī (*apud* Kessler, *Mani*), 371 ll.11–13.

262 Fitzmyer – Harrington, *Manual*, 77.

[263] Milik, *Books of Enoch*, 306.

[264] J. Cantineau, "Tadmorea," *Syria* 14 (1933), 183–84; F. Rosenthal, *Die Sprache der palmyrenischen Inschriften* (Leipzig, 1936), 91. For examples of Syriac *byt 'rk'*, cf. Brockelmann, *Lexicon Syriacum*, 49.

[265] According to an oral communication from Elisha Qimron, there is one *possible* Greek loan within a yet unpublished Qumran text.

[266] Beyer, *Texte*, 265.

[267] Note the other Targumim to this verse as well as Mekhilta, *Beshallaḥ* 5 *ad loc.* Exodus 15:6 (Horovitz – Rabin, 133); Aboth de R. Natan A 32; Midrash Tanḥuma, *Noaḥ* §5. See also Targum Habakkuk 3:1–2: *ṣlwt' dṣly ḥbqwq nby' kd 'tgly lyh 'l 'rk' dyhb lršy'y' ... d't yhyb 'rk' lršy'y' d'm ytwbwn l'wrytk wl' tbw w'nwn mrgzyn qdmk ... d'mrt' lḥdt' 'lm' l'tpr'' mršy'y' d'brw 'l mymrk.* Another manuscript (Codex Kissingensis) relates this *'rk'* specifically to the *dr' dṭwpn'.* These passages are reproduced in Merx, *Chrestomathia Targumica*, 105. Compare also 1 Peter 3:20: ἡ τοῦ θεοῦ μακροθυμία ἐν ἡμέραις Νῶε....

[268] Merx, *Chrestomathia Targumica*, 254: "procella."

[269] Targum Pseudo-Jonathan to Numbers 21:14 refers to *'l'wl' dsgyrwt'* "the calamity of leprosy."

[270] Layton, *Gnostic Scriptures*, 69.

[271] Also Sokoloff, *MAARAV* 1/2 (1978–79), 211.

[272] Ibid., 215.

[273] Compare *hamidbar hagadol* of Deuteronomy 1:19; 2:7; 8:15. The "great desert" of these passages refers to the wilderness between Egypt and Canaan wherein the Israelites wandered for forty years. Contrast 1QM 2:12, where *hamidbar hagadol* refers to the Syrian desert (*contra* A. Dupont-Sommer, *The Essene Writings from Qumran* [Gloucester, 1973], 173 n.1 and Y. Yadin, *The Scroll of the War of the Sons of Light Against the Sons of Darkness* [Oxford, 1962], 32 n.5), as in 1QapGen.

[274] Cf. Milik, *Books of Enoch*, 289–91. For the *prds qwšṭ'*, see 4QEn^{e} 1 xxvi 21 (= 1 Enoch 32:3), ibid., 232.

[275] 1 Enoch 6:6; 13:7–9. See G.W.E. Nickelsburg, "Enoch, Levi, and Peter: Recipients of Revelation in Upper Galilee," *JBL* 100 (1981), 575–600.

[276] Cf. Genesis 2:8; Jubilees 4:23; 8:16; 1 Enoch 32:2–6 (but contrast 70:3!); 2 Enoch 31:2. Comprehensive discussions of this tradition are provided by A.J. Wensinck, *Tree and Bird as Cosmological Symbols in Western Asia* (Amsterdam, 1921), 4–5 and P. Grelot, *RB* 65 (1958), 33–69. See also P.S. Alexander, "Notes on the *Imago Mundi* of the Book of Jubilees," *JJS* 33 (1982), 197–213; M. Tardieu, *Trois mythes gnostiques: Adam, Eros et les animaux d'Egypte dans un écrit de Nag Hammadi (II,5)* (Paris, 1974), 178–82.

[277] Milik, *Books of Enoch*, 306.

[278] Beyer also translates in this way; cf. his *Texte*, 265.

[279] Milik, *Books of Enoch*, 306; Beyer, *Texte*, 265.

[280] So Milik, *Books of Enoch*, 306, and Beyer, *Texte*, 265.

[281] Milik, *Books of Enoch*, 306. Cf. Henning, *BSOAS* 11 (1943), 66, reproduced below.

282 Beyer, *Texte,* 265. See QG4A 10 above.

283 Henning, *BSOAS* 11 (1943), 65, citing A. von Le Coq, "Türkische Manichaica aus Chotscho III," *APAW,* Phil.-hist. Kl., II (1922), 23, and W. Bang, "Manichäische Erzähler," *Le Muséon* 44 (1931), 13–17. The latter is reprinted in G. Widengren, ed., *Der Manichäismus* (Darmstadt, 1977), 268–71. See also Klimkeit, *ZRGG* 32 (1980), 367–68.

284 That is, Mahaway. See nn.202–4 above.

285 "Enoch, the apostle" is Henning's rendering of Uighur *xonuǧ burxan.* The word *burxan* translates the concept of "Buddha" in Uighur versions of Buddhist texts. See Bang, *Muséon* 44 (1931), 23 (= Widengren, ed., 282); A. von Gabain, *Alttürkische Grammatik* (Leipzig, 1950[2]), 305; Klimkeit, *ZRGG* 32 (1980), 367; S.N.C. Lieu, *Manichaeism in the Later Roman Empire and Medieval China: A Historical Survey* (Manchester, 1985; repr. 1988), 202–13.

286 Henning suggests that the Kögmän mountains (identified by von Gabain as the Sayan range of southern Siberia) may reflect an original Mount Hermon; cf. *BSOAS* 11 (1943), 55; also Klimkeit, *ZRGG* 32 (1980), 373.

287 Henning, *BSOAS* 11 (1943), 66, originally published by *idem,* "Ein manichäisches Henochbuch," *SPAW* (1934), 29.

288 Presumably a reference to the *šr*] *šyn rbrbyn npqw mn ʿqrhn* of QG4A 8 above.

289 The loan-word *ʿyr* (= Aramaic *ʿyr* "Watcher") is a clear indication of this Middle Persian text's dependence upon an Aramaic substrate. See Henning, *SPAW* (1934), 30. On the identification of "trees of paradise" and "angels," compare the notice of Hippolytus regarding the teaching of the Gnostic Justin: "The company of all these angels together, he says, is the Paradise of which Moses says: «God planted a paradise in Eden towards the East» (Gen 2:8), that is, in front of Eden, that Eden might for ever see the paradise, that is, the angels. The angels of this paradise are allegorically called «trees» ..." (Hippolytus, *Refutatio* 5.26.5–6 [ed. Marcovich, 202]). Translation taken from W. Foerster, *Gnosis: A Selection of Gnostic Texts* (Oxford, 1972), I 53.

290 In the Qumran Book of Giants, the "garden" (*prdsʾ*) seems to represent the created order (including humanity) and the "great shoots" tended by the "gardeners," the Giants. By contrast, Middle Persian D interprets the "trees" (= "great shoots"?) to be *both* Watchers and Giants.

291 Although the "two tablets" are not explicitly mentioned here, it is clear from both the succeeding Aramaic fragments and the later Manichaean recensions that Mahaway indeed bore Enoch's message to the Giants in this form.

292 According to a Middle Persian fragment of the Book of Giants that was recently published by W. Sundermann, Mahaway was actually commanded by an unnamed speaker (Enoch? Shemiḥazah?) to transmit his message *first* to Narīmān (= Hahyah) before imparting it to the assembled Giants. See Sundermann, "Ein weiteres Fragment" (cf. n.122 above), 495–96. Were ʾOhyah and Hahyah confused during the transmission of this work?

293 See Henning Fragment c and Sogdian C cited below.

[294] Fitzmyer – Harrington, *Manual*, 337. Note that Milik mistakenly enters this word under the stem *mrt* in his glossary.

[295] Compare, for example, Targum Pseudo-Jonathan to Deuteronomy 20:3b: *l'yzwḥ lybkwn l'tydḥlwn wl' tyrttwn wl' ttyr'wn mn qdmyhwn* "do not be faint-hearted, do not fear, do not tremble, and do not be afraid of them."

[296] Milik, *Books of Enoch*, 209.

[297] Henning, *ZDMG* 90 (1936), 4.

[298] Henning, *BSOAS* 11 (1943), 60.

[299] Fitzmyer, *Genesis Apocryphon*², 60.

[300] Cf. Daniel 3:32–33; 6:28.

[301] Milik, *Books of Enoch*, 300–301; also Beyer, *Texte*, 262. Milik (followed by Beyer) calls attention to Jubilees 37:20–23 wherein Esau expresses the impossibility of a reconciliation with Jacob by pronouncing a series of improbable conditional occurrences (e.g., "if a pig can alter its skin and soften its bristles to be like wool ... then I will observe brotherhood with you").

[302] Sundermann, "Ein weiteres Fragment" (see n.292 above), 495–96.

[303] An introductory superscription identifying the content of this leaf.

[304] The speaker is apparently Māhawai.

[305] The scribe responsible for the tablets is undoubtedly Enoch, as lines 10–12 (not reproduced here) make clear. On the difficult readings in this line see Sundermann, "Ein weiteres Fragment," 496 n.21 and n.34.

[306] The message of Enoch is apparently inscribed upon "two tablets" (Middle Persian *dw txtg*; Aramaic *try lwḥy'*). These "tablets" appear in the Qumran Book of Giants in QG7 and QG8, and are apparently also alluded to in QG5 7 above. The word *txtg* also occurs in Henning Fragment j. There Henning interpreted the word as a proper name ("Taxtag") in light of its confusing context. Given the new evidence of the Qumran texts and the Sundermann fragment, the word should probably also be understood as "tablet" in Henning fragment j. See Milik, *Books of Enoch*, 334; W. Sundermann, *Mitteliranische manichäische Texte kirchengeschichtlichen Inhalts* (Berlin, 1981), 124 l.2070.

[307] Note that Māhawai consults Narīmān first before delivering his message to the Giants. In QG6, by contrast, he initially encounters 'Ohyah (= Middle Persian Sām!). Sundermann plausibly suggests that one tablet contains an interpretation of Narīmān's dream and the other bears a general message addressed to all the Giants.

[308] Compare QG6 3: *wl' mrtt* "do not be afraid."

[309] Henning, *BSOAS* 11 (1943), 60. The following passage brings Sām and Māhawai into conjunction.

[310] Compare QG6 4: *brq'l 'by 'my hwh* "Baraq'el my father was with me."

[311] The expression "one of thousands" is curious. Henning interpreted it on the basis of later Persian usage to connote that Māhawai did not expressly communicate all the information that he potentially could. See for example the introductory lines of *Škand-Vimānīk Vičār* 16: "Furthermore, is (here) written about the heresy of Mani *one (thing only) of a thousand (and) ten thousand*, for I am unable to write in a more fundamental way of the heresy, prating, and deceit of

Mani and the Manichaeans, and much trouble and long daily work would be necessary for me therein." (A.V.W. Jackson, *Researches in Manichaeism* [New York, 1932; repr. New York, 1965], 177). One might compare, however, logion 23 of the Coptic Gospel of Thomas: "Jesus said: I shall choose you, one out of a thousand, and two out of ten thousand, and they shall stand as a single one." Perhaps the expression is not an idiom, as Henning believed, but a literal indication of how few individuals would survive the impending catastrophe of the Deluge. The translation of the Gospel of Thomas is cited from A. Guillaumont, et al., *The Gospel According to Thomas* (Leiden and New York, 1959), 19. For another instance of the same expression, see now Sundermann, *Kirchengeschichtlichen Inhalts*, 117 ll.1925–26.

[312] Henning, *BSOAS* 11 (1943), 66. Henning's order for these two pages has been reproduced here even though it seems clear that the sequence should be reversed. The warnings and promises on Henning's "second page" make better narrative sense if they precede the actions described on his "first page." Henning himself noted that his suggested sequence was "uncertain."

[313] Compare n.308 above.

[314] Is the speaker Virōgdād (= Baraq'el)?

[315] This is presumably the import of the curious sentence in QG6 4, "Baraq'el my father is/was with me," as well as Henning Fragment c 14, "as my father Virōgdād was [with me?] ...."

[316] A discussion of this unusual form can be found in Fitzmyer, *Genesis Apocryphon*^{2}, 97.

[317] The text of 4QTLevi ar^a is cited from J.T. Milik, "Le testament de Lévi en araméen," *RB* 62 (1955), 400. With regard to the siglum, note the comments of Fitzmyer – Harrington, *Manual*, 203.

[318] See pages 132–36 above and notes 119–23.

[319] Another possibility would be to interpret 4Q Testuz in light of the confrontation of Mahaway by 'Ohyah that is recounted in QG6 and its parallel narratives. In this case, the speaker of lines 1–3 would be Mahaway, and the reference to "distress" in line 4 might reflect 'Ohyah's reaction to the consternating news of universal destruction.

[320] Recall as well the reference to a "second (tablet?)" (*tnynwt*) in QG5 7 above.

[321] The word *pršgn* (variant *ptšgn*) belongs to the vocabulary of Achaemenid administration and scribal bureaucracy, and is derived from Old Iranian **patičagnya-* by W. Hinz, *Altiranisches Sprachgut der Nebenüberlieferung* (Wiesbaden, 1975), 186. See Ezra 4:11,23; 5:6; 7:11; Esther 3:14; 4:8. Note also the prologue to 4Q Amram: *pršgn ktb mly ḥzwt ʻmrm br qht br lwy* "copy of the book (containing) the contents of the vision of Amram bar Qahat bar Levi" (Beyer, *Texte*, 211). This usage of *pršgn* is paralleled in the opening clause of each of the Testaments of the Twelve Patriarchs, wherein Greek ἀντίγραφον apparently renders an original *pršgn* in the heading of each of these testaments. M. Philonenko has perceptively suggested that "ces prologues [of the Testaments] paraissent vouloir s'inspirer de formules juridiques réelles." (idem, "Testa-

ments des douze patriarches," in A. Dupont-Sommer – M. Philonenko, eds., *La Bible: écrits intertestamentaires* [Paris, 1987], 817 n.1.)

[322] Milik, *Books of Enoch*, 315; Beyer, *Texte*, 261.

[323] Sundermann, "Ein weiteres Fragment," 496. See especially his n.36.

[324] Milik suggests that *qdyš'* refers to a "heavenly Watcher"; see his *Books of Enoch*, 316.

[325] Flemming restores *yebē* "(he) said" on the basis of the Greek versions of 1 Enoch 10:1, but there is no need for his emendation.

[326] The spelling *šmyḥzh* is attested in 4QEn^{a} 1 iii 6 (= 1 Enoch 6:7), 4QEn^{a} 1 iv 1 (= 1 Enoch 8:3), and QG8 5. A variant *šm*[*yḥz*] 'apparently occurs in 4QEn^{b} 1 iv 9 cited above.

[327] Knibb, *Enoch*, II 67–68; Sokoloff, *MAARAV* 1/2 (1978–79), 207; M. Black, "The Twenty Angel Dekadarchs at I Enoch 6.7 and 69.2," *JJS* 33 (1982), 229; *idem*, *The Book of Enoch*, 119; Beyer, *Texte*, 740; Uhlig, *Henochbuch*, 516. These authors explain the *yod* of *šmyḥzh* as a relic of an ancient case-ending. By contrast, Milik (*Books of Enoch*, 152) interprets the *yod* as a pronominal suffix, translating "My Name has seen." Knibb and Uhlig reproduce Milik's rendering as a possible option in translation.

[328] A. Caquot, "I Hénoch," in Dupont-Sommer – Philonenko, eds., *La Bible* (see n.320 above), 477. Caquot was anticipated in this suggestion by N. Schmidt who proposed a possible retroversion of the name Shemiḥazah to *šmy' ḥz'* "he surveys the heavens." See N. Schmidt, "The Original Language of the Parables of Enoch," in R.F. Harper, F. Brown, and G.F. Moore, eds., *Old Testament and Semitic Studies in Memory of William Rainey Harper* (Chicago, 1908), II 344.

[329] bT Yoma 67b: חנא דבי רבי ישמעאל עזאזל שמכפר על מעשה עוזא ועזאל.

[330] This was recognized by Rashi in his commentary to Yoma 67b: "Uzza and Azael: (They were) angels of destruction who descended to earth during the time of Na'amah sister of Tubal-Qain, and about them Scripture states: And the sons of God beheld the daughters of man ... (Genesis 6), therefore (the goat) makes atonement for sexual transgressions."

[331] For a comprehensive collection of the allusions in rabbinic literature to the story of Uzza/Azza and Azael, see R. Margolioth, ed., *Mal'akey 'elyon* (Jerusalem, 1945; repr. Jerusalem, 1964), 274–80.

[332] See Jellinek, *Bet ha-Midrasch*, V xlii; M. Schwab, *Vocabulaire de l'angélologie d'après les manuscrits hébreux de la Bibliothèque Nationale* (Paris, 1897), 209 and 256; Heller, *REJ* 60 (1910), 205; Ginzberg, *Legends of the Jews*, V 152; A. Kahana, "Sefer Ḥanokh I," in idem, ed., *Hasefarim haḥiṣonim* (Tel Aviv, 1936–37), I 31. Compare also the remarks of Dillmann, *Henoch*, 93.

[333] This possibility was suggested by J. Halévy, "Recherches sur la langue de la rédaction primitive du livre d'Enoch," *JA* 6th sér., IX (1867), 359.

[334] bT Niddah 61a: סיחון ועוג בני אחיה בר שמחזאי הוו "Sihon and Og were the sons of Ahyah (= 'Ohyah?) bar Shemhazai."

[335] Targum Pseudo-Jonathan to Genesis 6:4: *šmḥz'y w'wzy'l hynwn npylyn mn šmy' whww b'r'' bywmy' h'ynwwn* "Shemhazai and Azael fell from heaven and were on the earth in those days."

336 See S.P. Brock, "A Fragment of Enoch in Syriac," *JTS* 19 (1968), 626–31.

337 *wḥtymyn b'yzqth dšmḥyz' mry' bgd'n'* "and they (i.e., the evil spirits) are sealed with the name of Shemhazai (?) lord of Bagdana (?)." Cf. J.A. Montgomery, "A Magical Bowl-Text and the Original Script of the Manichaeans," *JAOS* 32 (1912), 433–38; idem, ed., *Aramaic Incantation Texts From Nippur* (Philadelphia, 1913), 198 and 273.

338 Henning Fragment c lines 6 and 15 (Henning, *BSOAS* 11 [1943], 60); Sundermann Fragment L I Recto line 10 (Sundermann, "Ein weiteres Fragment," 496).

339 Henning Sogdian H line 9 (Henning, *BSOAS* 11 [1943], 70).

340 Driver, *Aramaic Documents* (see n.86 above), 25 and 29. E. Benveniste has suggested a possible Iranian exemplar for this phrase; see his "Elements perses en araméen d'Egypt," *JA* 242 (1954), 305.

341 Note the remark of Sokoloff, *MAARAV* 1/2 (1978–79), 205, and the translation of Fitzmyer – Harrington, *Manual*, 73.

342 A. Dillmann, *Lexicon Linguae Aethiopicae* (Leipzig, 1865), 1041–42; C. Brockelmann, *Grundriss der vergleichenden Grammatik der semitischen Sprachen* (Berlin, 1908–13), I 232.

343 Milik (*Books of Enoch*, 315) and Sokoloff (*MAARAV* 1/2 [1978–79], 207) specify Raphael as the subject, but the context of this line and of the fragment as a whole makes their interpretation unlikely.

344 Beyer, *Texte*, 261.

345 See Henning, *BSOAS* 11 (1943), 71–72, reproduced below.

346 Milik, *Books of Enoch*, 315–16.

347 God issues his judgment to the four archangels (1 Enoch 10), who in turn commission Enoch to carry the news of the judgment to the Watchers and Giants (1 Enoch 12). Enoch performs this mission, but after he delivers the news of condemnation, the Watchers persuade Enoch to intercede on their behalf before God (1 Enoch 13). Enoch is granted a "throne-room" vision wherein the condemnation and ensuing punishment of the Watchers and Giants is repeated (1 Enoch 14–16). Nowhere in this narrative does the *actual* binding of the Watchers and slaughter of their progeny occur. It is always treated as a future event.

348 " ... all ... carried off ... severally they were subjected to tasks and services. And they ... from each city ... and were ordered to serve the ... The Mesenians [were directed] to prepare the Khuzians to sweep [and] water, the Persians to ...." The preceding page of Fragment i had described the descent of the Watchers and their pursuit of mortal women. See Henning, *BSOAS* 11 (1943), 62.

349 Henning Fragment j line 33; Sogdian G lines 1–2; and Parthian T lines 4–5. Note also QG11 VI 3 below.

350 Sundermann, "Ein weiteres Fragment," 496–97.

351 Henning, *BSOAS* 11 (1943), 61.

352 Compare 1 Enoch 12:5–6; 13:1; 16:4.

353 This is probably a reference to the length of time (*'rk'*) that God allowed

the Watchers and Giants to "rule" over the earth. According to the traditional interpretation of Genesis 6:3, this period was prolonged in order to give earthly inhabitants an opportunity to repent of their wickedness. See the Targumim and medieval commentaries to Genesis 6:3, as well as n.267 above.

354 Henning, *BSOAS* 11 (1943), 66.

355 This "apostle" is presumably Enoch, given the frequent occurrence of this attribute with Enoch's name in the Manichaean fragments. It will be recalled that in the extant Aramaic remains and in the Sundermann fragment, it is Mahaway who acts as the messenger of Enoch. Here it appears that Enoch himself acts as messenger. It is possible that this fragment describes a different scene from that depicted in QG7–8 and in the Sundermann fragment. Given the hostile reception granted Enoch's message in QG9 (and parallels), it is not unlikely that Enoch paid a personal visit to the Watchers and Giants in order to prevent further rebellion.

356 Beyer (*Texte*, 262) identifies the speaker as Shemiḥazah, but in light of the emphasis placed upon the speaker's "strength" and "power" in line 3, it would seem more likely that the speaker is a Giant.

357 Text and translation cited from Greenfield–Porten, *The Bisitun Inscription* (cf. n.117 above), 34.

358 See Beyer, *Texte*, 719.

359 Milik, *Books of Enoch*, 308. See Sokoloff, *MAARAV* 1/2 (1978–79), 221 n.84.

360 For *'ns* in this sense, see especially Daniel 4:6: *wkl rz l' 'ns lk* "and no mystery is too baffling for you."

361 Milik, *Books of Enoch*, 313; Beyer, *Texte*, 263.

362 Sumerian King List Column iii 17–20: "divine Gilgameš — his father (was) a *lillû*-demon — a high priest of Kullab, reigned 126 years" (T. Jacobsen, *The Sumerian King List* [Chicago, 1939], 89–91). Elsewhere Gilgamesh is called the son of the goddess Ninsun and Lugalbanda, king of Uruk. Note the references in Jacobsen as well as D.O. Edzard, "Gilgameš," in H.W. Haussig, ed., *Wörterbuch der Mythologie Band I: Götter und Mythen in vorderen Orient* (Stuttgart, 1965), 69–73.

363 Transliteration cited from R.C. Thompson, ed., *The Epic of Gilgamish* (Oxford, 1930), 11 and 50. See also J.H. Tigay, *The Evolution of the Gilgamesh Epic* (Philadelphia, 1982), 142 and 264.

364 J. Friedrich, "Die hethitischen Bruchstücke des Gilgameš-Epos," *ZA* 39 (1930), 3–5. See Tigay, *Gilgamesh*, 153 and A. Heidel, *The Gilgamesh Epic and Old Testament Parallels*[2] (Chicago, 1949; repr. Chicago, 1971), 17.

365 See Tigay, *Gilgamesh*, 251. Two cuneiform fragments (BM 35174 + 35628) previously published by D.J. Wiseman and dated by him to the Achaemenid period (see his "Additional Neo-Babylonian Gilgamesh Fragments," in P. Garelli, ed., *Gilgameš et sa légende* [Paris, 1960], 131–35) have been plausibly situated in the Arsacid period by J. Oelsner, "Ein Beitrag zu keilschriftlichen Königstitulaturen in hellenistischer Zeit," *ZA* 56 (1964), 262–64.

366 Compare the international popularity of the Ahiqar Romance, a story

which almost surely originated in Mesopotamia. Note also the recent discovery that a story about Ashurbanipal and his brother Shamash-shum-ukin forms part of the content of an Aramaic text written upon papyrus in demotic script (R.A. Bowman, "An Aramaic Religious Text in Demotic Script," *JNES* 3 [1944], 219–31). This papyrus apparently dates from the late second century B.C.E., and is obviously dependent upon an earlier Aramaic exemplar. For the story of the Assyrian rulers, see R.C. Steiner – C.F. Nims, "Ashurbanipal and Shamash-shum-ukin: A Tale of Two Brothers from the Aramaic Text in Demotic Script," *RB* 92 (1985), 60–81.

367 Aelian, *On Animals* 12.21.

368 M. Lewin, *Die Scholien des Theodor bar Koni zur Patriarchengeschichte (Genesis XII–L)* (Berlin, 1905), 2 ll.8–9.

369 Al-Suyūṭī, [*Kitāb*] *al-raḥma fi 'l-ṭibb wal-ḥikma* (repr. Beirut, 1983), 337. This reference has been heretofore overlooked in the standard discussions of Gilgamesh. Translations of the relevant lines can be found in H.A. Winkler, *Salomo und die Ḳarīna* (Stuttgart, 1931), 25, and V. Haas, *Magie und Mythen in Babylonien* (Gifkendorf, 1986), 217.

370 Cf. *Maqlû* I 37–38: *ÉN irṣitum*^{tum} *irṣitum*^{tum} *irṣitum*^{tum}*-ma* ^{d}*Gilgameš bēl ma-mi-ti-ku-nu* "Beschwörung. Erde, Erde, ja Erde! Gilgameš (ist) der Herr eures Bannes." Text and translation cited from G. Meier, *Die assyrische Beschwörungssammlung Maqlû* (Berlin, 1937; repr. Osnabrück, 1967), 8. See also *Maqlû* IV 54. For a discussion of Gilgamesh in such contexts and a representative sampling of the evidence, see W.G. Lambert, "Gilgameš in Religious, Historical and Omen Texts and the Historicity of Gilgameš," in Garelli, ed., *Gilgameš* (see n.365 above), 39–56.

371 Sundermann, "Ein weiteres Fragment," 497–98.

372 One presumes that the "sorrow" of the Giants stems from their reception of Enoch's oracle of doom. By contrast, Sām's behavior expresses his defiance of the heavenly judgment.

373 The Giant Atambīš appears in another fragment of the Manichaean Book of Giants (M 5900; cf. M. Boyce, *A Catalogue of the Iranian Manuscripts in Manichaean Script in the German Turfan Collection* [Berlin, 1960], 116) that was published by Sundermann. See his *Kosmogonische Texte* (cf. n.93 above), 77–78. Sundermann initially thought that Atambīš was one of the fallen Watchers and suggested an identification with Tamiel, the fifth Watcher mentioned in the list at 1 Enoch 6:7. He now thinks it more likely that the name designates a Giant. See his "Ein weiteres Fragment," 495 n.19. Given the presence of Gilgamesh and Humbaba in the Book of Giants, it seems possible that the name "Atambīš" is a reflex of Mesopotamian "Utnapishtim," here transformed from Flood hero to Giant.

374 Corresponding to the narrative sequence of QG9 9ff.

375 An allusion to the Deluge?

376 Compare the analogous expression in QG4A 16: *h' šlṭn šmy' l'r'' nḥt.*

377 Henning, *BSOAS* 11 (1943), 61.

378 Ibid., 70.

[379] Compare QG9 3: *wbtqwp hyl dr'y wbhsn gbwrty.*

[380] Genesis 6:19–20; 7:1–3.

[381] Henning Fragment l 50–53 (*BSOAS* 11 [1943], 61).

[382] Beyer, *Texte*, 267.

[383] Henning, *BSOAS* 11 (1943), 69.

[384] This line perhaps refers to those "archons" of Darkness who, in Manichaean cosmogony, were affixed (literally "crucified") upon the newly created firmament. See *Acta Archelai* 8: Τὸ Ζῶν Πνεῦμα ... κατελθὸν ἀνήνεγκε τοὺς ἀρχοντας καὶ ἐσταύρωσεν ἐν τῷ στερεώματι (Hegemonius, *Acta Archelai* edited by C.H. Beeson [Leipzig, 1906], 11 ll.4–6); also Epiphanius, *Panarion* 66.32. Both sources are conveniently reproduced by W. Bousset, *Hauptprobleme der Gnosis* (Göttingen, 1907; repr. Göttingen, 1973), 46. Apparently two hundred archons managed to escape this imprisonment and fled to earth. Cf. *Kephalaia* 92:20–28 for the equation of these "bound archons" with the Watchers (ἐγρήγοροι) of 1 Enoch 6–16 and the Book of Giants.

[385] According to Indian tradition, Mount Mēru or Sumēru ("Good Mēru") was the great mountain which stood at the center of the earth. See *Mahābhārata* 1(5)15.5ff.: "There is an all-surpassing mountain that blazes like a pile of fire and casts forth the splendor of the sun with its golden glowing peaks — Mount Meru! It is the many-splendored ornament of gold that is cherished by Gods and Gandharvas, immeasurable and unattainable by those of little merit of Law. Awesome beasts of prey range over it, divine herbs illumine it, and the great mountain rises aloft to cover with its heights the vault of heaven. To others inaccessible even in their imaginings, it abounds in rivers and trees and resounds with the most beautiful flocks of many-feathered birds." Translation taken from J.A.B. van Buitenen, ed., *The Mahābhārata: 1. The Book of the Beginning* (Chicago, 1973), 72. See also H. Zimmer, *Myths and Symbols in Indian Art and Civilization* (Princeton, 1946; repr. Princeton, 1974), 52.

[386] Compare *Kephalaia* 117:5–8: "Before the sons of the Giants were born, who knew neither righteousness nor piety among themselves, *thirty-six towns had been prepared and [built] for them* so that the sons of the Giants might dwell in them ...." Henning notes that the number was changed to "thirty-two" to conform with Indian tradition (Henning, *BSOAS* 11 [1943], 55–56).

[387] *Aryān-waižan* is Iranian *Airyanəm Vaējah* "Aryan expanse," the legendary homeland of the ancient Indo-Iranian peoples. "In the Zoroastrian works Airyanəm Vaējah often appears as a mythical land, the place where all the great events of world «history» took place." (Boyce, *A History of Zoroastrianism* [see n.116 above], I 144). For a fuller discussion, see E. Benveniste, "L'Ērān-vēž et l'origine légendaire des Iraniens," *BSOS* 7 (1933–35), 265–74. Note also E. Yarshater, "Iranian Common Beliefs and World-View," in idem, ed., *The Cambridge History of Iran: Volume 3(1): The Seleucid, Parthian and Sasanian Periods* (Cambridge, 1983), 351–52.

[388] Henning, *BSOAS* 11 (1943), 62.

[389] The motifs of the 400,000 "pious ones" and destruction by fire are also found in the Gnostic *Apocalypse of Adam.* Therein Sakla (the incompetent

Demiurge) attempts to destroy 400,000 descendants of Ham and Japhet by raining upon them "fire and sulfur and asphalt," but they escape this threat through the intervention of heavenly emissaries (73:13–76:7). Compare the reference, unfortunately very fragmentary, to "400,000 Righteous (δίκαιος)" in *Homilies* 68:18. A similar statement is found in *Psalm-Book* 142:7–8: "The Righteous (δίκαιος) who were burnt in the fire ... This multitude that were wiped out — four thousand ...," where "four thousand" should probably be emended to "four *hundred* thousand." One wonders whether the cipher 400,000 might have originally referred to the number of Giants who perished in the Flood. A suggestive tradition found in the *Greek Apocalypse of Baruch* (so-called *3 Baruch*) states that "409,000 Giants" drowned in the Flood. For further discussion of this motif, see Stroumsa, *Another Seed*, 85–88.

390 Compare 1 Enoch 87:3–4; 70:3.

391 The two principal grades of Manichaean adherence; i.e., the "elect" and the "hearers."

392 Sundermann, *Kosmogonische Texte*, 77–78. He now restores the internal heading to this text as follows: /v/ [*o gw*] *'yšn o* /v/ *o m*(*'*) [*zyndr'n o*] "the discourse about the Māzendarān," that is, "the Giants." (personal communication from Professor Sundermann).

393 Henning, *BSOAS* 11 (1943), 73.

394 Ibid., 72.

395 This passage can be viewed as a synopsis of either 1 Enoch 6–16 or the Book of Giants.

396 Milik, *Books of Enoch*, 313.

397 See the texts cited in Tigay, *Gilgamesh*, 32–33; 93–95. For an excellent discussion of the figure of Humbaba, see E. Cassin, *La splendeur divine: Introduction à l'étude de la mentalité mesopotamienne* (Paris, 1968), 53–64.

398 Note the references in Tigay, *Gilgamesh*, 79–80 nn.25–26, as well as C. Wilcke, "Ḫuwawa/Ḫumbaba," in E. Ebeling – B. Meissner *et al.*, eds., *Reallexikon der Assyriologie* (repr., Berlin & New York, 1972–), IV 534.

399 Cf. Knibb, *Enoch*, II 94; Spiegel, "Noah, Danel, and Job" (see n.172 above), 336–37.

400 T. Bauer, "Ein viertes altbabylonisches Fragment des Gilgameš-Epos," *JNES* 16 (1957), 256 recto l.13 and 260; J. Day, *God's Conflict with the Dragon and the Sea: Echoes of a Canaanite Myth in the Old Testament* (Cambridge, 1985), 117–18.

401 Henning Fragment j 24 (*BSOAS* 11 [1943], 60); Milik, *Books of Enoch*, 311.

402 Lucian, *De Dea Syria* 19–27. The text employed is that of H.W. Attridge – R.A. Oden, *The Syrian Goddess (De Dea Syria) Attributed to Lucian* (Missoula, 1976).

403 P. Jensen, *Assyrisch-babylonische Mythen und Epen* (Berlin, 1900), 437–38; E. Schrader – H. Zimmern – H. Winckler, eds., *Die Keilinschriften und das Alte Testament* 3. Auflage (Berlin, 1903), 570 n.2; A. Ungnad – H. Gressmann, *Das Gilgamesch-Epos* (Göttingen, 1911), 111–12; E. Benveniste, "La légende de

Kombabos," in *Mélanges syriens offerts à Monsieur René Dussaud* (Paris, 1939), I 249–58; R.A. Oden, *Studies in Lucian's De Syria Dea* (Missoula, 1977), 36–40. The identity of Humbaba and Kombabos is disputed by H. Stocks, "Studien zu Lukians »De Syria Dea«," *Berytus* 4 (1937), 12–13; C. Clemen, *Lukians Schrift über die syrische Göttin* (Leipzig, 1938), 39 n.1.

[404] Al-Jāḥiẓ states that among the contents of the Manichaean writings are "stories of Shaqlūn, *Hummāmah*, and *hdrw'y* (?)" (*Kitāb al-Ḥayawān apud* Kessler, *Mani*, 368–69). Al-Nadīm explicitly identifies Hummāmah as the "Spirit of Darkness" (روح الظلمة); cf. the text of his *Fihrist apud* Flügel, *Mani*, 58 l.5. Compare al-Māturidī, *Kitāb al-Tawḥīd*: "The Spirit of Darkness is named Hummāmah and is alive" (G. Vajda, "Le témoignage d'al-Māturidī sur la doctrine des Manichéens, des Dayṣānites et des Marcionites," *Arabica* 13 [1966], 4 l.10; cf. also l.12). Al-Shahrastānī states that there exists within the Realm of Darkness four "physical" entities and one "spiritual" entity, the latter of which is named "Hummāmah" (*Kitāb al-milal wa-al-niḥal* [ed. Cureton], 189 l.18). For further references to Hummāmah in Muslim polemic, see Vajda, *Arabica* 13 (1966), 18–21; 116; 126.

[405] Ibn Abī l-Ḥadīd (13th century), cited by Vajda, *Arabica* 13 (1966), 20. One should note that the translations of Haarbrücker (see Chapter One n.112) and Dodge (see Chapter One n.55) fail to recognize the term "Hummāmah" as a proper name, the justification for which is provided by Flügel, *Mani*, 240. See also H.-C. Puech, "Le Prince des Ténèbres en son royaume," in *Satan* (Paris, 1948), 159. With regard to Hummāmah, a recent anthology states: "Es gibt für den Namen bis jetzt keine überzeugende Erklärung." (J.P. Asmussen – A. Böhlig, eds., *Die Gnosis III: Der Manichäismus* [Zürich and München, 1980], 327 n.144). For a recent ingenious attempt to explain this noun, see W. Sundermann, "Some More Remarks on Mithra in the Manichaean Pantheon," in J. Duchesne-Guillemin, ed., *Etudes mithraiques* (Leiden, 1978), 491–92 n.46.

[406] Note already Adam, *Texte*², 124 n.21. See the remarks of G. Monnot, *Penseurs musulmans et religions iraniennes: 'Abd al-Jabbār et ses devanciers* (Paris, 1974), 123–25. He includes some observations upon this proposed identification by the eminent Assyriologist J. Bottéro. Neither Monnot nor Bottéro seem aware that Humbaba is already present in the Book of Giants, a circumstance that indicates that the Book of Giants was probably the transmissional link between the Mesopotamian and Islamic traditions.

[407] 1 Enoch 10:4–6: "Moreover, the Lord said to Raphael: Bind Azazel hand and foot (and) cast him into darkness. Break open the wilderness which is in Dudāēl (and) cast him there. Cast upon him sharp, jagged stones and cover him with darkness, and let him abide there forever. Cover his face so that he will not see light. And on that great Day of Judgment he will be dispatched into the conflagration." Compare a fragment of Mani's eschatological teaching reported in the *Fihrist* (Flügel, *Mani*, 58 ll.3–9):

> Mani says: This conflagration will last for a period of 1468 years. Mani further says: When this step is completed, and Hummāmah, the Spirit

> of Darkness, sees the deliverance of the Light and the ascension of the angels, warriors, and guardians, (Hummāmah) will become submissive, (for Hummāmah) beholds the battle, and the warriors who surround (Hummāmah) will drive (Hummāmah) back. Then (Hummāmah) will withdraw to a tomb that has been prepared, and the tomb will be blocked with a boulder as large as the world, thus burying (Hummāmah) in it. Then the Light will be delivered from the Darkness and its damage at that time.

One might make the following observations: 1) Aza[z]el is cast into "darkness"; Hummāmah is identified as the "Spirit of Darkness," 2) both entities are sequestered in a "cavity," 3) both entities are buried by a mass of "stone," and 4) both entities are separated from all contact with "light."

408 Al-Shahrastānī explicitly credits Abū 'Isā al-Warrāq as the source of the former's report on Manichaeism (*Milal* [ed. Cureton], 188 l.14).

409 Al-Nadīm, *Fihrist* (*apud* Flügel, *Mani*, 78 l.14) identifies Abū 'Isā al-Warrāq as a *zindiq* "heretic." For further information regarding this figure and his reputation as a "crypto-Manichaean", see S.M. Stern, "Abū 'Isā Muḥammad b. Harūn al-Warrāḳ," *EI²* I 130; H. Ritter, "Philologika III. Muhammedanische Häresiographen," *Der Islam* 18 (1929), 35–36; G. Vajda, "Les zindiqs en pays d'Islam au début de la période Abbaside," *RSO* 17 (1938), 196–97; C. Colpe, "Anpassung des Manichäismus an den Islam (Abū 'Isā al-Warrāq)," *ZDMG* 109 (1959), 82–91.

410 Vajda, *Arabica* 13 (1966), 6 and 116 n.3.

411 Milik, *Books of Enoch*, 150 and 188.

412 M. Yoma 6:8. Compare Targum Pseudo-Jonathan to Leviticus 16:10 (*byt ḥrwry, byt ḥdwry*). This identification was first suggested by A. Geiger, "Einige Worte über das Buch Henoch," *Jüdische Zeitschrift für Wissenschaft und Leben* 3 (1864–65), 200–201. See also S. Landersdorfer, *Studien zum biblischen Versöhnungstag* (Münster, 1924), 21–23; H. Speyer, *Die biblischen Erzählungen im Qoran* (Gräfenhainichen, 1931; repr. Hildesheim, 1988), 424; and M. Delcor, "Le mythe de la chute des anges et de l'origine des géants comme explication du mal dans le monde dans l'apocalyptique juive: Histoire des traditions," *RHR* 190 (1976), 37.

413 Note the incipit to the text of this *Midrash* in Jellinek (see n.165 above): "Rab Joseph was asked by his students: Who is Azazel? ...," to which query the story recounted in the *Midrash* supplies the explanation.

414 4Q180 1 ll.7–8: [ו]פשר על עזזאל והמלאכים אש[ר באו אל בנות האדם וי]לדו להם גברים ועל עזזאל [... "[and] a pesher on Azazel and the angels wh[o came unto mortal women, and they bo]re to them Giants, and regarding Azazel ...." The restorations within the brackets are based upon 4Q181 2 l.2 and the suggestion of J. Strugnell, "Notes en marge du volume V des Discoveries in the Judaean Desert of Jordan," *RQ* 7 (1969–71), 253. 4Q180–181 was initially published by J.M. Allegro, "Some Unpublished Fragments of Pseudepigraphical Literature from Qumran's Fourth Cave," *The Annual of Leeds University Oriental Society* 4

(1962–63), 3–5. For the most recent edition of 4Q180, see D. Dimant, "The «Pesher on the Periods» (4Q180) and 4Q181," *Israel Oriental Studies* 9 (1979), 77–102. For Islamic testimonies about 'Azāzīl, usually interpreted as an alternative designation for Iblīs (i.e., "Satan"), see G. Vajda, "'Azāzīl," *EI*², I 811; M.J. Kister, "Legends in *tafsīr* and *hadīth* Literature: The Creation of Adam and Related Stories," in A. Rippen, ed., *Approaches to the History of the Interpretation of the Qur'ān* (Oxford, 1988), 90–91.

Chapter Three

Severus of Antioch and the Book of Giants

Another possible witness to the original contents of the Manichaean Book of Giants is provided within a sixth-century homily authored by Severus of Antioch. Severus, who served as Patriarch of Antioch from 512 to 518, was a leader of the Monophysite movement[1] in eastern Christianity, an affiliation which led to the condemnation of his writings by a Byzantine synod in 536.[2] As a result of this censure, his homilies no longer survive in their original Greek form, but they were preserved among the Monophysites by two Syriac translators.[3]

Important for our present purpose is his 123rd homily,[4] a treatise which, according to its heading, "deals with the abominable impiety of the Manichaeans." This text intersperses, among its florid exhortations and strident polemic, extracts which were apparently excerpted from a Manichaean work. The quotations are relatively simple to identify, being set off formally from the remainder of the admonition by phrases such as "he says" (*'mr*), "for he says" (*'mr gyr*), "they say regarding (these) matters" (*'mryn bhyn bml'*), and the like. The excerpts themselves apparently stem from a work which focused upon certain cosmogonical doctrines of the Manichaeans. However, these fragments exhibit little correspondence in content to what is known about Manichaean cosmogony from the classical transmitters of this information, Theodore bar Konai and Ibn al-Nadīm.

The first scholars to call attention to the significance of the Severus fragments for the recovery of a Manichaean text were F. Cumont and M.-A. Kugener.[5] Their *Recherches sur le manichéisme* included an edition of that portion of the 123rd homily which contained the Manichaean quotations, accompanied by a translation and brief discussion.[6] Cumont and Kugener suggested that the discrepancies which distinguish the cosmogonical reports of Theodore bar Konai and Severus could be attributed to those writers' reliance upon two different works of Mani.[7] Apparently, the source which undergirds the testimony of Severus was also utilized previously by the Byzantine heresiologist Theodoret (451–458 C.E.), for not only is there a general similarity in theme among the extracts contained in both works, but in some cases identical expressions and phrases appear.[8] The evidence supplied by these two independent witnesses assures the authenticity of this alleged Manichaean work. Unfortunately, neither writer identifies the source that he is using.

Earlier researchers had speculated that the unnamed source was possibly Mani's "Book of Mysteries,"[9] but the synopsis of the contents of the "Book of Mysteries" preserved in the *Fihrist* of al-Nadīm does not mention a cosmogonical narrative within that work.[10] Relying upon internal allusions within the 123rd homily, Cumont and Kugener cautiously proposed that the work refuted by Severus was in fact the Book of Giants.[11] In support of their suggestion, they appeal to 1) a brief description which characterizes some of the evil entities who rebel against God as "limitless in size" (*brbwt' 'ytyhwn hww dl'sk'*); and 2) an allusion by Severus to the pagan gigantomachy (presumably that of Hesiod) as "inferior in scope to his (i.e., Mani's) blasphemy."[12] It thus seemed possible to Cumont and Kugener that the extracts attested by Theodoret and Severus were taken from Mani's Book of Giants.[13]

Despite the caution displayed by Cumont and Kugener, and the tenuous nature of their evidence, almost all subsequent commentators have jumped to the uncritical conclusion that the Severus fragments are actually citations from Mani's Book of Giants.[14] This state of affairs persists in spite of the subsequent discovery and publication of authentic fragments of the Book of Giants from Turfan and Qumran. In fact, as we have seen above, V. Arnold-Döben and H.-J. Klimkeit rely upon this identification to support their contention that iconographic representations of the Manichaean Tree of Life in Central Asia are dependent upon the textual depiction of the Tree of Life contained in the Severus fragments.[15] Klimkeit has gone so far as to suggest that the tree "with three shoots" that functions as a symbol for Noah and his three sons in an Aramaic fragment of the Qumran Book of Giants is the ultimate source for the Tree of Life imagery that figures in the Manichaean quotations preserved by Severus. If Klimkeit's hypothesis of such a link can be verified, a significant step forward would be taken toward the confirmation of the Cumont-Kugener proposal.[16]

The importance of the Severus fragments for a possible determination of the content of the Manichaean Book of Giants requires their presentation at this juncture. The following translation is based upon the edition of the text provided by Cumont-Kugener,[17] and the numbers which introduce each new quotation refer to the pages of their edition. Only the actual excerpts of the Manichaean treatise are translated here.

Severus of Antioch: 123rd Homily

Homily of admonition whose topic and theme are profession of an orthodox belief, but which deals especially with the abominable impiety of the Manichaeans. It provides warning so that no man will fall into their snares, because certain individuals have indeed made trial of this sort of destructive error.

(89–90) From whence did it come into the minds of these extraordinarily perverse Manichaeans that there are two principles which are uncreated and which have no beginning;[18] (namely) Good and Evil, Light and Darkness, which latter is also named Hyle?[19]

(91–92) Yet he says: Each one of them is uncreated and has no origin, both the Good, which is also Light, and the Evil, which is also Darkness and Hyle; and they had no association one with the other.

(96) And they say: That which is Good, also named Light and the Tree of Life, possesses those regions which lie to the east, west, and north; for those (regions) which lie to the south and to the meridian belong to the Tree of Death,[20] which they also call Hyle,[21] being very wicked and uncreated.

(97–98) And they say regarding (these) matters: The difference and the relationship between these two principles is comparable to that between a king and a pig. The one conducts itself in localities which are suitable for it, as in royal palaces; but the other is like a pig wallowing in filth and feeding upon and even rejoicing over foulness; or it is like a serpent who has crawled into its hole.[22] They add furthermore that the pig and snake are both self-originating.

(99–102) For he says in one of his books (those which are secret); or rather, those which deserve (to be named) "darkness" and "error," thusly: These are they which are unceasing and which have existed eternally from the beginning — he speaks here of Hyle and God — everything in its essence has come about from them. Likewise does the Tree of Life exist,[23] which is there adorned with every sort of pleasing and lovely, beautiful thing. It is filled and covered with all sorts of good things, and it is stable and invariable with regard to its "essential nature." Its land encompasses three regions: that of the north[24] which extends both beyond and below, and that of the east and west (also) extending both beyond and below. And below there is nothing that has sunk or has withdrawn from it not even into any of the regions; rather, it extends infinitely both beyond and below. No foreign body exists there or even near it or below it or in any place among these three regions; only (the Tree) itself (extending) both beyond and below to the north, east, and west. There is nothing that encompasses or encloses it within these three regions,[25] only what belongs to (the Tree) itself, for its fruits cover it, and majesty belongs to it.

(103) And, he says, it (the Tree) is not visible in the southern region, and those (things) which are within (the Region of Light) are hidden, for God enclosed that place with a wall.[26]

(104–105) Its light and its bounty are concealed, so as to not grant a cause for desire to the Tree which is evil which is in the south,[27] or that there be a cause for that (evil Tree) to be disturbed or vexed or to bring (the good Tree) into danger. Rather, it is enclosed by splendor, and does not give a pretext (for mischief) on account of its goodness. It preserves itself in righteousness and remains in this splendor, retaining continually its magnificent "nature" in those three regions. (However), the Tree of Death has no life in its "nature," nor does it (produce) fruits of goodness on any of its branches. It exists eternally in the region of the south, having its own locality which it is over.

(117–118) The Tree of Death[28] is divided into many (parts);[29] war and bitterness characterize them, for they are strangers to (the concept of) peace, and are full of every sort of wickedness. Good fruits are never upon them.[30] (The Tree) is divided against its fruits, and the fruits are also (divided) against the Tree, and they do not become reconciled with that which bore them, but rather all of them form rottenness for the corruption of their place. They do not submit themselves to that which bore them. The Tree is wholly evil, and it never produces any good thing, but remains divided against itself, and all of its parts corrupt whatever draws near to it.[31]

(122–128) These things (are written) about Hyle and about its fruits and members. The cause that led them to ascend from here up to the "worlds" of light[32] was their turbulence.[33] In actuality, these members of the Tree of Death had no knowledge of each other. Rather than having perception of each other, each one of them was aware of nothing more than their individual sound(s), and saw only what was before their eyes.[34] When a certain one cried out, they heard (it), and perceived in this (way), and would (then) proceed hastily toward the cry. Some of the others (however) had no knowledge of anything.[35] Thus they provoked and stirred each other up until they came unto the boundaries of the glorious land of Light. When they beheld that marvelous and surpassingly beautiful sight, which was a much more excellent (place) than their own (abode), they gathered together — namely (the members) of Hyle or Darkness — and plotted against the Light regarding how they could mix themselves with it. Due to (their) frenzy, they were unaware that the mighty and powerful God dwelt in it (the region of Light). Nevertheless, they sought to ascend to the upper (region), despite their having no knowledge of the goodness of the divinity or ever having perceived who (indeed) was God. Rather, they frantically beheld, fueled by desire, the appearance of those blessed Aeons, and thought that it (the region of Light) could become theirs. Therefore all of the parts of the Tree of Darkness rose up — namely Hyle which produces corruption — and ascended with many powers whose total number cannot be reckoned. They were all clothed with the substance[36] of fire.[37] Moreover, these (powers) had different parts. Some had tough bodies and were of limitless size,[38] while others were incorporeal and imperceptible to (the sense of) touch, possessing only a slight perceptibility in the manner of demons and apparitions. And having raised itself up, the whole of Hyle ascended together with its winds, storms, waters, fire, its demons and apparitions, and its princes and powers — all of those who had been in the depth — so that they could place themselves in the Light.[39] Because of this disturbance which was brought to pass from the depth against the region of Light and against the holy fruits, it was unavoidable that some portion of the Light came to be mixed with those evil entities, whereby the enemies (of Light) by means of "mixture" ensnared them.

Yet tranquility endures among that which is Good, for the essence of the Good will be preserved when this blessed essence is delivered from the fire of Hyle and the worm of corruption.[40] Moreover, these particles of Light will be purified[41] of the Hyle — the power that was mixed — so that Hyle will be expunged from (its) midst. Then the Tree of Life will be God, among all and above all.[42]

In the Aeon of Light there is no burning fire which could be discharged against that which is evil. There is neither an iron (weapon) for cutting, nor overwhelming waters,[43] nor any other evil substance like those.[44] Instead, all is Light and (every) place is noble. There is no defect (within Light) to oppose it (i.e., Darkness), only its egress or passage (i.e., into the Darkness), so that through a portion of the Light having come forth (to submit to mixture), the enemies were dispersed, they desisted from (further) violence, and were ensnared by means of mixture.

(144) As a type of bait[45] for tumult and error was this portion (of Light) given over to Hyle, so that afterwards those that are mixed — as you say — will be purified, and the Light will become more (and more) pure ... and after the purification Hyle will be reduced to complete destruction.

As we have seen above, the initial identification of the source of the Manichaean quotations within this homily as the Book of Giants rested upon two items: 1) the description of some of the inhabitants of the Realm of Darkness as "limitless" in size; and 2) explicit knowledge of a Manichaean gigantomachy by Severus. To these factors, Arnold-Döben and Klimkeit have added a third possible correlation — the designation "Tree of Life" as an alternative name for the Realm of Light. When we consider, however, the actual content of the Book of Giants available to us in both its Qumran and

Middle Iranian recensions, a topic explored at length above in chapter two, the validity of this generally accepted correspondence must be questioned.

To be sure, the gargantuan size of the Giants is explicitly emphasized in Jewish literature of the Second Temple era. 1 Enoch 7:2 states: "And they (i.e., human women) became pregnant and bore *great Giants, having heights of three thousand cubits.*" The Damascus Covenant characterizes the Giants as having "statures like the height of cedar trees, and whose bodies were like mountains," an image derived partially from the description of the Amorites found in Amos 2:9.[46] The exegetical background of the Damascus Covenant tradition is discernible in Jubilees 29:9–11. That passage reads: "However, in former days they called the land of Gala'ad (Gilead) the land of the Rephai<m>, for it was the land of the Rephaim, and (there) the Rephaim were born, *Giants whose stature was ten, nine, eight, and not less than seven cubits* ... and God destroyed them on account of their evil behavior, for they were exceedingly perverse. *The Amorites settled (there) in their place,* (an) evil and sinful (people) ...." A reference to the bodily size of the Giants is absent in our extant copies of the Book of Giants, but in light of the fragmentary nature of the surviving witnesses, one cannot rule out the possibility that such information was originally included in the text.[47]

However, the common motif of the large size of the rebels is not sufficient evidence for concluding that Severus has excerpted from Mani's Book of Giants. There remains a crucial difference between the testimonies of Severus and the Jewish texts, including the Qumran Book of Giants. In Jewish tradition, the Giants are the result of illicit sexual intercourse between the fallen Watchers and mortal women. They are the products of an unsanctioned mingling between separate realms. By contrast, in Severus the "Giants" (if we may use that term) are already present in the Realm of Darkness prior to that Realm's assault upon the Land of Light. These "Giants" are not the result of mixture, but are indeed part of its cause. In light of these divergent settings, it seems preferable to regard these creatures of "limitless size" as simply immortal entities whose divine status is expressed by means of their superhuman dimensions.[48]

Furthermore, it is unclear how much weight we should grant to Severus' comparative observation about the relative complexities of the "wars of the Giants" in Greek and Manichaean literature. Severus is not quoting from his Manichaean source at this point, but is instead concerned with demonstrating the absurdity of Mani's theological reasoning. His mention of a Manichaean gigantomachy indicates that Severus had knowledge of a Manichaean work which included among its contents a "war of the Giants." However, it does not necessarily follow that the work he is excerpting throughout his homily is the same text that features this war.

Similarly, the prominence of the designation "Tree of Life" in the Manichaean citations of Severus does not automatically necessitate a dependence upon the Book of Giants. Neither the extant Qumran nor the extant Middle Iranian recensions of the Book of Giants explicitly mention the phrase "Tree of Life," either as a symbol for Noah and his progeny, or as a circumlocution for the heavenly realm. While the Qumran fragments do employ arboreal symbolism for the depiction of Noah and his posterity, the equation of this "righteous plant" with a "Tree of Life" rests upon later Jewish exegetical traditions which may or may not have been known by Mani.[49] It, of course, remains possible that the Qumran imagery of the "tree with three shoots" was later developed by Mani, under the stimulation of Jewish tradition, into his distinctive "Tree of Life" symbolism. In this event, we might reasonably expect to uncover traces of this interpretation in the Middle Iranian versions of the Book of Giants, recensions of the earlier Qumran work which are replete with Manichaean allegory and mythological motifs. Such, however, is not the case.

When we reconsider the Severus fragments from the perspective of the new textual evidence, there arise further difficulties with the accepted identification of the source of the quotations. As we have seen, the patriarch Enoch plays an important role in the Book of Giants, and his name survives in both the Qumran and Manichaean fragments of that work. No trace of Enoch is visible in the Severus citations. Indeed, as we have seen, a whole host of *dramatis personae* figure in the Book of Giants; most of their names are preserved in both versions of our textual witnesses. We, however, search in vain for figures corresponding to Shemiḥazah, Azazel, Baraq'el, 'Ohyah, Hahyah, or Mahaway within the testimony of Severus. There is, by contrast, almost no trace of anthropomorphism in these citations.

Neither the members of the Realm of Darkness nor those of the Realm of Light are identified by name in Severus. Instead, the narrative supplied by Severus has an abstract, almost philosophical flavor that contrasts sharply with the aggadic nature of the known portions of the Book of Giants.[50]

This observation perhaps provides a clue for the resolution of the relationship between the two sets of texts under discussion. Both sets describe a course of events which produces "mixture" between two separate realms of reality. These events, however, transpire at two different points in primal history. The Severus fragments situate the "mixture" in the era before the creation of the earth. The Book of Giants describes an unsanctioned "mixture" that took place during the era of the antediluvian patriarchs. While the motif of "mixture" typologically unites these disparate narratives, they nevertheless exhibit two distinct settings.

The Severus fragments are, furthermore, rather abstract and impersonal in comparison to the mythological narrative of the Book of Giants. In place of actors like Shemiḥazah, Mahaway, or Enoch are unidentified "entities" (*kyn', 'yt'*), "members" (*hdm'*), or "fruits" (*p'r'*). The domain of God is qualified by substantives like "Goodness" (*ṭb'*) and "Light" (*nhwr'*), while the locale where the forces of wickedness sojourn is "Evil" (*byš'*) and "Darkness" (*ḥšwk'*). The prominent use of the Greek loanword "Hyle" (*hwl'*) as an alternative designation for the lower realm should also be remarked. Attention is given to the spatial orientation, intellectual capacity, and sensory powers of each region and its inhabitants. This quasi-philosophical exposition is augmented by a metaphorical description of each of these realms as, respectively, the "Tree of Life" and the "Tree of Death."

The employment and development of this latter imagery is somewhat surprising in its context, suggesting that an exegetical treatment of the Eden narrative found in Genesis 2–3 may underlie the structure of this exposition. In addition to this possibility, it will be recalled from our discussion above that the Manichaean "Tree of Life" is frequently linked with the periodic "flowering" of authentic Apostles of Light upon earth, notably figures like Seth, Enoch, Noah, Jesus, and Mani himself. They are "shoots," so to speak, of the original Tree of Life in the realm of Light that are "transplanted" to earth for the purpose of instructing humankind regarding the preservation and redemption of the captured elements of Light.[51] The identification of the Tree of Life with God underscores the divine mission of these messengers. The tragic consequences of the mixing of Light and Darkness will eventually be overcome with human assistance.

The Book of Giants also depicts the deleterious effects of a forbidden "mixture" of two disparate realms of existence. As we have seen, the Book of Giants develops this idea by means of a mythological story based upon Genesis 6:1–4 and related works such as 1 Enoch 6–11. In chronological terms, the event described by the Book of Giants occurs well after the initial mixture recounted in the Severus fragments. This raises the suspicion that the Severus citations and the Book of the Giants should be viewed as a narrative continuum. The Severus fragments might properly be characterized as "prehistory" in relation to the "historical" discourse of the Book of Giants. Severus transmits the theological prolegomenon to the event depicted in the Book of Giants. Other witnesses to Manichaean cosmogonical teaching affirm that there was a narrative continuitv between the initial mixture which occured in "prehistory" and subsequent attempts by the forces of Darkness to retain and further disperse the captured elements of Light. One of these attempts is presumably recounted in the Book of Giants.

The Severus fragments therefore need no longer be identified with Mani's Book of Giants. They instead set the scene for further efforts on the part of the realm of Darkness to maintain and intensify the initial mixture that was achieved.

Notes to Chapter Three

[1] H. Chadwick refers to Severus as "the greatest of the Monophysite theologians" (cf. his *The Early Church* [Baltimore, 1967], 207). Discussions of the importance of Severus, with further references, are provided by E. Honigmann, *Evêques et évêchés monophysites d'Asie antérieure au VIe siècle* (Louvain, 1951), 19–25; B. Spuler, "Die westsyrische (monophysitische/jakobitische) Kirche," in *Religionsgeschichte des Orients in der Zeit der Weltreligionen* (*Handbuch der Orientalistik* Bd.8, Ab.2) (Leiden, 1961), 180–83; A.S. Atiya, *A History of Eastern Christianity* (Notre Dame, 1968), 179; W.S. McCullough, *A Short History of Syriac Christianity to the Rise of Islam* (Chico, 1982), 81–82; and especially W.H.C. Frend, *The Rise of the Monophysite Movement* (Cambridge, 1972), 201–76. Early biographies of Severus were composed by Zacharias Scholasticus (cf. M.-A. Kugener, ed., "Vie de Sévère," *PO* 2 [1907], 7–115) and John of Beit-Aphthonia (cf. M.-A. Kugener, ed., "Vie de Sévère," *PO* 2 [1907], 207–64).

[2] The synod proceedings are conveniently reproduced by M.-A. Kugener, "Textes grecs relatifs à Sévère," *PO* 2 (1907), 336–61. See also A. de Halleux, "La chronique melkite abrégée du Ms. Sinaï Syr. 10," *Le Muséon* 91 (1978), 38–39.

[3] An early translation of the homilies of Severus was made in the sixth century by Paul of Callinicus. This recension, known from four manuscripts, was published by I.E. Rahmani, *Studia Syriaca IV* (Beirut, 1909). A description of these manuscripts is provided by M. Brière in the introduction to his edition (see next note) of the last five homilies of Severus, 18–33. A later revision of Paul's translation was carried out at the beginning of the eighth century by the renowned polymath Jacob of Edessa.

[4] The complete text of the 123rd homily is available in Rahmani, 48–89 (text), and M. Brière, "Les Homiliae Cathedrales de Sévère d'Antioche, traduction syriaque de Jacques d'Edesse CXX à CXXV," *PO* 29 (1960), 124–89.

[5] F. Cumont and M.-A. Kugener, *Recherches sur le manichéisme* (Bruxelles, 1908–12), 83–172.

[6] Syriac text with translation on pages 89–150. The published text is based upon British Museum Add. 12159, dated 867/8 C.E. Cf. W. Wright, *Catalogue of the Syriac Manuscripts in the British Museum* (London, 1870–72), II 534–46.

[7] Cumont-Kugener, *Recherches*, 151.

[8] Conveniently set forth in tabular form in ibid., 152–56. For the complete text of Theodoret's remarks on Manichaeism, see Migne, *Patrologia Graecae* 83, cols. 377–81.

[9] I. de Beausobre, *Histoire critique de Manichée et du manichéisme* (Amsterdam, 1734–39; repr. Leipzig, 1970), I 221–23 and 427–28; G. Flügel, *Mani, seine Lehre*

und seine Schriften (Leipzig, 1862; repr. Osnabrück, 1969), 355–56; K. Kessler, *Mani: Forschungen über die manichäische Religion* (Berlin, 1889), 197–98.

[10] Flügel, *Mani*, 72–73 (text); 102–3 (translation). Cumont and Kugener also point out that the identification of this work as the "Book of Mysteries" relies upon a misinterpretation of Epiphanius by Beausobre. Cf. their *Recherches*, 157–58.

[11] Cumont-Kugener, *Recherches*, 160–61.

[12] "... that the many gods of the pagans and the conflict of the Giants are modest, even miniscule, alongside his (i.e., Mani's) blasphemy" (Cumont-Kugener, *Recherches*, 138 ll.2–4; Brière, *PO* 29 [1960], 170 ll.20–21).

[13] They, however, caution: "Mais dans l'ignorance où nous sommes du contenu exact des divers ouvrages manichéens, il convient d'être très réservé." (Cumont-Kugener, *Recherches*, 161).

[14] P. Alfaric, *Les écritures manichéennes* (Paris, 1918–19), II 27–33; A. Adam, "Manichäismus," in *Religionsgeschichte des Orient in der Zeit der Weltreligionen* (cf. n.1 above), 106 (but note that page 110 expresses more reserve); idem, *Texte zum Manichäismus* (Berlin, 1969[2]), 11 (the extracts from Severus are presented under the rubric "Aus dem «Buch der Giganten»"); B. Aland, "Mani und Bardesanes — Zur Entstehung des manichäischen Systems," in A. Dietrich, ed., *Synkretismus im syrisch-persischen Kulturgebiet* (Göttingen, 1975), 129; P. Nagel, "Die apokryphen Apostelakten des 2. und 3. Jahrhunderts in der manichäischen Literatur," in K.-W. Tröger, ed., *Gnosis und Neues Testament* (Gütersloh, 1973), 164; S.N.C. Lieu, *Manichaeism in the Later Roman Empire and Medieval China: A Historical Survey* (Manchester, 1985; repr. 1988), 9.

[15] V. Arnold-Döben, *Die Bildersprache des Manichäismus* (Köln, 1978), 8–9; 37–39; H.-J. Klimkeit, "Der dreistämmige Baum: Bemerkungen zur manichäischen Kunst und Symbolik," in *Kulturwissenschaften: Festgabe für Wilhelm Perpeet zum 65. Geburtstag* (Bonn, 1980), 253; idem, *Manichaean Art and Calligraphy* (Leiden, 1982), 31. See the discussion of Qumran Book of Giants fragment QG4B above.

[16] It is true that the designation "Tree of Life" does not figure in the extant remains of the Qumran Book of Giants, but the synonymity of the concepts "tree of life" and "righteous plant" is well attested in contemporaneous Jewish literature. According to the ideology of 1 Enoch 6–16, Noah is the "righteous plant" spared by the Flood.

[17] Aside from Cumont-Kugener and a rendering of the entire homily by Rahmani (Latin) and Brière (French), translations of the Severus "Giants" fragments also appear in Alfaric, *Les écritures*, II 27–30; Adam, *Texte*[2], 11–14; and J.P. Asmussen – A. Böhlig, eds., *Die Gnosis III: Der Manichäismus* (Zürich and München, 1980), 133–37.

[18] The ontological primacy of the "two principles" is a fundamental tenet of Manichaean ideology and is stressed in practically all extant sources. The "two principles" (here designated *ryšnwt'*) are frequently termed the "two roots" in Manichaean literature; cf. J.J. Overbeck, ed., *S. Ephraemi Syri ... Opera Selecta* (Oxford, 1865), 64 l.20: *try 'qryn*. H.-C. Puech has suggested that the subsequent

symbolism of the "two roots" as "Trees" represents a natural development of this botanical metaphor; cf. his *Le manichéisme* (Paris, 1949), 159–61 n.285. Note already Cumont-Kugener, *Recherches*, 162 n.1. One might recall the motif of "shoots" (*šršyn*) in the Giant Hahyah's dream recounted in QG4A and 4B above.

[19] *hwl'* = Greek ὕλη, literally "matter." The use of "Hyle" as a designation for the second of the two Manichaean uncreated "principles" is already attested in Alexander of Lycopolis. Cf. his *contra Manichaei* VI (A. Brinkmann, ed., *Alexandri Lycopolitani contra Manichaei opiniones disputatio* [Leipzig, 1895], 9 l.17): Δύο ἀρχὰς ὑποτίθεται, θεὸν καὶ ὕλην; also II–III (Brinkmann, 4 l.24–6 l.22), and Brinkmann's index *s.v.* ὕλη. Note E. Beck, ed., *Des heiligen Ephraem des Syrers: Hymnen contra Haereses* CSCO 169 (Louvain, 1957), 52 ll.3–8. For further discussion and references, see H.H. Schaeder, "Urform und Fortbildungen des manichäischen Systems," in F. Saxl, ed., *Vorträge der Bibliothek Warburg IV* (Leipzig, 1927), 112–18; reprinted in H.H. Schaeder, *Studien zur orientalischen Religionsgeschichte* (Darmstadt, 1968), 62–68; Puech, *Le manichéisme*, 161 n.286.

[20] Compare the testimony of the *Chronicon Maroniticum*: "Mani says in his teaching that there were two original beings: God and Hyle. The former was good and possessed the east, north, west, and upper regions; and the latter being which he called Hyle which was evil possessed the southern regions" (I. Guidi, ed., *Chronica Minora* [Paris, 1903], 60 ll.10–13), essentially repeated by Michael the Syrian in his universal chronicle (cf. J.-B. Chabot, ed., *Chronique de Michel le Syrien patriarche jacobite d'Antioche (1166–1199)* [Paris, 1899–1924], IV 118). For similar statements in other sources, see F.C. Baur, *Das manichäische Religionssystem nach den Quellen neu untersucht und entwickelt* (Tübingen, 1831), 27.

[21] Cf. *Kephalaia* 22:32: "But [the] evil Tree is Hyle ...." See *Kephalaia* 16–23 *passim* for the dualistic schema of the "good tree" and the "worthless tree." Note also W. Sundermann, *Mitteliranische manichäische Texte kirchengeschichtlichen Inhalts* (Berlin, 1981), 91 ll.1440–41.

[22] Compare the imagery used in the so-called "Naassene Psalm" that is preserved by Hippolytus (*Refutatio* 5.10.2) concerning the plight of the "soul" (ψυχή) upon earth: "Sometimes she [i.e., the soul] would live in a royal palace and look at the light; but sometimes she is being thrown in a den, and there she weeps." Translation taken from M. Marcovich, "The Naassene Psalm in Hippolytus (*Haer.* 5.10.2)," in B. Layton, ed., *The Rediscovery of Gnosticism ... Volume II: Sethian Gnosticism* (Leiden, 1981), 771.

[23] Cf. *Acta Archelai* 10: "that tree in Paradise by which men know what is good is Jesus himself ...." Note the curious statement contained in the 21st *memra* of the *Liber Graduum*, a fourth-century Syriac treatise of uncertain provenance: "The Good Tree who is in that World of Light, invisible to the sight of mortal man, Jesus our Lord; and he is the Tree of Life, granting life to all by his fruits" (M. Kmosko, ed., "Liber Graduum," in R. Graffin, ed., *Patrologia Syriaca* [Paris, 1894–1926], III 589 ll.3–6).

[24] For "north" as the location of the Tree of Life, note especially the

Ethiopic version of 1 Enoch 25:5: "From its fruit (i.e., of the Tree of Life) life will be given to the elect, and toward the north it will be planted, in a sacred place by the abode of the Lord, the Eternal King." The Greek version of this verse reads "food" (εἰς βοράν) instead of "north" (εἰς βορρᾶν), understanding the fruit of the Tree as sustenance for the elect. The Aramaic is unfortunately not extant for this passage. One might compare the statement found in the Coptic Gnostic treatise *On the Origin of the World* that both the Tree of Life and the Tree of Knowledge are situated "in the *north* of Paradise" (J.M. Robinson, ed., *The Nag Hammadi Library in English* [San Francisco, 1977; repr., 1981], 169). For a thorough discussion of this latter tradition, see M. Tardieu, *Trois mythes gnostiques: Adam, Eros et les animaux d'Egypte dans un écrit de Nag Hammadi (II,5)* (Paris, 1974), 190–93. "North" is also the locus of the Mandaean "World of Light"; see *Right Ginza* 7:11 and especially 280:28–281:22 (M. Lidzbarski, ed., *Ginzā: Der Schatz oder das grosse Buch der Mandäer* [Göttingen, 1925]) and the remarks of E.S. Drower, *The Mandaeans of Iraq and Iran* (Oxford, 1937), 18–19 n.9, and E. Peterson, "Urchristentum und Mandäismus," *ZNW* 27 (1928), 94–95. While West Semitic religions traditionally situate the dwelling-place of the deities in the north (*ṣaphon*), later Jewish tradition identified the "north" as the locale of evil spirits and darkness, usually citing Jeremiah 1:14 as a proof-text. Note *Pirkei de Rabbi Eliezer* 3 (M. Higger, ed., *Horeb* 8 [1944], 89–90) which serves as the source for the identical assertion in the medieval *Chronicle of Jerahmeel* (cf. M. Gaster, *The Chronicles of Jerahmeel* [London, 1899; repr. New York, 1971], 6–7). Compare also bT Baba Bathra 25a–b; *Pesiqta Rabbati* 46 (ed. Friedmann 188b); *Bamidbar Rabba* 2:9; *Midrash Konen* (*apud* A. Jellinek, ed., *Bet ha-Midrasch* [Leipzig, 1853–77; repr. Jerusalem, 1938], II 30). Note too *Bahir* §162 (R. Margolioth, ed., *Sefer ha-Bahir* [Jerusalem, 1951], 70–71 = §109 Scholem): כל רעה אשר היא באה לכל יושבי הארץ מצפון היא באה, discussed by G. Scholem, "Kabbalah und Mythus," *Eranos-Jahrbuch* 17 (1949), 295 (English translation "Kabbalah and Myth," in G. Scholem, *On the Kabbalah and its Symbolism* [New York, 1965; repr. New York, 1978], 92). A prophecy contained in the *Book of Elchasai* (Hippolytus, *Refutatio* 9.16.4) which predicts an eschatological battle "among the wicked angels of the north" (μεταξὺ τῶν ἀγγέλων τῆς ἀσεβείας τῶν ἄρκτων) is probably based upon the Gog and Magog tradition of Ezekiel 38–39, the attribute *mlk* "king," granted to Gog by Ezekiel 38:2 and LXX Amos 7:1 and Magog in the Syriac Cave of Treasures (see n.27 below), perhaps being corrupted to *ml'k* "angel." Cf. W.Bousset, *Hauptprobleme der Gnosis* (Göttingen, 1907; repr. Göttingen, 1973), 156 n.1.

[25] That is, the Kingdom of Light is of infinite extension on every side *except that one* which adjoins the Kingdom of Darkness. Compare the statement of Augustine, *Contra epistulam fundamenti* 22: "If then on one side of the region of Light there was the race of Darkness, what bounded it on the other side or sides? The Manichaeans say nothing in reply to this; but when pressed, they say that on the other sides of the region of Light, as they call it, is infinite, that is, extends throughout boundless space." Translation adapted from that of R. Stothert, "St. Augustin: Against the Epistle of Manichaeus called Fundamental," in P. Schaff,

ed., *A Select Library of the Nicene and Post-Nicene Fathers of the Christian Church, First Series Volume IV: St. Augustin: The Writings Against the Manichaeans, and Against the Donatists* (repr. New York, 1901), 138. Presumably the "wall" (*šwr'*) mentioned in the next fragment lies only upon the southern frontier of the Region of Light.

[26] The so-called *Apocalypse of Moses*, actually a Greek recension of the *Life of Adam and Eve*, mentions "walls" surrounding Paradise: καὶ εὐθέως ἐκρεμάσθη παρὰ τῶν τειχῶν τοῦ παραδείσου ... "And immediately he (the serpent) dangled himself from *the walls of Paradise*" (17:1). Text cited from D.A. Bertrand, ed., *La vie grecque d'Adam et Eve* (Paris, 1987), 80. Compare, however, the testimony of al-Nadīm in his *Fihrist*: "Mani said: The Luminous World adjoins the Dark World, *(having) no barrier between them*. The Light contacts the Darkness on its surface" (Flügel, *Mani*, 53 ll.4–6). For discussions of the nature of the "boundary" dividing Light from Darkness, with citations from relevant sources, see Flügel, *Mani*, 187–92; Puech, *Le manichéisme*, 162–63 n.293; and A.V.W. Jackson, *Researches in Manichaeism* (New York, 1932; repr. New York, 1965), 200–201. According to *Acta Archelai* 24, Mani identified the separating "boundary" or "wall" (τεῖχος) with the *raqia'* of Genesis 1:6–8.

[27] The association of the southern quarter with "evil" has some basis in tradition-history. As A. Adam has pointed out (*Texte*^{2}, 11 n.6), Magog is termed the "king of the south" in the Syriac Cave of Treasures: "And when Magog, the king of the south, heard (the news of the foundation of Jerusalem), he came to him (i.e., Melchizedek) and beheld his form and spoke with him and gave to him offerings and gifts." Text translated from C. Bezold, ed., *Die Schatzhöhle »Mĕ'ārath Gazzē«* (Leipzig, 1883–88; repr. Amsterdam, 1981), 152 ll.1–3. Compare also Sibylline Oracles 3.319–20: "Woe to you, *land of Gog and Magog*, situated in the midst of *Ethiopian* rivers." J.J. Collins suggests that the location of Gog and Magog in Ethiopia is probably an exegetical development of the reference to Cush in Ezekiel 38:5; cf. his "Sibylline Oracles," in J.H. Charlesworth, ed., *The Old Testament Pseudepigrapha* (New York, 1983–85), I 369. Gog ha-Magog (later Gog *and* Magog) is normally understood as an eschatological threat emanating from the *north*. Note in particular Ezekiel 39:2: "and I shall bring you (i.e., Gog) *from the far north*" (*myrkty ṣpwn*), as well as Genesis 10:2, 1 Chronicles 1:5–7, and the discussion in n.24 above.

[28] The *Zohar* also refers to a "Tree of Death" (*'yln' dmwt'*) as the polar opposite of a "Tree of Life" (*'yln' dḥyy*). When night falls, the Tree of Death has dominion over this world, and the Tree of Life is removed to the heavenly heights. The "darkness" of the night is produced by the Tree of Death, which unfurls its branches at this time. Cf. *Sefer ha-Zohar* (repr. of Vilna edition, New York, 1954), III 119a, 120b–121a.

[29] For an enumeration of some of the denizens of Darkness, see the following fragment from Severus as well as the text of Augustine quoted in n.31 below. See also n.37 below.

[30] Compare *Acta Archelai* 17: "Fornications, adulteries, murders, avarice, and all evil deeds are the fruits of that evil root." This image is doubtlessly derived from texts like Matthew 7:17–18 (quoted by Mani in *Acta Archelai* 5 and

13): "Thus every healthy tree (πᾶν δένδρον ἀγαθόν) produces good fruit (καρποὺς καλούς), but the diseased tree (τὸ σαπρὸν δένδρον) produces rotten fruit (καρποὺς πονηρούς)"; cf. also Matthew 12:13; Luke 6:43. The last text is explicitly quoted in the *Kephalaia* (17:2ff.) when Mani's disciples question their master concerning the proper interpretation of the "two trees" described in the Christian Gospel (εὐαγγέλιον). The usage of the adjectives *ṭb'* "good" and *byš'* "evil" in the fragments preserved by Severus is paralleled in the Old Syriac and Peshitta versions of the New Testament verses.

[31] Compare the description of the Realm of Darkness provided in Augustine, *Contra epistulam fundamenti* 19:

> In one direction on the border of this bright and holy land there was a Land of Darkness deep and vast in extent, where abode fiery bodies, destructive races. Here was boundless darkness, flowing from the same source in immeasurable abundance, with the productions properly belonging to it. Beyond this were muddy turbid waters with their inhabitants; and inside of them winds terrible and violent with their prince and their progenitors. Then again a fiery region of destruction, with its chiefs and peoples. And similarly inside of this a race full of smoke and gloom, where abode the dreadful prince and chief of all, having around him innumerable princes, himself the mind and source of them all. Such are the five natures of the pestiferous land.

(Trans. Stothert [see n.25 above], 136.) The concept of Darkness "flowing" from a source might be compared with a similar metaphor contained in the Qumran *Serek ha-Yaḥad*: במעין אור תולדות האמת וממקור חושך תולדות העול "from a spring of light are the generations of truth, but from the fountain of darkness are the generations of wickedness" (1QS 3:19). See also 1QM 16:1; 1QH 18:29.

[32] *'lm' dnwhr'* "worlds of Light" or perhaps "Aeons of Light." Compare the terminology used by the Father of Greatness (the Manichaean supreme deity who dwells in the Region of Light) in Theodore bar Konai's account of the Manichaean cosmogonic myth: "The Father of Greatness took thought and said: I will not send any of the Five Shekinahs from these Aeons (*'lmy hlyn*; cf. H.J. Polotsky, "Manichäismus," in *Paulys Real-Encyklopädie der klassischen Altertumswissenschaft* Supplementband VI [Stuttgart, 1935], 251, reprinted in G. Widengren, ed., *Der Manichäismus* [Darmstadt, 1977], 115) to do battle, because they were created by me for tranquility and peace" (ed. Scher, 313 ll.23–26). The same word describes the five "worlds" or "Aeons" of Darkness (ibid., ll.18–21). See Cumont-Kugener, *Recherches*, 11 n.3.

[33] The random "turbulence" (*šgwšy'*) of the "members" of the Region of Darkness might be compared to the chaotic, undirected motion of the four (or more) uncreated "elements" (*'yty'*) of Bardaiṣanite cosmology. See especially Aland, "Mani und Bardesanes" (cf. n.14 above), 130–31, and H.J.W. Drijvers, *Bardaiṣan of Edessa* (Assen, 1966), 96–126. *Šgwšy'* also possesses the connotation

of "sedition" or "rebellion," and one is tempted to connect with the present context the occasional references to the "rebels" in Manichaean literature; see *CMC* 16:7; 29:4; *Psalm-Book* 1:25–27; 9:29–30; 213:6–9; Theodore bar Konai (ed. Scher), 318 ll.2–4.

[34] Note the phrasing of *Kephalaia* 32:12–13.

[35] Compare the statement of al-Nadīm regarding the beliefs of the Dayṣānīyah; i.e., followers of the teachings of Bardaiṣan: "[Some of the Dayṣānīyah] relate that Light is a living entity, possessing senses (and) cognizance, but that Darkness by contrast is blind, having no sense perception or cognizance ..." (Flügel, *Mani*, 161 ll.11–13).

[36] Literally "hyle" (*hwl'*), employed here not as a proper name, but in the common Greek connotation of "stuff" or "material." Note Wisdom of Solomon 11:17a: "For your powerful hand, which created the world out of amorphous matter (ἐξ ἀμόρφου ὕλης) ...."

[37] Compare Augustine, *Contra epistulam fundamenti* 19 (cited in n.31 above): "... a Land of Darkness deep and vast in extent, where abode fiery bodies, destructive races." According to some Jewish traditions, (based ultimately upon Psalm 104:4), the angels were created from fire, and those angels who abide in God's presence are clad in garments of fire. See 2 Enoch 29; 2 Baruch 21:6–7; bT Hagigah 14a; *Pirkei de Rabbi Eliezer* 4 and note especially ibid. 22 with reference to the fiery nature of the "fallen angels": רבי יהושע אומר המלאכים אש לוהט הם שנאמר (Psalm 104:4) משרתיו אש לוהט והוא בא כבעלת בשר ודם ואינה נשרפת את הגוף אלא בשעה שנפלו ממקום קדושתן חזר כחן וקומתן כבני אדם ולבושו גוש ועפר שנאמר (Job 7:5) לבש בשרי רמה וגוש עפר, cited from the edition of M. Higger, *Horeb* 9 (1946), 146.

[38] *lhlyn mn gyr 'yt hw' lhwn gwšm' qšy' wbrbwt' 'ytyhwn hww dl' sk'*. See notes 11–13 above. With regard to *gwšm' qšy'*, compare *Kephalaia* 31:8–16; 68:4–5.

[39] For similar rosters of the inhabitants of the primordial Land of Darkness, commonly transmitted as a pentad, see the citation of Augustine in n.31 above, as well as Augustine, *De haeresibus* 46 (*apud* Adam, *Texte*², 66 l.45); Theodoret, *Compendium haereticarum fabularum* 1.26 (*apud* Cumont-Kugener, *Recherches*, 152 ll.26–28); Theodore bar Konai (ed. Scher, 313 ll.19–21); al-Nadīm, *Fihrist* (*apud* Flügel, *Mani*, 53 ll.3–4; 54 ll.13–14; 55 l.8–56 l.5); al-Shahrastānī, *Milal* (ed. Cureton, 189 ll.15–19); Ibn al-Murtaḍā (*apud* Kessler, *Mani*, 347 ll.4–8). Important discussions of these lists are those of Flügel, *Mani*, 205–6; Puech, *Le manichéisme*, 75; and especially idem, "Le Prince des Ténèbres en son royaume," in *Satan* (Paris, 1948), 136–74. *Kephalaia* 21:28–29 speaks of "five members (μέλος)" of the "worthless tree"; cf. also *Kephalaia* 30–34.

[40] *ss' hy mḥblnyt'*. Adam (*Texte*², 14 n.11) refers to Mark 9:44, a passage not contained in many New Testament manuscripts. There we read that among the terrors of Gehenna are numbered "the worm (σκώληξ) that never dies, and the unquenchable fire," a manifest borrowing from Isaiah 66:24. Whether this passage is the source of Mani's "worm of corruption" remains unclear.

[41] Literally "strained," from *šḥl*. See C. Brockelmann, *Lexicon Syriacum* 2nd edition (Halle, 1928; reprint Hildesheim, 1982), 768–69. Compare the use of *ṣll* in Theodore bar Konai (ed. Scher, 315 ll.18–22): "Then the Living Spirit

revealed his forms (*sic*) to the sons of Darkness, *and he strained out (some) light* from the light that these had consumed from those five luminous divinities, and made (from it) the sun and moon ...."

[42] Adam (*Texte*^{2}, 14 n.12) calls attention to the language of Romans 9:5 ("the Messiah, *who is God over all*," Greek ὁ Χριστὸς ... ὁ ὢν ἐπὶ πάντων Θεός; Syriac *mšyḥ' ... d'ytwhy 'lh' d'l kl*).

[43] Was God then not responsible for the Flood of Noah's day? There seems to be a reflection here of the Gnostic concept that the Deluge was the work of an incompetent, malevolent Demiurge in an effort to extirpate representatives of the "righteous seed of Seth." See *Apocalypse of Adam* 69:2ff. (Robinson, ed., *Nag Hammadi Library*, 258); *Gospel of the Egyptians* 61:2–5 (ibid., 202); and in general A.F.J. Klijn, "An Analysis of the Use of the Story of the Flood in the Apocalypse of Adam," in R. van den Broek – M.J. Vermaseren, eds., *Studies in Gnosticism and Hellenistic Religions presented to Gilles Quispel on the Occasion of his 65th Birthday* (Leiden, 1981), 218–26. How this conception of the Flood could be harmonized with its purgative function in the Jewish story of the Giants is problematic. Note Theodoret, *Compendium haereticarum fabularum* 1.26 (*apud* Cumont-Kugener, *Recherches*, 152 ll.31–32): οὔτε ὕδωρ ἵνα κατακλυσμὸν ἐπενέγκῃ. κατακλυσμός is of course the Greek word used for Noah's Flood. See LXX Genesis 6–9 *passim*; Josephus, *Antiquities* 1.92–93; *Contra Apionem* 1.130; Berossus (*apud* Josephus, *Ant.* 1.158); Nicolaus of Damascus (*apud* Josephus, *Ant.* 1.95); Pseudo-Eupolemus (*apud* Eusebius, *Praeparatio Evangelica* 9.17.2; *Testament of Reuben* 5:6; *Testament of Naphtali* 3:5; *Testament of Benjamin* 7:4.

[44] This passage is quoted in Greek by Theodoret, ibid., ll.30–34.

[45] Compare the statement of Theodore bar Konai (ed. Scher, 314 ll.6–10): "Then Primal Man gave himself and his five sons as food to the five sons of Darkness, just as a man who has an enemy mixes deadly poison in a cake (and) gives (it) to him"; also, the Chinese Manichaean treatise published by Chavannes and Pelliot: "Les cinq sortes de démons se collèrent aux cinq corps lumineaux, telle la mouche qui s'attache au miel, tel l'oiseau qui est retenu par la glu, tel le poisson qui a avelé l'hameçon" (E. Chavannes – P. Pelliot, eds., *Un traité manichéen retrouvé en Chine* [Paris, 1913], 18). See further Puech, *Le manichéisme*, 77; Jackson, *Researches*, 226 n.17.

[46] CD 2:19: כרום ארזים גבהם וכהרים גויותיהם. Compare Amos 2:9a: ואנכי השמדתי את האמרי מפניהם אשר כגבה ארזים גבהו וחסן הוא כאלונים.

[47] Presumably this information could have figured in QG1 2–5. Note also 6Q14 1: [*yg*] *bh lgb*[*h*] *kpyl*, perhaps a reference to the height of the Flood waters in comparison with the height of the Giants. This latter text is cited from K. Beyer, *Die aramäischen Texte vom Toten Meer* (Göttingen, 1984), 268.

[48] For example, see 1 Chronicles 21:16, and note the remarks of R. Otto, *The Idea of the Holy* trans. J.W. Harvey (Oxford, 1923; repr. 1973), 40.

[49] See the discussion of Fragments QG4A and QG4B in Chapter Two above.

[50] "The [Manichaean] system is expressed both in a mythical and in an abstract-philosophical form, the latter, however, never being able to liberate

itself completely from its mythical presuppositions." Quotation taken from G. Widengren, "Manichaeism and its Iranian Background," in E. Yarshater, ed., *The Cambridge History of Iran, Volume 3(2): The Seleucid, Parthian and Sasanian Periods* (Cambridge, 1983), 972.

[51] See n.49 above, and especially Chapter Two, n.259.

Chapter Four

Manichaean Cosmogony and Jewish Traditions

We have seen from the foregoing analysis of the Qumran Book of Giants the close relationship that these fragments have with the parallel narratives about the descent of the Watchers and birth of the Giants in both Jewish and Jewish-Christian literature. We have also had occasion to notice the correspondences that exist between the Qumran and Manichaean recensions of that work. Mani's dependence upon a text like that of the Qumran Book of Giants for his own canonical production is clearly evident.[1] There are, however, further indications that the Jewish legend about the coming of the Watchers and the deeds of the Giants played a decidedly fundamental role in the origin, structure, and development of Mani's cosmogonical teaching. An exploration of the structural analogues between the Jewish sources on the one hand and the most important testimony concerning Manichaean cosmogony on the other will form the subject of this chapter.

The story of the Watchers and their Giant progeny can be shown to exhibit at least three distinct forms in Jewish and Christian tradition. The chronological relationship among the three versions of the story is difficult to determine due to the fact that the surviving narratives or allusive summaries conflate elements from two or more of the distinct forms. These forms, however, can be unraveled with relative ease from the narratives wherein they figure.

The first form of the story of the Watchers places emphasis upon the sin of the Watchers and its (that is, the sin's) locus in heaven. In this version, the Watchers perceive the beauty of mortal women from their station in heaven and are led into immoral activity by their resultant lust for these women. Classic representatives of this version are 1 Enoch 6, 1 Enoch 86–88, and 1 Enoch 106–107 (= 1QapGen 2).

Sometimes combined with this first form is another version of the story of the Watchers which gives a different motivation for the descent of the heavenly beings. According to this second version, the Watchers do not commit any sin while in heaven, and their descent to earth has an originally benevolent intention. It is stated that the Watchers were commissioned by God to instruct humanity in matters of morality and piety, but that after they arrived on earth, they were seduced by the beauty of mortal women and so led astray. Thus the Watchers were not originally motivated by evil intentions, but instead became exposed to sin only after an unspecified sojourn upon earth among human beings. A further development of the "instructional" motif also is connected with this version of the story. Originally commissioned to teach humanity the rules of justice, righteousness, and piety, the Watchers instead instruct humans in various arts and technologies which increase the spread of lawlessness and impiety upon earth. These "forbidden sciences" include metallurgy, herbology, magic, and astrology. Linked with the proliferation of these techniques is the appearance of idolatry. Allusions to the originally benevolent mission of the Watchers occur in Jubilees, the *Clementine Homilies*, medieval Jewish and Islamic folklore, and perhaps the Qumran Book of Giants. Emphasis upon the teaching of "forbidden secrets" appears in those sources as well as in 1 Enoch 7–8.

A third form of the story of the Watchers surfaces primarily in Christian sources. In this version, the heavenly Watchers are transformed into the human descendants of the patriarch Seth. Similarly, the mortal women are designated the "daughters of Cain," and responsibility for the corruption of the *beney Seth* is laid at the feet of the latter group. Herein we observe an attempt by exegetes to absolve heavenly beings of any possible wrongdoing by denying that the *beney ha'elohim* were angels at all. Analogous interpretive tendencies occur in the classical Jewish exegeses of Genesis 6:1–4. Although this particular interpretation of the *beney ha'elohim* as "sons of Seth" and the *benot ha'adam* as "daughters of Cain" is attested most frequently in patristic literature,[2] it has been argued that the groundwork for such an exegesis was already laid in Jewish texts, and that therefore this interpretation could very well be Jewish in origin.[3]

A common concern uniting all three versions of the story of the Watchers and the Giants is the question of the presence of evil in the created order. Of particular importance for the compilers of these stories is the role played by the heavenly Watchers in the dissemination of evil upon earth. An obsession with the origin of evil in the cosmos lies, as G.A.G. Stroumsa has stressed, "at the root of the Gnostic rejection of the material world."[4] However, the forms of the myth of the Watchers and Giants that we have noted so far do not exhibit the strident polemic against the cosmos and its creator featured in classic Gnostic texts. There is no dualistic division between a "true God" and an incompetent or malevolent Demiurge. Yet the initial steps toward this eventual bifurcation within the divine realm are already discernible within the forms of the story of the Watchers and the Giants.[5]

In the first version of the story, as represented by 1 Enoch 6, the responsibility for the introduction of evil into the world is placed upon the heavenly Watchers. The Watchers perceive the physical beauty of human women, lust is aroused in them, and they resolve to descend from heaven to consummate their evil desires. Necessarily presupposed in this explanation for corruption is the inherent potential for the manifestation of evil throughout the entire created order, whether in heaven or upon earth. The Watchers or "angels" are the agents by whom this evil first achieves real existence. As a result of their decision to commit sin, evil is introduced into the human realm.

This conception of the origin of evil in the cosmos should be contrasted with the explanation offered in the second form of the story of the Watchers. There, it will be recalled, the Watchers only encounter the corrupting influence of evil after they descend to earth at the behest of God. Evil is thus present upon earth prior to the arrival of the Watchers. In light of their original commission to instruct humankind in the ways of righteousness and justice, it would appear that God was already taking steps to combat the presence of evil upon earth through these heavenly emissaries, only to be thwarted when the Watchers also succumb to its pernicious influence. Within this form of the story, the responsibility for the introduction of evil into the cosmos probably belongs to either Adam and Eve (their disobedience in the Garden) or Cain (his murder of Abel). Interestingly, one should note that no trace of either of these stories figures in the narratives which ascribe the introduction of evil to the Watchers (form 1). One should also observe that the Watchers are affected by evil only after they depart from heaven.[6] This is an important contrast to the conception found in the first form of the story. There, evil knows no spatial limitations: it can occur either in heaven or on earth, and indeed appears first in heaven. Here evil is spatially localized, manifesting itself only on earth. A significant step is thus taken toward the Manichaean demarcation of spheres of influence, as we shall see below.

The third form of the story advances the tendency to delimit the operation of evil by redefining the identity of the Watchers themselves. Apparently appalled that evil behavior could be ascribed to any being that participated in the divine economy, the promulgators of this form of the story deny that the Watchers are angels. In its most popular version, the Watchers are identified as the human progeny of the pious patriarch Seth. These worthies are led into ruin by the descendents of the wicked Cain. Thus evil is entirely removed from the divine realm.

Concern with both the problem of evil and redemption of that which is by nature good and pure from the power of evil also forms a central focus of Manichaean religious ideology. This concern is expressed most clearly in the accounts preserved of Manichaean cosmogonical teaching. There are four basic sources from which we can derive an accurate depiction of Mani's system. The first and most important is the account provided by the eighth-century Nestorian bishop Theodore bar Konai in his *Book of Scholia.* The eleventh and final *memra* of Theodore's theological treatise consists of an exposition and short description of the various heresies and sects known to Theodore either from the literary reports of earlier Christian heresiologists or from his personal acquaintance with the literature and practices of contemporary religious communities in Mesopotamia. Theodore's discussion of the Manichaean "heresy" is one of the longest and most detailed accounts contained in his tractate,[7] and it merits particular attention in light of its Syriac composition. Since we presume that Mani's native tongue was an eastern Aramaic dialect, it seems likely that Theodore employs terminology traceable to Mani himself in his description of Mani's teachings.

A second account of Manichaean cosmogonical teaching is found in the tenth-century encyclopaedia of knowledge prepared by al-Nadīm entitled *Kitāb al-Fihrist*.[8] This description, probably based upon Arabic translations of Manichaean literature, largely confirms the accuracy of the report supplied by Theodore bar Konai, but it also contains additional material that supplements and clarifies the information provided by the Nestorian bishop.[9]

Less voluminous but equally significant for the description of Manichaean cosmogonical doctrine are several Middle Persian and Sogdian fragments recovered from Turfan.[10] These testify regarding the Manichaean tradition as it was promulgated within Manichaean communities in Central Asia during the final half of the first millenium C.E. Aside from obvious terminological differences arising from the exigencies of translation, these accounts of primeval events attest the verity of the hostile testimonies transmitted by Theodore bar Konai and al-Nadīm. Finally, there are some allusions to cosmogonical events in Coptic Manichaean literature.[11] These allusions do not contradict what is found in the later testimonies and serve to confirm their essential authenticity.

In order that a comparison between the Jewish literature mentioned above and the Manichaean cosmogonical tradition might be readily effected, we insert at this point an English translation of the most important source for the recovery of Manichaean cosmogony, that of Theodore bar Konai.[12]

Theodore bar Konai on the Manichaeans

Regarding his abominable teaching: It is however proper that we set down in this book a little of the absurd blasphemy of Mani the wicked in order to confound[13] the Manichaeans. He (Mani) says that before heaven and earth and all that they contain came into being, there were Two Essences:[14] one Good and the other Evil. The Good Essence dwelt in the region of Light, and he terms him the Father of

Greatness,[15] and he says that there were dwelling (there) in addition to him (the Father) his five Shekinahs:[16] mind, knowledge, intellect, thought, reflection.[17] The Evil Essence he terms the King of Darkness,[18] and he says that he dwelt in the land of Darkness with his five Aeons: the Aeon of smoke, the Aeon of fire, the Aeon of wind, the Aeon of water, and the Aeon of darkness.[19] He says that when the King of Darkness contemplated ascending to the region of Light, those five Shekinahs (there) became agitated, and he says that at that time the Father of Greatness took thought and said: I will not send any of the five Shekinahs from these Aeons to do battle because they were created by me for tranquility and peace. Instead, I myself will go and make battle.

He says that the Father of Greatness evoked[20] the Mother of Life,[21] and the Mother of Life evoked the Primal Man,[22] and Primal Man evoked his five sons, like a man who puts on armor for battle.[23] He says that an angel whose name was *Nḥšbṭ* went out in front of him, holding in his hand a crown of victory,[24] and he says that he spread (or shed) light before Primal Man. When the King of Darkness saw him, he (the King) took thought and said, The thing that I desired which was distant, I have discovered nearby. Then Primal Man gave himself and his five sons as food to the five sons of Darkness,[25] just as a man who has an enemy mixes deadly poison in a cake (and) gives (it) to him.

And he says that when they had eaten them, the reasoning power of the five luminous deities was removed, and they became like a man bitten by a rabid dog or a serpent due to the venom of the sons of Darkness. He says that Primal Man regained his rationality and prayed seven times[26] to the Father of Greatness, and he (the Father) evoked the Second Evocation, the Friend of the Luminaries.[27] The Friend of the Luminaries evoked the Great *Ban*,[28] and the Great *Ban* evoked the Living Spirit.[29] The Living Spirit evoked his five sons: the Ornament of Splendor from his mind, the Great King of Honor from his knowledge, the Adamos of Light from his intellect, the King of Glory from his thought, and the Porter from his reflection.[30] They came to the land of Darkness and found Primal Man and his five sons engulfed by Darkness. Then the Living Spirit cried out with his voice, and the voice of the Living Spirit was like a sharp sword, and it uncovered the form of Primal Man, and he said to him: "Greetings to you, O Excellent One among evil entities, O Luminous One in the midst of Darkness, O Divine One dwelling among wrathful beasts who have no knowledge of his[31] glory!" Then Primal Man answered him and said: "Come in peace, O bringer of the merchandise of tranquility and peace!" And he said: "How do our fathers, the sons of Light,[32] fare in their city?"[33] The Caller[34] answered him: "They are faring well!" The Caller and the Respondent joined together and ascended to the Mother of Life and the Living Spirit.[35] The Living Spirit clothed himself with the Caller, and the Mother of Life clothed herself with the Respondent, her beloved son, and they descended to the land of Darkness where Primal Man and his sons were.

Then the Living Spirit commanded three of his sons,[36] that each should kill and should skin the archons,[37] the sons of Darkness, and bring (them) to the Mother of Life. The Mother of Life stretched out the heavens from their skins, and she made eleven heavens (*sic*!).[38] They threw down their bodies to the land of Darkness, and they made eight earths. And the five sons of the Living Spirit each completed their task — the Ornament of Splendor is the one who holds the five luminous deities by their loins, and below their loins the heavens were spread out, and the Porter is the one who bends upon one of his knees and supports the earths. After the heavens and earths were made, the Great King of Honor took a seat in the midst of the heavens and kept watch over the whole.[39]

Then the Living Spirit revealed his forms (*sic*)[40] to the sons of Darkness,[41] and he strained out (some) light from the light that these had consumed from those five luminous deities, and made (from it) the sun and the moon, and from the light which remained (after making these) vessel(s)[42] he made "wheels" (for) wind, water, and fire. He descended (and) forged them near the Porter. The King of Glory evoked and raised over them (the archons) a covering[43] so that they (the sun and moon?) can ascend over those archons who are subjugated[44] in the earths, so that they may serve the five luminous deities and not be harmed by the venom of the archons.

He says then the Mother of Life and Primal Man and the Living Spirit rose in prayer and beseeched the Father of Greatness. The Father of Greatness hearkened to them and evoked the Third Evocation, the Messenger.[45] The Messenger evoked twelve virgins[46] with their garments, crowns, and attributes — the first is majesty, the second wisdom, the third victory, the fourth persuasion, the fifth chastity, the sixth truth, the seventh faith, the eighth patience, the ninth uprightness, the tenth grace, the eleventh justice, and the twelfth light. When the Messenger came to those vessels (i.e., sun and moon), he appointed three servants to make the vessels move. He commanded the Great *Ban* to construct a new earth and three wheels for their (the vessels') ascending. When the vessels moved and reached the midst of heaven, the Messenger then revealed his male and female forms and became visible to all the archons, the sons of Darkness, both male and female.[47] At the appearance of the Messenger, who was beautiful in his forms, all of the archons became excited with desire, the males for the female image and the females for the male image. They began to eject as a result of their desire the light which they had consumed from the five luminous deities. Then the sin that was in them devised a plan. It mixed itself with the light[48] that came forth from the archons like hair in bread-dough, and sought to enter within (the emitted light).[49] Then the Messenger concealed his forms, and separated the light of the five luminous deities from the sin that was with them, and it (the sin) fell back upon the archons from whom it had issued, but they did not receive it back, just like a man who feels loathing for his own vomit. It (the sin) thereupon fell upon the earth, half of it upon moist ground and half of it upon dry. (The half which fell upon moist ground) became an odious beast in the likeness of the King of Darkness, and the Adamos of Light was sent against her (*sic*!) and he did battle with her and defeated her, and turned her over upon her back, and struck her with a spear[50] in her heart, and thrust his shield over her mouth, and set one of his feet upon her thighs and the other upon her breast. That (half) which fell upon dry ground sprouted up into five trees.

He says that these daughters of Darkness were previously pregnant of their own nature, and when they beheld the beautiful forms of the Messenger, their embryos aborted and fell to the earth.[51] These ate the buds of the trees. Then the abortions took counsel together and recalled the form(s) of the Messenger that they had seen and said, "Where is the form(s) that we saw?" And Ashaqlūn,[52] son of the King of Darkness, said to the abortions: "Give me your sons and daughters, and I will make for you a form like the one you saw." They brought (them) and gave (them) to him. He ate the males, and the females he gave to Namrael[53] his wife. Namrael and Ashaqlūn then united together, and she became pregnant from him and gave birth to a son, naming him Adam. She (again) became pregnant and bore a daughter, naming her Eve.

He (then) says that Jesus the Luminous[54] approached the unsuspecting Adam[55] and roused him from the sleep of death, that he might be delivered from the great spirit.[56] As (when) one who is righteous discovers a man possessed by a strong demon and calms him by his skill, so likewise it was with Adam when the Beloved One found him prostrate in deep sleep. He roused him and shook him and awakened him,[57] and chased away from him the deceptive demon, and bound apart from him the great (female) archon. Then Adam examined himself and recognized who he was, and (Jesus) showed him the Fathers on high, and (revealed to him) regarding his own self all that which he had fallen into — into the teeth of leopards and the teeth of elephants, swallowed by voracious ones and absorbed by gulping ones, consumed by dogs, mixed and imprisoned in all that exists, bound in the stench of Darkness. He says that he (Jesus) raised him up[58] and made him taste of the Tree of Life. Then Adam cried out[59] and wept, and raised his voice loudly like a lion that roars and tears (prey). He cast (himself down) and beat (his breast) and said, "Woe, woe to the one who formed my body, and to the one who bound my soul, and to the rebels who have enslaved me."

A closer examination of the structural motifs within the Jewish versions of the story of the Watchers and Giants and the mythological narrative transmitted by Theodore bar Konai reveals several distinct correspondences that cannot be ascribed to chance. A tabular outline clarifies this structural relationship.

1 Enoch	*Mani I (1st stage)*	*Mani II (2nd stage)*
1. Coexistence of *two* realms — Heaven & Earth	Coexistence of *two* realms — Light & Darkness	Coexistence of *two* realms — Heaven & Earth

2. Watchers *see beauty* of women; *lust* after them	Darkness *sees* Light; *desires* to unite with it	Archons *see* Messenger; *lust* after his beauty
3. Watchers *descend* and *mix* with women	Darkness *ascends* and *mixes* with Light	[Union has already taken place]; *sexual emission* of light & "sin"
4. Result of mixture: *Giants*, corruption, bloodshed upon *Earth*	Result of mixture: Primal Man and his five "sons" captured within *Darkness*	Result of mixture & emission: *abortions*, who "fall" to *earth*
5. *Distress* upon Earth perceived *above*	*Distress* within Darkness perceived *above*	Abortions magnify distress by producing Adam & Eve; their *distressful state* perceived above
6. Angels *sent to imprison & slay*; *purify* earth	Emissaries *sent to slay, bind, & purify*	Jesus the Luminous *sent* to awaken Adam
7. Means of purification: the *Deluge*	Means of purification: *creation* of cosmos (Heaven & Earth)	Means of purification: adherence to Manichaean precepts
8. Watchers bound; Giants slain; Earth *renewed* via Noah	Primal Man rescued; five luminous deities remain bound in archons; need for further purification initiates second stage (see next column)	Final purification accomplished at End of Days via *fire*; cosmos *renewed*

The first column provides an outline of the principal sequence of events that characterizes the story of the Watchers and Giants reported in 1 Enoch 6–11, the narrative that presumably underlies the more expansive Book of Giants. The second and third columns recount the main episodes in Manichaean cosmogonical teaching as recovered from the reliable testimonies of Theodore bar Konai and al-Nadīm. The latter narrative divides into two "stages." The first stage is initiated by the attack of Darkness upon Light, and concludes with the rescue of Primal Man from Darkness and the fabrication of the physical "heavens" and "earth." However, due to the continued imprisonment of members of the realm of Light within Darkness (the five luminous deities), a second stage of actions is initiated to effect the release of these captives. From a structural perspective, the sequence of events outlined in the third column parallels the succession of actions presented in the second column. The third column concludes with a justification for the observance of the distinctive Manichaean commandments until the eschaton.

A comparison of all three columns reveals that 1 Enoch 6–11, or a narrative based upon the events related in that pericope, forms the essential "scriptural" foundation for the subsequent Manichaean cosmogony. This appears to be the case not only with regard to the succession of events presented by Mani, but extends even to the specific content of his cosmogonical narrative. These correspondences are emphasized in the above table by italic type. One notes the "dualistic" setting presupposed in both narratives, the role of visual perception of beauty and the lust for mixture which this sight engenders, the calamitous results of the ensuing mixture, the affliction of the mixed elements alongside the corruption of the surrounding environment, the dispatch of emissaries to remedy the distress that has been created, and the concern for renewal to a previously unsullied state of existence. Many of these events involve identical actors (Watchers = sons of Darkness = archons; Giants = abortions; Noah = Adam [?][60]) and equivalent actions (for example, the charge to the emissaries to slay, bind, and purify).

One also observes that certain details of the Enochic substrate have been adjusted to accord with the dogmas of Manichaean belief. While the Enoch tradition records that the Watchers *descended* from heaven in order to unite with mortal women, the first stage of the Manichaean cosmogony "inverts"[61] the direction of this motif by depicting the forces of Darkness *ascending* for the purpose of union. This alteration conforms with the spatial orientation of the realm of Light "above" and the realm of Darkness "below" found in Severus, and is presumably due to Mani's strict exclusion of any "evil" substance, quality, or tendency from the realm of Light.[62] The "original" direction of motion surfaces in the second stage of his cosmogony, when the archons who are bound upon the firmament produce "abortions" which *fall* (*npl*) to earth.[63]

Indeed, although both stages of the Manichaean cosmogony possess demonstrable structural links with the Enochic material, it is the second stage that displays the clearest evidence of such dependence with regard to actual narrative content. Both stories are concerned with the preservation and eventual delivery of "heavenly" representatives who are threatened with extermination — respectively, Noah and his seed, and the remnants of Light entrapped within corporeal life. Watchers ("archons") and Giants ("abortions") play fundamental roles in both traditions, promulgating and aggravating corruption and wickedness. The four heavenly archangels of 1 Enoch 10 and the figure of Jesus the Luminous in Manichaean cosmogony also exercise parallel functions. According to 1 Enoch 10, each of the archangels receives a specific divine commission for the restoration of order upon earth. Uriel (Aramaic fragments: Sariel) is sent to warn Noah about the coming Deluge and to instruct him regarding the means for his preservation. Raphael is enjoined to bind Aza(z)el, Michael to bind Shemhazai and the remaining Watchers, and Gabriel to foment internecine warfare among the Giants. The educational mission of Uriel/Sariel is apparently paralleled in the Manichaean cosmogony by the instruction imparted to Adam by Jesus the Luminous. Moreover, the accounts of Theodore bar Konai and al-Nadīm report the binding of one or both of the principal abortions, Ashaqlūn and Namrael (named only in Theodore). It would seem that at least in this particular version of Manichaean cosmogony, Jesus the Luminous has assimilated the originally separate commissions of the Enochic archangels to himself.[64]

Noticeably absent from this roster of parallels is an explicit description of a war among the Giants/abortions. Nevertheless, there are two episodes within the story recounted by Theodore bar Konai that may utilize material from the Book of Giants. One is the short notice of a battle between the Adamos of Light and a frightful beast that appeared upon the "moist ground" (*rṭb'*) on earth. The monster is summarily vanquished and slain by the heavenly emissary. Interestingly, a cryptic line in a Parthian Manichaean commentary alludes to a story wherein Ohyah, Leviathan, and Raphael engage in battle.[65] The mention of Ohyah, a prominent character in the Qumran and Manichaean Books of Giants, suggests that the allusion is to an episode in the Book of Giants. More intriguing, however, is the appearance of Leviathan, a primeval sea-monster familiar from both biblical and later Jewish legend. It appears likely that Leviathan of Jewish lore was identified by Manichaean tradition with the unnamed monster of the present story. Such an association is strengthened by the evidence of another Middle Iranian text which narrates the same episode found in Theodore bar Konai, but which explicitly links the fearsome beast with the sea: "And that one part [of 'sin'] *that had fallen into the sea,* from that there became one hideous, cruel and terrible Mazan (i.e., 'monster'); and he tottered *out of the sea* and began sinning in the world."[66] Here the same odious beast which the Adamos of Light slays is expressly characterized as a "sea-monster," thus betraying its ancestry as the Jewish monster Leviathan.[67]

A second episode reminiscent of material belonging to the Book of Giants is the brief notice concerning the consumption of the progeny of the abortions by Ashaqlūn and Namrael. As we have seen, references to the voracious and undiscriminating appetites of the Giants appear in most strata of the Book of Giants tradition.[68] More significantly, cannibalism among the Giants themselves is specifically remarked. 1 Enoch 7:4–5 relates: "The Giants turned upon them (i.e., humans) (and) devoured humankind. And they began ... *devouring one another's flesh* and drinking blood as well." Similarly, Jubilees 7:22 notes that the Giants "*devoured one another.*" The identical consumptive activity of Ashaqlūn and Namrael may reflect this earlier motif.

In light of these observations, it appears that the Manichaean cosmogonical tradition preserved by Theodore bar Konai (and parallel tradents) displays considerable reliance upon the Jewish traditions about the Watchers and Giants found in Enochic literature. The structural features of Mani's cosmogony, as we have seen, are essentially identical with those of the earlier Jewish legends. We have also discovered that specific narrative motifs, such as the roles of the Watchers and the Giants, are common to both traditions. The Jewish story of the Watchers and Giants was thus an essential component of Mani's teachings about the presence of evil in the created order.

Notes to Chapter Four

[1] B. Aland cautions that more complete editions of both the Qumran Book of Giants and the Turfan fragments of the Manichaean Book of Giants are needed before anything definite about the relationship of these two works can be said. See her "Mani und Bardesanes — Zur Entstehung des manichäischen Systems," in A. Dietrich, ed., *Synkretismus im syrisch-persischen Kulturgebiet* (Göttingen, 1975), 124. In light of the present investigation her caution would seem to be unwarranted.

[2] Apparently the first Christian author who asserted the identification of the *beney ha'elohim* and the Sethites was Julius Africanus (third century C.E.). His interpretation of Genesis 6:1–4 survives in an excerpt contained in the *Chronographica* of Syncellus; see A.A. Mosshammer, ed., *Georgii Syncelli Ecloga Chronographica* (Leipzig, 1984), 19–20. See also Aphrahat, *Demonstratio* 13.5 (R. Graffin, ed., *Patrologia Syriaca* [Paris, 1894–1926], I 549 ll.17–18); Pseudo-Clementine *Recognitions* 1.29: "octava generatione *homines iusti qui angelorum vixerant vitam,* inlecti pulchritudine mulierum, ad promiscuos et inlicitos concubitus declinarunt;" but contrast ibid., 4.26: "*angeli* quidam relicto proprii ordinis cursu *hominum favere vitiis coeperunt,*" an anomaly pointed out by J. Bergmann, "Les éléments juifs dans les Pseudo-Clémentines," *REJ* 46 (1903), 94. Citations from the *Recognitions* depend upon B. Rehm, ed., *Die Pseudoklementinen II: Rekognitionen in Rufins Uebersetzung* (Berlin, 1965). For a list of further Christian sources which utilize this exegesis, see especially A.F.J. Klijn, *Seth in Jewish, Christian and Gnostic Literature* (Leiden, 1977), 41–80; and W. Adler, *George Syncellus and His Predecessors: Ante-Diluvian History in the Chronicle of Syncellus and His Acknowledged Authorities* (Ph.D. Diss., University of Pennsylvania, 1982; repr. Ann Arbor, 1984), 233–36.

[3] G.A.G. Stroumsa, *Another Seed: Studies in Gnostic Mythology* (Leiden, 1984), 126–34.

[4] Ibid., 17.

[5] "A tendency toward dualism can already be found in the Book of the Watchers ... and in Jubilees ..." (J.J. Collins, "Messianism in the Maccabean Period," in J. Neusner – W.S. Green – E.S. Frerichs, eds., *Judaisms and Their Messiahs at the Turn of the Christian Era* [Cambridge, 1987], 101–2).

[6] A clear expression of this demarcation occurs in Pseudo-Seder Eliahu Zuta 25: מה אעשה לבשר ודם שהוא שרוי במקום טומאה ויצר הרע שולט בו ואתם [i.e., המלאכים] שרויים במקום טהרה ואין יצר הרע שולט בכם "What can I do to human beings, for they dwell in an unclean place and the evil inclination rules over them, *but you dwell in a pure place where there is no evil inclination ruling over you.*" Text cited from

edition of M. Friedmann, ed., *Pseudo-Seder Eliahu Zuta* (Wien, 1904), 49.

[7] H. Pognon, *Inscriptions mandaïtes des coupes de Khouabir* (Paris, 1898), 125–31 (text); Theodore bar Konai, *Liber Scholiorum*, ed. A. Scher, CSCO scrip. syri, ser. II, t.66 (Paris, 1912), 311–18 (text).

[8] See G. Flügel, *Mani: seine Lehre und seine Schriften* (Leipzig, 1862; repr. Osnabrück, 1969), 49–80 (text).

[9] This material will be included in the following notes when appropriate.

[10] See especially M. Boyce, *A Reader in Manichaean Middle Persian and Parthian* (Leiden & Teheran, 1975), 60–74 (text), which contains references to earlier publications; J.P. Asmussen, ed., *Manichaean Literature* (Delmar, N.Y., 1975), 121–32; J.P. Asmussen – A. Böhlig, eds., *Die Gnosis III: Der Manichäismus* (Zürich & München, 1980), 108–18; W.B. Henning, "A Sogdian Fragment of the Manichaean Cosmogony," *BSOAS* 12 (1948), 306–18; W. Sundermann, *Mittelpersische und parthische kosmogonische und Parabeltexte der Manichäer* (Berlin, 1973), 11–80.

[11] *Kephalaia* 30:27–33; 55:26–31; 56:17–29; 58–60; 66–70; 87:7–9;92:12–94; 113–17; 137–44; 171:16ff.; 243; 246; 268:15–18; *Psalm-Book* 9:2–11:32.

[12] Translations of Theodore's account of Manichaeism have previously been provided by Pognon, *Inscriptions*, 181–93; F. Cumont – M.-A. Kugener, *Recherches sur le manichéisme* (Bruxelles, 1908–12), 7–49 (extracts interspersed within a running commentary); R. Reitzenstein – H.H. Schaeder, *Studien zum antike Synkretismus aus Iran und Griechenland* (Leipzig, 1926), 342–47; A.V.W. Jackson, *Researches in Manichaeism* (New York, 1932; repr. 1965), 222–54; A. Adam, ed., *Texte zum Manichäismus* 2. Auflage (Berlin, 1969), 15–23; Asmussen – Böhlig, *Die Gnosis III*, 103–8. We have omitted Theodore's introductory paragraph regarding the life of Mani from our translation.

[13] *lbhtt 'pyhwn*, literally "to shame the faces."

[14] *kynyn*. Compare al-Nadīm, *Fihrist*: كونين (Flügel, *Mani*, 52 l.13). For the significance of this expression, see H.H.Schaeder, "Urform und Fortbildungen des manichäischen Systems," in F. Saxl, ed., *Vorträge der Bibliothek Warburg IV* (Leipzig, 1927), 77 n.2, reprinted in H.H. Schaeder, *Studien zur orientalischen Religionsgeschichte* (Darmstadt, 1968), 27 n.2; H.-C. Puech, *Le manichéisme: son fondateur — sa doctrine* (Paris, 1949), 159–61 n.285.

[15] *'b' drbwt'*. For other attestations of this title in Manichaean literature, see especially Reitzenstein – Schaeder, *Studien* (cf. n.12 above), 277; Puech, *Le manichéisme*, 164 n.295. This title is perhaps derived from Ephesians 1:17: ὁ πατὴρ τῆς δόξης; cf. the Syriac lexica *s.v. rbwt'*. Compare 1QapGen 2:4: *b'ly' bmrh rbwt' bmlk kwl* '[*lmyn* ... "by the Most High, by the Lord of Greatness, by the E[ternal] King ...." Text cited from J.A. Fitzmyer, *The Genesis Apocryphon of Qumran Cave 1* 2nd revised ed. (Rome, 1971), 50. Compare the Mandaean "Lord of Greatness" (*marā ḏrabbūtā*); cf. K. Rudolph, *Die Mandäer* (Göttingen, 1960–61), I 185 n.5.; idem, *Theogonie, Kosmogonie und Anthropogonie in den mandäischen Schriften* (Göttingen, 1965), 82 n.3.

[16] *ḥmš škynth*. See Cumont – Kugener, *Recherches*, 9–10.

[17] For similar rosters detailing the companions of the Father of Greatness,

see Reitzenstein – Schaeder, *Studien*, 285–86.

[18] Scher's text reads *ml'k ḥšwk'* "Angel of Darkness," but other manuscripts have *mlk ḥšwk'* "King of Darkness," and this latter designation is in accord with the testimonies of other sources. Compare *Acta Archelai* 12.4: princeps tenebrarum = Epiphanius, *Panarion* 66.30.2: ὁ ἄρχων τοῦ σκότους; *Kephalaia* 31:2: *prrŏ nnapkĕkĕ*. In the *Fihrist* this personage is termed "Satan" (الشيطان) or "Ancient Devil" (ابليس القديم); cf. Flügel, *Mani*, 192–97. For still other designations, see M. Tardieu, *Le manichéisme* (Paris, 1981), 103. Interestingly, the designation *ml'k ḥwšk* "Angel of Darkness" is attested in Qumran literature. See 1QS 3:20–22: "And under the power of the Angel of Darkness are all the wicked, and in the ways of Darkness they walk, and all the righteous are led astray (*t'wt*!) by the Angel of Darkness ...."

[19] See the discussion of H.-C. Puech, "Le Prince des Ténèbres en son royaume," in *Satan* (Paris, 1948), 150–56.

[20] *qr'*, literally "called forth." This mode of divine creation expresses the Manichaean abhorrence of sexual generation. See Jackson, *Researches*, 224 n.8; S.N.C. Lieu, *Manichaeism in the Later Roman Empire and Medieval China: A Historical Survey* (Manchester, 1985; repr. 1988), 11–12.

[21] *'m' dḥy'*. For other synonymous titles of this personage, see Jackson, *Researches*, 321–31; Tardieu, *Le manichéisme*, 104. The name "Mother of Life" is apparently based on Genesis 3:20 (*'m kl ḥy*), but it should be noted that "Eve" as the first human female also plays a role in Manichaean myth.

[22] *'nš' qdmy'*. Compare *Acta Archelai* 7: τὸν πρῶτον ἄνθρωπον; Ephrem: *'nš' qdmy'* (J.J. Overbeck, ed., *S. Ephraemi Syri ... Opera Selecta* [Oxford, 1865], 65 ll.11–12); al-Nadīm, *Fihrist*: الانسان القديم (Flügel, *Mani*, 54 l.6). This name is reminiscent of the title(s) frequently accorded Adam in rabbinic literature; namely, *'dm qdmwny*, *'dm qdm'h*, or *'dm hr'šwn*. L. Ginzberg explicitly equates the Manichaean title with the Jewish designations; see his "Adam Ḳadmon," in *The Jewish Encyclopaedia* (New York & London, 1901–6), I 182. That the Manichaeans were familiar with this Jewish terminology is now confirmed from *Cologne Mani Codex* 48:16, where we read [οὕτ]ω πρῶτο[ς ὁ] Αδαμ ... "t[hus] the *first Adam* ...."; see also W. Sundermann, *Mitteliranische manichäische Texte kirchengeschichtlichen Inhalts* (Berlin, 1981), 97 l.1515. The "Primal Man" of the Manichaeans is nevertheless distinct from the first created human being ("Adam"), as we shall see later in Theodore bar Konai's narrative.

[23] Compare *Acta Archelai* 7 and al-Nadīm, *Fihrist* (Flügel, *Mani*, 54 ll.6–8): "He (Mani) said: Primal Man armed himself with five kinds (of things) which are five deities ... and used them as armor." Cf. Reitzenstein – Schaeder, *Studien*, 252–54.

[24] The name of this crown-bearing angel, *Nḥšbṭ*, is not attested in any other source. This figure, however, corresponds to an entity termed Στεφανοφόρος "crown-bearer" in the Byzantine "great abjuration formula"; see Adam, *Texte*², 97–98 ll.13–14.

[25] *bnwhy dḥšwk'*. Cf. *bny ḥšwk'* in Ephrem (ed. Overbeck), 62 l.20; 65 l.12; 66 l.22; etc.; Parthian *ṯ'rz'dg'n* (cf. Sundermann, *Kirchengeschichtlichen Inhalts*,

66 l.898). Aphrahat turns the sobriquet *bny ḥšwk'* upon the Manichaeans themselves; see his *Demonstratio* 3.9 (ed. Graffin [cf. n.2 above]), 116 ll.12–17. The expression "sons of Darkness" recalls the recurrent Hebrew designation *beney ḥoshek* used by members of the Qumran sect for hopelessly corrupt individuals who were misled by the "Angel of Darkness" (*ml'k ḥwšk*; 1QS 3:19–21). Cf. 1QS 1:10; 1QM 1:1,6–7,10,16; 3:6,9; 13:16; 14:17; 16:9. Compare the designation "sons of Light" for the inhabitants of the Realm of Light in the text below.

[26] It is interesting to note in this connection that the Manichaean *electi* were required to pray seven times daily. See Flügel, *Mani,* 64 ll.14–15; E. Chavannes – P. Pelliot, *Un traité manichéen retrouvé en Chine* (Paris, 1913), 300; Puech, *Le manichéisme,* 183 n.367; N. Sims-Williams, "The Manichaean Commandments: A Survey of the Sources," in *Papers in Honour of Professor Mary Boyce* (Leiden, 1985), 578 n.43.

[27] *qryt' dtrtyn lḥbyb nhyr'.* For a thorough discussion of this figure, see Jackson, *Researches,* 273–83.

[28] *bn rb'.* Note *bn* in Ephrem (ed. Overbeck), 60 ll.21–22. The name presumably derives from *bn'* "to build, construct." See Jackson, *Researches,* 283–87; Tardieu, *Le manichéisme,* 105.

[29] *rwḥ' ḥy'.* See Jackson, *Researches,* 288–95; Tardieu, *Le manichéisme,* 105.

[30] For a discussion of these five entities, see Cumont – Kugener, *Recherches,* 22–23; Jackson, *Researches,* 296–313. A list of the designations used for these five in other testimonies is provided by Tardieu, *Le manichéisme,* 105–6. With regard to the title *mlk' rb' d'yqr'* "Great King of Honor," compare Peshitta Psalm 24:7–10 *mlk' d'yqr'* (= Hebrew *mlk hkbwd;* cf. 1QM 12:8; 19:1). The "Porter" (*sbl'*) is identified in other texts as "Atlas"; cf. Cumont – Kugener, *Recherches,* 69–75; C. Brockelmann, *Lexicon Syriacum* 2. Auflage (Halle, 1928; repr. Hildesheim, 1982), 455. For the "Adamos of Light," see A. Adam, *Die Psalmen des Thomas und das Perlenlied als Zeugnisse vorchristlicher Gnosis* (Berlin, 1959), 42.

[31] All manuscripts read here "*their* glory" (*'yqrhyn*), but this would suggest that the evil inhabitants of Darkness possessed "glory" or "honor," which is absurd. I therefore follow the emendation *'yqrh* "his glory" first suggested by M. Lidzbarski and published in Reitzenstein–Schaeder, *Studien,* 352.

[32] *bny nwhr'.* Cf. *bny nwhr'* in Ephrem (ed. Overbeck), 67 l.20. Compare the Qumranic *beney 'or* and n.25 above.

[33] "Dass wir hier ein originales Stück von Manis Dichtung vor uns haben, ist nicht zu bezweifeln." (Reitzenstein–Schaeder, *Studien,* 265). See further H.H. Schaeder, "Ein Lied von Mani," *OLZ* 29 (1926), 104–7.

[34] *qry'.* The "voice" of the Living Spirit is personified as a separate hypostasis, the "Caller," as is the answering voice of Primal Man, the "Respondent" (*'ny'*). Note al-Nadīm, *Fihrist* (Flügel, *Mani,* 55 ll.6–7): "He (Mani) says: Then the Living Spirit called to Primal Man in a loud voice as quick as lightning, *and it (the voice) became another deity.*"

[35] All manuscripts have "And the Living Spirit ..." at the beginning of this sentence, which does not accord with the destination of the ascension.

[36] Presumably the Great King of Honor, the Adamos of Light, and the King of Glory, since the Ornament of Splendor and the Porter are given separate tasks below.

[37] *'rkwnṭ'* = Greek ἄρχοντα (> ἄρχων). This is a common designation in Gnostic literature for prominent evil spirits, and was similarly used in Manichaean literature for the same entities. See *Acta Archelai* 8; Ephrem, ed. Overbeck, 66 ll.16,18; Epiphanius, *Panarion* 66.32; *Kephalaia* 50:22,24; 51:25–27; al-Nadīm, *Fihrist* (Flügel, *Mani,* 58 ll.12,14, and *passim*); al-Shahrastānī, *Kitāb al-milāl wa-al-niḥāl,* ed. W. Cureton (London, 1842–46), 190 l.9: "*archontic* satans."

[38] Thus two manuscripts; another reads "twelve." Based upon other testimonies, the correct number should be "ten." Note particularly al-Nadīm, *Fihrist* (Flügel, *Mani,* 56 l.14): "He (an angel) constructed ten heavens and eight earths"; also *Kephalaia* 115:7. See Jackson, *Researches,* 234–35 n.48; 314–20; Andreas–Henning, *Mir. Man. I,* 177 n.7. However, according to a Turkish fragment published by Le Coq, the zodiac was counted as an "eleventh" heaven. See *Mir. Man. I,* 183 n.2; Boyce, *Reader* (cf. n.10 above), 60.

[39] The Great King of Honor apparently guards an unspecified number of archons who were not killed and flayed, but are rather held captive in the heavens. According to *Kephalaia* 92:24–31, the Great King of Honor had his seat in the third heaven, and it was from this district that the "Watchers" (ἐγρήγοροι) escaped and fled to earth. Compare al-Nadīm, *Fihrist* (Flügel, *Mani,* 56 ll.9–10): "He (Mani) says: Then he (Primal Man) commanded some of the angels to pull out this mixture to an area apart from the land of Darkness, next to the land of Light. They thereupon hung them (the archons) in the heights." See the remarks of Flügel, *Mani,* 216–17 on this passage. Note too the Syriac *Chronicon Maroniticum,* ed. I. Guidi, 60 ll.18–19: "When God saw them (the attacking archons), he bound (*'sr*) them there (i.e., in heaven)," a statement repeated verbatim in the *Chronicle* of Michael the Syrian, IV 118. For the *Chronicon Maroniticum,* see I. Guidi, ed., *Chronica Minora* CSCO script. syri series 3, vol.4 (Paris, 1903). Citations from Michael the Syrian rely upon J.-B. Chabot, ed., *Chronique de Michel le Syrien, patriarche jacobite d'Antioche,* 1166–1199 (3 vols., Paris, 1899–1924; repr. in 4 vols., Brussels, 1963).

[40] The Living Spirit, like the Messenger below, is presumably hermaphroditic.

[41] That is, the captive archons in the heavens. See n.39 above.

[42] *'lp'* "ship, vessel." Note the *Chronicle* of Michael the Syrian, ed. Chabot, IV 118: "They (the Manichaeans) say that the sun and moon are ships (*'lp'*) which receive human souls." Interestingly, the Hebrew phrase *kly 'wr* "vessels of light" refers to the heavenly luminaries in a fragmentary prayer text from Qumran. See 4Q503 col. III:9, published by M. Baillet, ed., *Discoveries in the Judaean Desert VII: Qumrân grotte 4, III (4Q482–4Q520)* (Oxford, 1982), 106. See also the remarks of M. Kister, "Beshulley Sefer Ben Sira," *Leshonenu* 47 (1983), 142.

[43] *mškb',* literally "bed, couch." See Jackson, *Researches,* 240 n.72.

[44] *kbyšyn.* A manuscript variant reads *ḥbyšyn* "confined, imprisoned." One

would expect "in the heavens" in place of "in the earths"; cf. n.39 above.

[45] *qryt' dtlt l'yzgd'.* For further references to this figure, see Tardieu, *Le manichéisme,* 106.

[46] Usually identified with the twelve signs of the zodiac. For a recent discussion of these entities, see Sundermann, *Kirchengeschichtlichen Inhalts,* 50–52.

[47] As observed above, these archons are clearly imprisoned in the heavens.

[48] All manuscripts have *shr'* "moon" here, which makes little sense, since the moon was not produced by the archons. I follow the emendation *nwhr'* suggested by J.-B. Chabot, as printed in Scher, 316 n.4.

[49] This passage is very difficult, and many proposals have been made regarding possible emendations. I have sought to translate the text here with minimal recourse to these suggestions. Compare the remarks of Pognon, *Inscriptions,* 190 nn.4–5; Cumont – Kugener, *Recherches,* 39 n.1; Reitzenstein–Schaeder, *Studien,* 345–46; Jackson, *Researches,* 244–45; Adam, *Texte²,* 20–21 nn.60–61.

[50] Text reads *'wrṭy'* "aorta(?)," but one should probably emend to *dwrṭy'* "lance, spear." See Cumont – Kugener, *Recherches,* 39 n.3; Brockelmann, *Lexicon Syriacum,* 166.

[51] *yḥṭ 'wlyhyn wnplw 'l 'r''.* Note the prominence of the stem *npl,* recalling the *nephilim* of Genesis 6:4.

[52] *'šqlwn.* This figure is identical to Greek, Coptic, and Latin "Sakla(s)," a name appearing in both Manichaean and other Gnostic writings. Note *Kephalaia* 137:15–22; 138:1–5,17–18, where Saklas is designated "the archon who is the ruler of the [abortions]." See further the Greek and Latin testimonies cited by Cumont – Kugener, *Recherches,* 73 n.3; *Chronicle* of Michael the Syrian, ed. Chabot, IV 118: "They (the Manichaeans) say that Adam and Eve derive from Saqla (*sql'*), the ruler of Hyle (*šlyṭ' dhwl'*), and Nebruel (*nbrw'yl*)."; al-Jāḥiẓ, *Kitāb al-Ḥayawān* (*apud* K. Kessler, *Mani: Forschungen über die manichäische Religion* [Berlin, 1889], 368): "... and narratives about *Shaqlun* (شقلون) and Hummāmah ...." For further discussion of Saklas, see n.75 in Chapter Two above. I therefore reject the Iranian derivation of Ashaqlūn from Ashōqar advocated by A. Adam, "Ist die Gnosis in aramäischen Weisheitsschulen entstanden?" in U. Bianchi, ed., *Le origini dello gnosticismo: Colloquio di Messina, 13–18 aprile 1966, testi e discussioni* (Leiden, 1967), 291–301; idem, *Texte²,* 21 n.65.

[53] There are several textual variants for this name: *nqb'yl, 'qb'yl, nmr'yl* (adopted here), *nbrw'yl* (see preceding note). In some Western sources, this name is transmitted as Νεβρώδ or biblical Nimrod; cf. F.C. Baur, *Das manichäische Religionssystem nach den Quellen neu untersucht und entwickelt* (Tübingen, 1831), 66 n.14 and 137–8 n.10; Cumont – Kugener, *Recherches,* 42 n.3; H.H. Schaeder, "Hasan al-Baṣri: Studien zur Frühgeschichte des Islam," *Der Islam* 14 (1925), 9 n.1. Interestingly, both "Sakla" and "Nebrouel" figure as angelic rulers of "chaos and Hades" in the Coptic *Gospel of the Egyptians,* a Gnostic composition recovered from Nag Hammadi. See NHC III 57:5–58:21 (B. Layton, *The Gnostic Scriptures* [Garden City, 1987], 113–14.

[54] *yšw' zywn'.* Compare the fuller narrative of al-Nadīm, *Fihrist* (Flügel, *Mani*, 58 l.15–59 l.5): "He (Mani) says: When the five angels saw the divine Light and Goodness which Desire had plundered and bound as captive within those two who had been born, they asked al-Bashīr (= the Messenger), the Mother of Life, Primal Man, and the Living Spirit to send to this first-born creature someone to release and deliver him, to teach him knowledge and piety, and to deliver him from the satans. He (Mani) says: They thus sent Jesus, along with (another) deity. They approached the two archons, confined them, and rescued the two who had been born."

[55] *'dm tmym'.* Literally "the innocent Adam"; i.e., in the sense that he was unaware of the circumstances of his creation or of the heavenly world. Compare al-Nadīm, *Fihrist* (Flügel, *Mani*, 59 ll.5–9): "He (Mani) says: Then Jesus came and spoke to the one who had been born, who was Adam, and explained to him (about) the gardens (of Paradise), the deities, Gehenna, the satans, earth, heaven, sun, and moon. He also made him fear Eve, showing him how to suppress (desire) for her, and he forbade him to approach her, and made him fear to be near her, so that he did (what Jesus commanded)."

[56] Presumably referring to Ashaqlūn.

[57] *wrddh.* See Pognon, *Inscriptions*, 192 n.3; T. Nöldeke, [Review of Pognon, *Inscriptions*], *WZKM* 12 (1898), 358.

[58] *'qymh.* G. Widengren has argued that this verb signifies "baptism" in this context, and appeals to unidentified Mandaic references (*Mesopotamian Elements in Manichaeism* [Uppsala, 1946], 123–24). No confirmation for Widengren's proposal can be gathered from E.S. Drower – R. Macuch, eds., *A Mandaic Dictionary* (Oxford, 1963), 407–8. In light of Mani's known hostility to "baptism," and the previous prone state of Adam, the idea of being raised to a standing position is surely intended.

[59] *n'r.* Literally "roar, growl."

[60] Note the epithet *'dm tmym'* (Scher, 317 l.16) and compare Genesis 6:9: *nḥ 'yš ṣdyq tmym hyh bdrtyw.* Is there a possible connection between these two texts? Noah is arguably the "second Adam" of primeval history, whose righteous behavior assures the preservation of human life upon the renewed earth. Similarly, the Manichaean Adam through his righteous behavior (i.e., adhering to Manichaean precepts) assures the preservation and final liberation of the entrapped particles of Light. Compare Tanḥuma Buber, *Bereshit* §32, where Adam is granted a vision of his righteous descendants, among whom is *nḥ wkl htmymym.* Text cited from S. Buber, ed., *Midrash Tanḥuma 'al ḥamishah ḥumshey Torah* (repr. New York, 1946).

[61] The role of "motif-inversion" among Gnostic sects, and particularly with regard to interpretations of Genesis 6:1–4, has been stressed by Y. Janssens, "Le thème de la fornication des anges," in Bianchi, ed., *Le origini dello gnosticismo* (cf. n.52 above), 488–95; B.A. Pearson, "Jewish Sources in Gnostic Literature," in M.E. Stone, ed., *Jewish Writings of the Second Temple Period* (Assen & Philadelphia, 1984), 443–81; Stroumsa, *Another Seed, passim.*

[62] W.B. Henning, "The Book of the Giants," *BSOAS* 11 (1943), 53; Asmussen,

Manichaean Literature, 103.

[63] According to *Kephalaia* 92:24ff., "Watchers" (ἐγρήγοροι) escaped from their guardian in the third heaven and descended to earth together with the "abortions." Compare also *Kephalaia* 117:1–9.

[64] It should be remarked that in the tradition preserved by al-Nadīm Jesus is accompanied by a second unnamed "divinity" who assists the former in the binding of the two archons (see n.54 above). Does this feature represent a transitional stage in the progression from the four emissaries of 1 Enoch 10 to the single authoritative messenger of Theodore bar Konai?

[65] "... like unto (the fight in which) Ohya, Lewyatin, and Raphael lacerated each other, and they vanished ...." Cf. Henning, *BSOAS* 11 (1943), 71–72.

[66] Asmussen, *Manichaean Literature,* 124.

[67] For a more detailed exploration of this possibility, see J.C. Reeves, "An Enochic Motif in Manichaean Tradition," in A. van Tongerloo and S. Giversen, eds., *Manichaica Selecta: Studies Presented to Professor Julien Ries on the Occasion of his Seventieth Birthday* (Louvain, forthcoming).

[68] See the commentary to QG1 5–6 in Chapter Two.

Chapter Five

Conclusions

Did Jewish traditions exert a determinative influence upon the formulation of Mani's cosmogonical system? Our preceding investigation points toward an affirmative response. Mani made the Enochic legend of the Watchers and the Giants a cornerstone of his theological speculations. He seems to have utilized this Jewish story in two ways. First, it serves as the major structural element in Mani's exposition of the events which led to the creation of the physical cosmos, and as such, remains a paradigm for Mani's subsequent depictions of the hostile intercourse between the realms of Light and Darkness. Secondly, the Book of Giants survives as a narrative entity in its own right because it illustrates the deleterious results of unsanctioned mixture at a particular point within human history. Mani thus employed it as a parable in the service of his own theological system. The Book of Giants therefore plays a central role in the formation and elaboration of Mani's distinctive world-view.

How did Mani become acquainted with this literature? Thanks to the recent decipherment and publication of the *Cologne Mani Codex*, we are now in possession of an important primary source for the life and thought of Mani prior to his travels through the ancient Orient. The *Codex* tells us that Mani spent his childhood and early adult years among Elchasaites, a heterodox Jewish-Christian sect emanating from the "baptist" milieu of late first-century Palestine. In this autobiographical report, Mani recounts his growing dissatisfaction with and eventual opposition to the teachings revered by the Elchasaites. His discontent was fueled by a series of "revelations" which he claims to have received from a heavenly messenger. When the Elchasaites discovered that he was undermining the community on the basis of these "revelations," they summoned him before their *sanhedrin* and expelled him from their midst. Mani thereupon began his travels for the purpose of propagating his "revelations."

According to the *Codex*, therefore, Mani formulated the core of his distinctive system during his sojourn among the Elchasaite sect. Did Mani peruse the Qumran Book of Giants or a later recension thereof during this period? The Codex informs us that the Elchasaites esteemed the teachings of a group termed the "forefathers" (οἱ πρόγονοι πατέρες), and it occasionally quotes passages from their writings. Among the cited "forefathers" are biblical personages such as Adam, Seth, Enosh, Shem, and Enoch. Elchasaite reverence for these ancient worthies should probably be connected with their concept of the recurrent appearance upon earth of an authoritative "teacher," termed by some heterodox circles a "True Prophet." Biblical figures such as Adam, Seth, Enoch, and Noah are often identified as part of this series of teachers. Given the Elchasaite esteem for the "forefathers," and the presence of literary quotations from patriarchal "fathers" in the *Codex*, it appears reasonable that the Elchasaite community among whom Mani lived possessed a library containing writings allegedly authored by these biblical "forefathers." Included among these books may have been writings ascribed to Enoch, as well as compositions depicting the exemplary life and deeds of Enoch. The Qumran Book of Giants fits into this latter category of writings. It seems plausible to conclude that Mani encountered the Book of Giants during his sojourn among the Elchasaites. His study of that narrative then stimulated the development of his own theological system.

If Mani had already formulated his new teachings during his Elchasaite period, then the extent of Iranian religious influences upon Mani's thought should be reassessed. The Elchasaites were not a Zoroastrian sect. They espoused a peculiar amalgam of Judaism and Christianity. They combined concern for ritual purity and devotion to the Mosaic Law with a recognition of Jesus as one link in the chain of authoritative "teachers." Yet despite their recognition of Jesus, their Judaic roots remained strong. According to the *Codex*, the Elchasaite community among whom Mani lived was a "closed" society whose members were extremely suspicious of what they termed "gentile" mores and customs. The entertainment of "gentile" ideas was sufficient reason for banishment from the community. One doubts, therefore, whether Zoroastrian ideas or "writings" (if such were extant at this period) were studied or discussed among Mani's Elchasaites.

It nevertheless remains possible that Mani could have assimilated some rudimentary knowledge of Iranian traditions via cultural osmosis. His cosmogonical employment of Light-Darkness symbolism might be adduced as a possible borrowing of the ancient attributes of Ahura Mazda and Ahriman, respectively. However, as we have seen, the dualistic employment of the concepts of "Light" and "Darkness" is also present in Jewish literature, being particularly evident in the sectarian compositions of the Second Temple period. Recensions of some of these writings may also have been available to Mani in the Elchasaite library. An examination of the Codex does not uncover any indubitable evidence pointing to Mani's adaptation of identifiably Iranian motifs. His arguments with his Elchasaite brethren rely upon the "revelations" which he claimed to have received from God. When the Elchasaites question the authenticity of his "revelations," Mani cites the teachings of biblical personages and recognized Elchasaite authorities. Zoroaster does not figure in Mani's series of prophetic "revealers" at this stage of his ideological development. If Mani was influenced by Zoroastrian concepts during this period of his life, he does not communicate that information to either his Elchasaite adversaries or the later readers of his *vita*.

One therefore concludes that the extent of Zoroastrian influence upon the young Mani has been overrated. The new textual evidence which has appeared over the last twenty years supplies a valuable corrective to earlier expositions of Mani's thought. These texts indicate that heterodox Jewish thought, particularly that embodied in Enochic literature, was a powerful stimulus in the formulation of Mani's theology. The impact of Jewish literary traditions upon the youthful Mani will necessarily occupy a central place in future studies dealing with the origins of Manichaeism.

Bibliography

PRIMARY SOURCES

Adam, A., ed. *Texte zum Manichäismus.* 2nd ed. Berlin, 1969.

Albeck, Ch., ed. *Midrash Bereshit Rabbati.* Jerusalem, 1940.

————., ed. *Shishah sidrey Mishnah.* Jerusalem & Tel Aviv, 1952–59.

Allberry, C.R.C., ed. *Manichaean Manuscripts in the Chester Beatty Collection, vol. II: A Manichaean Psalm-Book, pt. II.* Stuttgart, 1938.

Andreas, F.C., and Henning, W.B. "Mitteliranische Manichaica aus Chinesisch-Turkestan. I." *Sitzungsberichte der Preussischen Akademie der Wissenschaften in Berlin.* Berlin, 1932: 175–222.

————. "Mitteliranische Manichaica aus Chinesisch-Turkestan. II." *Sitzungsberichte der Preussischen Akademie der Wissenschaften in Berlin.* Berlin, 1933: 294–363.

————. "Mitteliranische Manichaica aus Chinesisch-Turkestan. III." *Sitzungsberichte der Preussischen Akademie der Wissenschaften in Berlin.* Berlin, 1934: 846–912.

Arnim, H. von. *Stoicorum Veterum Fragmenta.* Leipzig, 1903–24.

Augustinus. *Contra epistulam quam vocant fundamenti.* Edited by J. Zycha. CSEL 25. Vienna, 1891–92, pp. 191–248.

Baillet, M., ed. *Discoveries in the Judaean Desert VII: Qumrân grotte 4, III (4Q482–4Q520).* Oxford, 1982.

Baillet, M., Milik, J.T., and Vaux, R. de. *Discoveries in the Judaean Desert of Jordan III: Les "petits grottes" de Qumrân.* Oxford, 1962.

Barthélemy, D., and Milik, J.T. *Discoveries in the Judaean Desert of Jordan I: Qumran Cave I.* Oxford, 1955.

Beck, E., ed. *Des heiligen Ephraem des Syrers: Hymnen contra Haereses.* CSCO 169. Louvain, 1957.

Benoit, P., Milik, J.T., and Vaux, R. de. *Discoveries in the Judaean Desert II: Les grottes de Murabba'at.* Oxford, 1961.

Bezold, C. *Die Schatzhöhle «Mĕ'ārath Gazzē».* Leipzig, 1883–88; reprint ed., Amsterdam, 1981.

Al-Bīrūnī. *Al-Athār al-bāqiya 'ani'l-qurūn al-khāliya.* Edited by C.E. Sachau [Chronologie orientalischer Völker von Alberuni]. Leipzig, 1878.

Black, M., ed. *Apocalypsis Henochi Graece.* Leiden, 1970.

Brière, M. "Les Homiliae Cathedrales de Sévère d'Antioche, traduction syriaque de Jacques d'Edesse CXX à CXXV." *Patrologia Orientalis* 29 (1960): 124–89.

Brinkmann, A., ed. *Alexandrii Lycopolitani contra Manichaei opiniones disputatio.* Leipzig, 1895.

Buber, S., ed. *Midrash Tanḥuma 'al ḥamishah ḥumshey Torah.* 2 vols.; reprint ed., New York, 1946.

Chabot, J.-B., ed. *Chronicon ad annum Christi 1234 pertinens.* CSCO script. syri series 3, vol. 14. Paris, 1920.

————. *Chronique de Michel le Syrien, patriarche jacobite d'Antioche, 1166–1199.* 3 vols. Paris, 1899–1924; reprint ed. in 4 vols., Brussels, 1963.

Charles, R.H., ed. *Maṣhafa Kufalē, or the Ethiopic Version of the Hebrew Book of Jubilees.* Oxford, 1895.

Cyrillus Hierosolymitanus. *Catechesis VI.* In *Patrologiae Graeca,* vol. 33, cols. 537–604. Edited by J.P. Migne. Paris, n.d.

Dedering, S., ed. "Apocalypse of Baruch." In *Vetus Testamentum Syriace iuxta simplicem Syrorum versionem.* Pars IV, fasciculus iii. Leiden, 1973.

Denis, A.-M., ed. *Fragmenta Pseudepigraphorum quae supersunt Graeca.* Leiden, 1970.

Diels, H., ed. *Die Fragmente der Vorsokratiker.* 2 vols. 3. Aufl. Berlin, 1912.

Eisenstein, J.D. *Otzar midrashim.* 2 vols. New York, 1915.

Eusebius. *Praeparatio Evangelica.* 2 vols. Edited by K. Mras. Berlin, 1956.

Finkelstein, L., ed. *Sifra on Leviticus according to Vatican Manuscript Assemani 66 ...* New York, 1983– .

Flemming, J., ed. *Das Buch Henoch: Æthiopischer Text.* Leipzig, 1902.

Friedmann, M., ed. *Midrash Pesiqta Rabbati.* Wien, 1880.

————, ed. *Pseudo-Seder Eliahu Zuta.* Wien, 1904.

Georgius Cedrenus. *Compendium Historiarum.* Edited by I. Bekker.

Bonn, 1838.

Graffin, R., et al., eds. *Patrologia Syriaca.* 3 vols. Paris, 1894–1926.

Guidi, I., ed. *Chronica Minora.* CSCO script. syri series III, vol. 4. Paris, 1903.

Guillaumont, A., et al. *The Gospel According to Thomas.* Leiden and New York, 1959.

Hegemonius. *Acta Archelai.* Edited by C.H. Beeson. GCS 16. Leipzig, 1906.

Henrichs, A., and Koenen, L. "Der Kölner Mani-Kodex (P. Colon. inv. nr. 4780). ΠΕΡΙ ΤΗΣ ΓΕΝΝΗΣ ΤΟΥ ΣΑΜΑΤΟΣ ΑΥΤΟΥ. Edition der Seiten 1–72." *Zeitschrift für Papyrologie und Epigraphik* 19 (1975): 1–85.

————. "... Edition der Seiten 72,8–99,9." *Zeitschrift für Papyrologie und Epigraphik* 32 (1978): 87–199.

————. "... Edition der Seiten 99,10–120." *Zeitschrift für Papyrologie und Epigraphik* 44 (1981): 201–318.

————. "... Edition der Seiten 121–192." *Zeitschrift für Papyrologie und Epigraphik* 48 (1982): 1–59.

Hieronymus. *De virus illustribus.* In *Patrologiae Latina,* vol. 23, cols. 603–759. Edited by J.P. Migne. Paris, 1883.

————. *S. Hieronymi Presbyteri Opera: Pars II: Opera Homiletica.* Edited by G. Morin. CCSL 78. Turnholt, 1958.

Higger, M., ed. "Pirqey de Rabbi Eliezer." *Horeb* 8 (1944): 82–119; 9 (1946): 94–165; 10 (1948): 185–294.

Hippolytus. *Refutatio omnium haeresium.* Edited by M. Marcovich. Berlin and New York, 1986.

Holl, K., ed. *Epiphanius: dritter Band.* GCS 37. Leipzig, 1935.

Horowitz, H.S., and Rabin, I.A., eds. *Mekhilta de-Rabbi Ishmael.* Breslau, 1931; reprint ed., Jerusalem, 1970.

Jacoby, F., ed. *Die Fragmente der griechischen Historiker.* Leiden, 1923–; reprint ed., Leiden, 1957– .

Jellinek, A., ed. *Bet ha-Midrasch: Sammlung kleiner Midraschim und vermischter Abhandlungen aus der ältern jüdischen Literatur.* 6 vols. Leipzig, 1853–77; reprint ed., Jerusalem, 1938.

Jonge, M. de. *The Testaments of the Twelve Patriarchs.* Leiden, 1978.

Kmosko, M., ed. "Liber Graduum." Volume 3 of *Patrologia Syriaca.* Edited by R. Graffin, et al. Paris, 1926.

Koenen, L., and Römer, C. *Der Kölner Mani-Kodex: Abbildungen und diplomatischer Text.* Bonn, 1985.

———. *Der Kölner Mani-Kodex: Kritische Edition.* Opladen, 1988.

Kotter, B., ed. *Die Schriften des Johannes von Damaskos IV.* Berlin, 1981.

Lagarde, P. de. *Hagiographa Chaldaice.* Leipzig, 1873.

———. *Prophetae Chaldaice e fide codicis reuchliniani edidit.* Leipzig, 1872.

Landauer, S., ed. *Kitāb al-Amānāt wa'l-I'tiqādāt von Sa'adja b. Jūsuf al-Fajjūmī.* Leiden, 1880.

Margolioth, R., ed. *Sefer ha-Bahir.* Jerusalem, 1951.

Al-Mas'ūdī. [*Kitāb al-tanbih*]. *Le livre de l'avertissement et de la revision.* Translated by B. Carra de Vaux. Paris, 1896.

Mosshammer, A.A., ed. *Georgii Syncelli Ecloga Chronographica.* Leipzig, 1984.

Al-Nadīm. *Kitāb al-Fihrist.* Edited by G. Flügel. Leipzig, 1871–72.

Nau, F., ed. "Bardesanes: Liber Legum Regionum." In *Patrologia Syriaca,* vol. 2, cols. 492–657. Edited by R. Graffin, et al. Paris, 1907.

Overbeck, J.J., ed. *S. Ephraemi Syri ... Opera Selecta.* Oxford, 1865.

Pognon, H. *Inscriptions mandaïtes des coupes de Khouabir.* Paris, 1898.

Polotsky, H. *Manichäische Handschriften der Sammlung A. Chester Beatty, Band I: Manichäische Homilien.* Stuttgart, 1934.

Polotsky, H., and Böhlig, A. *Manichäische Handschriften der Staatlichen Museen Berlin,* Band 1: *Kephalaia, 1. Hälfte.* Stuttgart, 1934–40; *2. Hälfte (Lfg. 11/12).* Stuttgart, 1966.

Rahmani, I.E. *Studia Syriaca IV. Documenta de antiquis haeresibus.* Beirut, 1909.

Rehm, B., ed. *Die Pseudoklementinen II: Rekognitionen in Rufins Uebersetzung.* Berlin, 1965.

Rieder, D. *Targum Jonathan ben Uziel on the Pentateuch.* Jerusalem, 1974.

Schechter, S., ed. *Aboth de-Rabbi Natan.* Wien, 1887.

Sefer ha-Yashar. Reprint ed., Brooklyn, 1960.

Sefer ha-Zohar. 3 vols. Reprint of Vilna ed., New York, 1954.

Serapion Thmuitanus. *Adversus Manichaeos.* Edited by R.P. Casey, *Serapion of Thmuis Against the Manichees.* Cambridge, MA, 1931.

Al-Shahrastānī. *Kitāb al-milal wa-al-nihal: Book of Religious and Philosophical Sects.* Edited by W. Cureton. London, 1842–46.

Sperber, A., ed. *The Bible in Aramaic.* 4 vols. Leiden, 1959–68.

Sundermann, W. *Mittelpersische und parthische kosmogonische und Parabeltexte der Manichäer.* Berlin, 1973.

———. *Mitteliranische manichäische Texte kirchengeschichtlichen Inhalts.* Berlin, 1981.

Theodor, J., and Albeck, Ch., eds. *Midrash Bereshit Rabba.* 3 vols. Berlin, 1903–29; reprint ed., Jerusalem, 1965.

Theodore bar Konai. *Liber Scholiorum.* Edited by A. Scher. CSCO script. syri series II, vol. 66. Paris, 1912.

Thompson, R.C., ed. *The Epic of Gilgamish.* Oxford, 1930.

Timotheus Presbyter Constantinopolitanus. *De receptione haereticorum.* In *Patrologiae Graeca,* vol. 86.1, cols. 11–74. Edited by J.P. Migne. Paris, 1865.

Titus Bostrensis. *Adversus Manichaeos.* In *Patrologiae Graeca,* vol.18, cols. 1069–1264. Edited by J.P. Migne. Paris, 1857.

Weiss, I.H., ed. *Sifra deBey Rab.* Wien, 1862; reprint ed., New York, 1946.

Ya'qūb al-Qirqisānī. *Kitāb al-Anwār wa-l-marāqib.* 5 vols. Edited by L. Nemoy. New York, 1939–43.

Al-Ya'qūbī. *Ibn Wadih qui dicitur al-Ja'qubi historiae ....* 2 vols. Edited by M.T. Houtsma. Leiden, 1883.

SECONDARY SOURCES

Abraham ben Elijah of Vilna. *Sefer Rab Pe'alim.* Warsaw, 1894.

Adam, A. "Ist die Gnosis in aramäischen Weisheitsschulen entstanden?" In *Le origini dello gnosticismo: Colloquio di Messina, 13–18 aprile 1966, testi e discussioni,* pp. 291–301. Edited by U. Bianchi. Leiden, 1967.

———. "Manichäismus." In *Religionsgeschichte des Orients in der Zeit der Weltreligionen,* pp. 102–119. Handbuch der Orientalistik Bd.8, Ab.2. Leiden, 1961.

———. *Die Psalmen des Thomas und das Perlenlied als Zeugnisse vorchristlicher Gnosis.* Berlin, 1959.

Adler, W. *George Syncellus and His Predecessors: Ante-Diluvian History in the Chronicle of Syncellus and His Acknowledged Authorities.* Ph.D. dissertation, University of Pennsylvania, 1982. Ann Arbor, 1984.

Aland, B. "Mani und Bardesanes — Zur Entstehung des manichäischen Systems." In *Synkretismus im syrisch-persischen Kulturgebiet,* pp. 123–43. Edited by A. Dietrich. Göttingen, 1975.

Albright, W.F. *From the Stone Age to Christianity.* 2nd ed. Garden City, 1957.

Alexander, P.S. "Notes on the *Imago Mundi* of the Book of Jubilees." *Journal of Jewish Studies* 33 (1982): 197–213.

————. "The Targumim and Early Exegesis of 'Sons of God' in Genesis 6." *Journal of Jewish Studies* 23 (1972): 60–71.

Alfaric, P. *Les écritures manichéennes.* 2 vols. Paris, 1918–19.

Allberry, C.R.C. "Das manichäische Bema-Fest." *Zeitschrift für die neutestamentliche Wissenschaft* 37 (1938): 2–10.

Allegro, J.M. "Some Unpublished Fragments of Pseudepigraphical Literature from Qumran's Fourth Cave." *The Annual of Leeds University Oriental Society* 4 (1962–63): 3–5.

Alon, G. "The Levitical Uncleanness of Gentiles." In his *Jews, Judaism and the Classical World,* pp. 146–89. Jerusalem, 1977.

Andrae, T. *Mohammed: The Man and his Faith.* New York, 1936; reprint ed., New York, 1960.

Arnold-Döben, V. *Die Bildersprache des Manichäismus.* Köln, 1978.

Asmussen, J.P. *Manichaean Literature.* Delmar, NY, 1975.

Asmussen, J.P., and Böhlig, A., eds. *Die Gnosis III: Der Manichäismus.* Zürich & München, 1980.

Atiya, A.S. *A History of Eastern Christianity.* Notre Dame, 1968.

Attridge, H.W., and Oden, R.A., eds. *The Syrian Goddess (De Dea Syria) Attributed to Lucian.* Missoula, 1976.

Augustine. "Against the Epistle of Manichaeus called Fundamental." In *A Select Library of the Nicene and Post-Nicene Fathers of the Christian Church, First Series Volume IV: St. Augustin: The Writings Against the Manichaeans, and Against the Donatists,* pp. 129–50. Translated by R. Stothert. Series edited by P. Schaff. Reprint ed., New York, 1901.

Baḥya ben Asher. *Be'ur 'al hatorah.* 3 vols. Reprint ed., Jerusalem, 1966–68.

Bang, W. "Manichäische Erzähler." *Le Muséon* 44 (1931): 1–36.

Barc, B. "Samaél-Saklas-Yaldabaôth: Recherche sur la genèse d'un mythe gnostique." In *Colloque international sur les textes de Nag Hammadi (Quebec, 22–25 août 1978),* pp. 123–50. Edited by B. Barc. Quebec and Louvain, 1981.

Barr, J. "Aramaic-Greek Notes on the Book of Enoch." *Journal of Semitic Studies* 23 (1978): 184–98; 24 (1979): 179–92.

Bauer, T. "Ein viertes altbabylonisches Fragment des Gilgameš-Epos." *Journal of Near Eastern Studies* 16 (1957): 254–62.

Baumstark, A. "Der Text der Mani-Zitate in der syrischen Uebersetzung des Titus von Bostra." *Oriens Christianus* series 3, no.6 (1931), 23–42.

Baur, F.C. *Das manichäische Religionssystem nach den Quellen neu untersucht und entwickelt.* Tübingen, 1831.

Beausobre, I. de. *Histoire critique de Manichée et du Manichéisme.* Amsterdam, 1734–39; reprint ed., Leipzig, 1970.

Beer, B. *Das Buch der Jubiläen und sein Verhältniss zu den Midraschim.* Leipzig, 1856.

Beer, G. "Das Buch Henoch." In *Die Apokryphen und Pseudepigraphen des Alten Testaments.* Vol. 2: *Die Pseudepigraphen des Alten Testaments,* pp. 217–310. Edited by E. Kautzsch. Tübingen, 1900.

Benveniste, E. "Eléments perses en araméen d'Egypt." *Journal Asiatique* 242 (1954): 297–310.

————. "L'Erān-vēž et l'origine légendaire des Iraniens." *Bulletin of the School of Oriental Studies* 7 (1933–35): 265–74.

————. "La légende de Kombabos." In *Mélanges syriens offerts à Monsieur René Dussaud,* vol. 1, pp. 249–58. Paris, 1939.

Berger, K. *Das Buch der Jubiläen.* Gütersloh, 1981.

Bergmann, J. "Les éléments juifs dans les Pseudo-Clémentines." *Revue des études juives* 46 (1903): 89–98.

Bertrand, D.A., ed. *La vie grecque d'Adam et Eve.* Paris, 1987.

Beyer, K. *Die aramäischen Texte vom Toten Meer.* Göttingen, 1984.

Bickerman, E.J. *The Jews in the Greek Age.* Cambridge, MA, 1988.

Bidez, J. "Les écoles chaldéennes sous Alexandre et les Séleucides." *Annuaire de l'institut de philologie et d'histoire orientales (Bruxelles)* 3 (1935): 41–89.

Bidez, J., and Cumont, F. *Les mages hellénisés.* 2 vols. Paris, 1938.

Black, M. *An Aramaic Approach to the Gospels and Acts.* 3rd edition. Oxford, 1967.

————. *The Book of Enoch or I Enoch.* Leiden, 1985.

————. "The Twenty Angel Dekadarchs at I Enoch 6.7 and 69.2." *Journal of Jewish Studies* 33 (1982): 227–35.

Böhlig, A. "Der Synkretismus des Mani." In *Synkretismus im syrisch-persischen Kulturgebiet,* pp. 144–69. Edited by A. Dietrich. Göttingen, 1975.

Boilot, D.J. "al-Bīrūnī." In *The Encyclopaedia of Islam* (new edition), 1:1236–38. Leiden, 1960.

Bousset, W. *Hauptprobleme der Gnosis.* Göttingen, 1907; reprint ed. Göttingen, 1973.

————. "Die Testamente der zwölf Patriarchen." *Zeitschrift für die neutestamentliche Wissenschaft* 1 (1900): 141–75; 187–209.

Bousset, W., and Gressmann, H. *Die Religion des Judentums im spät-hellenistischen Zeitalter.* 3rd ed. Tübingen, 1926.

Bowman, R.A. "An Aramaic Religious Text in Demotic Script." *Journal of Near Eastern Studies* 3 (1944): 219–31.

————. "An Interpretation of the Asshur Ostracon." In *Royal Correspondence of the Assyrian Empire: Part IV*, pp. 275–82. Edited by L. Waterman. Ann Arbor, 1936.

Boyce, M. *A Catalogue of the Iranian Manuscripts in Manichaean Script in the German Turfan Collection.* Berlin, 1960.

————. *A History of Zoroastrianism.* Leiden, 1975– .

————. "The Manichaean Middle Persian Writings." In *The Cambridge History of Iran*, vol. 3(2): *The Seleucid, Parthian and Sasanian Periods*, pp. 1196–1204. Edited by E. Yarshater. Cambridge, 1983.

————. *A Reader in Manichaean Middle Persian and Parthian.* Leiden & Teheran, 1975.

Brandt, W. *Elchasai: ein Religionsstifter und sein Werk.* Leipzig, 1912.

Brauner, R.A. *A Comparative Lexicon of Old Aramaic.* Ph.D. dissertation, Dropsie University, 1974. Ann Arbor, 1984.

Brock, S.P. "A Fragment of Enoch in Syriac." *Journal of Theological Studies* 19 (1968): 626–31.

Brockelmann, C. *Grundriss der vergleichenden Grammatik der semitischen Sprachen.* 2 vols. Berlin, 1908–13.

————. *Lexicon Syriacum.* 2nd ed. Halle, 1928; reprint ed. Hildesheim, 1982.

Büchler, A. "The Levitical Impurity of the Gentile in Palestine Before the Year 70." *Jewish Quarterly Review* 17 (1926–27): 1–81.

Burkitt, F.C. *The Religion of the Manichees.* Cambridge, 1925.

Burstein, S.M. *The Babyloniaca of Berossus.* Malibu, CA, 1978.

Cantineau, J. "Tadmorea." *Syria* 14 (1933): 169–202.

Caquot, A. "I Hénoch." In *La Bible: écrits intertestamentaires*, pp. 465–625. Edited by A. Dupont-Sommer and M. Philonenko. Paris,

1987.
Cassin, E. *La splendeur divine: Introduction à l'étude de la mentalité mesopotamienne.* Paris, 1968.
Chadwick, H. *The Early Church.* Baltimore, 1967.
Charles, R.H., ed. *The Apocrypha and Pseudepigrapha of the Old Testament.* 2 vols. Oxford, 1913.
———. *The Book of Enoch.* Oxford, 1893.
———. *The Book of Jubilees.* London, 1902.
———. *The Greek Versions of the Testaments of the Twelve Patriarchs.* Oxford, 1908.
Charles, R.H., and Cowley, A. "An Early Source of the Testaments of the Patriarchs." *Jewish Quarterly Review* o.s. 19 (1906–7): 566–83.
Charlesworth, J.H., ed. *The Old Testament Pseudepigrapha.* 2 vols. New York, 1983–85.
———. "The SNTS Pseudepigrapha Seminars at Tübingen and Paris on the Books of Enoch." *New Testament Studies* 25 (1979): 315–23.
Chavannes, E., and Pelliot, P. *Un traité manichéen retrouvé en Chine.* Paris, 1913.
Christensen, A. *L'Iran sous les Sassanides.* Copenhagen, 1936.
———. *Les Kayanides.* Copenhagen, 1931.
Clemen, C. *Lukians Schrift über die syrische Göttin.* Leipzig, 1938.
Collins, J.J. "The Development of the Sibylline Tradition." In *Aufstieg und Niedergang der römischen Welt,* Teil II: Principat, Band 20.1, pp. 421–59. Edited by W. Haase. Berlin, 1987.
———. "Messianism in the Maccabean Period." In *Judaisms and Their Messiahs at the Turn of the Christian Era,* pp. 97–109. Edited by J. Neusner, W.S. Green, and E.S. Frerichs. Cambridge, 1987.
———. "Sibylline Oracles." In *The Old Testament Pseudepigrapha,* vol. 1, pp. 317–472. Edited by J.H. Charlesworth. New York, 1983.
Colpe, C. "Anpassung des Manichäismus an den Islam (Abu 'Isa al-Warraq)." *Zeitschrift der Deutschen Morgenländischen Gesellschaft* 109 (1959): 82–91.
———. "Das Siegel der Propheten." *Orientalia Suecana* 33–35 (1984–86): 71–83.
Coomaraswamy, A.K. *History of Indian and Indonesian Art.* New York, 1927; reprint ed., New York, 1965.

Cornill, C. *Das Buch des Propheten Ezechiel.* Leipzig, 1886.
Cothenet, E. "Le document de Damas." In *Les textes de Qumran,* vol. 2, pp. 131–204. Edited by J. Carmignac, et al. Paris, 1963.
Cowley, A. *Aramaic Papyri of the Fifth Century B.C.*. Oxford, 1923; reprint ed., Osnabrück, 1967.
Cross, F.M. "The Development of the Jewish Scripts." In *The Bible and the Ancient Near East: Essays in Honor of William Foxwell Albright,* pp. 170–264. Edited by G.E. Wright. New York, 1961; reprint ed., Garden City, 1965.
Crum, W.E. *A Coptic Dictionary.* Oxford, 1939.
Cumont, F. "La fin du monde selon les mages occidentaux." *Revue de l'histoire des religions* 103 (1931): 29–96.
——————. *Textes et monuments relatifs aux mystères de Mithra.* 2 vols. Bruxelles, 1896–99.
Cumont, F., and Kugener, M.-A. *Recherches sur le manichéisme.* Bruxelles, 1908–12.
Dalman, G. *Grammatik des jüdisch-palästinischen Aramäisch.* Leipzig, 1905; reprint ed., Darmstadt, 1960.
Davenport, G.L. *The Eschatology of the Book of Jubilees.* Leiden, 1971.
Davies, P.R. *Behind the Essenes: History and Ideology in the Dead Sea Scrolls.* Atlanta, 1987.
——————. *The Damascus Covenant: An Interpretation of the "Damascus Document."* Sheffield, 1983.
Day, J. *God's Conflict with the Dragon and the Sea: Echoes of a Canaanite Myth in the Old Testament.* Cambridge, 1985.
Delcor, M. "Le mythe de la chute des anges et de l'origine des géants comme explication du mal dans le monde dans l'apocalyptique juive: Histoire des traditions." *Revue de l'histoire des religions* 190 (1976): 3–53.
Denis, A.-M. *Introduction aux pseudépigraphes grecs d'ancien testament.* Leiden, 1970.
Dexinger, F. *Henochs Zehnwochenapokalypse und offene Probleme der Apokalyptikforschung.* Leiden, 1977.
——————. *Sturz der Göttersöhne oder Engel vor der Sintflut?* Vienna, 1966.
Dillmann, A. *Das Buch Henoch.* Leipzig, 1853.
——————. *Lexicon Linguae Aethiopicae.* Leipzig, 1865.
Dimant, D. "The «Pesher on the Periods» (4Q180) and 4Q181."

Israel Oriental Studies 9 (1979): 77–102.

Dobschütz, E. von, ed. *Das Decretum Gelasianum: De libris recipiendis et non recipiendis.* TU 38. Leipzig, 1912.

Dodge, B. *The Fihrist of al-Nadim.* 2 vols. New York, 1970.

Donner, H., and Röllig, W., eds. *Kanaanäische und aramäische Inschriften.* 3 vols. Wiesbaden, 1962–64.

Dozy, R., and De Goeje, M.J. "Nouveaux documents pour l'étude de la religion des Harraniens." In *Actes de la sixième session du congrès international des orientalistes à Leide,* pt. II sect. I, pp. 283–366. Leiden, 1884–85.

Drews, R. "The Babylonian Chronicles and Berossus." *Iraq* 37 (1975): 39–55.

Drijvers, H.J.W. *Bardaiṣan of Edessa.* Assen, 1966.

Driver, G.R. *Aramaic Documents of the Fifth Century B.C..* Oxford, 1957.

Drower, E.S. *The Mandaeans of Iraq and Iran.* Oxford, 1937.

Drower, E.S., and Macuch, R. *A Mandaic Dictionary.* Oxford, 1963.

Dunlop, D.M. *Arab Civilization to A.D. 1500.* New York, 1971.

Dupont-Sommer, A. *The Essene Writings from Qumran.* Translated by G. Vermes. Cleveland, 1961; reprint ed., Gloucester, MA, 1973.

————. "L'Ostracon araméen d'Assour." *Syria* 24 (1944–45): 24–61.

Dupont-Sommer, A., and Philonenko, M., eds. *La Bible: écrits intertestamentaires.* Paris, 1987.

Edzard, D.O. "Gilgameš." In *Wörterbuch der Mythologie Band I: Götter und Mythen in vorderen Orient,* pp. 69–73. Edited by H.W. Haussig. Stuttgart, 1965.

Endres, J.C. *Biblical Interpretation in the Book of Jubilees.* Washington, 1987.

Fahd, T. "Anges, démons et djinns en Islam." In *Génies, anges et démons,* pp. 155–214. «Sources Orientales VIII». Paris, 1971.

————. *Le panthéon de l'Arabie centrale à la veille de l'Hégire.* Paris, 1968.

Finkelstein, L. "Pre-Maccabean Documents in the Passover Haggadah." *Harvard Theological Review* 36 (1943): 1–38.

Fitzmyer, J.A. *The Dead Sea Scrolls: Major Publications and Tools for Study.* Missoula, 1977.

————. *The Genesis Apocryphon of Qumran Cave 1.* 2nd revised ed.

Rome, 1971.

————. "The Study of the Aramaic Background of the New Testament." In his *A Wandering Aramaean: Collected Aramaic Essays*, pp. 1–27. Chico, CA, 1979.

Fitzmyer, J.A., and Harrington, D.J. *A Manual of Palestinian Aramaic Texts.* Rome, 1978.

Flügel, G. *Mani: seine Lehre und seine Schriften.* Leipzig, 1862; reprint ed. Osnabrück, 1969.

Flusser, D. "The Apocryphal Book of *Ascensio Isaiae* and the Dead Sea Sect." *Israel Exploration Journal* 3 (1953): 30–47.

Foerster, W., ed. *Gnosis: A Selection of Gnostic Texts.* 2 vols. Oxford, 1972.

Fraenkel, S. *Die aramäischen Fremdwörter im Arabischen.* Leiden, 1886.

Frend, W.H.C. *The Rise of the Monophysite Movement.* Cambridge, 1972.

Friedrich, J. "Die hethitischen Bruchstücke des Gilgameš-Epos." *Zeitschrift für Assyriologie* 39 (1930): 1–82.

Fujita, S. "The Metaphor of Plant in Jewish Literature of the Intertestamental Period." *Journal for the Study of Judaism* 7 (1976): 30–45.

Gabain, A. von. *Alttürkische Grammatik.* 2nd ed. Leipzig, 1950.

Gaster, M. *The Chronicles of Jerahmeel.* London, 1899; reprint ed., New York, 1971.

Geiger, A. "Einige Worte über das Buch Henoch." *Jüdische Zeitschrift für Wissenschaft und Leben* 3 (1864–65): 196–204.

————. *Was hat Mohammed aus dem Judenthum aufgenommen?* Bonn, 1833; reprint ed., Leipzig, 1902.

Geyer, R. *Gedichte von Abû Başîr Maimûn Ibn Qais al-'A'šâ.* London, 1928.

Gimaret, D., and Monnot, G., eds. *Shahrastani: Livre des religions et des sectes I.* N.p., 1986.

Ginzberg, L. "Adam Ḳadmon." In *The Jewish Encyclopaedia,* 1:181–83. New York & London, 1901.

————. *The Legends of the Jews.* 7 vols. Philadelphia, 1913–38.

Giversen, S. *Apocryphon Johannis.* Copenhagen, 1963.

Glasson, T.F. *Greek Influence in Jewish Eschatology.* London, 1961.

Golb, N. "The Qumran Covenanters and the Later Jewish Sects." *Journal of Religion* 41 (1961): 38–50.

Goldstein, J.A. "The Date of the Book of Jubilees." *Proceedings of the American Academy of Jewish Research* 50 (1983): 63–86.

Greenfield, J.C. Prolegomenon to reprint of *3 Enoch or The Hebrew Book of Enoch*, by H. Odeberg. New York, 1973.

————. Review of the 3rd ed. of *An Aramaic Approach to the Gospels and Acts*, by M. Black. *Journal of Near Eastern Studies* 31 (1972): 58–61.

Greenfield, J.C., and Porten, B. *The Bisitun Inscription of Darius the Great: Aramaic Version.* Corpus Inscriptionum Iranicarum. Part I, Volume V, Text I. London, 1982.

Greenfield, J.C., and Stone, M.E. "The Books of Enoch and the Traditions of Enoch." *Numen* 26 (1979): 89–103.

————. "The Enochic Pentateuch and the Date of the Similitudes." *Harvard Theological Review* 70 (1977): 51–65.

Grelot, P. "La géographie mythique d'Hénoch et ses sources orientales." *Revue biblique* 65 (1958): 33–69.

————. "Hénoch et ses écritures." *Revue biblique* 82 (1975): 481–500.

Gressmann, H. *Die orientalischen Religionen im hellenistisch-römischen Zeitalter.* Berlin & Leipzig, 1930.

Grünbaum, M. *Gesammelte Aufsätze zur Sprach- und Sagenkunde.* Berlin, 1901.

Gruenwald, I. "Manichaeism and Judaism in Light of the Cologne Mani Codex." *Zeitschrift für Papyrologie und Epigraphik* 50 (1983): 29–45.

Grünwedel, A. *Altbuddhistische Kultstätten in Chinesisch-Turkistan.* Berlin, 1912.

Gunkel, H. *Genesis.* 5th ed. Göttingen, 1922.

Guttmann, J. *Die Religionsphilosophie des Saadia.* Göttingen, 1882.

Haarbrücker, T. *Abu-'l-Fath' Muhammad asch-Schahrastâni's Religionspartheien und Philosophen-Schulen.* Halle, 1850–51.

Haas, V. *Magie und Mythen in Babylonien.* Gifkendorf, 1986.

Hackin, J. *Recherches archéologiques en Asie centrale* (1931). Paris, 1936.

Halévy, J. "Recherches sur la langue de la rédaction primitive du livre d'Enoch." *Journal Asiatique* 6th series, IX (1867): 352–95.

Halleux, A. de. "La chronique melkite abrégée du Ms. Sinaï Syr. 10." *Le Muséon* 91 (1978): 5–44.

Haloun, G., and Henning, W.B. "The Compendium of the Doctrines and Styles of the Teaching of Mani, the Buddha of Light." *Asia Major* 3 (1953): 188–212.

Hambis, L., and Bussagli, M. "Manichaean Art." In *Encyclopaedia of World Art*, 9:433–43. New York, 1968.

Hamilton, E., and Cairns, H. *The Collected Dialogues of Plato.* Princeton, 1961.

Hanson, P.D. "Rebellion in Heaven, Azazel, and Euhemeristic Heroes in 1 Enoch 6–11." *Journal of Biblical Literature* 96 (1977): 195–233.

Harnack, A. *Geschichte der altchristlichen Literatur bis Eusebius.* 3 vols. Leipzig, 1893–1904.

Hatch, E., and Redpath, H.A. *A Concordance to the Septuagint.* 2 vols. Oxford, 1897.

Hedrick, C.W. *The Apocalypse of Adam: A Literary and Source Analysis.* Chico, CA, 1980.

Heidel, A. *The Gilgamesh Epic and Old Testament Parallels.* 2nd ed. Chicago, 1949; reprint ed., Chicago, 1971.

Heinemann, I. *Altjüdische Allegoristik.* Breslau, 1936.

Heller, B. "La chute des anges: Schemhazai, Ouzza et Azaël." *Revue des études juives* 60 (1910): 202–12.

Hengel, M. *Judaism and Hellenism.* 2 vols. Translated by J. Bowden. Philadelphia, 1974.

Henning, W.B. "The Book of the Giants." *Bulletin of the School of Oriental and African Studies* 11 (1943): 52–74.

————. "Ein manichäisches Henochbuch." *Sitzungsberichte der Preussischen Akademie der Wissenschaften in Berlin* (Berlin, 1934): 27–35.

————. "Neue Materialen zur Geschichte des Manichäismus." *Zeitschrift der Deutschen Morgenländischen Gesellschaft* 90 (1936): 1–18.

————. "A Sogdian Fragment of the Manichaean Cosmogony." *Bulletin of the School of Oriental and African Studies* 12 (1948): 306–18.

————. "Two Manichaean Magical Texts with an Excursus on the Parthian ending *-endeh*." *Bulletin of the School of Oriental and African Studies* 12 (1947): 39–66.

Henrichs, A. "The Cologne Mani Codex Reconsidered." *Harvard Studies in Classical Philology* 83 (1979): 339–67.

————. "Mani and the Babylonian Baptists: A Historical Confrontation." *Harvard Studies in Classical Philology* 77 (1973): 23–59.

Henrichs, A., and Koenen, L. "Ein griechischer Mani-Codex (P. Colon. inv. nr. 4780)." *Zeitschrift für Papyrologie und Epigraphik* 5 (1970): 97–217.

Hinz, W. *Altiranisches Sprachgut der Nebenüberlieferung.* Wiesbaden, 1975.

Honigmann, E. *Evêques et évêchés monophysites d'Asie antérieure au VIe siècle.* Louvain, 1951.

Horgan, M.P. *Pesharim: Qumran Interpretations of Biblical Books.* Washington, 1979.

Horovitz, J. *Koranische Untersuchungen.* Berlin & Leipzig, 1926.

Hultgård, A. "Théophanie et présence divine dans le judaïsme antique." In *La littérature intertestamentaire: Colloque de Strasbourg (17–19 octobre 1983)*, pp. 43–55. Edited by A. Caquot. Paris, 1985.

Jackson, A.V.W. *Researches in Manichaeism.* New York, 1932; reprint ed. New York, 1965.

Jacobsen, T. *The Sumerian King List.* Chicago, 1939.

Janssens, Y. "Le thème de la fornication des anges." In *Le origini dello gnosticismo: Colloquio di Messina, 13–18 aprile 1966, testi e discussioni*, pp. 488–95. Edited by U. Bianchi. Leiden, 1967.

Jean, C.-F., and Hoftijzer, J. *Dictionnaire des inscriptions sémitiques de l'ouest.* Leiden, 1965.

Jeffery, A. *The Foreign Vocabulary of the Qur'an.* Baroda, 1938.

Jensen, P. *Assyrisch-babylonische Mythen und Epen.* Berlin, 1900.

Jerome. *The Homilies of Saint Jerome: Volume I (1–59 On the Psalms).* Translated by M.L. Ewald. Washington, 1964.

Jonas, H. *Gnosis und spätantiker Geist,* Teil 1: *Die mythologische Gnosis.* Göttingen, 1934.

Jung, L. *Fallen Angels in Jewish, Christian and Mohammedan Literature.* Philadelphia, 1926.

Kahana, A. "Sefer Ḥanokh I." In his *Hasefarim haḥiṣonim,* vol. 1, pp. 19–101. Tel Aviv, 1936–37.

Kaufman, S.A. *The Akkadian Influences on Aramaic.* Chicago, 1974.

Kent, R.G. *Old Persian: Grammar — Texts — Lexicon.* 2nd revised ed. New Haven, 1953.

Kessler, K. *Mani: Forschungen über die manichäische Religion.* Berlin,

1889.

Kister, M. "Beshulley Sefer Ben Sira." *Leshonenu* 47 (1983): 125–46.

Kister, M.J. "Legends in *tafsir* and *hadith* Literature: The Creation of Adam and Related Stories." In *Approaches to the History of the Interpretation of the Qur'an*, pp. 82–114. Edited by A. Rippen. Oxford, 1988.

Klijn, A.F.J. "An Analysis of the Use of the Story of the Flood in the Apocalypse of Adam." In *Studies in Gnosticism and Hellenistic Religions presented to Gilles Quispel on the Occasion of his 65th Birthday*, pp. 218–26. Edited by R. van den Broek and M.J. Vermaseren. Leiden, 1981.

————. *Seth in Jewish, Christian and Gnostic Literature.* Leiden, 1977.

Klijn, A.F.J., and Reinink, G.J. *Patristic Evidence for Jewish-Christian Sects.* Leiden, 1973.

Klimkeit, H.-J. "Der Buddha Henoch: Qumran und Turfan." *Zeitschrift für Religions- und Geistesgeschichte* 32 (1980): 367–77.

————. "Der dreistämmige Baum: Bemerkungen zur manichäischen Kunst und Symbolik." In *Kulturwissenschaften: Festgabe für Wilhelm Perpeet zum 65. Geburtstag*, pp. 245–62. Bonn, 1980.

————. *Manichaean Art and Calligraphy.* Leiden, 1982.

Knibb, M.A. "The Date of the Parables of Enoch: A Critical Review." *New Testament Studies* 25 (1979): 345–59.

————. *The Ethiopic Book of Enoch.* 2 vols. Oxford, 1978.

Köbert, R. "Die Einführung Birunis zu seinem Verzeichnis der Schriften Rāzīs." *Orientalia* 27 (1958): 198–202.

————. "Orientalistische Bemerkungen zum Kölner Mani-Codex." *Zeitschrift für Papyrologie und Epigraphik* 8 (1971): 243–47.

Koenen, L. "Manichäische Mission und Klöster in Ægypten." In *Das römisch-byzantinische Ægypten*, pp. 93–108. Mainz am Rhein, 1983.

Koffmahn, E. *Die Doppelurkunden aus der Wüste Juda.* Leiden, 1968.

Kosmala, H. "Gābhar." In *Theological Dictionary of the Old Testament*, 2:373–77. Edited by G.J. Botterweck and H. Ringgren. Grand Rapids, MI, 1977.

Kraus, P. *Epître de Beruni, contenant le répertoire des ouvrages de M. b. Zakariya' ar-Razi.* Paris, 1936.

Kraus, P., and Pines, S. "al-Rāzī." In *Enzyklopaedie des Islam*, 3:1225–27. Leiden, 1936.

Küchler, M. *Frühjüdische Weisheitstraditionen*. Göttingen, 1979.

Kugener, M.-A. "Textes grecs relatifs à Sévère." *Patrologia Orientalis* 2 (1907): 336–61.

————. "Vie de Sévère [John of Beit-Aphthonia]." *Patrologia Orientalis* 2 (1907): 207–64.

————. "Vie de Sévère [Zacharias Scholasticus]." *Patrologia Orientalis* 2 (1907): 7–115.

Kuhn, K.G. *Konkordanz zu den Qumrantexten*. Göttingen, 1960.

Lagarde, P. de. *Materialen zur Kritik und Geschichte des Pentateuchs*. Leipzig, 1867.

Lambert, W.G. "Gilgameš in Religious, Historical and Omen Texts and the Historicity of Gilgameš." In *Gilgameš et sa légende*, pp. 39–56. Edited by P. Garelli. Paris, 1960.

Landersdorfer, S. *Studien zum biblischen Versöhnungstag*. Münster, 1924.

Lawlor, H.J. "Early Citations From the Book of Enoch." *Journal of Philology* 25 (1897): 164–225.

Layton, B. *The Gnostic Scriptures*. Garden City, NY, 1987.

Leander, P. *Laut- und Formenlehre des Ægyptisch-aramäischen*. Göteborg, 1928.

Le Coq, A. von. *Die buddhistische Spätantike in Mittelasien II: Die manichäischen Miniaturen*. Berlin, 1923.

————. *Buried Treasures of Chinese Turkestan*. London, 1928.

————. "Türkische Manichaica aus Chotscho III." *Abhandlungen der Preussischen Akademie der Wissenschaften in Berlin*, Phil.-hist. Kl., Nr.2. Berlin, 1922.

Leemhuis, F., Klijn, A.F.J., and van Gelder, G.J.H. *The Arabic Text of the Apocalypse of Baruch*. Leiden, 1986.

Levy, J. *Chaldäisches Wörterbuch über die Targumim und einen grossen Teil des rabbinischen Schrifttums*. 2 vols. Leipzig, 1867–68.

Lewin, M. *Die Scholien des Theodor bar Koni zur Patriarchengeschichte (Genesis XII–L)*. Berlin, 1905.

Lidzbarski, M. "Ein aramäischer Brief aus der Zeit Ašurbanipals." *Zeitschrift für Assyriologie* 31 (1917–18): 193–202.

————, ed. *Ginzā: Der Schatz oder das grosse Buch der Mandäer*. Göttingen, 1925.

————. "Warum schrieb Mani aramäisch?" *Orientalistische Literaturzeitung* 30 (1927): 913–17.

Lieu, S.N.C. "An Early Byzantine Formula for the Renunciation of Manichaeism — The Capita VII Contra Manichaeos of <Zacharias of Mitylene>." *Jahrbuch für Antike und Christentum* 26 (1983): 152–218.

————. *Manichaeism in the Later Roman Empire and Medieval China: A Historical Survey.* Manchester, 1985; reprint ed., Manchester, 1988.

Littmann, E. "Hārūt und Mārūt." In *Festschrift Friedrich Carl Andreas,* pp. 70–87. Leipzig, 1916.

Luttikhuizen, G.P. *The Revelation of Elchasai.* Tübingen, 1985.

McCullough, W.S. *A Short History of Syriac Christianity to the Rise of Islam.* Chico, CA, 1982.

MacKenzie, D.N. "Mani's Šabuhragan." *Bulletin of the School of Oriental and African Studies* 42 (1979): 500–534; 43 (1980): 288–310.

Maimonides. *The Guide for the Perplexed.* Translated by M. Friedländer. London, 1904; reprint ed., New York, 1956.

Mann, J. *The Bible as Read and Preached in the Old Synagogue.* Volume 1: *The Palestinian Triennial Cycle: Genesis and Exodus.* Cincinnati, 1940; reprint ed., New York, 1971.

Marcovich, M. "The Naassene Psalm in Hippolytus (Haer. 5.10.2)." In *The Rediscovery of Gnosticism: Proceedings of the International Conference on Gnosticism at Yale ... Volume II: Sethian Gnosticism,* pp. 770–78. Edited by B. Layton. Leiden, 1981.

Margolioth, R., ed. *Mal'akey 'elyon.* Jerusalem, 1945; reprint ed., Jerusalem, 1964.

Marmorstein, A. "Midrash 'Abkir." *Debir* 1 (1923): 113–44.

Martin, F. *Le livre d'Hénoch.* Paris, 1908.

Martini, R. *Pugio Fidei adversus Mauros et Judaeos.* Leipzig, 1687.

Mayer, M. *Die Giganten und Titanen in der antike Sagen und Kunst.* Berlin, 1887.

Mayer, R. *Die biblische Vorstellung vom Weltenbrand.* Bonn, 1956.

Mearns, C.L. "Dating the Similitudes of Enoch." *New Testament Studies* 25 (1979): 360–69.

Meier, G. *Die assyrische Beschwörungssammlung Maqlû.* Berlin, 1937; reprint ed., Osnabrück, 1967.

Merx, A. *Chrestomathia Targumica.* Berlin, 1888.

Meyer, E. "Die Gemeinde des neuen Bundes im Lande Damaskus: eine jüdische Schrift aus der Seleukidenzeit." *Abhandlungen der Preussischen Akademie der Wissenschaften in Berlin,* Phil.-hist. Kl. IX (1919): 1–65.

————. *Ursprung und Anfänge des Christentums.* 3 vols. Stuttgart, 1921–23.

Milik, J.T. *The Books of Enoch: Aramaic Fragments of Qumrân Cave 4.* Oxford, 1976.

————. "Ecrits préesséniens de Qumrân: d'Hénoch à Amram." In *Qumrân: sa piété, sa théologie et son milieu,* pp. 91–106. Edited by M. Delcor. Paris, 1978.

————. "Les papyrus araméens d'Hermoupolis et les cultes syro-phéniciens en Egypte perse." *Biblica* 48 (1967): 546–622.

————. "«Prière de Nabonide» et autres écrits d'un cycle de Daniel." *Revue biblique* 63 (1956): 407–15.

————. "Problèmes de la littérature hénochique à la lumière des fragments araméennes de Qumrân." *Harvard Theological Review* 64 (1971): 333–78.

————. *Ten Years of Discovery in the Wilderness of Judaea.* Translated by J. Strugnell. London, 1957.

————. "Le testament de Lévi en araméen." *Revue biblique* 62 (1955): 398–406.

————. "Turfan et Qumran, Livre des Géants juif et manichéen." In *Tradition und Glaube: Das frühe Christentum in seiner Umwelt,* pp. 117–127. Edited by G. Jeremias, H.-W. Kuhn, and H. Stegemann. Göttingen, 1971.

Mohaghegh, M. "Razi's Kitab al-Ilm al-Ilāhi and the Five Eternals." *Abr-Nahrain* 13 (1972–73): 16–23.

Molenberg, C. "A Study of the Roles of Shemihaza and Asael in 1 Enoch 6–11." *Journal of Jewish Studies* 35 (1984): 136–46.

Monnot, G. *Penseurs musulmans et religions iraniennes: 'Abd al-Jabbar et ses devanciers.* Paris, 1974.

Montgomery, J.A., ed. *Aramaic Incantation Texts From Nippur.* Philadelphia, 1913.

————. "A Magical Bowl-Text and the Original Script of the Manichaeans." *Journal of the American Oriental Society* 32 (1912): 433–38.

Morard, F. *L'Apocalypse d'Adam (NH V,5)*. Quebec, 1985.

Mosheim, J.L. *De rebus christianorum ante Constantium Magnum commentarii.* Helmstedt, 1753.

Müller, F.W.K. "Handschriften-Reste in Estrangelo-Schrift aus Turfan, Chinesisch-Turkistan." *Sitzungsberichte der Preussischen Akademie der Wissenschaften in Berlin* (1904): 348–52.

Murray, G. *Five Stages of Greek Religion.* 3rd ed. Boston, 1951; reprint ed., Garden City, 1955.

Nagel, P. "Die apokryphen Apostelakten des 2. und 3. Jahrhunderts in der manichäischen Literatur." In *Gnosis und Neues Testament,* pp. 149–82. Edited by K.-W. Tröger. Gütersloh, 1973.

Nickelsburg, G.W.E. "Apocalyptic and Myth in 1 Enoch 6–11." *Journal of Biblical Literature* 96 (1977): 383–405.

————. "The Bible Rewritten and Expanded." In *Jewish Writings of the Second Temple Period,* pp. 89–156. Edited by M.E. Stone. Assen & Philadelphia, 1984.

————. "Enoch, Levi, and Peter: Recipients of Revelation in Upper Galilee." *Journal of Biblical Literature* 100 (1981): 575–600.

————. *Jewish Literature Between the Bible and the Mishnah: A Historical and Literary Introduction.* Philadelphia, 1981.

————. Review of *Textual and Historical Studies in the Book of Jubilees,* by J.C. VanderKam. *Journal of the American Oriental Society* 100 (1980): 83–84.

————. "Some Related Traditions in the Apocalypse of Adam, the Books of Adam and Eve, and 1 Enoch." In *The Rediscovery of Gnosticism: Proceedings of the International Conference on Gnosticism at Yale ... Volume II: Sethian Gnosticism,* pp. 515–39. Edited by B. Layton. Leiden, 1981.

Nöldeke, T. *Das iranische Nationalepos.* 2nd ed. Berlin, 1920.

————. "Die Namen der aramäischen Nation und Sprache." *Zeitschrift der Deutschen Morgenländischen Gesellschaft* 25 (1871): 113–31.

————. Review of *Inscriptions mandaïtes des coupes de Khouabir,* by H. Pognon. *Wiener Zeitschrift für die Kunde des Morgenlandes* 12 (1898): 353–61.

————. Review of *Mani: Forschungen über die manichäische Religion,* by K. Kessler. *Zeitschrift der Deutschen Morgenländischen*

Gesellschaft 43 (1889): 535–44.

Nötscher, F. *Zur theologischen Terminologie der Qumran-Texte.* Bonn, 1956.

Nyberg, H.S. "Forschungen über den Manichäismus." *Zeitschrift für neutestamentliche Wissenschaft* 34 (1935): 70–91.

Oden, R.A. *Studies in Lucian's De Syria Dea.* Missoula, 1977.

Oelsner, J. "Ein Beitrag zu keilschriftlichen Königstitulaturen in hellenistischer Zeit." *Zeitschrift für Assyriologie* 56 (1964): 262–74.

Oppenheim, A.L. *The Interpretation of Dreams in the Ancient Near East.* Philadelphia, 1956.

Otto, R. *The Idea of the Holy.* Translated by J.W. Harvey. Oxford, 1923; reprint ed., Oxford, 1973.

Payne Smith, R. *Thesaurus Syriacus.* 2 vols. Oxford, 1879–1901.

Pearson, B.A. "Jewish Sources in Gnostic Literature." In *Jewish Writings of the Second Temple Period*, pp. 443–81. Edited by M.E. Stone. Assen & Philadelphia, 1984.

————. "The Problem of 'Jewish Gnostic' Literature." In *Nag Hammadi, Gnosticism, & Early Christianity*, pp. 15–35. Edited by C.W. Hedrick and R. Hodgson, Jr. Peabody, MA, 1986.

Pellat, C. "al-Djāḥiẓ." In *The Encyclopaedia of Islam* (new edition), 2:385–87. Leiden, 1965.

————. "Le témoignage d'al-Jāḥiẓ sur les manichéens." In *Essays in Honor of Bernard Lewis: The Islamic World, From Classical to Modern Times*, pp. 269–79. Edited by C.E. Bosworth, et al. Princeton, 1989.

Pelliot, P. "Two New Manichaean Manuscripts from Tun-Huang." *Journal of the Royal Asiatic Society* (1925): 113.

Pépin, J. *Mythe et allégorie: Les origines grecques et les contestations judéo-chrétiennes.* 2nd ed. Paris, 1976.

Peterson, E. "Urchristentum und Mandäismus." *Zeitschrift für die neutestamentliche Wissenschaft* 27 (1928): 55–98.

Polotsky, H.J. "Manichäismus." In *Paulys Real-Encyklopädie der klassischen Altertumswissenschaft*, Supplementband VI, cols. 240–71. Stuttgart, 1935.

Porten, B., and Greenfield, J.C. *Jews of Elephantine and Aramaeans of Syene.* Jerusalem, 1974.

Puech, H.-C. "Fêtes et solemnités manichéennes: le Bêma." *Annuaire du Collège de France* 72 (1972): 322–26.

————. *Le manichéisme: son fondateur — sa doctrine.* Paris, 1949.

————. "Le Prince des Ténèbres en son royaume." In *Satan*, pp. 136–74. Paris, 1948.

Qimron, E. *The Hebrew of the Dead Sea Scrolls.* Atlanta, 1986.

Rabin, C. *The Zadokite Documents.* 2nd revised ed. Oxford, 1958.

Reeves, J.C. "The 'Elchasaite' Sanhedrin of the Cologne Mani Codex in Light of Second Temple Jewish Sectarian Sources." *Journal of Jewish Studies* 42 (1991): 68–91.

————. "An Enochic Motif in Manichaean Tradition." In *Manichaica Selecta: Studies Presented to Professor Julien Ries on the Occasion of his Seventieth Birthday.* Louvain, forthcoming.

Reitzenstein, R. "Eine wertlose und eine wertvolle Ueberlieferung über den Manichäismus." *Nachrichten von der Gesellschaft der Wissenschaften zu Göttingen,* phil.-hist. Kl. (1931): 28–58.

Reitzenstein, R., and Schaeder, H.H. *Studien zum antike Synkretismus aus Iran und Griechenland.* Leipzig, 1926.

Ries, J. "La fête de Bêma dans l'église de Mani." *Revue des études augustiniennes* 22 (1976): 218–33.

Ritter, H. "Philologika III. Muhammedanische Häresiographen." *Der Islam* 18 (1929): 34–55.

Robinson, J.M., ed. *The Nag Hammadi Library in English.* San Francisco, 1977; reprint ed., San Francisco, 1981.

Rose, H.J. *A Handbook of Greek Mythology.* London, 1928; reprint ed., New York, 1959.

Rosenthal, F. *Die aramaistische Forschung seit Th. Nöldeke's Veröffentlichungen.* Leipzig, 1939; reprint ed., Leipzig, 1964.

————. *Die Sprache der palmyrenischen Inschriften.* Leipzig, 1936.

Rowley, H.H. *The Relevance of Apocalyptic.* 3rd ed. New York, 1964.

Rudolph, K. *Gnosis: The Nature and History of Gnosticism.* Translation edited by R. McL. Wilson. San Francisco, 1983.

————. *Die Mandäer.* 2 vols. Göttingen, 1960–61.

————. *Theogonie, Kosmogonie und Anthropogonie in den mandäischen Schriften.* Göttingen, 1965.

Ruska, J. "Al-Bīrūnī als Quelle für das Leben und die Schriften al-Rāzīs." *Isis* 5 (1923): 26–50.

Russell, D.S. *The Method and Message of Jewish Apocalyptic.* Philadelphia, 1964.

Saadia Gaon. *The Book of Beliefs and Opinions.* Translated by S. Rosenblatt. New Haven, 1948.

Sachau, C.E. *Alberuni's India.* London, 1888; reprint ed., London, 1910.

———. *The Chronology of Ancient Nations.* London, 1879.

Saunders, E.D. *Mudrā: A Study of Symbolic Gestures in Japanese Buddhist Sculpture.* New York, 1960.

Schaeder, H.H. "Hasan al-Başri: Studien zur Frühgeschichte des Islam." *Der Islam* 14 (1925): 1–75.

———. "Ein Lied von Mani." *Orientalistische Literaturzeitung* 29 (1926): 104–7.

———. Review of "Ein Mani-Fund," by C. Schmidt and H. Polotsky. *Gnomon* 9 (1933): 337–62.

———. *Studien zur orientalischen Religionsgeschichte.* Edited by C. Colpe. Darmstadt, 1968.

———. "Urform und Fortbildungen des manichäischen Systems." In *Vorträge der Bibliothek Warburg IV*, pp. 65–157. Edited by F. Saxl. Leipzig, 1927.

Schall, A. *Studien über griechische Fremdwörter im Syrischen.* Darmstadt, 1960.

Schechter, S. *Aspects of Rabbinic Theology.* New York, 1909; reprint ed., New York, 1961.

Scheftelowitz, I. *Die Entstehung der manichäischen Religion und des Erlösungsmysteriums.* Giessen, 1922.

Schmidt, C., and Polotsky, H. "Ein Mani-Fund in Ægypten." *Sitzungsberichte der Preussischen Akademie der Wissenschaften in Berlin* (Berlin, 1933): 4–90.

Schmidt, N. "The Original Language of the Parables of Enoch." In *Old Testament and Semitic Studies in Memory of William Rainey Harper*, vol. 2, pp. 327–50. Edited by R.F. Harper, F. Brown, and G.F. Moore. Chicago, 1908.

Schnabel, P. *Berossos und die babylonisch-hellenistische Literatur.* Leipzig, 1923; reprint ed., Hildesheim, 1968.

Scholem, G. "Kabbalah und Myth." *Eranos-Jahrbuch* 17 (1949): 287–334.

———. *On the Kabbalah and its Symbolism.* New York, 1965; reprint ed., New York, 1978.

———. *Origins of the Kabbalah.* N.p., 1987.

Schrader, E., Zimmern, H., and Winckler, H., eds. *Die Keilinschriften und das Alte Testament.* 3rd ed. Berlin, 1903.

Schulthess, F. *Umajja ibn Abi ṣ Ṣalt.* Beiträge zur Assyriologie 8.3. Leipzig, 1911.

Schwab, M. *Vocabulaire de l'angélologie d'après les manuscrits hébreux de la Bibliothèque Nationale.* Paris, 1897.

Schwartz, E. "Berossos." In *Paulys Real-Encyclopädie der klassischen Altertumswissenschaft,* Band 3:1, cols. 309–16. Stuttgart, 1897.

Schwarz, E. *Identität durch Abgrenzung: Abgrenzungsprozesse in Israel im 2. vorchristlichen Jahrhundert und ihre traditionsgeschichtlichen Voraussetzungen.* Frankfurt am Main, 1982.

Seeliger, K. "Weltalter (Weltjahr)." In *Ausführliches Lexikon der griechischen und römischen Mythologie,* 6:426–30. Edited by W.H. Roscher. Leipzig, 1924–37.

Sezgin, F. *Geschichte des arabischen Schrifttums.* 9 vols. Leiden, 1967–.

Sims-Williams, N. "The Manichaean Commandments: A Survey of the Sources." In *Papers in Honour of Professor Mary Boyce,* pp. 573–82. Leiden, 1985.

Skinner, J. *A Critical and Exegetical Commentary on Genesis.* Revised ed. New York, 1925.

Sokoloff, M. "Notes on the Aramaic Fragments of Enoch From Qumran Cave 4." *MAARAV* 1/2 (1978–79): 197–224.

———. *The Targum to Job From Qumran Cave XI.* Ramat-Gan, 1974.

Speyer, H. *Die biblischen Erzählungen im Qoran.* Gräfenhainichen, 1931; reprint ed. Hildesheim, 1988.

Spiegel, J.S. "Ha'edut ha'aḥaronah le-Midrash 'Abkir." *Kiryat Sefer* 45 (1970): 611–14.

Spiegel, S. "Noah, Daniel, and Job: Touching on Canaanite Relics in the Legends of the Jews." In *Louis Ginzberg Jubilee Volume,* English section, pp. 305–55. New York, 1945.

Spuler, B. "Die westsyrische (monophysitische/jakobitische) Kirche." In *Religionsgeschichte des Orients in der Zeit der Weltreligionen,* pp. 170–216. Handbuch der Orientalistik Bd.8, Ab.2. Leiden, 1961.

Steiner, R.C., and Nims, C.F. "Ashurbanipal and Shamash-shum-ukin: A Tale of Two Brothers from the Aramaic Text in Demotic Script." *Revue biblique* 92 (1985): 60–81.

Stern, S.M. "Abū 'Isā Muḥammad b. Harūn al-Warrāḳ." In *The*

Encyclopaedia of Islam (new edition), 1:130. Leiden, 1960.

Stocks, H. "Studien zu Lukians »De Syria Dea«." *Berytus* 4 (1937): 1–40.

Strack, H.L. *Introduction to the Talmud and Midrash.* New York, 1931; reprint ed., New York, 1980.

Strecker, G. "Elkesai." In *Reallexikon für Antike und Christentum,* 4:1171–86. Stuttgart, 1959.

Stroumsa, G.A.G. *Another Seed: Studies in Gnostic Mythology.* Leiden, 1984.

————. "Aspects de l'eschatologie manichéenne." *Revue de l'histoire des religions* 198 (1981): 163–81.

Stroumsa, S., and Stroumsa, G.G. "Aspects of Anti-Manichaean Polemics in Late Antiquity and Under Early Islam." *Harvard Theological Review* 81 (1988): 37–58.

Strugnell, J. "Notes en marge du volume V des Discoveries in the Judaean Desert of Jordan." *Revue de Qumran* 7 (1969–71): 163–276.

Sundermann, W. "Some More Remarks on Mithra in the Manichaean Pantheon." In *Etudes mithraiques,* pp. 485–99. Edited by J. Duchesne-Guillemin. Leiden, 1978.

————. "Ein weiteres Fragment aus Manis Gigantenbuch." In *Orientalia J. Duchesne-Guillemin emerito oblata,* pp. 491–505. Leiden, 1984.

Suter, D.W. "Fallen Angel, Fallen Priest: The Problem of Family Purity in 1 Enoch 6–16." *Hebrew Union College Annual* 50 (1979): 115–35.

————. *Tradition and Composition in the Parables of Enoch.* Missoula, 1979.

Al-Suyūṭī. [*Kitāb*] *al-raḥma fi 'l-ṭibb wal-ḥikma.* Reprint ed., Beirut, 1983.

Tardieu, M. *Le manichéisme.* Paris, 1981.

————. "Ṣābiens coraniques et «Ṣābiens» de Ḥarrān." *Journal Asiatique* 274 (1986): 1–44.

————. *Trois mythes gnostiques: Adam, Eros et les animaux d'Egypte dans un écrit de Nag Hammadi (II,5).* Paris, 1974.

Taūbler, E. "Jerusalem 201 to 199 B.C.E.: On the History of a Messianic Movement." *Jewish Quarterly Review* 37 (1946–47): 1–30; 125–37; 249–63.

Testuz, M. "Deux fragments inédits des manuscrits de la Mer Morte." *Semitica* 5 (1955): 37–38.

————. *Les idées religieuses du Livre des Jubilés.* Geneva, 1960.

Thomas, J. *Le mouvement baptiste en Palestine et Syrie.* Gembloux, 1935.

Tigay, J.H. *The Evolution of the Gilgamesh Epic.* Philadelphia, 1982.

Till, W.C., and Schenke, H.-M. *Die gnostische Schriften des koptischen Papyrus Berolinensis 8502.* 2nd ed. Berlin, 1972.

Tisserant, E. "Fragments syriaques du livre des Jubilés." *Revue biblique* 30 (1921): 55–86; 206–32.

Tubach, Jürgen. "Spuren des astronomischen Henochbuches bei den Manichäern Mittelasiens." In *Nubia et Oriens Christianus: Festschrift für C. Detlef G. Müller zum 60. Geburtstag,* pp. 73–95. Edited by P.O. Scholz and R. Stempel. Köln, 1988.

Uhlig, S. *Das äthiopische Henochbuch.* Gütersloh, 1984.

Ungnad, A., and Gressmann, H. *Das Gilgamesch-Epos.* Göttingen, 1911.

Vajda, G. "ʿAzāzīl." In *The Encyclopaedia of Islam* (new edition), 1:811. Leiden, 1960.

————. "La démonstration de l'unité divine d'après Yūsuf al-Baṣīr." In *Studies in Mysticism and Religion Presented to Gershom G. Scholem on his Seventieth Birthday,* pp. 288–306. Jerusalem, 1967.

————. "Hārūt wa-Mārūt." In *The Encyclopaedia of Islam* (new edition), 3:236–37. Leiden, 1971.

————. "Le témoignage d'al-Māturidī sur la doctrine des Manichéens, des Dayṣānites et des Marcionites." *Arabica* 13 (1966): 1–38; 113–28.

————. "Les zindiqs en pays d'Islam au début de la période Abbaside." *Rivista degli Studi Orientali* 17 (1938): 173–229.

Vajda, G., and Blumenthal, D.R. *Al-Kitāb al-Muḥtawī de Yūsuf al-Baṣīr.* Leiden, 1985.

van Buitenen, J.A.B., ed. *The Mahabharata: 1. The Book of the Beginning.* Chicago, 1973.

van der Horst, P.W., and Mansfeld, J. *An Alexandrian Platonist Against Dualism.* Leiden, 1974.

VanderKam, J.C. *Enoch and the Growth of an Apocalyptic Tradition.* Washington, 1984.

————. "Enoch Traditions in Jubilees and Other Second-Century Sources." In *Society of Biblical Literature Seminar Papers*

1978, 1:229–51.

———. "Some Major Issues in the Contemporary Study of 1 Enoch." *MAARAV* 3 (1982): 85–97.

———. *Textual and Historical Studies in the Book of Jubilees.* Missoula, 1977.

Vermes, G. "The Archangel Sariel: A Targumic Parallel to the Dead Sea Scrolls." In *Christianity, Judaism and Other Greco-Roman Cults: Studies for Morton Smith at Sixty*, vol. 3, pp. 159–66. Edited by J. Neusner. Leiden, 1975.

Vian, F. *La guerre des géants.* Paris, 1952.

Villey, A. *Alexandre de Lycopolis: Contre la doctrine de Mani.* Paris, 1985.

Volz, P. *Die Eschatologie der jüdischen Gemeinde im neutestamentlichen Zeitalter.* Tübingen, 1934.

Wacholder, B.Z. "The Date of the Eschaton in the Book of Jubilees." *Hebrew Union College Annual* 56 (1985): 87–101.

———. *The Dawn of Qumran: The Sectarian Torah and the Teacher of Righteousness.* Cincinnati, 1983.

Wagner, S. *Die Essener in der wissenschaftlichen Diskussion.* Berlin, 1960.

Wansbrough, J. *Quranic Studies.* Oxford, 1977.

Wensinck, A.J. "Muhammed und die Propheten." *Acta Orientalia* (Copenhagen) 2 (1924): 168–98.

———. *Tree and Bird as Cosmological Symbols in Western Asia.* Amsterdam, 1921.

Westermann, C. *Genesis 1–11: A Commentary.* Translated by J.J. Scullion. Minneapolis, 1984.

Widengren, G. *The Great Vohu Manah and the Apostle of God: Studies in Iranian and Manichaean Religion.* Uppsala, 1945.

———. *Mani und der Manichäismus.* Stuttgart, 1961.

———. "Manichaeism and its Iranian Background." In *The Cambridge History of Iran*, Volume 3(2): *The Seleucid, Parthian and Sasanian Periods*, pp. 965–90. Edited by E. Yarshater. Cambridge, 1983.

———, ed. *Der Manichäismus.* Darmstadt, 1977.

———. "Der Manichäismus: Kurzgefasste Geschichte der Problem-forschung." In *Gnosis: Festschrift für Hans Jonas*, pp. 278–315. Edited by B. Aland. Göttingen, 1978.

————. *Mesopotamian Elements in Manichaeism.* Uppsala, 1946.

————. *Muhammad, the Apostle of God, and his Ascension.* Uppsala, 1955.

Wilcke, C. "Ḫuwawa/Ḫumbaba." In *Reallexikon der Assyriologie,* 4:530–35. Edited by E. Ebeling, et al. Reprint ed., Berlin & New York, 1972–.

Winkler, H.A. *Salomo und die Ḳarīna.* Stuttgart, 1931.

Winternitz, M. *A History of Indian Literature.* Translated by V.S. Sarma. Delhi, 1981.

Wiseman, D.J. "Additional Neo-Babylonian Gilgamesh Fragments." In *Gilgameš et sa légende,* pp. 123–35. Edited by P. Garelli. Paris, 1960.

Wright, W. *Catalogue of the Syriac Manuscripts in the British Museum.* 3 vols. London, 1870–72.

————. *A Grammar of the Arabic Language.* 3rd ed. Cambridge, 1896–98; reprint ed., Cambridge, 1979.

Yadin, Y. *The Scroll of the War of the Sons of Light Against the Sons of Darkness.* Oxford, 1962.

Yaron, R. "The Murabba'at Documents." *Journal of Jewish Studies* 11 (1960): 157–71.

Yarshater, E. "Iranian Common Beliefs and World-View." In *The Cambridge History of Iran,* vol. 3(1): *The Seleucid, Parthian and Sasanian Periods,* pp. 343–58. Edited by E. Yarshater. Cambridge, 1983.

————. "Iranian National History." In *The Cambridge History of Iran,* vol. 3(1): *The Seleucid, Parthian and Sasanian Periods,* pp. 359–477. Edited by E. Yarshater. Cambridge, 1983.

Zimmer, H. *Myths and Symbols in Indian Art and Civilization.* Princeton, 1946; reprint ed., Princeton, 1974.

Zunz, L., and Albeck, Ch. *Haderashot beyisrael.* Jerusalem, 1946.

Index of Citations

I. HEBREW SCRIPTURES

Jeremiah

1:14 — 178
22:3 — 150

Ezekiel

31:1–14 — 90
32:27 — 70
38–39 — 178
38:2 — 178
38:5 — 179
39:2 — 179
45:9 — 150

Amos

2:9 — 171, 182
7:1 (LXX) — 178
7:4 — 146

Zephaniah

1:18 — 146
3:8 — 146

Malachi

3:19 — 146

Psalms

1 — 99, 100
1:1–2 — 149
24:7–10 — 202
29:10 — 140
92:14 — 100
92:15 — 100
104:4 — 181

Job

4:12–16 — 141
7:5 — 181
21:6 — 108
40:10 — 83

Ecclesiastes

8:1 — 91

Esther

3:14 — 155
4:8 — 155
6:1 — 85

Daniel

2:1 — 85
2:9–11 — 90
2:23 — 146
2:24 — 90
2:31 — 72, 85
2:34 — 143
3:18 — 114
3:32–33 — 154
4:1–25 — 90
4:6 — 158
4:7 — 72
4:10 — 70, 72
4:12 — 143
4:13 — 104
4:14 — 70
4:20 — 104, 143
4:22 — 104
4:23 — 143, 147
4:27 — 82
4:29 — 104
4:33 — 82
5:7 — 90
5:12 — 91
5:16 — 91
5:18 — 82
6:4 — 79
6:5 — 73
6:11 — 146
6:18 — 83
6:19 — 85
6:28 — 154
7:2 — 72, 85
7:4 — 143
7:5 — 72
7:6 — 72, 85
7:7 — 72
7:8 — 72
7:9–10 — 92, 146

7:13 — 72, 115
7:21 — 119
7:28 — 143
10:7 — 141

Ezra

4:11 — 93, 155
4:12 — 85, 114, 142
4:13 — 114
4:17 — 93
4:18 — 76, 93
4:23 — 155
5:3 — 85, 142
5:6 — 93, 155
5:7 — 93
5:8 — 114
5:15 — 94
5:17 — 93
7:11 — 155

1 Chronicles

1:5–7 — 179
1:18 (LXX) — 44
20:4 — 135
21:16 — 182

II. NEW TESTAMENT

Matthew

7:15–20 — 149
7:17–18 — 179
12:13 — 180

Mark

9:44 — 181

Luke

3:36 — 44
6:43 — 179
6:43–44 — 149
17:26–30 — 146

Romans

9:5 — 182

1 Corinthians

9:2 — 4

2 Corinthians

12:1–5 — 5

Galatians

1:1 — 5
1:11–12 — 5

Ephesians

1:17 — 200

1 Peter

3:20 — 152

2 Peter

2:4–6 — 146
3:5–13 — 145

Jude

6 — 132–133
6–7 — 146

III. APOCRYPHA AND PSEUDEPIGRAPHA

2 Baruch

21:6–7 — 181
56:2 — 78
56:9–16 — 78

1Q Hodayot (1QH)

3:29–36 — 145
8:4–14 — 151
18:29 — 180

1Q Milḥamah (1QM)

1:1 — 202
1:6–7 — 202
1:16 — 202
2:12 — 152
3:6 — 202
3:9 — 202
9:14–16 — 142
12:8 — 202
13:16 — 202
14:17 — 202
16:1 — 180
16:9 — 202
19:1 — 202

1Q Serekh ha-Yaḥad (1QS)

1:10 — 202
3:19 — 180
3:19–21 — 202
3:20–22 — 201
8:4–7 — 151

1Q23
51, 52, 57, 59, 60, 62, 64, 65, 136

1Q24
51, 129

2Q26
51, 129, 147

4QAJa (Visions de Jacob)
140

4Q Amram
155

4QDan[c]
53

4QEn[a]

1 ii 8–9 — 90
1 ii 13 — 67
1 iii 6 — 156
1 iii 7 — 138
1 iii 9 — 126
1 iii 18–19 — 75
1 iii 19 — 74
1 iv 1 — 156
1 iv 7 — 79
1 v 4 — 150

4QEn[b]

1 iii 7 — 142
1 iii 8 — 79
1 iv 9 — 112, 156

4QEn[c]
52, 53

1 ii 26 — 126
1 v 19 — 136
4 10 — 75
5 ii 18 — 132
5 ii 26 — 107
5 ii 29 — 94

4QEn[e]

1 xxii 1 — 75
1 xxii 4 — 75
1 xxvi 21 — 152
2–3 — 51, 57, 62, 80, 129
4 i 16 — 85

4QEn[g]

1 ii 23 — 75
1 iii 25 — 78
1 v 17 — 75
1 v 22 — 75

V. RABBINIC LITERATURE

VI. GRAECO-JEWISH LITERATURE

VII. PATRISTIC LITERATURE

62–65 — 37
62.6 — 36

Hippolytus

Refutatio

5.10.2 — 177
5.26.5–6 — 153
6.31.2 — 136
6.36.3 — 136
9.13.1–2 — 6
9.13.2–3 — 6
9.15.1 — 6
9.16.4 — 178
9.27.3 — 145–146

Jerome

De viris illustribus

72 — 37

Tractatus de Psalmo CXXXII
43, 44

John of Damascus

De haeresibus

53 — 6

Justin Martyr

First Apology

1.20 — 145
5.2 — 133

Origen

Contra Celsum

1.19–20 — 146
4.11–12 — 146
4.20–21 — 146

Socrates

Historia ecclesiastica
1.22 — 37

Titus of Bostra

Adversus Manichaeos

I 14 — 33

Theodoret

Haereticarum fabularum compendium

1.26 — 181, 182
2.7 — 6

VIII. MANICHAEAN LITERATURE

Cologne Mani Codex (CMC)

16:7 — 181
29:4 — 181
47:1–48:15 — 47
48:16 — 201
48:16–50:7 — 5
48:16–60:12 — 49
50:8–52:7 — 5
52:8–55:9 — 5
55:10–58:5 — 5
58:6–60:7 — 5
60:18–23 — 5
61:2–14 — 5
61:16–22 — 5
64:8–65:22 — 5
66:4–68:5 — 5
68:6–69:8 — 5
69:9–70:10 — 5
72:6–7 — 4
94:10–12 — 6
104:10–105:8 — 34
124:6–15 — 34

Homilies

25:2–5 — 10

IX. MISCELLANEOUS TEXTS

Ancient and Imperial Aramaic Literature

Index of Ancient and Medieval Authors

Index of Modern Authors

Sundermann, W. — 6, 7, 34, 36, 39, 75, 109, 111, 117, 119, 121, 123, 137, 140, 153, 154, 155, 156, 157, 158, 159, 161, 162, 177, 200, 201, 204
Suter, D.W. — 49, 133, 134, 135
Tardieu, M. — 34, 35, 47, 49, 152, 178, 201, 202, 204
Taübler, E. — 131
Testuz, M. — 130, 139
Theodor, J. — 44, 130, 135, 149
Thomas, J. — 6
Thompson, R.C. — 158
Tigay, J.H. — 158, 161
Till, W.C. — 136
Tisserant, E. — 45
Tongerloo, A. van — 206
Tröger, K.-W. — 176
Tubach, J. — 49
Uhlig, S. — 73, 77, 131, 138, 150, 156
Ungnad, A. — 161
Vajda, G. — 39, 144, 145, 162, 163, 164
Van der Horst, P.W. — 40, 41
VanderKam, J.C. — 49, 54, 129, 130, 131, 133, 139
Vaux, R. de — 129, 146
Vermaseren, M.J. — 182
Vermes, G. — 142
Vian, F. — 41
Villey, A. — 40
Volz, P. — 145
Wacholder, B.Z. — 130, 131, 139
Wagner, S. — 6
Wansbrough, J. — 4
Waterman, L. — 136
Weiss, I.H. — 134
Wensinck, A.J. — 5, 152
Westermann, C. — 134
Widengren, G. — 4, 5, 6, 33, 36, 44, 46, 48, 149, 151, 153, 180, 183, 205
Wilcke, C. — 161
Wilson, R. McL. — 136
Winckler, H. — 161
Winkler, H.A. — 159
Winternitz, M. — 43
Wiseman, D.J. — 158
Wright, G.E. — 129
Wright, W. — 33, 175
Yadin, Y. — 152
Yarshater, E. — 34, 43, 160, 183
Zimmer, H. — 160
Zimmern, H. — 161
Zunz, L. — 143
Zycha, J. — 38